Socio-historical linguistics its status and methodology

In this series

1 DAVID CRYSTAL: *Prosodic systems and intonation in English**
2 PIETER A.M.SEUREN: *Operators and nucleus*
3 RODNEY D.HUDDLESTON: *The sentence in written English*
4 JOHN M.ANDERSON: *The grammar of case**
5 M.L.SAMUELS: *Linguistic evolution**
6 P.H.MATTHEWS: *Inflectional morphology**
7 GILLIAN BROWN: *Phonological rules and dialect variation**
8 BRIAN NEWTON: *The generative interpretation of dialect**
9 R.M.W.DIXON: *The Dyirbal language of North Queensland**
10 BRUCE L.DERWING: *Transformational grammar as a theory of language acquisition**
11 MELISSA BOWERMAN: *Early syntactic development**
12 W.SIDNEY ALLEN: *Accent and rhythm*
13 PETER TRUDGILL: *The social differentiation of English in Norwich**
14 ROGER LASS and JOHN M.ANDERSON: *Old English phonology*
15 RUTH M.KEMPSON: *Presupposition and the delimitation of semantics**
16 JAMES R.HURFORD: *The linguistic theory of numerals*
17 ROGER LASS: *English phonology and phonological theory*
18 G.M.AWBERY: *The syntax of Welsh*
19 R.M.W.DIXON: *A grammar of Yidiɲ*
20 JAMES FOLEY: *Foundations of theoretical phonology*
21 A.RADFORD: *Italian syntax: transformational and relational grammar*
22 DIETER WUNDERLICH: *Foundations of linguistics**
23 DAVID W.LIGHTFOOT: *Principles of diachronic syntax**
24 ANNETTE KARMILOFF-SMITH: *A functional approach to child language**
25 PER LINELL: *Psychological reality in phonology*
26 CHRISTINE TANZ: *Studies in the acquisition of deictic terms*
27 ROGER LASS: *On explaining language change*
28 TORBEN THRANE: *Referential–semantic analysis*
29 TAMSIN DONALDSON: *Ngiyambaa*
30 KRISTJÁN ÁRNASON: *Quantity in historical phonology*
31 JOHN LAVER: *The phonetic description of voice quality*
32 PETER AUSTIN: *A grammar of Diyari, South Australia*
33 ALICE C.HARRIS: *Georgian syntax: a study in relational grammar*
34 SUZANNE ROMAINE: *Socio-historical linguistics*

**Issued in hard covers and as a paperback*

SOCIO-HISTORICAL LINGUISTICS

its status and methodology

SUZANNE ROMAINE
Department of Linguistics
University of Birmingham

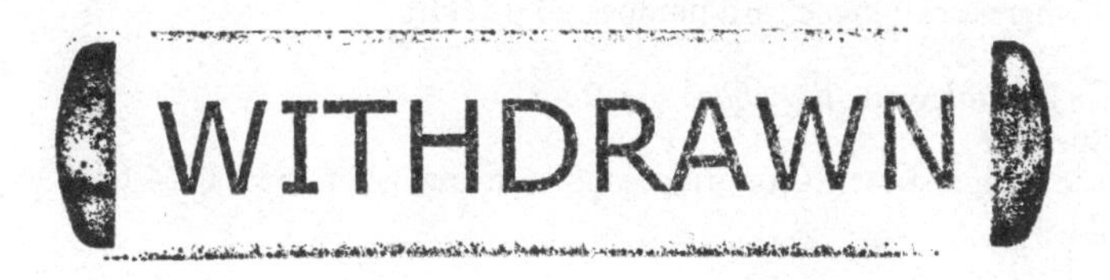

CAMBRIDGE UNIVERSITY PRESS
CAMBRIDGE
LONDON NEW YORK NEW ROCHELLE
MELBOURNE SYDNEY

Published by the Press Syndicate of the University of Cambridge
The Pitt Building, Trumpington Street, Cambridge CB2 1RP
32 East 57th Street, New York, NY 10022, USA
296 Beaconsfield Parade, Middle Park, Melbourne 3206, Australia

First published 1982

Printed in Great Britain at the University Press, Cambridge

Library of Congress catalogue card number: 81-12211

British Library Cataloguing in Publication Data
Romaine, Suzanne
Socio-historical linguistics. – (Cambridge studies in linguistics, ISSN 0068-676X)
1. Sociolinguistics
I. Title
401'.9 P40
ISBN 0 521 23750 5

Contents

Preface ix

1 Methodology and aims
1.1 Brief description of the proposed study 1
1.2 Sociolinguistics vs. linguistics 3
1.3 Written vs. spoken language 14
1.4 Diachronic variation – a sociolinguistic perspective 22
1.5 The use of the Cedergren–Sankoff variable rule program 26

2 Methods for a sociolinguistic study of historical syntax
2.1 The relevance of sociolinguistics to syntax 29
2.2 The nature of syntactic variation 31
2.3 A sociolinguistic study of historical syntax: the relative system 37
2.3.1 Treatment of the relatives in generative grammar 38
2.3.2 The Det-S or Art-S analysis 38
2.3.3 The NP-S analysis 40
2.3.4 The NOM-S analysis 41
2.3.5 Deep structure conjunction analysis 42
2.3.6 Rules for the introduction and deletion of relative markers 44
2.3.6.1 WH-rel attachment or relative clause formation rule 44
2.3.6.2 WH fronting 46
2.3.6.3 Relative *that* transformation 46
2.3.6.4 Relative *that* deletion 48
2.4 The derivation of relative clauses and pronouns 51

3 The history of the relative clause/markers in English with special reference to Middle Scots
3.1 The origin of the relative clause in the Germanic languages: a problem of general syntax 53
3.2 The Old English period 56
3.3 The Middle English period 59
3.4 The early modern English period 69
3.5 Relative markers in Middle Scots 69
3.6 The case of relative marker deletion/omission 72

4 The linguistic variables

4.1 Type of clause 81
4.2 Features of the antecedent or head NP 88
4.2.1 Animacy of the antecedent 88
4.2.2 Types of noun modification structures 89
4.3 Syntactic position or function of the relative marker 92
4.3.1 Subject relatives 92
4.3.2 Object and indirect object relatives 93
4.3.3 Predicate nominal relatives 94
4.3.4 Genitive or possessive relatives 95
4.3.5 Temporal and locative relatives 96
4.3.6 Prepositional or oblique relatives 97
4.4 Other factors affecting the choice of relative markers 99
4.5 Relativization and syntactic complexity 99

5 The extralinguistic variables: methods for the reconstruction of language in its social context

5.1 The problem of sampling 105
5.1.1 'Random' sampling and the problem of sample size 107
5.1.2 On the random nature of linguistic data 111
5.2 Type of text 114
5.2.1 Sociolinguistic definitions of style 115
5.2.2 The isolation of contextual styles 118
5.3 Reconstructing language in its social context 121
5.4 The intersection of stylistic and linguistic factors in the use of relative markers 126
5.4.1 Quirk's study of relative pronouns in modern educated English 128
5.4.2 Caldwell's (1974) study of the relative pronoun in Early Scots 131
5.5 Prescriptive grammar and the relative pronouns 132

6 Analysis of the data by two sociolinguistic techniques: cross-product analysis and implicational scaling

6.1 Where to start? 139
6.2 A linguistic description of the relative markers in Middle Scots (1530–50) 140
6.2.1 The effect of the animacy of the antecedent 142
6.2.2 The effect of different types of antecedents 143
6.2.3 The effect of syntactic position 144
6.3 Syntactic complexity 148
6.4 The measurement of syntactic complexity in individual texts 152
6.5 Syntactic complexity and stylistic differentiation 157
6.6 Index of relative marker deletion 160
6.7 The isolation of contextual styles and the language of individuals 165
6.7.1 Stylistic levels in *Ane Satyre of the Thrie Estaitis* 166
6.7.2 Stylistic levels in *The Scottish Correspondence of Mary of Lorraine* 167

6.8 Analysis of the data by implicational scaling 170
Appendix 174
Excursus 177

7 Variable rule analysis of the data
7.1 The Cedergren–Sankoff variable rule program 184
7.2 Variable rule analysis of Middle Scots relative clauses 188
7.3 Multivariate analysis of some data from modern English 198
7.4 The contribution of extralinguistic constraints to the study of diachronic change 200
7.5 The relationship between model and theory 209
7.6 Implications for synchronic and socio-historical grammars 214

8 The bearing of sociolinguistic data on linguistic hypotheses
8.1 Labov's analysis of contraction and deletion of the copula in BEV 218
8.2 The use of variable constraints in linguistic argumentation 221
8.3 The role of social factors in linguistic descriptions and argumentation 224
8.4 A sociolinguistic analysis of variation in word-final /r/ in Edinburgh: a case for integrative sociolinguistic description 228
8.5 What is a speech community? 234

9 On the epistemological status of sociolinguistic theory
9.1 On the nature and locus of variability 240
9.1.1 Idiolectal vs. sociolectal grammars 240
9.1.2 Is variability a matter of competence or performance? 247
9.2 Linguistic and social data: independent or dependent variables? 252
9.2.1 Transition 253
9.2.2 The social dimension of linguistic change 262
9.2.3 Constraints and actuation: what can be explained? 269
9.3 Is a sociolinguistic theory possible? 273
9.3.1 On the empirical foundations of a sociolinguistic theory 274
9.3.2 On falsification and the role of probability theories in linguistics 277
9.3.3 Defining a sociolinguistic methodology 280
9.4 Suggestions for a sociolinguistic research program 282
9.4.1 Avoiding scientism 282
9.4.2 Developing a non-deductivist epistemology 284
9.5 The place of sociolinguistic theory vis-à-vis linguistic theory 285

Bibliography 290
Index 310

FOR MY PARENTS
JOSEPH AND HELENE ROMAINE

Preface

A few years ago I became interested in claims made about the epistemological status of sociolinguistic methodology and, in particular, the so-called empirical foundations of a sociolinguistic theory. My concern with the nature of sociolinguistic methods and data grew out of some of the difficulties I encountered in trying to present a sociolinguistic description of some variables in Scottish English (cf. Romaine 1975). Some of the problems (e.g. continuous vs. discrete variation, levels of abstraction in the construction of sociolinguistic grammars, probabilistic rules) still bother me. I deal with them again here, but this time with reference to another descriptive problem, namely, variation in the relative marker in Middle Scots. This also leads to consideration of some new issues, e.g. the scope of sociolinguistic theory and the relevance of sociolinguistic methods to problems in historical syntax.

It will become apparent that I am using the term 'sociolinguistic' primarily in a narrow sense, i.e. to refer to the work which has derived from Labov (1966). I have concentrated on Labov's research program because it has been so influential; supported by a substantial body of empirical research, it represents one of the most concrete proposals yet made for a sociolinguistic theory. However, I also discuss Bailey's work; and I attempt to show that much of the controversy between the so-called quantitative (Labovian) and dynamic (Baileyan) paradigms results from a misunderstanding of the ontological status of some of the arguments and explanations which can be supported on the basis of sociolinguistic or variable data. I believe that both theories rest on shaky epistemological ground with respect to a number of claims, and most of what I have to say about both the major variationist theories is therefore critical.

I believe that a sociolinguistic theory of language provides a more comprehensive framework than an autonomous, e.g. 'asocial', one for dealing with dialect differentiation and language change, but that a sociolinguistic theory need not be completely (or even largely) empirical, or 'be' linguistics, i.e. replace an autonomous or asocial linguistic theory, in order to be successful. I reject, for example, Labov's (1975a: 228) claim that we appear to be entering a 'dramatic and critical period in the development of linguistics as a natural science'. Even if a sociolinguistic theory were largely empirical (and I argue that in its present state it is not), it would not anyway give us the kinds of explanations for certain sociolinguistic phenomena that we want; furthermore, its scope would be very restricted. I have tried therefore to suggest some directions (or better, methodological guidelines) for a sociolinguistic theory which will be less empirical, but also, I believe, less narrow in scope than that proposed by Labov.

My own view is that a sociolinguistic theory which is truly integrative in its approach must transcend the traditional concept of grammar represented by both Bailey's and Labov's models; in this I agree with Hymes (1974b: 434). I also think that the increasing tendency towards emphasis on quantitative models and methods, and the development of computer-assisted analysis to the exclusion of all else is misguided; but any serious sociolinguistic work or critique of methodology must assess the contributions of such techniques to a sociolinguistic theory in terms of the claims made for its analytical tools. Therefore, I have analyzed my data by both variable rule analysis and implicational scaling as a means of dealing critically with theoretical issues in each model with a new set of data.

Synchronic sociolinguistics has been particularly convincing in its use of quantitative models to demonstrate how the 'present might be used to explain the past' (cf. Labov, Yaeger and Steiner 1972). There have, however, been few attempts to cross-fertilize historical linguistics with sociolinguistics in order to 'use the past to explain the present'. This book tries to develop a methodological and theoretical framework for a field of research I refer to as 'socio-historical linguistics'. The main goal of such a discipline would be to investigate and provide an account of the forms/uses in which variation may manifest itself in a given community over time, and of how particular functions, uses and kinds of variation develop within particular languages, speech communities, social groups, networks and individuals. There are a great many methodological and theoretical problems arising from the nexus of sociolinguistics and historical linguistics. Owing to the preliminary nature of this field of enquiry I have focussed my attention on one particular problem, namely, the development of the relative clause marker in a non-standard dialect of English, in order to show in some detail how one might treat it in terms of a socio-historical approach. The diachronic analysis of social dialects is, however, only one task for a socio-historical linguistic theory.

This volume, therefore, tries to do a number of things simultaneously, namely, provide an account of variation in the Middle and modern Scots relative marker, lay the foundation for a socio-historical linguistic theory, and question the epistemological status of sociolinguistics. Not all the issues I have raised are resolved, but judging from the literature, some at least have not previously been recognized as issues and given the serious attention they merit.

I am very grateful to Roger Lass for his careful and critical reading of several versions of this book. His comments caused me to consider more deeply the implications of my research. I would also like to thank Bob Le Page, who very kindly read a first draft of the book; I have incorporated some of his suggestions and comments in this revised version. I am indebted to Nancy Dorian for commenting on an early version of the first chapter and, in general, for encouraging me to pursue this topic of enquiry at a time when no one else did. Since I completed a first draft of this book in 1978 I have had the chance to discuss a number of aspects of it with various people. I have particularly profited from my discussions with Elizabeth Traugott about socio-historical linguistics. There are no doubt some controversial points in this version; and I accept full responsibility for my own stubbornness, which compels me to retain them.

Birmingham 1980

All decisive advances in the history of scientific thought can be described in terms of mental cross-fertilization between different disciplines. Some of these historic bisociations appear even in retrospect as surprising as the combination of cabbages and kings.

Arthur Koestler 1975: 230

Dass nun gar das Unterfangen mit der Natur zu laborieren, sie zu Phänomenen zu reizen, sie zu 'versuchen', indem man ihr Wirken durch Experimente blossstellte, – dass das alles ganz nahe mit Hexeri zu tun habe, ja schon in ihr Bereich falle und selbst ein Werk des 'Versuchers' sei, war die Überzeugung früherer Epochen: eine respektable Überzeugung, wenn man mich fragt.

Thomas Mann, *Doktor Faustus*

Charlatans have existed at all times and in the most tightly-knit professions.

Paul Feyerabend 1978: 219

1 *Methodology and aims*

> In some areas of research it may appear possible to separate the linguistic from the socio-cultural, the synchronic from the diachronic or historical.
>
> Dell Hymes 1971: 423

1.1 Brief description of the proposed study

Thus far, sociolinguistics has concerned itself primarily with the analysis of synchronic variable speech data. If, however, sociolinguistics is to reach the final goal set for it by Hymes (1974a: 206), namely, that it should preside over its own liquidation, then clearly sociolinguistics should itself be an integrative mode of description. I take Hymes' comment to mean that the subject matter of linguistics should not be confined to the study of the conceptual function of language, but should also include its social function or communicative use. What he argues for, then, is a general theory of language which comprises both aspects. Such a theory would dispense with the need for a separate sociolinguistic theory; in other words, sociolinguistics would be 'redundant' (Labov 1972a: 183).[1]

The chances of sociolinguistics becoming such an integrative discipline are, in Hymes' opinion as well as my own, uncertain. Furthermore, I question whether a sociolinguistic theory in these terms is possible. My starting point is the assumption that if sociolinguistics is to meet the challenge given by Hymes, it must move beyond the treatment of synchronic phonetic and phonological data to a more general body of linguistic data. My study attempts to extend the application of variation theory from the domain of synchronic phonological variation to the study of a

1. Others have expressed similar views. For example, Kanngiesser has said (1972a: 14):

> Sofern die Linguistik aber eine bestimmte Form von Sprechhandlungen vollzieht, ist sie ipso facto auch 'Soziolinguistik' ... In einer Linguistik, die diesem Erklärungsanspruch genügt, kann es demzufolge keine spezielle Teildisziplin mit dem Namen 'Soziolinguistik' geben.

Cf. also Aracil (1974: 7) who says that sociolinguistics is complementary to linguistics proper, but is likely to absorb linguistics in the long run rather than the other way around.

problem in historical syntax. In this way, I hope not only to test the ability of sociolinguistics to deal with historical data, but also to examine what implications the results of this test have for the status of sociolinguistics.

The approaches to data collection and analysis are important dimensions here, not because they are novel or original – they are all well-tried, established procedures within the sociolinguistic literature – but because no studies on historical linguistics to date have claimed to have based themselves on a purely sociolinguistic approach. Interestingly, the diachronic analysis of social dialects was one of the seven dimensions of sociolinguistic research formulated by Bright (at the first conference to carry the title 'sociolinguistic', in 1964), and it is with this dimension that I am concerned.

As a specific illustration of the application of sociolinguistics to problems in historical syntax, I examine relativization in Middle Scots, using as a data base a sample of different types of texts written during the reign of James V. I have made an attempt to control possible extraneous sources of variation by limiting the texts to be sampled both chronologically and geographically to the Central Scots region during the period c. 1530–50.[2] The investigation focusses specifically on variation between WH forms (*quhilk* – *which*), TH (*that*) and Ø (instances of relative omission), which is characteristic of sixteenth-century texts. It was my hypothesis that the variation would correlate highly with a number of linguistic factors in the first instance, e.g. characteristics of the antecedent (animateness, definiteness, etc.), syntactic position of the relative marker in the relative clause (subject, direct object, etc.) and type of clause (restrictive/non-restrictive), as well as with a number of extralinguistic (or social) factors such as type of text (prose/verse), and style within a text (quoted speech/narrative prose).

If the validity of sociolinguistic research is to be measured in terms of its ability to relate sociolinguistic data to the central problems of linguistic theory, as Labov says (1972a: 183–4), then the results of this study should be relevant to models of historical change and not just to the more specific descriptive problem of providing an account of relativization in a dialect of English.

In laying the methodological and theoretical background to the socio-historical linguistic framework within which this study is presented, a number of questions are relevant; these will be discussed under the following headings:

2. Some recent comments by McIntosh lend support to my choice of this period. McIntosh (1978: 42–3) thinks that the most fruitful period to study is 1450–1550 since material from this time is sufficiently free of standardizing tendencies. In addition, he suggests that it is advisable to restrict the time span to less than a century to avoid possible confusion between chronological and regional patterns.

1. What is the scope of sociolinguistics? In particular, what is the relationship between sociolinguistics and linguistics, between sociolinguistics and other subdisciplines of linguistics such as stylistics, historical linguistics, and between sociolinguistics and other disciplines such as sociology?
2. What special problems, if any, arise in the adaptation of techniques used in the analysis of the spoken language to the written language? What are the implications for the application and relevance of sociolinguistic theory to historical studies?
3. How can one investigate the social or extralinguistic dimension of linguistic variation in the historical record of a language? Can the notion of 'stylistic continuum' be meaningfully applied to quantitative differences in the written language? To what extent do these different levels of usage of variable linguistic phenomena reflect differences in the spoken language?

In the latter part of the chapter the proposed investigation of relativization in Middle Scots will be outlined in terms of a socio-historical linguistic approach which suggests some possible models to account for the observed variation and a means for testing them.

1.2 Sociolinguistics vs. linguistics

It might reasonably be argued that once it has been decided to deal with a problem of historical syntax, we have already moved outside the scope of sociolinguistics and into the realms of philology, textual analysis, or even stylistics, since we have no data to draw on apart from what exists in the extant written records of a language which is no longer spoken. The question of whether such a study can in fact be called 'sociolinguistic' is in some respects fundamental,[3] and should not be dismissed as either trivial (and hence not relevant to the study), or totally utilitarian; for apart from practical questions of identity – i.e. what to call oneself, historical linguist, sociolinguist, etc., or just linguist – it is necessary to know what field one is working in. At some level one must decide what models of description are relevant to the problem at hand, or even what the problem is. As much as we might like to believe that we can avoid 'a priori theoretical considerations', it is impossible to argue that there can be a description without a theory.

I take Popper's (1972: 104) view that all knowledge is theory-impregnated. Popper (1972: 146) has argued that the epistemology of

3. Already at this stage I have probably departed from what might be called 'Labovian sociolinguistics proper'. This will become clearer however in the next section where I discuss what implications the study of the written records of a language has for the applicability of sociolinguistics.

induction breaks down before taking its first step. It cannot begin with perceptions and build theories upon them, since there are no such things as sense data or perceptions which are not built on theories. The conclusion which can be drawn from this is that the data are no guarantee for the theories.[4]

To take a linguistic example, our idea of 'the structure of a language' is based on what we think is in the real world and what constitutes a description (or an explanation) of it. It determines which observations are selected as being important, and hence the very shape of the description. The notion 'shape of the description' is indeed quite a real one. We 'know', for example, what a grammar or a phonology of a language looks like. A phonetic description of a language might include a classification of consonants in terms of place and manner of articulation. Such a classification embodies a theory of phonetics which tells us what to include as relevant and what to look for in the sound system of a language; for example, one does not expect to find a language with no stops or fricatives, although there is no reason why they should occur universally. Nor does one expect to find a language using sounds which for some reason do not fall within the descriptive categories, e.g. those which are thought to be physiologically impossible.[5]

It is in this sense that such a classification can be considered predictive; although languages may still surprise us, we generally look for what we have found before elsewhere, or what can be accommodated within the present descriptive model. A taxonomy then, linguistic or otherwise, does not serve as a classificatory scheme for ordering neutral facts or observations since it is already based on theory. There is, however, a distinction to be made between description and explanation; I assume that the function of a theory is to explain how the phenomena it describes have come about.

This illustration is not intended to point a finger at phonetic theory, since it could reasonably be argued that we 'know' more about phonetics than any other aspect of language. Yet to 'know' all the possible speech sounds

4. I am assuming that this position is not controversial, at least within the philosophy of science (cf. also the discussion in Harre 1976: 24–34); and I will not argue here against the so-called 'autonomy principle' with respect to the relationship between facts and theories.

5. There has been a tendency among some phoneticians to regard phonetic data as raw data. Pike's (1968: 57) comment, 'Phonetics gathers raw material; phonemics cooks it', reflects this view. Phonetics cooks too in the sense that it assumes that certain sounds, e.g. coughing, are to be classified as non-speech sounds, and hence not part of the data. Laver (1976: 55) has recently emphasized the fact that the phonetic level of analysis is a 'level of considerable abstraction from the phonic artefacts created by each act of speaking'.

which can be produced or describe how they can be produced is not to 'explain' them. Popper (1972: 195) has pointed out that every explanation can be further explained, so the idea of an ultimate explanation must be rejected.

It should now be clear that I reject the view that a successful sociolinguistic theory or progress towards a sociolinguistic theory involves transition to a theory which will provide direct empirical tests for most of its basic assumptions or explanations, although this would seem to be the view held by Labov (1972b: 114). In accepting a sociolinguistic framework for my study, I commit myself to a description of the imbrication of language structure and use, but reject the notion that this can be an explanation of an essence. I agree with Popper (1972: 195) that we must give up essentialism, i.e. asking what a thing is, what the true nature or essence is which causes something to be what it is or act as it does. Even though I make use here of some recent analytical tools, I do so without accepting that there is anything in the nature of language which entails a description of it in terms of a variable rule or other such formal expression of quantitative relations. Furthermore, apparent successes with such analytical devices cannot be regarded as an indication of truth or a correspondence with the nature of language. To believe this would be to subscribe to 'radical instrumentalism' (cf. Chalmers 1978).

Before returning to the question of the relevance of sociolinguistics to historical linguistics, the relationship between sociolinguistics and linguistics must be considered. The term 'sociolinguistics' immediately suggests an interconnection between two separate and distinct disciplines; though it is not to be assumed automatically that these disciplines are sociology and linguistics. Hymes (1974a: viii), for example, views sociolinguistics as a multidisciplinary field, which includes not only sociology and linguistics, but also social anthropology, education, poetics, folklore and psychology.

Hymes has made the interesting observation (1974a: 84) that such mixed or hyphenated terms linking linguistics with the social sciences and, in particular, anthropology have quite a long history; terms such as 'ethnographic philology', 'philological ethnology', 'linguistic anthropology', etc., occur from at least the nineteenth century. The form, relative chronology and prevalence of such terminology is revealing, as Hymes points out. Until World War II these mixed terms were generally phrasal formations, either coordinate, e.g. linguistics and anthropology; genitival, e.g. the sociology of language; or adjectival, e.g. anthropological linguistics. It is only since the war that compounds with 'linguistics' as the second member have come into use. Hymes concludes that this usage signifies that it is linguistics and linguistic concepts and methods which have become central.

It seems reasonable to suppose that the goals and scope of a sociolinguistic theory, if there is such a thing, could be stated in terms of the many disciplines whose interests converge in sociolinguistics; but this raises the issue of whether sociolinguistics can be said to merit any independent status in linguistics or whether it is merely an eclectic amalgam of ideas and procedures from disparate disciplines. The issue could be resolved to some extent through examination of the individual goals of a number of these disciplines; then an assessment of the progress towards these goals could be made.

At a simpler level, practitioners of these separate disciplines could be asked to state the goals of their respective disciplines; this can be done under the assumption that whatever the specific individual questions which exist in a discipline, there will be some general agreement among practitioners about what constitutes doing X (whether X is linguistics, anthropology, etc.). The entity X is a central and recognizable enterprise to all concerned with the discipline. Thus it may be said very simplistically that the description of languages is the occupation of linguistics just as the description of human cultures constitutes the enterprise of anthropology. In each case the professional of X understands it means to describe a language or a culture, etc., and that there is a method of enquiry upon which the answers depend. Perhaps even this seemingly simple assumption is not uncontroversial. It can be questioned whether sociolinguistics has reached such a level of definable autonomy.[6]

Sociolinguistics has gained a great deal from sociological methods of research. This is not surprising in view of the fact that sociology appears to have a long-standing connection between theory and empirical investigation, while linguistics has recently been going through a period when linguistic descriptions may be considered justifiable on the evidence of intuitions, even in the face of contradictory empirical data (not to mention conflicting intuitions).[7] However, the research aims of an independent sociolinguistics cannot be met by relying on the methodological perspec-

6. I am assuming that a discipline has to reach a certain level of maturity before it begins to define itself in terms of the activities of those who practice it, i.e. linguistics is what linguists do. Cf. Bailey (1971), Aracil (1974).

7. This is not to say that linguistics does not possess a tradition of this sort. For example, Hjelmslev (1953) considered his theory of language to be empirical in an important sense. Conversely, not all sociologists would accept the statement that there is a well-established connection between empirical investigation and major sociological theories (cf. e.g. Nisbet 1977; Adorno 1978). I discuss the extent to which a sociolinguistic theory can and should be empirical in Chapter 9.

tives drawn from linguistics and sociology. If the interdisciplinary perspective is to be fruitful, it cannot be merely an 'additive' one; it must be integrative.

Hymes (1974a: 76) takes essentially this view when he says that 'Adding a speechless sociology to a sociology-free linguistics can yield little better than post-hoc attempts at correlation between accounts from which the heart of the relevant data will be missing.' The whole must, in other words, equal more than the sum of its parts if any claim to independent status is to be made. Hymes has argued repeatedly, and perhaps in more eloquent terms than most, for an integrated theory of sociolinguistic description, i.e. a partially independent body of method and theory which is itself a mode of description in the same way that recognized autonomous disciplines like linguistics and anthropology are conceived.

A sociolinguistic mode of description would entail an organization of linguistic means fundamentally different from an abstract grammar of a single speech community. Hymes (1974b: 434) argues that the conception of grammar in terms of a more or less homogeneous norm is a frame of reference which must be transcended (cf. Romaine 1980b, 8.5 below). In its place he proposes that we begin with the sociolinguistic concept of a speech community organized in terms of styles. In this context 'style' is being used to refer to a way of doing something. A speech community would be characterized by both referential and stylistic features which must be considered with respect to structure on the one hand and use on the other. Referential and stylistic features represent two standpoints from which utterances may be the same in form or meaning (cf. Aracil 1974).

The contrast between linguistics proper and sociolinguistics lies in the fact that language structure constitutes the subject matter of linguistics, while language use is left to sociolinguistics. A sociolinguistic theory, however, presupposes a linguistic theory; if it is to be truly integrative, it must relate both structure and use. This obviously is no small task. Lomax's work on cantometrics (Lomax et al. 1968) and parlametrics (Lomax 1977) is perhaps the only detailed, and certainly the most concrete, example of how one might study the relationship between ways of speaking and types of speech communities.

Cantometrics refers to the study of the relationship between song style, dance style and social structure cross-culturally. Lomax's more recent work (1977) is an attempt to apply a parallel framework to the study of speaking style in its relationship to social structure. He has claimed that the presence of certain styling qualities such as repetitiveness, volume, etc., cluster together in different cultures as distinctive performance models, and that these speech styling qualities also correlate with song and dance style.

If sociolinguistics is not additively comprised or extended from linguistics or sociology, then what relation does it have to linguistics? Labov (1977: 3–4) has argued that there are many reasons to reject sociolinguistics as an independent discipline, hyphenated or otherwise; the most important of these from his standpoint is that the recognition of an independent sociolinguistics would implicitly endorse the existence of an asocial linguistics. In the preface to *Sociolinguistic Patterns* he comments: 'I have resisted the term sociolinguistics for many years, since it implies that there can be a successful linguistic theory or practice which is not social' (p. xiii).[8]

Furthermore, Labov suggests that, to be independent, sociolinguistics would have to be organized around theoretical questions distinct from those of the diverse disciplines whose interests fall within sociolinguistics. So far no such coherent framework of theoretical principles has emerged. He notes that until recently sociolinguistic studies were data-gathering exercises without reference to theoretical issues more general than the observation that a given individual or group spoke language X. The problem in unifying sociolinguistics is considerable due to the large number and diversity of subdisciplines assembled under it.

Labov claims, however, that in the past few years a body of sociolinguistic research has been developing which is addressed much more specifically to linguistic issues such as the linguistic organization of variation, constraints on optional rules, implicational relations and limits to variability. What is perhaps even more important to Labov is the systematization and elaboration of descriptive and analytical techniques, i. e. methodological innovations. It is at this point that we can begin to question whether there are any specifically sociolinguistic questions which would give a theoretical coherence to a mode of description which is recognized as constituting sociolinguistics rather than being a use of sociolinguistics.

There has also been a distinction made between sociolinguistics and the

8. There are of course a number of 'successful' asocial linguistic theories in the history of linguistics. Whether or not a theory is social or asocial does not determine its success. For example, Chomsky and Hjelmslev exclude language use from linguistic theory (cf. Chomsky 1976: 54–79). Hjelmslev has said (1953: 2–3):

> To establish a true linguistics, which cannot be a mere ancillary or derivative science . . . linguistics must attempt to grasp language not as a conglomerate of non-linguistic (e.g. physical, psychological, logical, sociological) phenomena, but as a self-sufficient totality, a structure *sui generis*. Only in this way can language in itself be subjected to scientific treatment.

In Chapter 9 I argue in more detail that the choice of categories or aspects of language for inclusion in a linguistic theory is not a matter for empirical decision.

sociology of language (cf. especially Fishman 1971; Dahlstedt 1973), both of which can be said to start with the data of one field to study problems which have a bearing on the other. For example, sociolinguistic research is intended to produce a linguistic description as its end result, although it uses social facts and even social methods to arrive at this end; the sociology of language uses linguistic information as a means of describing social behavior. The two approaches are by no means mutually exclusive (cf. Romaine 1975: 54f; Trudgill 1978a: 4–5). Labov's (1966) study of variation in New York City speech is by now considered a classic example of the genre of work which is recognized to be sociolinguistics; yet Labov himself professes to believe there is no such thing as sociolinguistics, but instead acknowledges the existence of linguistics only, which studies language as a form of social behavior. For Labov, then, there is no linguistics other than sociolinguistics, or, as Hymes has phrased this conception of linguistics, 'a socially constituted linguistics' (cf. Halliday 1978).

Since Labov's study however, others (especially most American linguists) have adopted the term 'sociolinguistics' as a cover term for variation studies (although there are some who call themselves 'variationists'). They tend to regard their field of study as a relatively 'new' aspect of linguistics, but there were certainly sociolinguists, in practice if not in name, before Labov, e.g. Quirk, Ulvestad and Fries, to name only a few. Indeed, there are still those who are engaged in what might be called sociolinguistics but who do not consider themselves sociolinguists. Crystal and Davy (1976: 11) say, for example, that the aim of 'stylistics' is to analyze language for the purpose of isolating those features which are restricted to certain kinds of social context and to classify these features into categories based on their function in the social context.

Lass (1976a: 219) has commented on this tendency to claim novelty for the study of variation in a review of Bailey and Shuy (1973). He notes that 'Freedom from static analysis has been around for a long time (certainly since Sapir) for anyone who wanted it, and some of the "new ways" are a good deal older than most of the bibliographies would lead one to suspect.'

Sociolinguists have no monopoly on the study of variation. What is true, however, is that more attention has been devoted recently to certain types of variation. Historical linguists and dialectologists have of course long been concerned with the study of variation through time and space respectively; and most linguists have dealt with variation in linguistic forms conditioned by linguistic context (cf. Bloomfield's concept of 'alternation'). For many linguists, however, the study and description of variation among speakers or variation in linguistic form which was not conditioned by linguistic context, i.e. 'free variation', was largely excluded.

It is of course in these latter two areas (and especially the last) that sociolinguists have attempted to fill the gap; what is really more novel is the acknowledgement of a linguistic conditioning that is relative rather than absolute as in traditional descriptions of morphophonemic alternations. Linguists have never been ignorant of variation; it has just been more convenient to assume as a pragmatic principle that languages and linguistic communities were homogeneous. This assumption of homogeneity has in fact been largely responsible for the provision of a sound descriptive base for linguistics, which has then been built upon by sociolinguists and made their work possible.

Martinet (1963: vii) has commented on both the necessity and utility of the homogeneity hypothesis:

> There was a time when the progress of research required that each community should be considered linguistically self-contained and homogeneous. Whether this autarchic situation was believed to be a fact or was conceived of as a working hypothesis need not detain us here. It certainly was a useful assumption. By making investigators blind to a large number of actual complexities, it has enabled scholars, from the founding fathers down to the functionalists and structuralists of today, to abstract a number of fundamental problems, to present for them solutions perfectly valid in the frame of the hypothesis and generally to achieve, perhaps for the first time, some rigor in a research involving man's psyche . . . Linguists will always have to revert at times to this pragmatic assumption. But we shall have to stress the fact that a linguistic community is *never* homogeneous and hardly ever self-contained.

Weinreich, Labov and Herzog (1968) argue quite strongly that the key to a rational conception of language itself lies in the possibility of describing orderly differentiation in a language by breaking down the identification of structuredness with homogeneity. They claim (1968: 101):

> nativelike command of heterogeneous structures is not a matter of multidialectalism of 'mere' performance, but is part of unilingual competence. One of the corollaries of our approach is that in a language serving a complex (i.e. real) community, it is the absence of structured heterogeneity that would be dysfunctional.

The homogeneity hypothesis is bound up with levels of abstraction, as Wunderlich (1974: 137–41, 391–4) has pointed out. The problem in taking the idiolect as the lowest level of abstraction is that an individual language system does not in itself represent the language of which it is a part. This is the difficulty Labov refers to as the 'Saussurean paradox'; to deal with it,

Labov recommends viewing the individual's fluctuating behavior against the background of the whole community. Wunderlich also maintains that the first level of abstraction relevant to linguistic theory is the sociolect. Whether one follows in the tradition of Labov (the quantitative paradigm) or Bailey (the dynamic paradigm), a claim of homogeneity with respect to some linguistic or sociolinguistic unit is assumed; the difference lies in the level of abstraction involved in each case.[9]

For example, Labov has assumed that persons who are sociologically similar are linguistically similar, i.e. they are characterized by regular linguistic patterns, while individuals (or idiolects) are not (cf. Weinreich et al. 1968: 188; Labov 1969: 759). Bailey, on the other hand, assumes that the individual is homogeneous and that variability results from the aggregation of internally consistent lects which are different from each other with respect to one or more linguistic features. The difference in competing linguistic theories lies not so much in the denial or admission of the existence of variation per se (as one might believe from reading the work of Labov, for example), but rather in disagreement about which types of variation can and are to be included within the scope of linguistic theory as fundamental to an understanding of questions which are indisputably linguistic. The remaining variation, i.e. the non-fundamental, is then excluded as irrelevant, or, at worst, non-existent.

If, however, social claims constitute the heart of sociolinguistics, and in particular its supposed novelty, then many studies, especially those of Bailey, would seem to fall outside the mainstream of both linguistics and sociolinguistics; Bailey's work is at odds with the former by virtue of providing an account of variation which is thought to be part of performance, and with the latter by concern with the distribution of linguistic variants without attending to their social meaning.

What is required of a sociolinguistic analysis is a broad descriptive and functional base within which the use of linguistic structure can be investigated. This cannot be done by conceiving of language in terms of a single communicative function, i.e. that of communicating conceptual information; the social and linguistic differentiation which forms the data of empirical work in sociolinguistics remains uninterpretable and paradoxical within such a narrow framework. A sociolinguistic analysis de-

9. Bailey seems to have begun the use of the term 'paradigm' in reference to variation studies (cf. especially Bailey 1971), and others have continued it (cf. e.g. Sankoff 1974). It seems to be intended to be understood in a Kuhnian sense (cf. Kuhn 1962), which is not appropriate here, as I will suggest in the final chapter (nor within the larger context of the history of linguistics; cf. Hymes 1974c; Percival 1976).

pends on the recognition of the difference between representational sameness and sociolinguistic choice. Labov (1977: 31) has said that the unity of sociolinguistics depends upon a different view of the functions of language. This sort of sociolinguistics presumes the existence of a linguistic analysis which has established a framework for dealing with and identifying the existence of alternate ways of saying the same thing and the social selection of variants as a principal mechanism of communication.[10]

Lass (1976a: 219) does, however, admit that there is some claim to novelty which might be made from a formal and methodological standpoint; indeed, he maintains that it is precisely the methodological and formal novelties of sociolinguistics which have produced the most solid empirical findings. Whether this methodology or formalism is solely the province of sociolinguistics and is capable of supporting a valid linguistic theory which will correspond to and in some way 'explain' sociolinguistic data is another question. Neither a descriptive model nor a theory which aims at being explanatory can be convincing if it cannot address itself to a new and more general body of data. In other words, once a theory is proposed which will account for a specific set of data, we want to see how wide a range of phenomena it can be applied to. There are, however, a number of philosophers of science (cf. e.g. Feyerabend 1978) who believe that theories typically account for only a few paradigmatic cases and have to be distorted to deal with new data.

I would argue that if linguistics is to be conceived of as sociolinguistic in nature, then sociolinguistics must be 'tested' on new and different kinds of data. Specifically, it must move beyond the description of synchronic variation to deal with fresh sets of data. Weinreich's remark (1966: 399) about the limited usefulness of restricted semantic theories – 'whether there is any point to semantic theories which are accountable only for special cases of speech – namely humorous, prosaic, banal prose – is highly doubtful' – applies here also. Sociolinguistics should be capable of integrating the major areas of research interest which have traditionally been considered the proper domain of linguistics if it is to be convincing; but there have been few demonstrations of how it might do this.

An area of vital importance to current linguistics, but one which has usually been considered marginal, is stylistics. Broadly conceived, stylistics can be almost indistinguishable from the 'ethnography of speaking' (cf. Chapter 5), but the literary applications of stylistics have assumed such

10. Theories which take into account different functions of language are of course not new (cf. e.g. Bühler 1934; Jakobson 1960).

importance that the term 'stylistics' has generally been restricted to textual analysis (where philology and stylistics go separate ways is also unclear). Recently, however, the analytical procedures of stylistics have been criticized for their inability to deal with variation (cf. Crystal and Davy 1976); and it is here that sociolinguistics is relevant.

Sociolinguistics developed partly out of the concern of linguists to describe variation found in the spoken language, but variation also occurs in written language in, one can assume, a patterned rather than a random way. Consequently, the techniques which sociolinguists have used to analyze the variation found in the speech of New Yorkers also have some relevance to variation in the use of relative markers in Middle Scots, and to historical problems in general.

Anyone can observe that two samples of speech or writing are different. Sociolinguistic analysis can show us that these differences are objectively measurable, and that there are patterns in the choices which a speaker/writer does make, on the one hand, and can make, on the other. Since the choices are not entirely free, we need to observe the conditions or factors that may influence them; and it is here that sociolinguistic methodology is applicable.

Past studies of variation tell us what to look for; for example, we know that there are a host of extralinguistic or social factors which may come into play in the selection of a particular variant, e.g. age, sex, social class, context, role, etc., as well as linguistic ones, which may be either universal or language-specific. Such studies provide us with descriptive models for looking at and organizing the variation into a meaningful structure which it is hoped has some 'explanatory' and predictive power. Turner (1973: 239) has argued that a theory of varieties is already a theory of styles, thus attesting the close connection between variation studies and stylistics and indicating how stylistics may be understood as part of sociolinguistics.[11] What I will be suggesting later is that historical linguistics and sociolinguistics have a similar close relationship, i.e. that in some respects the descriptive tasks of one coincide with those of the other. A large part of my preliminary work must be concerned with examining the connections between the two in order to determine how one might extrapolate from synchronic sociolinguistic findings insights which are relevant to diachronic problems.

11. Turner, however, is not sure whether a theory of stylistics ought to include the dimension of social class variation (1973: 162). In Turner's (as well as in Crystal and Davy's (1976)) terms my study could be subsumed under the heading of stylistics.

1.3 Written vs. spoken language

For some time now no one has questioned the primacy of the oral language over the written. Clearly people spoke languages before they wrote them; just as some languages exist today only in the written form (either because they are dead or fossilized), so there are also languages which exist only in the spoken form. Children of course learn the spoken language before they learn to write. Both phylogenetically and ontogenetically, this view is unchallengeable. Yet, with the prominence of descriptive linguistics in this century, this belief seems to have become more generalized and taken by some to mean that speech is the only 'true' manifestation of language; in this view, writing is only a speech surrogate or a poor reflection of the spoken language. While it is true that written language is a reflection of the spoken language to some extent, instances can be cited where the written language does not have or is not intended to have a corresponding spoken form, e.g. legal language. In other words, although there are obvious connections between spoken and written language and one may influence the other, something does not have to be spoken before it can be written (cf. Householder 1971: Chapter 13).

Nevertheless, the notion that 'speech' is synonymous with 'language' has been so influential that within the field of animal communication, for example, it was not thought paradoxical to consider the linguistic abilities of chimpanzees inferior to those of humans because they could not handle the vocal complexities of human spoken language. The only way in which Gua could have demonstrated her linguistic competence to the satisfaction of her human trainers would be to have spoken English. Subsequent work with chimpanzees using American sign language (Gardner and Gardner 1969) has demonstrated that previous approaches were misguided and very restricted.

In view of the independent nature of writing, it seems best to regard speech and writing as types of linguistic behaviors or events which may be realized in different channels; I would accept, in other words, the distinction made between language and medium (cf. Abercrombie 1967: 17–18) or between form and substance (cf. Saussure 1966; also Lyons 1977: 67–74). Thus it can be said that spoken and written language are instances of the same language embodied in different media, by assumption that a medium can have potential for full autonomy as a vehicle for language. This distinction is useful for many reasons. Since a medium is not itself a language, a distinction can be made between a linguistic pattern and its material embodiment, or between form and substance; in other words, language is form and medium is substance. Obviously this has great implications for linguistic theory as a whole; once we accept that the basic dichotomy exists between language and medium (and not between language and writing, or speech and writing), it can no longer be argued that all forms of the written language (or even sign language, for that matter) are outside the field of linguistics. The function of writing then is not merely to record the spoken language; writing has an independent existence.[12]

It may seem strange (and even tedious) to repeat this argument, since for centuries linguists were almost exclusively concerned with written texts; and for languages like Gothic written texts were the only evidence for the speech community. However, modern linguists who use the term 'language death' generally refer to the loss of the spoken form even though there are extant written records (cf. e.g. Dorian 1981).

The development of phonetic science in the nineteenth century lent support to the notion of the primacy of speech and also served to distance linguistics from philology. In the earliest stages of phonetics, however, the written language was taken as primary, and Grimm, for example, speaks of phonetics or phonology as the 'Lehre von den Buchstaben'.[13] Only later did phonetics concern itself with minute variations in the sounds of the spoken language. With the advent of the phonemic principle supposed insignificant variation was pushed aside, but the spoken language was still primary.

Sociolinguistics has always emphasized the primacy of the spoken language in its use of actual speech data, and indeed, there has been no explicit consideration of how one might attempt a sociolinguistic study of a written language. Only recently was sociolinguistics considered applicable to syntactic variation (cf. Sankoff 1973; Rickford 1975), and this issue is still not resolved (cf. Chapter 2). This is perhaps a reflection of the supposed relative novelty of a 'paradigm' which, in its classical form (e.g. Labov 1966), has only been tested and fully developed for dealing with phonetic/phonological variability. The fact that sociolinguistics has been considered a subdiscipline, or hybrid discipline, of linguistics has also had a limiting effect on its application to the written language, which seemed to belong more immediately to the domain of another subdiscipline, historical linguistics. If,

12. This point of view is basic to McIntosh's study of Middle English dialectology (cf. McIntosh 1969a, b).
13. We cannot be sure exactly what Grimm meant by the use of the term 'Buchstaben'. It seems likely that he may be using it partially in the sense of 'littera' (cf. Abercrombie 1965); if he were not, then we might have expected him to speak about 'Buchstabenverschiebung'.

however, the view is taken that linguistics is sociolinguistics, then if linguistics has any application to written texts, it must follow that sociolinguistics does also.

To return to the question of the relationship between the written and the spoken language, it can be said that if there is only a difference between form and substance, then written language, whether literary or non-literary, differs from the spoken language in substance. A further question, however, concerns the relationship between literary and non-literary written language, i.e. whether the literary language is a special type of written language, or whether, as McClure (1975) claims, it is the language of literature which constitutes the written language as a whole with non-literary language forming a limited compartment within it; it is wrong, he suggests, to conceive of the literary language as a special development or refinement (cf. also Turner 1973: 141). This view seems somewhat strange to me.

Whatever the connection between literary and non-literary language, both are still instances of language embodied in the same medium; and just as the contexts of speech exhibit characteristic patterns of variation, so do the contexts of writing. For example, the written hand shows regular variation in orthographic symbols which is conditioned by context in the same way that the spoken language displays allophonic variation. Characteristic organization of the written language into special schemata such as end-rhyming lines indicates that poetry rather than prose is intended. Language, in other words, qua language, exhibits the patterned organization that is a crucial property of language in whatever medium it is manifested. Both context and variation will be manifested in each medium.[14]

In the course of this study I will examine the extent to which literary and non-literary language and different types of prose styles and verse forms differ from each other. Presumably the extent of this variation is itself a variable; certainly languages differ from one another in this respect, and a single language may exhibit different degrees of variation in its life cycle. In Middle Scots it can be assumed that we are dealing with a fully elaborated

14. McIntosh (1969a, b, 1978) has pointed out that the problems involved in a dialectology of written Middle English and Middle Scots are in some respects similar to those of the modern language. He says (1978: 41):

> We must educate ourselves to recognize that the written word as such will often display its own regional habits and characteristics; a realisation of this will help to jolt us out of habitual obsession with spoken dialect characteristics and enable us to understand and interpret specifically written-dialect characteristics.

standard language which was in use in all domains of life during the period from 1530 to 1550, so that a great deal of stylistic variation would not be surprising (cf. Romaine, forthcoming a).

To what extent, however, these levels of literary usage corresponded to social or stylistic levels in the spoken language is an open question; the extent and type of correspondence no doubt varies over time. Current sociolinguistic studies, however, allow us to make some educated guesses about the nature of variation in the spoken language on the basis of repeated patterns of social and stylistic variation which occur today. Others have also speculated about this. Wyld (1920), for example, believes that the sixteenth century was linguistically relatively uniform, i.e. that the written and spoken language or colloquial and literary varieties were alike, but that in the seventeenth–eighteenth centuries the divergence was greater. Now perhaps it could be argued that there is a trend to minimize the difference between the colloquial and formal written standard. I take up such questions in more detail in Chapter 5.

Having established the distinction between language and medium, it may seem unnecessary to look for support for the belief that linguistic techniques (whether they are also sociolinguistic techniques) are applicable to the study of written texts. Indeed, Fowler claimed (1966: 157) that this should not be considered an issue since literature as language was evidently analyzable. But this was by no means the view taken by, among others, Halliday (1964) and Winter (1964); and recent works on stylistics (Leech 1969; Turner 1973; Crystal and Davy 1976) also discuss the question.

This can be taken as evidence that the study of the written language is in some sense still considered marginal to linguistics as a whole; and, similarly, that the use of linguistic techniques in the domain of literary analysis is still only marginally acceptable. A sociolinguistic theory which claimed to be coterminous with linguistic theory would certainly have to take a strong line on this issue. I cite Halliday who has said (1964: 302):

> It is part of the task of linguistics to describe texts; and all texts, including those, prose and verse, which fall within any definition of 'literature' are accessible to analysis by the existing methods of linguistics.

In more general terms, the position one would have to take is this: there exist linguistic methods of analysis which are already valid; if written language is an instance of language, then the same techniques apply to all instances of language. In other words, linguistic theory should not need to be *extended* to cover all relevant cases; it should just apply to these cases as it has done elsewhere.

In view of this, one would think that linguists would welcome studies which used both the theory and descriptive methods of linguistics to deal with forms of language in different media as a testing ground for linguistic theory itself. If these theories are not applicable, then the question arises: Why not? More fundamentally, we should also ask whether theories which cannot handle all the uses/forms in which language may manifest itself in a given speech community over time are actually acceptable. This is the test I maintain a socio-historical linguistic theory must face.[15] Studies of the written language will reveal not only patterning which is characteristic of the language itself, regardless of medium, but also that which may be peculiar to the medium itself; the findings may require us to revise certain views we have of present descriptive categories.

This view might, however, be regarded skeptically by some. Lass (1976a: 220), for example, notes that there was a wholesale extension of the formal apparatus and methodology of generative phonology into historical linguistics, which culminated in King (1969). He maintains this has led to a 'vast oversimplification of the problems of historical interpretation, a devaluation of important traditional concerns like reconstruction, and a host of other deleterious effects that we are just recovering from'.

Although there is to some extent a natural tendency for the insights developed within one field or subfield of a discipline to drift across its boundaries into another, Lass thinks there is a danger that this might happen in the case of variation studies, many of which seem to be carried out with a positivist slant. I would agree that 'transgressing boundaries' can be counter-productive unless one is sure that the theories, methods, etc., are relevant to phenomena on both sides of the boundary (cf. Romaine 1981a). However, the extension or application of the insights and procedures of one field to another may lead to important findings about the inadequacy of certain models, provided they are not allowed to assume such importance that they defeat the purpose for which they were adopted, i.e. what can we find out about language by pursuing a particular line of enquiry? More importantly, as I have pointed out earlier, if sociolinguistics is claimed to be a theory about language, then such 'extensions' provide crucial test cases.

15. I think that Labov and I definitely go separate ways here. His view of the written language is one which I am obviously rejecting. He says (1972b: 109):

> we retain the conviction of our predecessors in American linguistics that texts can be understood only in their relation to the spoken language – that the main stream of evolution of language is to be found in everyday speech . . . either our theories are about the language that ordinary people use on the street . . . or they are about very little indeed.

I comment in more detail on Labov's view of historical data in Chapter 5, and in Chapter 9 on the restricted view of sociolinguistic theory his ideas entail.

I think it can reasonably be said that sociolinguistic methodology has already demonstrated that there are interesting things about language which are revealed by the study of variation. Lass (1976a: 223) comments that it is almost entirely through the work of Labov that we have any information about how linguistic change might proceed in a functioning language system; namely, by internal and external structuring of inherent variability which shows directional gradience through social class, geographic space and time.

The fact that some work has now been done on American sign language from a sociolinguistic point of view is an encouraging and promising indication of the scope of sociolinguistics. The study of language in the manual – visual medium, as opposed to the oral–aural, from a variationist theoretical perspective has led to significant insights into its patterning and organization. Research into American sign language and other manual–visual codes has been influenced by the primacy of speech doctrine to the extent that they were regarded as auxiliaries to spoken languages; but they are now coming to be recognized as full-fledged languages in their own right (cf. especially Battison, Markowicz and Woodward 1975; Woodward 1975).

Something similar is happening in the field of pidgin/creole studies; linguists are discovering that the techniques of linguistics may also apply to what were considered 'marginal languages', and that these kinds of languages often shed light on important theoretical issues. At a time when sociolinguistics is expanding its scope and widening its perspectives, it seems to me that a re-examination of our attitude to the written language is in order. This will hopefully show that studies such as this one (as well as those on American sign language and pidgins/creoles) involve not so much seeing new ways to apply sociolinguistics (or linguistics) as recognizing what exactly constitutes linguistic data and how language manifests itself.

There is no apparent reason why a theory such as Hymes (1968: 110) has developed for the 'ethnography of speaking' might not be transformed into an 'ethnography of language', since the framework is sufficiently broad to include instances of language in other media (Hymes uses the term 'channel'); one could describe language events and not just speech events (cf. Basso (1974) for proposals on the 'ethnography of writing'). Uldall (1944) has proposed an etic/emic unit which is not medium-bound that could be used in such descriptions (cf. also Bloomfield's (1926) 'ceneme'). He has termed this distinctive unit of language which can apply across media the 'cenia'. Such a concept could override medium-specific concepts such as the phoneme, though it would not eliminate them for studies of specific media. In any event, where a choice exists between media in a community, one would want to know what kinds of messages were allocated to each channel and how; and furthermore, who had access to which channel(s).

Written language has of course always been a subject of study,[16] but my point is that sociolinguistic techniques (or at least techniques which are recognized as being specifically sociolinguistic) have not been employed, and that those who call themselves sociolinguists are not engaged in such studies. Halliday (1964) refers to the description of written texts by methods derived from general linguistic theory as 'linguistic stylistics'. Fowler (1966) regards this process, however, as only the first step, the other two being stylistics and criticism; and in this sense he feels that the analysis of written texts is an interdisciplinary study par excellence extending into two fields, linguistics and literary stylistics.

Fowler, however, sees the linguistic analysis as a part of criticism, i.e. as a means of getting something other than a linguistic description. In other words, a text must be examined first as an instance of language before any value statements can be made about it as literature. Halliday, on the other hand, being a linguist, is interested primarily in a linguistic description of a particular instance of language. It is worth noting that, although he considers the analysis of written texts a part of linguistics, he attaches the special name of 'linguistic stylistics' to it. If it is linguistics, why have a special name for it? This is of course Labov's view of the term 'sociolinguistics', namely that it is redundant because linguistics is already (or should be) sociolinguistics.

Fowler argues against Halliday's view of the task of linguistic stylistics and claims this approach is to a certain extent simply description conducted for its own sake. He does admit that such a description may have value in promoting awareness of the language or methodology used to investigate it. But basically he believes that (1966: 163):

> For a linguist to say that he will do the description or show the critic how to do it and leave the using of the description to the critic is not constructive. It implies that description is 9/10 of the task and that interpretation has to and can follow directly on.

At the risk of oversimplifying the argument, I would still say that we, as linguists, need not be concerned with what place objective formal descrip-

16. A number of Prague School linguists were of course concerned with the analysis of the written language (cf. especially Vachek 1964a, b).

tion has in literary studies, as Fowler is, or with the problem of how literary criticism ought to/could be incorporated into a linguistic description. The fact that written language, both literary and non-literary, is an instance of language is a datum of interest to both students of language and literature, though the use each will make of this fact will depend on the discipline or background from which they approach the problem. The territories are overlapping and not mutually exclusive; and there does not seem to be much point in arbitrary compartmentalization.

The linguist will be interested in the language as language in the first instance, while the literary critic is interested in the language as literature. This is reminiscent of the controversy over the boundary (or lack of one) between the sociology of language and sociolinguistics. Both cover the same territory, i.e. language as a social phenomenon, from different perspectives, with certain data as primary, and move to different descriptive ends. By the same token, it is perhaps true of virtually any discipline which deals with human phenomena that it will overlap in places with other disciplines, some more so than others.

Chomsky (1976: 36), for example, has claimed that linguistics is subsumed under cognitive psychology, or is at least part of it, while others, many of them linguists, consider psychology to be a part of linguistics, i.e. psycholinguistics.[17] It is difficult, however, to see how some of the subdisciplines of linguistics, for example historical linguistics (but cf. Andersen 1973) or phonetics, can be understood as cognitive psychology; and, similarly, there are areas of psychology which do not seem to fit into linguistic theory, for example animal ethology (which may or may not have a place in linguistics depending on how broad a view one takes of communication). It is not just subdisciplinary boundaries which may have a tendency to be fuzzy.

Fowler's remarks would therefore seem to represent an extreme position since description, whatever viewpoint one adopts, seems to be clearly a first and necessary step, whether the analysis is intended for linguistic and literary purposes, and not just as an exercise in methodology. The question of what to do with the description, if there need be such a question, can come after the description.

17. Chomsky has said (1976: 36) that 'The theory of language is simply that part of human psychology that is concerned with one particular "mental organ", human language.' Later in the same book he says (1976: 160) that 'Linguistics is simply that part of psychology that is concerned with one specific class of steady states, the cognitive structures that are employed in speaking and understanding.'

1.4 Diachronic variation – a sociolinguistic perspective

Any notion of homogeneity in Middle Scots was convincingly dispelled by Aitken (1971), who pointed out that Smith's list of the main characteristics of Middle Scots (1902: xviff.) contained many indications of variation and inconsistency, in spite of Smith's own claim that the most outstanding characteristic of this literary form was its uniformity. Smith's opinion was more strongly expressed by Wood (1933: xxxi), who claimed that Middle Scots was not a spoken historical dialect of the Scottish language at any period, but was instead an artificial language used by various writers of different social and geographical backgrounds. Aitken, on the other hand, maintains that Middle Scots is characterized by variety in usage at all levels, e.g. orthography, syntax and lexis, and that many of the departures from any standard that there was may reflect dialectal and colloquial forms and usages of which we otherwise have little contemporary indication.

Although not much work has been done on stylistic variation in Middle Scots, Aitken says that it is certainly possible on an impressionistic basis to delineate some general tendencies which characterize certain types of Middle Scots writing. For example, in literary prose, the principal historical records, legal and official texts there is a general preference for the use of hypotactic rather than paratactic structures, the Latin-derived 'accusative plus infinitive' construction, passives and impersonal constructions, free use of loanwords from Latin or literary French in addition to or instead of equivalent native vernacular expressions, the substitution of English terms for Scotticisms in later writings, the inflection of certain adjectives in plural concord, the employment of *quh-* forms of the relative pronoun instead of *that* or Ø, as well as an avoidance of certain constructions and phrases which perhaps had colloquial overtones. By way of contrast, more unlearned and unsophisticated writers and their works are characterized by paratactic, parenthetic and elliptical structures.

Aitken (1973) has also made a preliminary attempt to categorize different types of Older Scots poetry on the basis of features of theme and content, verse form, style and diction. He has set up a five genre classification as follows: 1. couplet–narrative verse; 2. alliterative verse; 3. courtly poetry; 4. comic, burlesque and vituperative verse; and 5. moralizing, religious, lyrical, personal and satirical poems. The first group is historically the earliest and contains narrative poems in octosyllabic or decasyllabic couplets, e.g. Barbour's *Brus*. The second category contains three relatively long narrative poems written in rhyming alliterative stanzas in the fifteenth century, the *Taill of Rauf Coilyear, how he harbreit King Charles*, *The buke of the Howlat*, and the *Knightly Tale of Sir Golagras and Sir Gawane*.

The next two categories, courtly poetry and comic verse, are major classes of poems which represent two opposite extremes of the Middle Scots stylistic spectrum. They have their own characteristic verse forms and vocabulary with virtually no overlap. The last category, moralizing verse, consists of poems in short stanzas for the most part; stylistically speaking, it lies in an intermediate position between the comic and courtly poetry. It shares some of the features of anglicization and Latinate overtones of the courtly style as well as some elements of the comic style. It is principally these latter three styles of verse that I will be concerned with here.

At the top of the stylistic continuum is the courtly poetry which has been called 'Scottish Chaucerian' because its typical features are the result of conscious imitation on the part of Scottish poets of Chaucer and his followers. The courtly poetry in Middle Scots is part of a larger general British or English tradition. Thematically speaking, courtly poetry is solemn and serious, saturated with classical overtones and allusions while, linguistically speaking, it is written in what Lewis (1954) calls the 'full-blown high style'. It is notable for its extremely low density of northern English or native Scottish words; as Aitken says, the diction of courtly verse was associated with a tradition of elegant and ornamental expression which was far removed from daily speech. In terms of syntax, this high or grand style is also highly elaborated; this is to say that it is characterized by a full syntax, e.g. ellipsis is avoided as are, in general, reduced forms. The syntactic relationship between clauses is explicitly indicated by formal markers such as the relative pronoun, complementizer *that* and coordinating conjunctions.

Comic verse represents a polar opposite to the courtly poetry. Aitken (1973: 3) says it is 'in every way the most distinctively Scottish of all Older Scots poetry ... It is by far the most consistently vernacular kind of Older Scots ... This is the colloquial style of Older Scottish writing.' Just as the courtly diction was no doubt valued and felt to be appropriate for dignified subject matter due to its association with foreign literary tradition and classical erudition, the vocabulary of comic verse, which Lewis (1954) has termed 'broadly and exaggeratedly Scotch', was used to convey native and homely or undignified subject matter of everyday life.

The type of vocabulary found in comic verse is the most densely northern or Scottish; among these words are a number which occur only once or several times, but never outside comic verse, except sometimes in strongly condemnatory passages in other verse and prose writings or in indirectly quoted speech in court records. Aitken suggests that these items belonged to an essentially colloquial or slang register, and therefore appeared only in the written language once this vernacular style of poetry came to be popular. He believes that the comic poetry drew on the latest in colloquial and folk speech. This is indicated in spellings that suggest phonetic reduction and the shortening of fuller forms, which was no doubt a reflection in writing of recent innovations in the pronunciation of spoken Scots. Syntactically speaking, the style of the comic poetry is parenthetic and elliptical. Successions of simple sentences are preferred to overtly marked syntactic structures such as subordination, and very often the formal features of connection are omitted altogether.

Aitken's categories are purely impressionistic ones which await detailed and systematic investigation. It is apparent, however, that this type of stylistic variation is very similar to the stylistic continuum which operates today in the spoken language, i.e. the most fully Scottish styles occur at the lower end of both the social class and stylistic continua, and the more anglicized styles are found at the top. Thus we can see in the written language of the sixteenth century a reflection of the modern linguistic situation. Anglicized forms established themselves early in verse as stylistic options which came to be associated with a more dignified and elite register, while the Scottish options were confined to homely, local and folksy types of writing. This situation was responsible for the great stylistic diversity which is present in the written language of this period.

In this study I look at different types of prose and verse texts forming a stylistic continuum ranging from the most fully Scottish styles to the most fully anglicized, in order to see how sociolinguistic methods of analysis may be used to examine variation in the realization of the relative marker in Middle Scots. Two of the reasons for selecting this particular problem of historical syntax were suggested by Aitken's (1971) essay.

1. Middle Scots contains a wealth of variable linguistic data which apparently correlates with the extralinguistic dimension of style. Aitken in fact specifically mentions that the employment of *quh-* forms of the relative (as opposed to *that* or Ø), might be correlated with stylistic levels. Moreover, a fully elaborated stylistic continuum of the type found during this period in Middle Scots makes it a more likely candidate for sociolinguistic analysis than most other varieties of English in use during the same period.

2. Both stylistic variation and syntax in particular are areas of study which have been neglected as far as Middle Scots is concerned. Caldwell's (1974) study of the relative pronoun in Early Scots made only a preliminary attempt at examining the usage of the relatives in relation to various levels of usage. Caldwell took into account only prose texts, i.e. non-literary prose (record and official) and literary prose; her main emphasis was in fact on literary prose. She also covered such a great time span, i.e. 1375–1500, that there is a lack of great detail in the data she presents for any given subsection of that period (cf. 5.4.2 for a more detailed discussion of the differences between this and Caldwell's study).

Apart from these considerations which are specific to Middle Scots, relativization is in itself an interesting syntactic process which has been the subject of much controversy among generative grammarians (cf. especially Stockwell et al. 1973: 419–501) and has attracted the attention of creolists (cf. e.g. Sankoff and Brown 1976; Dreyfuss 1977). Middle Scots data should therefore be of interest in comparison with other languages and in particular with other dialects of English. In addition, an account of relativization in Middle Scots could serve to illuminate the synchronic situation in Scottish English with respect to variation in the use of relative clause markers. In undertaking this study I hoped to demonstrate that variation in the relative system correlated with the stylistic levels suggested above and would fit in with Keenan's (1975) claims about the connection between syntactic complexity and relativization. If that were so, further studies of Middle Scots could use the relative markers as an independent variable characterizing a particular stylistic level; this would allow a point of departure for investigating other features which co-occur with the relative marker.

It is in fact in the area of linguistic change that I expect the analysis of variation by sociolinguistic methods to produce the most fruitful results. I hypothesized originally that the results would show that the incidence of Ø is for the most part a matter of register, and not, as sometimes suggested, of chronology or perceptual constraints, and that variation in the relative marker has for some time now been relatively stable in English. Hence the current use of Ø subject relatives and the alleged increase in the use of both *that* and Ø in a number of modern English dialects is not an innovation or an instance of 'change in progress'. The results should furthermore be relevant to models of historical change in general and may shed some light on the relation between synchronic variation and the mechanism of linguistic change.

1.5 The use of the Cedergren–Sankoff variable rule program

The Cedergren–Sankoff variable rule program is based on a theory of language variation which has been called the 'quantitative paradigm'; this framework assumes that variability is inherent in language and is best described by means of variable rules in the grammar of a speaker/ community. The program has been used to handle large quantities of data in order to estimate the underlying probabilities associated with a particular variable rule. Apart from this notion of variable rule, quantitative methods have been useful in locating systematicity in variable data in terms of purely linguistic environments or constraints; they must therefore be regarded as a powerful tool for sociolinguistic analysis. I discuss the mathematical and theoretical aspects of this program in Chapter 7.

The successful use of the Cedergren–Sankoff program in the analysis of sociolinguistic data has been well documented in the domain of phonological variation (cf. e.g. Cedergren 1973; and Cedergren and Sankoff 1974). There are a number of ways in which its use might be extended to deal not only with different kinds of linguistic data, e.g. syntactic and lexical, but also with extralinguistic variation, e.g. social class, age, sex, style, etc. Since I have been arguing that sociolinguistic techniques of analysis are not restricted to synchronic data, one potential and obvious area of application for the Cedergren–Sankoff program is in historical linguistics. In adapting the program to deal with variation in the relative marker in Middle Scots I hope to demonstrate its applicability in two areas simultaneously, syntactic and historical. Generally speaking, any variable linguistic data (i.e. lexical, phonological, etc.) in any channel (i.e. written, spoken, etc.) should be potentially analyzable in terms of the program.

This type of quantitative analysis makes the further assumption that 'performance consists essentially of samples of competence' (Sankoff 1974: 20); in other words, the claim is made that the underlying probabilities associated with variable rules will be reflected in actual speech as statistically observable fluctuations in the relative frequencies of the different variants.[18] This is at any rate Sankoff's view. I personally believe that the program can be used without strict adherence to the theoretical assumptions of the quantitative paradigm; it is not really an empirical issue whether there 'is' such a thing as a variable rule. The status of variable rules

18. This is a controversial assumption whose implications I ignore for the moment. I discuss Sankoff's views on competence and performance and their relation to the quantitative and dynamic paradigms in more detail in Chapters 7 and 9.

in sociolinguistic theory is nothing more than that of an analytical procedure or a useful heuristic device (cf. Romaine, 1981a) which can be used for dealing with the variable aspect of language. I intend its use in this study as a sorting procedure and a test of several models of variation. My ultimate aim is of course to see what bearing quantitative methods such as these have on hypotheses about language differentiation and change and what role they play in sociolinguistic theory. I am not using the program as a 'discovery procedure', a somewhat stronger term used by Guy (1975: 60), which suggests to me a greater commitment to the concept of variable rule. I accept only the following: Given a body of data which consists of observations of the frequency of occurrence of variants of a variable in different environments, the program can sort through the environments and correlate these with variants to give an idea of the extent to which this correlation holds, and in what order of importance the conditioning environments are arranged.

Cedergren and Sankoff have made more claims for their analysis than I am willing to accept. Although I do not wish to hold the position (untenable, in my opinion) that the method of analysis one chooses to use on a given body of data does not color the results of the study, I do not think the use of the program itself need be a 'theoretical issue' (again, to use Guy's phrase), which commits one to the concept of variable rule. It does of course entail that certain assumptions are accepted about the nature of variation in language, i.e. that language variation is embedded both in a linguistic and a social context, and the relationship between change and variation, i.e. that differentiation and change in the system is accomplished by successive reweightings in the environments which constrain or promote particular variants.

The variation in the Middle Scots relative marker which I will be concerned with here has its locus in the representation of the coreferential noun phrase in the relative clause.[19] There are three linguistic variants, WH, TH and ∅, which I define more precisely in the next three chapters.[20]

I will be using the Cedergren–Sankoff program to test some hypotheses about the description of variation in the relative system, e.g. what kinds of

19. I assume for the moment that relative clauses are to be considered as embedded sentences which have a constituent coreferential to one in the main clause. I discuss other possible analyses in Chapter 2.
20. I will not be concerned with the orthographic alternants of one and the same variant, although it would have been interesting to consider the problem of spelling variation. *Quh-* and *wh-* are Scots and English spelling options. I will be using the notation WH to refer to both Scots and English forms, e.g. *quhilk*, *which*, *quho*, *who*, etc., regardless of spelling. The notation TH refers to *that* (and its orthographic alternants, e.g. *þat*) and ∅ to the absence of a relative marker in the surface structure.

rules, and how many, are needed? what is the status of Ø? etc. Since the program was originally designed to handle only binary variables, I have set up two models with two rules each to account for the three variants of the relative marker. Each of the models, which I describe in detail in Chapter 7, makes different assumptions about the nature, number and order of operation of the rules involved in relativization in Middle Scots and English in general.

There is in fact some evidence that some kinds of phonological and syntactic data may be best analyzed in terms of two successively ordered rules each with its own set of environmental constraints. For example, Cedergren (1973) discussed the aspiration and deletion of /s/ in Panamanian Spanish as an 'extended process' whereby /s/ → /h/ → Ø. Since her treatment of it, Longmire (1976) has claimed there is some evidence in Venezuelan Spanish which suggests that the last stage of the process is a separate rule, i.e. /h/ → Ø, or /h/ deletion. Labov (1969) has also argued that contraction and deletion of the copula in BEV (Black English Vernacular) is best described by a two rule model in which the rules are ordered so that full forms are first contracted and then contracted forms are deleted (cf. Romaine 1979b, 8.1 below). I discuss the issues involved in dealing with syntactic variation and the special case of relativization in the next chapter.

2 *Methods for a sociolinguistic study of historical syntax*

2.1 The relevance of sociolinguistics to syntax

In this chapter I examine the contribution which variable data in historical syntax can be expected to make to descriptive and theoretical issues, with special reference to my study of the relative system in Middle Scots. A number of linguists have argued that variable data can be used in support of abstract linguistic analyses, and that quantitative relations bear directly on, and provide evidence for, 'deciding' some important theoretical issues. If such claims are tenable, then the argument put forward by both the quantitative and dynamic paradigms, that variation should form the core of linguistic theory, seems well justified.

Carden (1972), for example, has claimed that native speakers' judgements about the grammaticality or acceptability of sentences are crucial for determining the nature and operation of syntactic systems. He argues that by seeking out the patterns of variation in acceptability in and among speakers, we can confirm postulated abstract structures, since variation in the data results from rule differences and differences in rule ordering.[1] Likewise, Bailey (1970: 77) has maintained that an analysis of variable data allows us 'to confirm fairly abstract syntactic structures, rather than cast them into doubt'.

It was, however, Labov who first programmatically outlined the questions which the study of variation (in the form of variable rules) could address, thus suggesting contributions it might make to linguistic theory. These are (Labov 1969: 760):

1. What is the most general form of a linguistic rule? That is, what notations, conventions, schemata and interpretations allow us to account for the productive and regular patterns of linguistic behavior?
2. What relations hold between rules in a system? What principles of ordering, combination and parallelism prevail in systems . . . ?

1. Cf. however, Labov (1972d) as well as Carden (1976) on the reliability of native speaker intuition.

3. How are systems of rules related? What is the range of possible differences between mutually intelligible dialects? How do languages, originally diverse, combine within a bilingual speech community?
4. How do systems of rules change and evolve? This historical question is of course related to the last point:
5. How are rule systems acquired? How does the individual's system of rules change and develop as he acquires the norms of the speech community?

Furthermore, Labov (1969: 761) also says that the purpose of the paper, which deals with contraction and deletion of the copula in BEV (in which the above questions are raised), is threefold. The paper attempts 'to do more than solve this particular problem or enlarge a particular theoretical framework to deal with variation. It aims to provide a model for linguistic research which will arrive at decisive solutions.'

In the course of my study I hope to show that Labov has not done any of these things. Ignoring for the moment the analysis of contraction and deletion, which I take to be a descriptive problem (cf. Romaine 1979b, 8.1 below), I turn to the latter two claims since they involve questions which relate to the status of sociolinguistic theory. Although I concede that it is in principle possible to enlarge generative grammar to deal with variation, I do not think a satisfactory or coherent sociolinguistic theory results from the extension of the notion of rule of grammar to include variable rules, which is what Labov proposes (cf. also Romaine 1981a). Labov's last aim, however, to provide a model for linguistic research which will arrive at decisive solutions, is, in my opinion, neither realistic nor possible.

Since I do not accept the view that empirical hypotheses can be ultimately confirmed (cf. Popper 1972), or that linguistic issues can be decisively solved in the way Labov suggests, my purpose here will be to illustrate (and I twist Bailey's claim somewhat) how the data from variation can also be used to undermine rather than confirm the validity of abstract syntactic structures. I will examine specifically in this chapter how we can set up hypotheses which can be tested (but not, I would argue, confirmed) with sociolinguistic data and methods. My immediate concern, then, will be with the fourth area in which Labov says the study of variable rules has a contribution to make: namely, the question of how systems of rules change and evolve. However, this relates in an interesting way to the other issues, particularly the first three.

For an empiricist like Labov, success and progress in sociolinguistics are equated with the possibility of transition to a theory that can provide direct empirical tests for most of its basic methods and hypotheses. Therefore, a large part of my study will involve an examination of the possible theoretical arguments which can be and have been put forward to support the claim that new tools of analysis, e.g. the Cedergren–Sankoff program or implicational scales, provide a better or 'truer' picture of language.

I will be analyzing my data on variation in the relative system in Middle Scots by cross-product analysis and implicational scaling (cf. Chapter 6) as well as by variable rule analysis using the Cedergren–Sankoff program (cf. Chapter 7). Then I will see how my findings might be used as a test against the predictions of Labov's model of change and Bailey's wave model, and whether they have any bearing on linguistic arguments of the type Labov has indicated. These models differ not only in their formal representation of variation and change, but also in a number of important theoretical issues, which I treat in the final chapter with reference to my data and those from other sociolinguistic studies. Both agree, however, that linguistic change has its source in synchronic variation in the speech community.

2.2 The nature of syntactic variation

Sankoff (1973) has suggested that the scope of the study of language variation should include syntax and semantics; and she has demonstrated how the quantitative paradigm might be extended to deal with variability in levels of grammar above the phonological. She claims straightforwardly (1973: 58):

> The extension of probabilistic considerations from phonology to syntax is not a conceptually difficult jump . . . It seems clear to us that in the increasing number of situations which have been studied, . . . underlying probabilities are consistently and systematically patterned according to internal (linguistic) and external social and stylistic constraints. There is no reason not to expect similar patterning elsewhere in the grammar.

Sankoff's main purpose is to provide a demonstration of such an extension without giving much thought to the question of whether the nature of syntactic variation is sufficiently similar to that which takes place at the phonological level to justify such a wholesale transfer of method. Similarly, Rickford (1975), who has followed Sankoff's lead, is more concerned with the methods used in the collection of syntactic data, than with the larger, and in my opinion more important, issue of whether sociolinguistic methods are applicable in all respects to syntactic problems. The answer to this question has important implications for my study of historical syntax, since

I am dealing with transfer of method at two levels, i.e. from synchronic to diachronic (cf. Chapter 5), as well as from phonological to syntactic variation.

Lavandera (1978) has argued quite convincingly, I think, that one important methodological tool, the (socio-)linguistic variable, cannot be easily extended to the analysis of syntactic variation.[2] Some of her points are worth commenting on here since they lend support to my belief that the sociolinguistic findings to date seem to indicate that different kinds of problems are involved in syntactic variation.

Lavandera has observed that the three examples presented by Sankoff (1973) to support the extension of quantitative methods of analysis to syntax were all cases in which the variation seemed not to be the carrier of social and stylistic significance.[3] The problem is, says Lavandera, that phonological variables which can be shown to have social and stylistic variation do not have referential meaning. I take her use of the term 'referential meaning' to indicate what others have called 'cognitive', 'conceptual' or 'descriptive' meaning (cf. e.g. Leech 1974; Lyons 1977). Non-phonological variables, however, may have social and stylistic significance (or what Leech refers to as 'stylistic meaning') in a given case, but they always have cognitive meaning by definition. The difficulty is that the cognitive meaning must be assumed to be the same for all variants of the variable. The real dilemma, then, is the difference in defining or assuming sameness of meaning for phonological as opposed to syntactic variants.[4]

Within this context, it is easy to see why phonological variables were the safest starting point for quantitative analysis.[5] According to Labov, social and stylistic variation presuppose the option of saying the same thing in different ways, i.e. the variants of the variable have the same referential meaning but are somehow different with respect to their social or stylistic significance. The main contribution from quantitative studies which relied on the concept of the linguistic variable was the demonstration that dif-

2. It is important to note, as Lavandera herself is careful to point out, that her argument is not where *variation* stops (since it is an empirical issue whether syntax shows internally as well as externally conditioned variation), but where the linguistic variable stops, i.e. ceases to be a useful or meaningful concept.
3. To this, I add that the three cases involved both grammatical and phonological constraints rather than purely grammatical or syntactic ones.
4. Lavandera does not comment on the consequences of the conception of the linguistic variable as a continuous dimension of variation (cf. Romaine 1979c). Syntactic variation produces a finite number of discrete variants so that there is no surface continuum of realizations to be dealt with (cf. also Naro 1981).
5. In Chapter 8 I indicate how this concept of variation organized along a continuous phonetic dimension has proved difficult to apply even to certain types of phonological variation (cf. also Romaine 1979c).

ferences in phonetic form regarded as 'meaningless', i.e. 'free variation', were in fact carriers of social and stylistic information; Labov's work thus put the study of stylistic meaning on a par with that of cognitive meaning.

Lavandera's main objection to the extension of the variable to syntax is that it reverses the whole significance of the concept as originally defined and used by Labov (1966). She cites in particular Labov and Weiner's (1977) study of the agentless passive which depends on the assumption that the active and the passive can be used to say the same thing; or, in Labov and Weiner's words, the active and the passive, although different forms, are referentially identical.

It is not clear to me what is meant by the use of the term 'referential' by Labov and Weiner (or by Lavandera, who has adopted their terminology in her argument), and this lack of precision confuses the issue. Labov has defined the variants of a variable as 'alternative ways of saying the same thing from a truth-definitional point of view' (Labov and Weiner 1977: 6). Labov concludes that constancy of truth-value guarantees constancy of cognitive or descriptive meaning (what he imprecisely calls 'referential'). This is not really true. We can say that two or more expressions are synonymous, i.e. have the same sense or descriptive meaning if they are substitutable for one another in a range of utterances without affecting their descriptive value. Constancy of descriptive meaning implies constancy of truth-value, but the converse does not hold; we can substitute one expression for another which may result in an alteration of descriptive meaning, but not truth-value (cf. Lyons 1977: 202).

Labov's use of the term 'referential' is also problematic and misleading here since we are not dealing exclusively with referring expressions. I accept Lyons' (1977: Chapter 7) view of reference as an utterance-dependent notion, i.e. it applies to expressions in context and not to single word forms or lexemes. When Labov says that variants of a variable have the same meaning, what I think he should be saying (and meaning?) is that variant word forms don't change meaning. Here is where the trouble arises in talking about or defining syntactic and phonological variables in the same terms. If reference is a context- and utterance-bound concept, so that only expressions may have reference (lexemes have sense, and so do expressions), the study of syntactic variation must be concerned with the relationship between lexemes and expressions; the study of phonological variation, on the other hand, deals with the relationship between lexemes and forms. The sense of an expression can be thought of as a function of the senses of its component lexemes and of their occurrence in a particular grammatical

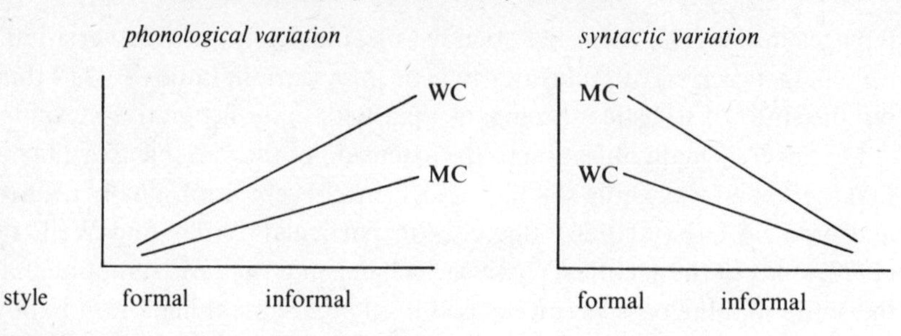

Figure 1

or syntactic structure; and the only reference an utterance can be said to have is to its truth-value.

In their study of the passive Labov and Weiner (1977) claimed that the choice between the agentless passive and the active under certain conditions was constrained entirely by syntactic factors, and carried neither social nor stylistic significance. A somewhat different result was obtained by Van den Broeck (1977), who studied the use of the passive in Flemish. He found that there were important social and stylistic differences, but that these were of a different type than those normally found for phonological variables. It is this aspect of the difference between phonological and syntactic variation that Lavandera seems concerned with. The fundamental difference between phonological and syntactic variation in Van den Broeck's study was that the former was more evident in informal, while the latter more so in formal situations.[6] I have sketched out this difference in patterning in Figure 1 (the convergent lines within the graphs represent the frequency with which the working and the middle class use a particular variable).

Van den Broeck concludes that sameness, rather than difference, may be the starting point from which to understand the interaction between language and social class. I suggest that what is needed to make sociolinguistic methods viable at the non-phonological level is a more careful consideration and specification of both sameness *and* difference as they relate to different levels of abstraction in the grammar as well as in sociolinguistic theory.

Lavandera (1978) hints at this issue, but does not produce a cogent or coherent argument. The kind of meaningfulness which Labov's study of

6. What is particularly interesting in Van den Broeck's study is the reversal of the social class relationships in the informal situation, i.e. the working class typically uses the complex syntactic structures more frequently than does the middle class.

phonological variables was originally concerned with relates to actual utterances in specific contexts. In other words, sameness and difference in meaning is assumed at a surface structure level of utterance in the case of phonological variables. In the case of syntactic variation, however, what is being assumed is equivalence of abstract syntactic structures. As Lavandera correctly points out, Labov and Weiner (1977) are really arguing that variation between the passive and active is meaningless in terms of three dimensions, referential (in the sense of 'cognitive' or 'descriptive'), social and stylistic. This amounts to saying that the observed frequency with which the active vs. the passive occurs relates only to surface structure constraints and does not convey any information (cf. Romaine, forthcoming c).[7]

Lavandera takes the argument in a somewhat different direction from here, which I will not pursue now because it is tangential to the issue at hand.[8] She seems to have become confused, or overly concerned with Labov's contradictory use of the linguistic variable, and hence misses what I consider to be the real issue. A variant must be understood as an alternative realization of an element on the next or some higher level of abstraction in the grammar. As long as the locus of variation is assumed to be superficial, e.g. in cases where variant word forms do not change cognitive meaning, but do alter stylistic meaning, assuming that cognitive and stylistic meaning is part of lexical meaning, no drastic alteration of generative grammar is required; and a strict division between competence and performance with respect to variability can be maintained by those who wish to. If, however, variation is assumed to exist at higher, non-superficial levels of the grammar, then Labov's views are incompatible with generative grammar. The problem becomes crucial in Labov's (1969) paper where the variable rule is proposed although, as far as I know, attention has not been drawn to the contradictions contained in it. It is strange that this

7. I have not taken account of Labov's (1978) reply to Lavandera, because (pace Labov) it does not really speak specifically to or shed light on the point she is making. It is merely a reiteration of methodology and Labov's position on the relevance of the study of variation to linguistic theory. He says, for example, (1978: 5):

> She [Lavandera] is right in not being persuaded by our arguments [i.e. that *they broke into the liquor closet* means the same thing as *The liquor closet was broken into*]. But we are not in the business of being persuasive: our enterprise demands conclusive demonstration.

I will make reference to this paper in Chapter 9, however, since it is a recent statement of Labov's views on methodology.

8. Lavandera observes that one of the reasons for restricting the study of sociolinguistic variation to cognitively meaningless surface variants is out of fear of providing a linguistically based argument for cognitive-deficit theories. One could avoid this problem of 'differential competence' by assuming that there are different ways of communicating the same cognitive meaning.

paper, which is of major theoretical importance, has received comparatively less attention than Labov's (1966) study of New York City.[9]

Since Labov proposed the concept of the variable rule there have been few detailed illustrations of how it might be integrated within generative grammar, which is the framework Labov considers himself to be working in. His use of the basic formalism of generative grammar in the rules for contraction and deletion of the copula seems to confirm, superficially at any rate, that this is the case, as does his discussion of abstract syntactic issues in terms of the evidence provided by variable rules for the existence of these. Yet, there is a contradiction in what Labov says about the nature of variable rules and their place in generative grammar. Neither of these issues is discussed explicitly, with the result that we are left confused by Labov's conflicting references to variation in abstract syntax as well as competence.

Labov (1969: 736) says that his goal is to incorporate variable rules such as those for contraction and deletion in BEV into the 'main body of generative rules'. By doing this he claims that 'we will be able to resolve questions of ordering and rule form which would otherwise remain undecidable. Furthermore, it will be possible to enlarge our current notion of the "linguistic competence" of a native speaker.'

It is evident, however, that Labov is doing more than 'extending' some of the notions of generative grammar. Thus he says about the competence/performance distinction (1969: 759):

> I am not sure whether this is a useful distinction in the long run ... Are the variable constraints discussed in this paper limitations on performance rather than competence? ... It is evident that rules 1–17 [i.e. rules responsible for contraction and deletion] are a part of the speaker's knowledge of the language, and if some of these rules are cast in a different form than traditional categorical rules, then we must clearly revise our notions of what it means to 'know' a language. It should be equally clear that we are in no way dealing with statistical statements or approximations to some ideal or true grammar. We are dealing with a set of quantitative RELATIONS which are the form of the grammar itself.

Labov concludes by saying that he does not regard his methods of analysis or formal treatment of variable rules as radical revisions of generative grammar. On the contrary, he maintains, his findings support Chomsky's position that dialects of English are likely to differ from each other in surface representations rather than in their underlying structures.

9. Weinreich et al. (1968: 167–70) mention the notion of a variable element within the system controlled by a single rule, but there is no detailed discussion of the concept of variable rule.

Furthermore, the fact that Wolfram's study of contraction and deletion among Black speakers in Detroit produced similar findings is taken by Labov (1969: 761) to support his claim that the 'convergence of such intricate quantitative findings on this abstract level is a compelling demonstration of the force of sociolinguistic method and theory'. I am puzzled by his reference to an 'abstract' level.[10]

The issue of competence/performance which I have raised here is a problem which goes beyond the scope of my discussion in this chapter, and I postpone treatment of it until the final chapter. It involves a consideration of the levels of abstraction relevant to the construction of grammar, i.e. idiolect, sociolect, speech community, etc. In the rest of this chapter I examine how my study of the relative system in Middle Scots relates to some of the issues mentioned here.

2.3 A sociolinguistic study of historical syntax: the relative system

Although it may seem odd in view of the above discussion, I take as my starting point a transformational generative analysis of the relatives in English. The most obvious reason for doing this is that Labov as well as other variationists such as Bailey consider themselves to be working within generative grammar, or at any rate somewhat extended or modified versions of it. The issues involved in a generative analysis of the relatives are of the type to which the study of variation, according to Labov, has important contributions to make, e.g. form of rules, rule ordering, relations with other rules in the system, etc. Since at least four different analyses have been proposed to account for the derivation and deletion of relatives in generative theory, this seems a likely testing ground for Labov's claims. In other words, the analysis of the relatives in English can be seen in Labov's terms as an area of the grammar which is in need of 'decisive solutions'. My question is: do sociolinguistic data bear on any of the issues or provide any evidence which would support one of the analyses over the others; and if so, how?

10. If the competence/performance dichotomy is not considered to be a necessary part of generative grammar, then perhaps Labov's departure from it is not as great as I suggest. I am indebted to Roger Lass for pointing this out to me. If we distinguish between generative grammar as a formal system and its interpretation as a theory about the speaker's competence, then Labov seems to be redefining the sort of knowledge a speaker has as a derived form of performance. Labov (1978: 13), for example, says that 'human linguistic competence includes quantitative constraints as well as discrete ones' (cf. Romaine 1981a).

2.3.1 Treatment of the relatives in generative grammar. Let us assume for the moment one of the views of relative clause formation current in generative grammar: namely, that relativization is a syntactic process whereby a sentence becomes embedded as a modifier in an NP, where the embedded sentence and the matrix sentence share an identical nominal constituent which is realized as a WH pronominal element (cf. Stockwell, Schachter and Partee 1973: 421). With this as background, we can see how an account of relativization will impinge on other aspects of English syntactic structure. For example, what is the relationship between interrogative and relative *which*, and between complementizer and relative *that*? Are these the same or different items in the grammar? The relatives are of course also related to the pronominal and determiner systems in English since relative clause formation involves the introduction of relative pronouns and the movement or re-arrangement of various constituents in pre- and post-nominal modification.

Three of the analyses referred to above assume that relative clauses are derived via a process of embedding, but they do not agree on the constituent in which the relative clause is embedded. The fourth analysis derives relative clauses from conjoined sentences. I give a brief summary of these proposals in the following four sections.[11]

2.3.2 The Det-S or Art-S analysis. The Det-S analysis goes back at least to Lees (1960), and continues into Chomsky's (1965) *Aspects of the Theory of Syntax*. In this analysis the relative clause is defined as a constituent of the determiner; this implies that its grammatical function is closely related to that of the other elements of the determiner system, i.e. delimitation of the potential domain of reference of the head noun. Stockwell et al. (1973: 423) give the P-marker for this analysis shown in Figure 2.

Two rules are needed to obtain the surface form: one that moves the clause around its head noun; and another that introduces the appropriate relative pronoun and deletes the coreferential NP from the clause. There are, however, a number of problems with this analysis, which have to do with the identity conditions which are claimed to exist between certain Ns or NPs in the derivation.

If we assume that the grammar has to account for stacked relatives, i.e. in which the first clause modifies the head noun as already modified in the first

11. Stockwell et al. (1973: 421–501) discuss the three embedding analyses and the problems involved in each in considerable detail. I have greatly simplified the issues here.

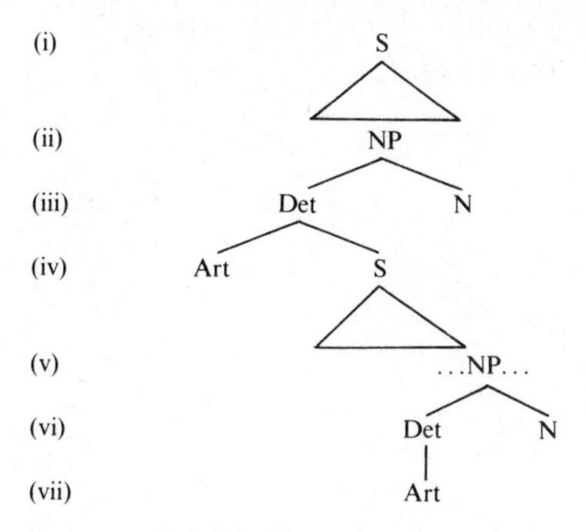

Figure 2 Phrase marker for the Det-S analysis

clause, etc., then the grammar must be more complex. It would need to add a rule which would reposition the clause in an embedded sentence after the new relative clause. The output of the grammar should produce sentences like (1) rather than (2) below:

(1) The house that is on the left that has three windows is John's.

(2) *The house that that is on the left has three windows is John's.

In one instance it is assumed that the identity condition holds between the N of (iii) and the N of (iv), and in the other, that the identity holds between the article and its head noun in the embedded sentence (i.e. (vii) and (vi)), and the article and its head noun (i.e. (iv) and (iii)). The latter double identity condition allows for the self-embedding of restrictive relative clauses, i.e. stacking as in (1), while the former produces a sentence like (2).

On the other hand, if the identity condition is stated to hold between the NP of (ii) and the NP of (v), then no relative clause can be generated at all because the NPs are not identical. The NP of (ii) contains the embedded S of (iv), which the NP of (v) cannot contain. Stockwell et al. conclude that identity between NPs is impossible under the Det-S analysis unless it can be defined in such a way as to exclude the embedded S which is being relativized.

It is not clear, however, whether the grammar should be expected to account for such instances of stacked relatives at all since their acceptability is variable. Stockwell et al. view this problem as a matter of dialect differentiation, while Bach (1974: 271) thinks that the phenomenon of

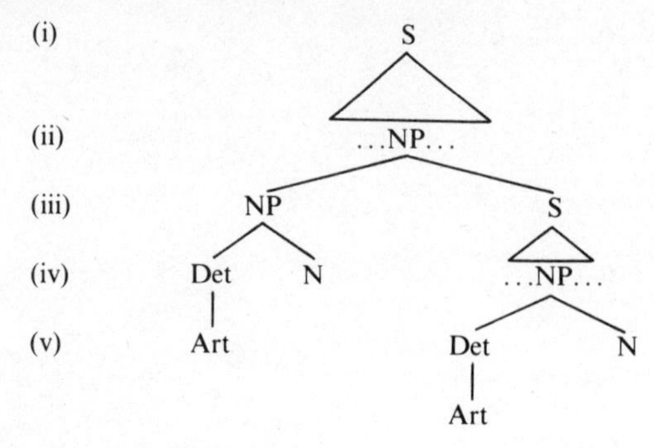

Figure 3 Phrase marker for the NP-S analysis

stacking must be accounted for in any adequate syntactic description of English.[12]

2.3.3 The NP-S analysis. Ross (1967) and Bach (1974), among others, have suggested that the NP-S analysis stands where the Det-S falls down; namely, in its ability to handle stacked relatives. Bach makes the point that this analysis would have to be made more complex to exclude stacked relatives.

This analysis also overcomes the derivational block mentioned earlier, which was that the NPs were not identical because one contained an embedded S and the other did not. In this case the identity condition can be stated on the shared NPs of (iii) and (iv). The P-marker for this analysis is given in Figure 3.

This condition of identity is in fact the strongest possible one, as Stockwell et al. (1973) point out. This condition of whole NP coreferen-

12. Bach also rejects this analysis because 'determiner' seems a much more language-specific category than NP or S. Although the Det-S analysis may be all right for English, Bach is interested in formulating a relativization rule which would operate in a universal grammar. Another reason why Bach favors the NP-S over the Det-S analysis has to do with the preposing rule, which is needed to order adjectival and other modifiers correctly with respect to their head nouns. This rule is based on the assumption that sentences such as the ones below are derivable from a common source.

(1) a. The house that is on the left.
 b. The house on the left. (But not: *The on the left house.)

(2) a. The house that is big.
 b. The big house (But not: *The house big.)

In the NP-S analysis modifiers can be preposed when the last element is a verb or an adjective, and is directly dominated by the highest VP or S in the relevant NP. In the Det-S analysis, however, the correct set of modifiers must be postposed by a more complex set of conditions or by postposing the clause, reducing it, and then preposing the correct set of modifiers before the noun. Here again Bach (1974: 272) suggests that there is some external motivation for taking this analysis (NP-S) as the correct underlying one in other languages. Languages that have verbs in final position prepose their relative clauses; this, he says, would argue for the existence of preposing as a universal transformation. Furthermore, even languages in which relative clauses precede their heads (i.e. S-NP, as in Japanese), can be considered to have the unaerlying NP-S structure.

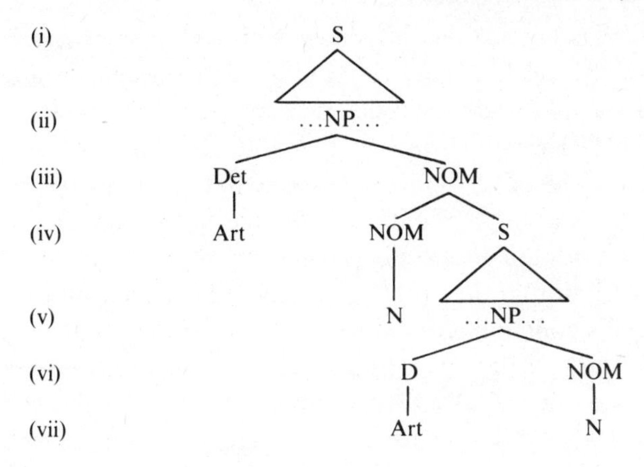

Figure 4 Phrase marker for the NOM-S analysis

tiality causes some difficulties. For example, a different source has to be devised for certain relative clauses with generic NPs as in:

(3) a. All students who can spell decently will pass the course.
 b. All students can spell decently.

It is clear that (3b) is not entailed by (3a). This could be avoided by imposing a constraint on relativization which states that if the shared NP of the relative clause is generic, then relativization is blocked, since a generic paraphrase cannot be entailed by the shared NP of any relative clause. Alternatively, one could exclude quantifiers and generic articles from inclusion in the category of NP at the time when the identity conditions are checked.

Stockwell et al. claim that the only correct paraphrase of relative clauses formed on generic heads is a conditional sentence as in (4).

(4) If they can spell decently, all students will pass the course.

Therefore, the surface structure of relative clauses may be derived from two distinct sources, i.e. either from the embedding of an S within a non-generic NP or from reduction of a conditional sentence that contains a shared generic NP. They suggest that genericness is somehow a sentence-level interpretation. In other words, this is a matter of surface structure interpretation of quantifier scope.

2.3.4 The NOM-S analysis. The NOM-S analysis was originally proposed by Schachter, and has been adopted by Stockwell et al. (1973); its P-marker is given in Figure 4. This analysis of relativization is dependent on a postulated element symbolized as NOM. It is dominated by NP and includes all of NP except the determiner. This view can be supported by the observation that relative clauses appear to modify the matrix noun and not the matrix NP as a whole as in the NP-S analysis.

The NOM-S derivation which Stockwell et al. put forward resembles to a great extent their NP-S analysis, but it avoids some of the latter's disadvantages. For example, it puts aside the question of coreferentiality since the identity condition does not have to be met between shared NPs. It also supplies a solution to the problem of deriving relative clauses on generic NPs and NPs containing quantifiers. Assuming that relative clauses on generic NPs are true relatives and not pseudo-relatives derived from if–then sentences, then the NOM-S analysis accounts for the fact that the shared NP of the relative clause cannot be interpreted as generic.[13]

2.3.5 Deep structure conjunction analysis. Thompson (1971) has argued that the appropriate underlying representation for relative clauses is not an embedded sentence at all, but rather a conjoined sentence. She attempts to justify her analysis in two ways. Firstly, she points out that those who claim that relative clauses are underlying embedded Ss do not agree on what the correct representation of nodes is to explain the relationship between the matrix and the embedded sentence. This, however, is not really an argument. Secondly, and certainly more importantly, Thompson argues that there is a set of structural distinctions between relative clauses and other complex sentences which are clearly relativizations of structures containing embedded sentences, namely, true nominalizations or complementation structures. In the latter case an embedding analysis, she claims, is well-motivated since the embedded sentence plays a role (either subject or object) with respect to the verb, without which it cannot stand. The verb governs the occurrence of the clauses and the type of clause which can occur.[14]

13. This analysis also avoids the problem of blocking relativizations on nominalizations, which the NP-S analysis would have to do by imposing an ad hoc condition on structures like:

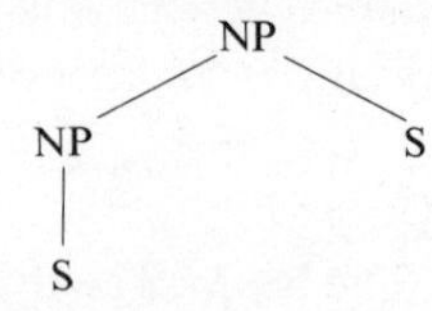

14. Most of the available literature on syntactic complexity assumes that the construction main clause + relative clause is a complex sentence, and that relativization is a process of embedding and subordination (cf. e.g. Noizet, Deyts and Deyts 1972).

Relative clauses, on the other hand, are equivalent to two independent predications on the same argument.[15] Thompson suggests that this basic distinction could be captured in an analysis which deals with relative clauses as superficially embedded structures. There is no distinction then in structural terms between the matrix and embedded sentences. Either of the two predications which are conjoined sentences in the deep structure may appear as the subordinate or modifier of the other in the surface structure, depending on what assumptions the speaker makes about the hearer's knowledge. The same assumptions on the part of the speaker also provide for the choice of the appropriate determiner for the head NP. Thompson gives the following examples to illustrate how this analysis works.

(5) *Deep structure:* I met girl. Girl speaks Basque.
(6) *Conjunction:* I met a girl and she speaks Basque.
(7) *Conjunction:* There's a girl who speaks Basque and I met her.
(8) *Indef. head N:* A girl I met speaks Basque.
(9) *Def. head N:* The girl I met speaks Basque.
(10) *Indef. head N:* I met a girl who speaks Basque.
(11) *Def. head N:* I met the girl who speaks Basque.

Thompson also believes that non-restrictive clauses are best derived from conjoined sentences. This idea goes back at least to Chomsky (1965), and is not as controversial as the argument for the derivation of restrictive relative clauses from conjoined sentences. The derivation of both restrictive and non-restrictive relative clauses from the same underlying source can be seen as having both advantages and disadvantages.[16] For one thing, a common derivation is more highly valued in generative grammar, since it

15. Leech (1974: 149–51) also shares the view that relative clauses have the structure of a predication, but for him relative clauses do not have independent status. They are instead 'downgraded predications', which are a kind of semantic unit equivalent to a feature in function, and which occur in an argument. It is characteristic of such downgraded predications that they always share part of the content of the argument in which they appear. One of the arguments within the predication has the same reference as the remainder of the argument in which the downgraded predication occurs. Thus, downgraded predications which qualify, i.e. occur within an argument, underlie many of the adjectival syntactic functions. The relative clause is the most explicit way for downgraded predications to be expressed, although shorter syntactic means are possible, e.g. a single word.

16. Smith (1974: 648) has suggested that the distinction between restrictive and non-restrictive clauses might be best characterized along a continuum of variable reference ranging in values from high to 0 variability. The variable portion of the continuum would be the domain of restriction and the constant portion, the domain of non-restriction. Somewhere in-between is a neutral type. The scale implies that there is a single core underlying the relative type that ranges over a continuum of variable reference (cf. also 4.4). This follows from Lakoff's (1970) suggestion that restrictive relatives identify a variable NP referent, while non-restrictives refer to a constant NP. Information in the second case is therefore irrelevant. As discourse continues, many of the variable NPs become constant. Relative clause formation is constrained by the constant–variable–constant shifts which must be monitored to avoid ambiguity.

provides a neat analysis in which the relationship between both types of clauses, restrictive and non-restrictive, is captured in a single structure.[17]

Others, however, have pointed out that it is not desirable to derive sentences which may have different meanings from the same source. Thompson, however, thinks that the differences between both types of relative clauses are not the sort of differences that ought to be represented structurally. They are instead differences of a different kind, i.e. in a speaker's decision about how to present to the hearer information present in the underlying representation. Thompson's analysis, then, depends on whether or not we accept this notion, which is an issue outside the grammar. Her interpretation touches, however, on a more fundamental issue, namely: what aspects of the meaning of a sentence should be represented in its underlying representation? In her analysis we can see a gradual extension of the locus of meaning to a non-deep structure level, e.g. surface structure interpretation.

2.3.6 Rules for the introduction and deletion of relative markers

2.3.6.1 WH-rel attachment or relative clause formation rule. In generative analyses which derive pronouns transformationally, one needs some sort of 'relative clause transformation rule' to attach the features [+ WH], [+ REL], [+ PRO] to a coreferential NP or NOM when coreferentiality or identity exists between the NP or NOM of the matrix and embedded sentence.

For the moment I am ignoring the problem of how the grammar will cope with the problem of assigning coreferentiality or identity. Two elements do not necessarily have to be identical in form or meaning to be coreferential; and coreference often involves correspondences which are not always one-to-one, but many-to-one. For example, when multiple coreferents occur in a sentence, how does the grammar decide which one undergoes the WH attachment rule and is then preposed to the front of the relative clause? Postal (1971: 243) refers to this as the 'pick-out problem'. Many syntacticians would now agree, I think, that reference is a matter of semantics and not grammar. Chomsky (1973), for example, eliminates conditions on rules such as coreference, i.e. where $NP_1 = NP_2$, so that the identity condition is not an issue in an X extended theory grammar.

17. Bach's (1968) argument that the reductions of relative clauses maintain the semantic difference between restrictive and non-restrictive adjectives could also be used in support of a conjunction analysis for the derivation of relative clauses.

However, the semantic representation of pronouns and their antecedents has been a source of controversy between the generative and interpretive semantics frameworks. Jackendoff (1972: 109–10), for example, argues for the superiority of the interpretive viewpoint on the basis of its handling of coreference. He claims that generative semantics (or indeed any theory which derives pronouns transformationally) cannot deal with crossing coreference, as in the example:

(12) The man who deserves it will get the prize he wants.

The problem here is this: assuming that the underlying source of a pronoun is a fully specified NP identical with its antecedent, such a sentence must have an infinite underlying semantic representation. Interpretive semantics avoids this by generating pronouns directly in the deep structure and establishing coreference by means of an interpretive rule.[18]

This WH-rel attachment rule raises the question of the relationship between the relative and interrogative pronouns *which* (and also *what*). Are these to be distinguished from one another by separate markers and, if so, how?

Some generativists have postulated the same WH marker for both relative and interrogative pronouns since in both cases, i.e. the formation of relative and interrogative clauses, a WH word is to be fronted or preposed; hence one transformational rule could suffice for both. Kuroda (1969) has examined this issue in detail to see whether an analysis of relativization which accounts for the morphological identity of the relative and interrogative pronouns adds any insight to a description of English grammar.

Kuroda objects to an analysis which posits the same marker for both relatives and interrogatives on the grounds that this is only done for the sake of convenience, and does not really account for the morphological identity of the forms. Koutsoudas (1968) claims that this is a completely ad hoc procedure because there is no apparent semantic equivalence of the two functions of the underlying WH.

Two 'solutions' are suggested: 1. Assign the same marker to both interrogatives and relatives on the basis that WH is one of a complex of features which determine the morphological shape of both, with the condition that if certain of these feature complexes are identical in the surface structure,

18. As Hastings and Koutsoudas (1976: 192–3) point out, however, Jackendoff's argument is not germane to the issue at hand, i.e. it does not demonstrate the superiority of interpretive semantics. The crucial point in dealing with crossing coreference is the assumption that the semantic representation of a pronoun need not be completely identical to the semantic representation of its antecedent. A transformational analysis of pronouns could still be preserved by deriving pronouns from fully specified NPs which are not distinct from their antecedents (cf. Karttunen 1971).

then the same phonological form results. This is at best a superficial attempt at 'explanation', which does not tackle the problem of semantic identity. Or 2. Posit an underlying WH attached to the questioned elements, but no Q; for relative clauses, the WH is introduced by transformation, so in the deep structure there is no relation between relative clauses and interrogatives. This analysis follows that of Stockwell et al. (1973).

Another factor in support of the second solution is that the WH in relative clauses is always predictable. Given the base configuration for a relative clause with the appropriate identity conditions, the grammar can obligatorily delete the identical head and attach the feature WH by the syntactic process of pronominalization; or, in other words, WH can be introduced transformationally like other pronouns.

2.3.6.2 WH fronting. Jacobs and Rosenbaum (1968) subsume both WH attachment and WH fronting under one rule of relative clause formation, but, following Stockwell et al. and others such as Smith (1964), I will treat them as separate rules to allow the possibility that the fronting rule may be optional, but not the WH attachment rule. The application of both these rules assumes that the appropriate identity conditions exist.

The WH fronting rule, which can occur in the same format for all three analyses, Det-S, NP-S and NOM-S, which assume deep structure embedding, moves the coreferential constituent, i.e. either Det, NP or NOM, to which WH has been attached, to the front of the sentence. The rule applies only to non-subject NPs in the embedded S. An additional clause positioning rule is necessary in the Det-S analysis to ensure that the relative clause is properly positioned as a constituent of the head NP. The tree diagrams in Figure 5 illustrate the application of the rules so far for a sentence with one relative clause such as:

(13) Jim liked the pictures that I took.

2.3.6.3 Relative 'that' transformation. The transformation which introduces relative *that* is optional. When it does apply, it must do so after WH fronting. This rule adds the feature [+ that] to the WH-attached element, provided that the element preceding is not a preposition. The latter condition prevents shifted prepositional structures of the type in (14) from being generated.

(14) *The rock on that he sat.

At this point the problem of the relation between relative and complementizer *that* can be raised. Can the same transformational rule handle

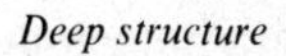

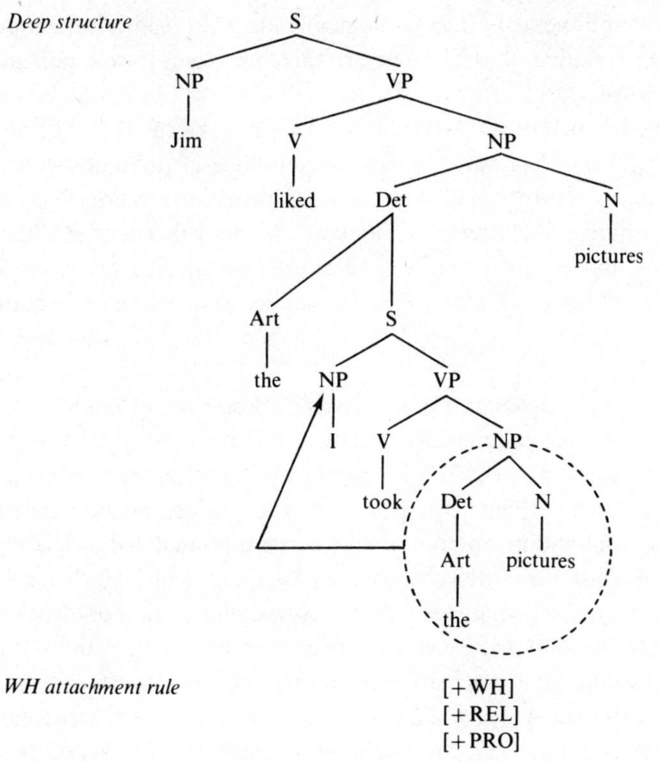

WH attachment rule

[+WH]
[+REL]
[+PRO]

WH fronting rule

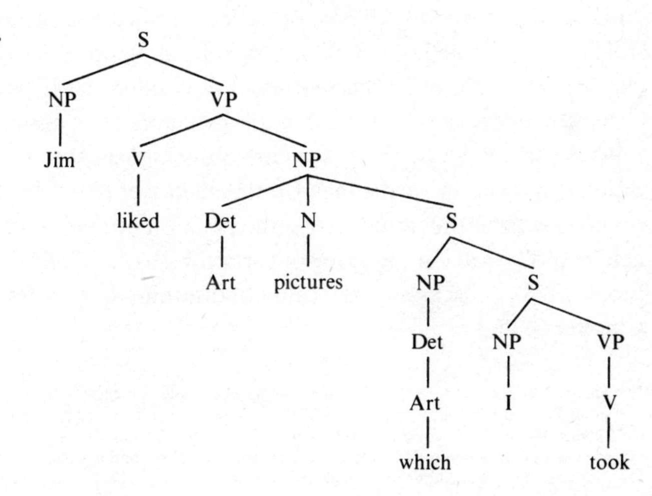

Figure 5

the deletion of a phonetically/morphologically identical *that* in both complementizer and relative clauses? There are some problems if we expect the grammar to do this.[19]

Apart from the surface similarity between a clause of the type, *the fact that she went* and *the fact that she mentioned* (which is ambiguous), it is evident that a complementizer clause may function as a subject or object in its own right, whereas a relative clause may not. It could also be argued that the conditions under which *that* is introduced and deleted are in both instances different (cf. e.g. Cofer 1972). I examine the question of deletion in the next section.

2.3.6.4 Relative 'that' deletion. Before looking specifically at relative *that* deletion, I would like to consider briefly the general phenomenon of deletion as a syntactic process. A basic premise of transformational grammar is that anything which is in principle recoverable can be deleted. Otherwise, an ambiguous sentence whose derivation included a deletion rule could have a number of different sources. Deletion can be seen in larger terms as a strategy which languages employ to avoid repetition of identical elements. Not all deletions, however, are prompted by repetition. For example, the deletion of a preposition before *that* takes place regardless of whether an identical preposition occurs elsewhere in the sentence. Generally speaking, however, the reduction or deletion of repeated constituents can normally take place under specified conditions of identity.

The kind of deletion which occurs in both complementizer and relative clauses is erasure under certain identity conditions. If we postulate that complementizer and relative *that* are deletable by the same rule, then we must somehow allow the grammar to distinguish the two since the conditions for deletion are distinct. Complementizer *that* deletion is dependent on at least three different factors: the position of *that* in the clause, type of clause and lexical conditioning of certain verbs (cf. Cofer 1972, Kroch and Small 1978). I discuss the relevant conditioning factors for relative *that* in Chapters 4 and 5.

19. There is also the question of the status of *that* as a linguistic element, i.e. is it a pronoun or a marker of subordination like complementizer *that*? (Cf. Chapter 3 where I discuss the history of the relatives in English.) It can be demonstrated that *that* is not a 'true' relative pronoun, i.e. it does not undergo the same syntactic processes as WH does. For example, *that* cannot occur as a relative with shifted prepositions as in the ungrammatical sentence:
(1) *The bank in *that* I put my money.
Shifted prepositions constitute an environment which has obligatory non-deletion of the relative; furthermore, the use of WH is categorical (cf. also 4.3.6). This fact together with the observation that TH's other than those derived from WH (i.e. complementizer *that*) may be deleted, could be taken to support the argument tnat TH $\rightarrow \emptyset$ has independent status as a rule of English grammar, i.e. both complementizer and relative *that* can be deleted by this one rule.

A number of considerations are relevant to the question of deletion, if we examine the status of the rules which must be applied to derive surface structure relative clauses which have neither WH or TH. Stockwell et al. (1973) and most others assume that WH attachment is an obligatory rule, and that rules which introduce and later delete *that* are optional. In any case, something must be introduced (whether it is *which* or *that* I will ignore for the moment), before we can speak of its subsequent deletion. Therefore, a rule for the insertion of a relative (i.e. the rel-attachment and rel-*that* rules) must apply in feeding order before a deletion rule can apply. The assumption behind this operation is that the absence of a constituent in the surface structure normally implies that something was present in the deep structure (provided, of course, that there is evidence that such a constituent exists elsewhere). In other words, the status of ∅ may be either that of something that was never there, or something that was added and then deleted. If the first case applies, then it is very difficult to argue for the existence of a category if no observable feature represents it. We must somehow distinguish absence and deletion as separate cases; otherwise, we are faced with the problem of not being able to recover the source of a ∅ in the surface structure, i.e. it may be either a deep structure ∅ or some other linguistic element.

If the presence of *that* on the surface structure is the result of both an optional insertion rule and an optional deletion rule, then it becomes difficult to specify under what conditions insertion of *that* applies since the absence of *that* in the surface structure may result from its never having been introduced in the first place or from its deletion after having been inserted. It seems pointless to postulate both attachment and deletion in cases where the forms do not appear on the surface.[20]

The standard theory allows only the following possible derivational histories for an instance of ∅ in the surface structure of a relative clause (as exemplified in Stockwell et al.'s summary): 1. either the deletion of *that* through the application of the rel-*that* deletion rule (and only in cases where *that* has been introduced previously); or 2. the deletion of a more abstract element, the WH-attached NP. We can easily do this by an optional deletion rule in the grammar which will delete the features [+ WH] [+ REL] [+ PRO] after the WH attachment rule applies (though again, it seems counter-productive to insert and delete). In the grammar constructed up to now, the only other possible source for a surface ∅ is an underlying *that*, since WH attachment was obligatory. To postulate the

20. I consider the problems involved in 'deletion' arguments in Chapter 8.

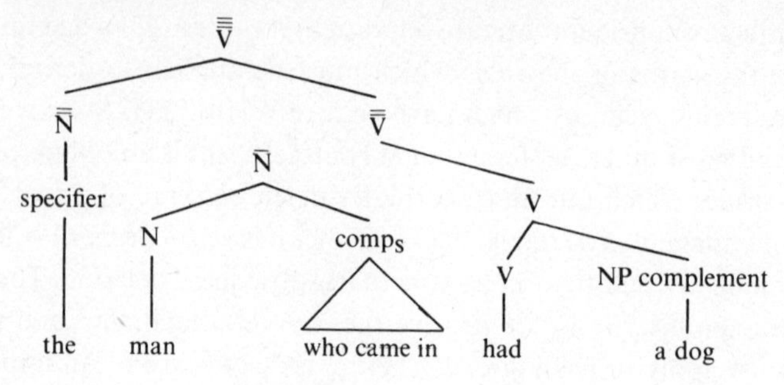

Figure 6

deletion of WH + NP however, we would need to make the rule of WH attachment optional and not obligatory, but then we face the same problem as we did in the case of *that* deletion, i.e. that of postulating an element in the deep structure which is later deleted when both rules are optional. Thus we may not be talking about relative pronoun deletion at all, but rather of shared nominal deletion. Peet (1974) has in fact made the claim that this is a more appropriate description of what happens in Hawaiian English Creole.

More recent analyses of relativization within a generative framework do not really differ radically from that presented in the standard theory; namely, it is still assumed that relative clauses marked with WH pronouns or *that* may be derived from the same underlying source. Emonds (1970) and Bresnan (1972), for example, claim that WH functions as a complementizer and is generated under the complementizer node. In other words, instead of postulating that the base generates an NP in sentence-initial position in subordinate clauses, they assume that it generates a complementizer which may take different forms, e.g. *that*. It may however be deleted or pronominalized. This allows Emonds to say that the WH fronting rule is structure-preserving; that is, a transformation which substitutes or introduces a constituent into a position in a phrase marker held by the complementizer node does not change or create a new structure. Thus, in the following sentence, *who* occupies a position generated by the base.

(15) I know a man who(m) we can buy a car from.

Jackendoff (1972, 1977) also departs from the early view that pronouns are derived from underlying full NPs; he proposes instead the generation of pronouns from the base. Within $\bar{X}$ syntax a relative clause may be generated as a complement of a noun (see Figure 6).

It is evident that the question of what elements, if any, are being introduced and deleted is an issue which can best be decided on the basis of language-specific evidence, in other words, by examining the data from Middle Scots. That is to say, we must first have an indication of the presence of a feature at some stage, either in the derivational history of a synchronic grammar or in the historical development of a language, before we can speak of its deletion. To answer the question of what the mechanism of deletion is we will have to consider briefly the history of the development of the relative clause/pronoun in English syntax with special reference to northern English. I take up this problem in the next chapter.

2.4 The derivation of relative clauses and pronouns

In this section I will indicate briefly some of the important questions involved in the derivation of relative clauses and pronouns. I take the major issues to be:

1. What is the relationship between restrictive and non-restrictive relative clauses?
2. Are relative clauses derived from underlying conjoined or embedded sentences?[21]
3. Are WH and TH strategies of relativization derived from the same underlying mechanism?
4. What types of rules (i.e. categorical, optional, or variable) and relationships of rule ordering are needed to describe variation in the distribution of surface relative markers?
5. What changes, if any, have taken place in the relative system from Middle to modern Scots? And does Scots have a different system for marking relative clauses from other English dialects?

Issues 1 and 2 are connected with each other as well as with the depth of analysis one assumes. I suggest in Chapter 6 that variable data add support to the argument that restrictive and non-restrictive clauses should be kept separate in the grammar.

Issues 3, 4 and 5, in particular, are of the type which Labov (1969) specifically mentions as being decidable on the basis of variable data and variable rule analysis, and are the ones that will be illuminated by a detailed examination of the historical record and comparison of it with the evidence

21. I consider this issue to be more important (or the larger one at any rate) than 'deciding' which constituent the relative clause is to be embedded in (if one chooses an embedding analysis). Both historical and functional considerations could be used to argue for the Det-S analysis.

from modern dialects of English and Scots. The complexity of the modern relative system reflects the fact that the present system is a conflation of what were historically two systems. In Chapter 7 I argue that the distribution of relative clause markers in dialects of modern English constitutes evidence against the derivation of WH and TH strategies from the same underlying source. This of course has some bearing on issues 4 and 5. If there has been substantial change in the relative system from the period in question, i.e. the first half of the sixteenth century to the present day, my task will be to show how a socio-historical linguistic account adds to our understanding of the process by which the change took place.

3 *The history of the relative clause markers in English with special reference to Middle Scots*

We are descended of ancient Families, and kept our Dignity and Honour many years till the Jacksprat *that* supplanted us.

Joseph Addison (1711)

3.1 The origin of the relative clause in the Germanic languages: a problem of general syntax

In his discussion of the relative clause as a problem of general syntax, Benveniste (1971) has commented that a comparison of relativization in languages cannot be based on formal elements alone since there are not always any comparable units; it must instead be approached from a functional viewpoint. He observes that the typical Latin construction with the relative pronoun *qui* governing a verbal clause has been taken to be the model for all relative clause constructions.

Nowadays, we are well aware of the dangers of adopting a Graeco-Latin point of view when dealing with historical syntax, and we avoid 'forcing' linguistic data into already existing models of description. However, the influence of Greek and Latin models on some of the older scholars of comparative syntax has been so pervasive that it deserves some mention. For example, quite a number of scholars (e.g. Curme) have commented that in early Germanic two basic types of sentence structure or relations between structures can be distinguished: *parataxis* and *hypotaxis*. These terms represent relative notions which are often somewhat vaguely used in the literature. In both parataxis and hypotaxis successive clauses may occur in sequence with no formal connecting link between them. Some have claimed that parataxis is a property of 'primitive' languages and is the simpler construction of the two because of its presence in the early stages of many languages. Jespersen (1926: 103) has observed, however, that parataxis is more frequently found in the spoken language, while hypotaxis is more often employed in the written literary style.[1]

1. There is some support for this idea in an experiment reported by Kroll (1977), who compared the use of

From this premise, i.e. that parataxis is a property of primitive languages, it is only a short step to the hypothesis that there is a transition from paratactic to hypotactic constructions which takes place in the evolution of a language; thus hypotaxis represents a stage of development which the 'more highly evolved' languages, like Greek and Latin, were alleged to have attained, and to which other languages in the course of their development aspired. Riecke (1884), for example, used the frequency of hypotaxis/parataxis as a yardstick to measure the development of a language (i.e. 'Je weniger die Sprache ausgebildet ist, desto mehr Parataxe, je höher, desto mehr Hypotaxe'). If we adopted this view, it would follow also that an author who made more use of hypotactic structure must somehow be a more 'highly developed' stylist than one who did not. Yet it does not seem likely that any critic would seriously claim today that Henry James, for example, was a better or more highly developed stylist than Ernest Hemingway simply on this basis (cf. Rynell 1952).

It seems to be largely under the influence of Greek and Latin tradition that the use of complex syntactic structures has come to be taken as an important, if not indeed the most significant, means by which ability in language is displayed and evaluated. Of the vast amount of literature on the subject of syntactic complexity, nearly all of it contains the implicit claim that syntactic complexity is something good.[2] Indeed, a number of sociolinguistic studies have proceeded on this assumption; for example, those of Bernstein (1973) and his followers, which have found that the lower social classes use more simple syntax and the middle classes more complex. Syntactic complexity is one hallmark of Bernstein's 'elaborated code'. The problem with the finding, among other things, is that Bernstein seems to have assumed that syntactic variation is directly related to cognitive ability, and can only be explained in terms of the cognitive function of language.[3]

coordinate and subordinate structures in samples of speech and writing. When subjects were asked to speak about an experience they used 74 percent coordinate structures; later, when writing about the same topic they used only 57 percent.

2. Jespersen (1894) is one of the few scholars writing at this time who connects 'progress' in linguistic evolution with simplicity rather than complexity. He argues that the long term syntactic tendency in a highly developed language like English is towards levelling rather than elaboration.
   Cf. also Labov's (1973) comparison of middle vs. working class speech in terms of 'logicality'. Labov is trying to make the point that differences in syntactic elaboration should not be equated with differences in cognitive ability.
3. Ontogenetically speaking, both in the life cycles of humans and languages, there do seem to be cases where differences of complexity/maturity correlate with cognitive ones, but this occurs only during language acquisition, language death, pidginization, etc. For example, children's language may be like some pidgins in its inability to convey particular concepts (cf. Bloom 1970; Labov 1970). One aspect of

I think we must reject external, aesthetic value judgements such as these, but at the same time realize that different degrees of syntactic complexity or elaboration exist as options, and as such have certain uses and functions in a language. Syntactically elaborated styles of speaking and writing have typically been valued in some languages in certain registers, e.g. scientific or legal writing, but negatively valued in other contexts, e.g. popular narratives.[4] From the end of the sixteenth century onwards, the writings of prescriptive grammarians provide a useful indication of the value placed on certain linguistic phenomena, and in Chapter 5 I will examine some of the prescriptive statements which have been made about the use of relative constructions in English.

What has not been accepted or recognized by all scholars who have made a distinction between parataxis and hypotaxis is the fact that there are clues to the relationship between two successive clauses other than the presence or absence of certain grammatical items, e.g. differences in rhythm, intonation, sentence stress, length and context; these are used in the spoken language today, and presumably always were. The presence of a subordinating marker is perhaps the most obvious of the forms of hypotaxis, but it does not follow from this that the absence of such a marker proves a construction to be paratactic (unless, of course, we take this as the defining characteristic of the distinction).[5] Today, of course, the conventions of punctuation are codified and to some extent substitute for some of the phonetic signals which would be employed in the spoken language; in older texts, however, where punctuation is erratic and cannot always be assumed

linguistic maturity is the reduction of potential clauses to single word or phrasal modifiers after the child has progressed through coordination, subordination and nominalization (cf. Hunt 1970a, b; Romaine 1979a). Similarly, during creolization conjoining seems to be replaced by embedding (cf. Dreyfuss 1977). In language death, on the other hand, speakers no longer utilize the full inflectional apparatus of a language and cannot do the more difficult things, syntactically speaking. Hill (1973), for example, cites the loss of patterns of subordination, and Dorian (1977) the differential failure of lenition in Gaelic (cf. Trudgill 1978b for a comparison between language death and creolization). I discuss some of these issues further in Chapter 4.

4. Here the difference may simply be that between written/spoken language in terms of preference for hypotactic/paratactic syntax. O'Neil (1976: 210) has suggested that the development of hypotactic structures is connected with the advent of literacy (cf. 3.3).
5. Cf. e.g. Schulz (1972), who has pointed out that the connective particles *ja* and *doch* in German are very often used to express logical – semantic relationships such as causality, just as the 'more highly valued' complex structures which use subordinating conjunctions and inverted word order (cf. also Van den Broeck 1977). Particles (or so-called *Füllwörter*) are therefore to be understood as functionally equivalent variables in the expression of discourse cohesion, i.e. the equation is between a paratactic construction with *Füllwort* and a hypotactic construction with a causal subordinating conjunction and transposed word order. Is the difference only functional, however? In other words, if a language/variety has only one marker which can be used in discourse to connect propositions in causal relationships, is the semantic relationship still there? Or, as Traugott (1979: 18) has queried, is a relatively paratactic stage of a language only syntactically and pragmatically different from a more hypotactic one, or is it also different semantically (cf. also Romaine, forthcoming c)?

to be the work of even one scribe or editor, let alone that of the author, this information is unavailable.

This distinction between parataxis and hypotaxis is a difficult one to apply in the case of the development of the relative clause in English, as in other languages, since when the relative pronouns do make their appearance, they are often not new linguistic devices but have the same formal marks as other elements already in use in the language. Scholars have differed in their opinions as to whether or not a word introducing a clause was being used with subordinative force, or whether it belonged to the second or first of two successive clauses. The latter question is connected with the depth of linguistic analysis one assumes. For example, it would be possible to analyze relative clauses as having an underlying paratactic structure (cf. Chapter 2).[6]

Curme (1912: 13) is one of the few earlier Germanic scholars writing about the relative pronouns who accepts that the distinction between parataxis and hypotaxis is not purely formal, since in each case two clauses or propositions may lie side by side. However, when the first formal signs of attempts to connect two expressions more closely begin to appear, some have claimed this is the origin of clear-cut relativization. In Old English, for example, either the demonstrative pronoun or the place adverb *þe*, *þær*, were used in a relative pronoun function. There is, however, the possibility that the second occurrence of the demonstrative in two successive clauses might have been used for repetition or emphasis, i.e. as a stylistic device. This, Curme has suggested, is an instance of *asyndetic hypotaxis*, and does not really involve the use of true relative pronouns at all. It seems best to consider this a transitional stage in the development of the relative pronoun system in English. In the following sections I will examine the history of the relatives in English beginning with the Old English period, i.e. roughly 800–1100.

3.2 The Old English period

The early Middle English relative pronouns which are the ancestors of the modern English relatives originate in certain uses of the Old English demonstrative and interrogative pronouns. In the first instance the Old English demonstrative and article *se*, *seo*, *þæt*,[7] either with or without a

6. This applies also to the issue of syntactic complexity (cf. n. 4 above), which is a function of the model of grammar one uses and the depth of analysis assumed.
7. Unless otherwise specified, I will use *se* to refer to the whole paradigm.

substantive in the initial clause, was repeated at the end of the clause to focus on some particular referent and point forward to some additional information which followed in the next clause, and thus in some way elaborated or restricted the referent in the first clause. An example (followed by a gloss in parentheses and a translation) is given in (1):[8]

(1) Þæt is se Abraham se him engla god naman niwan asceop. (*Exodus* 380–1; cited by Visser 1963: 522)
(That is Abraham that to him the angels' God name new made.)
'That is that Abraham for whom the God of the angels made a new name.'

It has been common practice among some of the traditional Germanic grammarians to call this extended use of the demonstrative an early instance of the relative. In examples such as these they explained that the demonstrative agreed with the case of the first demonstrative by 'attraction', instead of taking on the case marking that would indicate its syntactic position in the relative clause, which is what happens at a later stage. Curme (1912) maintains that the case of the extended demonstrative can be used as a criterion to indicate whether one is dealing with a true instance of a relative: once the demonstrative began to be felt as part of the second clause it no longer took the case required by the verb of the initial sentence or clause, but took the case required by the second. This of course cannot work in the case of nominatives, since the case form would be the same. So strictly speaking, it does not make sense to speak of relativization as a distinctively marked syntactic category; and it is not certain whether true relative status can be claimed for the demonstrative *se* in this context.

There was also the possibility in Old English of placing *þe*, an indeclinable particle, or *þær*, the locative adverb meaning 'there' after a substantive or pronominal element, which could serve the same function as the demonstrative.[9] Curme (1912) again feels that these instances cannot be

8. Traugott (1972: 86–7) says that *se* + proper noun complexes seem to be used as a 'singling out' construction in Old English, and that *se* also seems to indicate previous mention. Thus, modern English *the* grew out of such uses of *se* through the weakening of the dual sense of 'specific' and 'previous mention' to just previous mention.

9. The observation that it is characteristic of languages for expressions of spatial or deictic relationships to acquire extended use as expressions of more abstract relationships is incorporated into the localist view of case grammar (cf. e.g. Anderson 1971: 2–10). For example, in Latin, *ad* and *de* designated spatial relationships as do certain uses of their modern French reflexes *a* and *de* (compare also English *of* and *to*). But the modern reflexes also mark purely syntactic relationships of genitive and dative. It remains to be investigated in more detail how common a syntactic phenomenon it is for markers of such spatial relationships to provide the means of 'creating' other syntactic and grammatical categories (cf. 3.3). From a functionalist point of view, this can be seen to be a reinterpretative strategy which languages have for renewing or creating indispensable syntactic categories, which are either lost through sound change or developed in the process of creolization. Bickerton's (1975) work is particularly insightful, as is Lavandera's (1975) discussion of developments in contrary-to-fact conditional sentences in the Romance languages.

taken as examples of true relatives; and in this case there are no formal signs of agreement since these markers were indeclinable particles. He cites the fact that *þe* was carefully avoided by the glossarists after a noun where the Latin version used a relative pronoun; here they used instead *se* or the combination form *seþe*, where *se* took the case of the verb of the relative clause and was therefore a true relative pronoun. Both *se* and *seþe* by this time, he says, became extended from demonstrative use into true relative pronouns. An example of a *seþe* relative construction is given in (2):

(2) Þa com he on morgenne to þam tungerefan se þe his ealdormon wæs. (cited by Mitchell 1965: 74)
(Then came he in morning to that steward that one that his superior was.)
'Then he came in the morning to the steward who was his superior.'

It is perhaps useful at this point to introduce a technical distinction between relative pronouns and relative markers. We can define a relative marker as a linguistic element which does not vary according to some feature of the coreferential NP, e.g. case, animacy, etc., and which is not felt to be derived from it via a process of pronominalization. Up to this point I have been attempting to use the term 'relative marker' in a neutral sense, i.e. in describing my study as an examination of variation in the relative marker in Middle Scots, I wished to leave open the question of what status *that* has vis-à-vis WH forms. And I have been restricting my use of the term 'relative pronoun' to instances in which I am discussing the ideas, works, etc. of others who use it.

A number of linguists have argued that modern English *that* in relative clauses is not a pronoun (cf. e.g. Jespersen 1909–49; Bresnan 1972; Stahlke 1976; and also Lightfoot 1979: 314, who cites six factors in support of this position). There are however really two issues at stake here: What is a *true* relative pronoun and what is a *true* relative clause? Even if the marking of concord is essential for a true relative pronoun, there can still be true relative clauses which are not introduced by relative pronouns. That is, if the clause shows any marks of subordination, then there is very little reason to take constructions such as (1) with characteristic OV word order as 'pre-relatives', or anything other than true relative clauses. In other words, non-pronominal relativizers can introduce genuine relative clauses.

These issues are however by no means always separate. For example, in the development of relative clauses in Hawaiian Pidgin English, there is frequent ambiguity in grammatical relationships. It is difficult to tell whether some embedding (therefore relativizing) or merely conjoining process has taken place. The surface marker which may eventually be used in a relativizing function is not a specialized relative pronoun, but a simple pronoun. Bickerton (1977: 126) for example cites the following sentence:

Da boi jas wawk aut fram hia, hiz a fishamaen.

'The boy who just walked out of here, he's a fisherman.'

Bickerton (1977: 274) suggests that the pronouns are an intermediate stage between zero forms and the full range of English relative pronouns.

It seems to be clear, however, that *þe* is a relative marker and is probably best analyzed as a complementizer or, in more traditional terms, a subordinating conjunction. In fact, O'Neil (1976) has claimed that relativization was introduced into the Germanic languages as an adjunctive process. He argues, for example, that there is little evidence in Old English to support the view of relative clauses being embedded Ss under NP. It makes more sense, he says, to speak of 'clause adjunction', because the most striking characteristic of the relative clause (and in fact of all subordinate clauses) in Old English is the fact that they are almost always at the margins of the main clause (and almost never flanked by material from the main clause). In late Old English, however, and certainly by the early Middle English period, relative clauses are found flanked by the major constituents of the main clause; so at some point it becomes necessary to postulate a change from adjunction, i.e. $[_S$ ... NP ... S], to actual embedding under an NP, i.e. $[_{NP}$ NP S] (assuming the latter is justified). I will return to O'Neil's explanation of this historical change after I have discussed the Middle English period.

3.3 The Middle English period

Developments in Middle English will be a major concern here not only because this study concerns a dialect of late Middle English, i.e. Middle Scots,[10] but also because the complexity of the relative system of modern English has its origin in the Middle English period. During the early Middle English period *þe* and *þæt* (the neuter form of the demonstrative pronoun in Old English) are used to introduce relative clauses until *þat* (< *þæt*) gradually supplants *þe*. This seeming trend towards simplification is offset by the simultaneous introduction of the interrogative pronouns, the ancestors of modern English *who*, *which*, etc., in a relative function.

10. The terms 'middle', 'early', etc. are of course relative. Middle Scots refers to a period later than Middle English, namely 1450–1650, so that it overlaps with late Middle English and early modern English.

This set the scene for the present modern English system, which contains *who*, *which*, and *that*.

In the beginning of the Middle English period there was variation between *þe* and *þat*. McIntosh (1948) has attempted to show that there was some principle which governed the choice of *þe* and *þat* in certain contexts, i.e. that the two were not merely in free variation. As evidence for the partial complementary distribution of *þe* and *þat*, McIntosh has cited the fact that different versions of the same text generally agree in the choice of the relative, even though they may not agree in other details. This, he says, is an indication that there were in fact some general rules for their selection in certain syntactic environments.

Furthermore, McIntosh claims that these rules are evidently in operation from at least as early as the last part of the *Peterborough Chronicle* (1132 onwards). The rule seems to be that *þe* refers only to animate antecedents, while *þat* refers to inanimate antecedents. He also suggests that the origin of the functional distribution between *þe* and *þat*, which he has observed for Midland dialects of Middle English (not all of which are entirely uniform), lies in the Old English prose differentiation of the indeclinable particle *þe* and the demonstrative *se*; *þe* occurred mainly after demonstrative antecedents, while *se* occurred with antecedents of a more definite character.[11] *Þat* had come to be used in Middle English both where it was the reflex of OE *þæt*, i.e. in the same environments where OE *þæt* would have been used, and also where it had been generalized to include the environments which would have required the masculine *se* or the feminine *seo* form of the declined demonstrative.

The situation with plural antecedents was somewhat different; *þe* and *þa* (the plural nominative of *se* as well as the singular feminine accusative), were used with inanimate plural antecedents instead of *þat*. McIntosh suggests that there was probably some initial reluctance to extend *þat* to the plural since there had never been a way in the plural to express the

11. Old English *þe* shared many of the characteristics of modern English *that*, despite the latter's formal resemblance to OE *þæt*. For example, relativization both by *þe* and *that* involves movement of the noun which they pronominalize to the left of the clause and stranding any preposition in construction with that noun in its original position. In some cases *þe* also appeared at the beginning of the relative clause while the underlying noun was pronominalized as a personal pronoun. *Se*, on the other hand, does not appear to occur with the personal pronoun form of the relativized underlying noun; furthermore, if the relativized noun has a preposition associated with it, the preposition is shifted with the relative pronoun to the beginning of the relative clause. In modern English, however, the preposition may retain its original position. In this regard, *se* resembles modern English *who*, *which*. Traugott (1972: 153) has argued on the basis of the functional similarity between *se* and *who* on the one hand, and *þe* and *that* on the other, for the origin of the modern English *that* in the complementizer *þæt*, which in ME became generalized to all subordinate structures, and was then used in conjunction with any other subordinator, e.g. *if that*, *whether that*, etc.

distinction between masculine, feminine/neuter for any of the pronouns. Thus he says that the need for expressing a formal distinction between animate/inanimate in the plural was felt less strongly than in the singular, where the presence of *þat* already suggested an available means for doing so.

These rules were not observed with 100 percent regularity; and, as indicated above, they do not hold for all dialects of Middle English. Even within the Midland dialects McIntosh notes that *þat* was also used after some animate antecedents (some of which were originally neuter in Old English), after indefinite pronouns and pronominal adjectives, and with antecedents which were personal names or personal pronouns.

After the disappearance of *þe*, *þat* took over as the Middle English relative and was used with both animate and inanimate antecedents in both restrictive and non-restrictive clauses. When the interrogative pronouns *which*, *who*, etc. began to be used as relatives, there arose a tendency to confine *þat* to restrictive clauses. The simple interrogatives seem to have been used first as generalizing relatives in a generic sense (even in the Old English period, particularly in connection with *swa*); they had the meaning *whoever*, *whatever*, *whichever*, etc. as in this early Middle English example:

(3) Hwam mai he luve treweliche hwa ne luves his broþer. (*Wooing of Lord* 275; cited by Mustanoja 1960: 192)
(Whom may he love truly, who (-ever) does not love his brother.)

This use continued into the Middle English period where these 'relatives' were used in combination with *that* as well as *so*, *soever*, *some*, etc., also in a generic sense. Mustanoja (1960: 191) says that the transition from interrogative into relative pronoun began in types of indirect questions where the interrogative character of the pronoun became weakened and the pronouns so used were generalizing relatives. The final stage in the development occurred when the pronoun referred to a clearly definable antecedent and was used with a strictly relative function.

Mustanoja indicates that this use of the interrogative pronouns as relatives may have been prompted by Latin influence and no doubt was strengthened in Middle English under French influence. *Which* gradually began to supplant the relative *that* and was used with both animate and inanimate antecedents in the singular and plural as well as with sentential antecedents, i.e. it could have reference to whole clauses or sentences.[12]

12. Mustanoja (1960: 191) says that with the exception of the combination *all what*, which is recorded in Old English, interrogative pronouns do not occur in strictly relative use until the twelfth century.

What is interesting about the entrance of the interrogatives into the relative system (see further below) is that they were first used as relatives in the genitive case or as objects of prepositions. The WH form *who* was the last to establish itself as a relative on a par with *which* and *that*, although the inflected forms *whose* and *whom* had been in use since the earliest part of the Middle English period. In the first half of the fifteenth century *who* appears in a strictly relative use in a few stereotyped closing phrases of letters, but the use of *who* (instead of *which* or *that*) with personal antecedents was confined to this epistolary use until the sixteenth century. There are several hypotheses about the reasons for its origin and expansion in the system of relative pronouns as well as for the delay of its use for so long. Steinki (1932), for example, cites its epistolary use as evidence that the form had its origin in popular speech since letters of this period are a good source of colloquialisms.

Meier, on the other hand, claims that Latin models provided the major influence; he says (1967: 280) that even in the early uses of *who* in letters the authors will have followed letter-writing manuals which were traditional notarial form books largely in Latin. According to Meier, the development of *who* as a relative pronoun with a personal antecedent was delayed by the very use of *who* as a bridge or transition between its earlier and later expanded use. The use of the indefinite or generic *who* in both *who ... he* and *he who* (note also *he that* in use at the same time) was probably the basis for the breakthrough of the nominative forms into the relative system proper. This can be seen in example (4) from Middle Scots, where the same type of construction was used:

(4) Quha hapynt in to that fycht to fall, I trow agane he suld nocht rys. (Barbour's *Brus* 13/174)
(Whoever happened to fall in that fight, I believe he should not rise again.)

This can be compared with the following example from Chaucer:

(5) Whoso that first to mille comth, first grynt.
(*Canterbury Tales* D (III) 389)
(Whoever comes to the mill first, grinds first.)

There was also, no doubt, the influence of symmetry from the interrogative pronoun paradigm; although, at the same time it must be said that there was no formally marked distinction in the relatives *which* and *that*. Meier thinks that these two factors were operating counter to one another; while the former encouraged the use of *who*, the latter delayed it. Curme (1912) attributed the delay of *who* to the fact that the genitive and dative

Table 3.1. *The development of the relatives in English*

<table>
<tr><th></th><th>Old English</th><th colspan="2">Middle English</th><th>Modern English</th></tr>
<tr><td>Demonstratives</td><td>se, seo, þæt, seþe, etc.</td><td>þat</td><td rowspan="2">þat</td><td rowspan="2">that</td></tr>
<tr><td>Relative particle</td><td>þe</td><td>þe</td></tr>
<tr><td>Interrogatives</td><td>hwa, etc.
hwilc, etc.</td><td colspan="2">who, etc.
which</td><td>who, etc.
which</td></tr>
</table>

forms of the demonstratives (i.e. *þæs* and *þæm*) were similar to the corresponding forms of the interrogatives (i.e. *hwæs* and *hwæm*), while the nominative form of the demonstrative, *se*, was quite different from the nominative interrogative *hwa*.

Curme's 'explanation' does not however fit in well with the fact that in modern Dutch the interrogative relative pronouns are still limited to the genitive (i.e. *wiens* and *wier*) and objects of prepositions (i.e. *wie*). In other cases the masculine/feminine demonstrative (*die*) and the neuter demonstrative (*dat*) are used. Furthermore, the case, number and gender marking of the interrogative *wie* is exactly parallel to that of the demonstrative *die* (cf. Allen 1977: 199–200), and this was also true during Middle Dutch when the interrogative pronouns began to be used in relative clauses along with the demonstratives.

The use of *who* in the nominative was eventually established however, probably partly on the basis of internal symmetry, i.e. it completed the paradigm of *whose*, *whom*. Its entry into the relative system also had the effect of making English structurally more similar to Latin and French, which would have been considered desirable. In any event, the availability of *who* alongside *which/that* provided another option which could be exploited for stylistic as well as functional purposes. It created the basis for distinguishing antecedents in terms of animacy, and thus completed the paradigm which became established in early modern English. Table 3.1 outlines the developments discussed so far (cf. Kock 1897 for a more complete picture), which we can conveniently summarize in the following points:

1. Expansion and use of demonstrative pronouns and place adverbs as relatives in Old English.
2. Replacement of *þe*, a relative particle, by the subordinator *þat* in Middle English.

3. Replacement of the demonstrative pronouns by the interrogatives in Middle English.

O'Neil (1976: 207) has suggested that what we can see happening between the Old and Middle English periods is the working out of a syntactic strategy for the incorporation of sentences into sentences, i.e. a change from adjunction to embedding. His 'explanation' for this phenomenon is the advent of literacy among the Germanic peoples, which forced a change in adjunction. And he links the change specifically with performance strategies and perceptual factors, i.e. adjunction poses a burden by allowing the build-up of perceptually difficult sentences. Heavy modifiers in a sentence are delayed to the end and not allowed to break up the integrity of the sentence. Once the process of subordination or embedding was well developed, it was utilized to reduce the burden of adjunction; literacy afforded the Old English writers a means for the composition and decomposition of sentences.

O'Neil has further speculated that there were no relative clauses at all in the Germanic languages that preceded in time the earliest recorded Germanic languages commonly designated as 'Old', e.g. Old English, Old Norse, Old High German, etc. And he concludes that it is probably the case that there are never any dependent clauses in the early pre-literate stages of a language. This is particularly interesting in connection with the fact that there are no relative pronouns or particles common to the Germanic languages, although the replacement of demonstrative pronouns used as relatives in early stages of some of the languages, e.g. English and Dutch, by interrogatives can be seen as a Germanic strategy for creating relative pronouns. Typologically, the modern Germanic languages can be divided into two groups on the basis of their relative clause formation strategies: 1. those which use an invariant relativizing particle, e.g. Frisian (which uses the locative adverb *diar-* 'there', 'where') and Norwegian (which uses the particle *som*);[13] and 2. those which have a mixed system, e.g. English (which uses the subordinator *that* and the interrogatives), Swedish (which uses the invariant particle *som* and the interrogatives) and Dutch (which uses both demonstrative and interrogative pronouns). A language like modern German, which has no invariant relative particle, but uses the demonstratives as relative pronouns, could be considered to be a special case of type 1; that is, if we assume that the most relevant typological

13. Norwegian used to employ interrogatives in a relative function in certain syntactic positions as modern Swedish and Danish do today; the usage survives however only in older written usage (cf. Haugen and Chapman 1964).

distinction is between mixed/unmixed strategies. If, however, the relevant criterion for the grouping is the use/development of true relative pronouns, i.e. a strategy of relativization which involves pronominalization, even if this strategy is not available for use in all syntactic positions, then German belongs to type 2. A language like Dutch, which I have put as type 2, is of course 'mixed' only in the sense that it uses both demonstrative and interrogative pronouns rather than one or the other set exclusively; otherwise, Dutch has one strategy for relativization, namely, pronominalization. Perhaps then a third type consists of languages like Dutch and German which seem to have reached a later stage in the development of relativization as a syntactic category distinct from subordination.[14]

We can hypothesize that there is a developmental continuum consisting of three stages, beginning with the marking of relative clauses with invariant relative particles and culminating in the creation of relativization via a stage in which two strategies coexist. This progression is however not Germanic-specific, even though Germanic has examples of all three types. The fact that there are Germanic dialects like Frisian (and as I will point out later, dialects of English like Scots) which use only a subordinating strategy in relativization makes suspect the link between literacy and the shift from adjunction to embedding under NPs postulated by O'Neil. (I will have more to say about perceptual factors in the final section of this chapter.)

Although the Germanic languages have arrived at similar means for marking relative clauses which cannot be related to a common historical relative pronoun or marker, it is evident that the similarities are functional, i.e. they have to do with the syntactic task of relativizing. This will become clear if we examine other cases in which relativization is not a syntactically distinct category, e.g. pidgins, creoles and dying languages. An examination of what happens in creolization, which involves, among other things, development of greater distinctiveness in marking relativization, sheds some light on Germanic events and, in particular, English.

Sankoff and Brown (1976) have studied the process of how speakers of Tok Pisin, a New Guinea English-based pidgin, have created a relativizer

14. The typological split between those Germanic languages which have invariant relative particles and those which do not also coincides with the incidence of preposition stranding. It appears that an indeclinable relative particle is a necessary precondition for preposition stranding in relative clauses. This is furthermore connected with deletion; languages which have only pronominal relatives, like Dutch and German, have no pronoun deletion rule, while the languages which have an invariant particle, like English and Swedish, do (cf. Allen 1977: 355–6). Even though an indeclinable relative particle may be a necessary condition for stranding, it is not sufficient. Yiddish, for example, which has an indeclinable relative, *vos*, does not allow stranding.

from the place adverbial *ia* meaning 'there' (also spelled *hia*). The following examples illustrate the use of *ia/hia* in its adverbial function (Sankoff and Brown 1976: 639).

(6) tispela haus hia 'this house'

(7) yu stap hia 'you stop here'

In previous grammatical descriptions of Tok Pisin, *ia* has been treated as a place adverbial derived from English *here*; and it is fairly clear from what others have said that it had not been used as a relativizer or relative particle throughout the history of Tok Pisin. So far the English WH forms seem to be used only in indirect questions, and from what Sankoff and Brown report, it does not seem likely that they will expand to create a full system of relatives in the way that *who*, *which*, etc. did in Middle English.

Instead, what is happening in Tok Pisin is that the lexical item, *ia*, which originated as a place adverbial, has been extended to a demonstrative or generalized deictic function in discourse, as the following example (Sankoff and Brown 1976: 632) illustrates:

(8) Meri ia [em i yangpela meri, draipela meri ia] em harim istap.
(This girl, who was a young girl, big girl, was listening.)

In this sentence *ia* is being used to bracket an embedded clause from a matrix S by virtue of its placement after both the head noun and the embedded clauses.

Sankoff and Brown suggest that *ia*, while preserving its deictic function, has been extended to another structural possibility; namely, it has become a focussing particle which is backward-looking, i.e. it alerts listeners to a previous item in discourse or focusses on a particular referent and marks it as different from another referent. But at the same time *ia* has taken on a more general deictic function; it is also forward-looking in that it points to the slot where new material will be inserted.[15] In Tok Pisin then we have a nice illustration of how an original place adverbial used as a focussing particle becomes, in Sankoff and Brown's terms, a likely candidate for doing the syntactic work of separating an NP from an embedded sentence.

A chain of events similar to those which Sankoff and Brown have presented for Tok Pisin, i.e. from a situation in which a place adverbial is transformed in function to a postposed deictic or demonstrative and then is used as a relativizer, is represented synchronically in Buang, where the deictic particle *ken* is used as a place adverbial, postposed demonstrative

15. It is interesting to note that in American sign language nouns are marked deictically with a hand gesture when they are the topic of discourse, i.e. a speaker signs a noun and points somewhere. Thereafter, when referring to that NP the speaker points to the place he has marked (cf. Dreyfuss 1977: 167).

and a relativizer. Sankoff and Brown reject a strictly syntactic view of relativization in favor of a functional one which shows some of the properties which relative clauses share with other constructions. The case of Tok Pisin indicates, I think, the value of Benveniste's (1971: 192) approach to relativization as a problem of general syntax (cf. 3.1). He has commented (speaking of developments in the use of the Indo-European pronouns as determiners of nouns or adjectives and as relative pronouns) that in both cases the role or function of the pronoun is the same, i.e. that of a determiner, whether it is determining a nominal or has been extended to determine a complete verbal clause.[16] The relative clause, no matter how it is attached to the antecedent, he concludes, behaves like a determined syntactic adjective, and the relative pronoun plays the role of a determinate syntactic article.

I would suggest that what happened in Tok Pisin has some relevance to relativization in English (and Germanic). In the case of the extension of *se* in a relativizing function and the use of the locative adverb *þær* to mark relative clauses in Old English, we can note a trend similar to Tok Pisin.[17] This should not be too surprising since Tok Pisin is an English-based pidgin; but Tok Pisin did not just borrow the superstrate system of relativization. This suggests that there might be a universal principle governing the process of creating relativization.[18]

There seems to be support for this hypothesis in a study by Dreyfuss (1977), which compared the relative clause formation strategies in four creoles (Haitian Creole, Tok Pisin, Sango and Sranan). She found that all four languages used the order NP-S (with SVO word order), and that three of the languages used a deictic marker as a relativizer. According to Dreyfuss (1977: 150), the choice of the deictic in a relativizing function is an independent innovation, i.e. the languages have not borrowed from the superstrate (though there has been considerable influence from French in the case of Haitian Creole). The fact that the languages are creoles does not seem to have influenced the kind of marker; none uses true relative pro-

16. This also suggests the inadequacy (or at any rate, the restrictiveness) of defining relativization as a process applying to or on a noun (cf. Chapter 4 where I discuss the difficulty this poses in establishing coreference in the case of certain sentential relatives).
17. Braunmüller (1978) has argued that there is neither a functional nor an original historical difference between pronominal/deictic expressions and conjunctions in the Germanic languages, so that the functions of conjunctions can be described in terms of a deictic theory of discourse reference.
18. Kay and Sankoff (1974) view creolization as a process of adding grammatically marked categories in which a universal principle determines the order of addition. Certain semantic notions may become more psychologically salient or functionally necessary. A creole may create new categories by borrowing or calqueing on forms in the superstrate, or by drawing on possibilities in universal grammar.

Table 3.2. *Case marking in four creoles (from Dreyfuss 1977: 170)*

	HC	TP	SG	SN	English
Subject	1	2, 3	2, 3	2	1 (2)
Direct object	2	2, 3	2, 3	2	1, 2
Oblique and Genitive	3	3	3	3	1 (2)

1 = coding on relative marker
2 = deletion
3 = pronominalization

nouns that vary with case, animacy or other characteristics of the antecedents.

Resumptive pronouns occur in all four languages, but there are differences in the positions in which these occur. All the languages use them in obliques and genitives however. Dreyfuss (1977: 170) suggests that this may be evidence that pronominalization is the most favored of the three possible mechanisms of marking the case of a coreferential NP. The other possibilities would be marking the case on the relative pronoun or deletion. Where the relativized NP is a subject or direct object the languages use a variety of means for encoding case. These possibilities are summarized in Table 3.2, where modern English is included for comparison. If we just consider the WH relatives (i.e. the true relative pronouns), then English can be thought of as using only the first two strategies for coding case, namely either by marking case on the pronoun or by deletion. I have put parentheses around the deletion strategy to indicate that it is not always possible to delete relatives in subject, genitive and oblique positions. The use of resumptive pronouns in modern English is very limited (but does occur in some dialects like Scots), which allows for relativization of NPs which are otherwise in inaccessible positions, e.g. *the man that I knew his wife*. Resumptive pronouns do not seem to be used with WH relatives in any variety of spoken English; they may occur in certain registers of the written language, e.g. legal language.

We might expect further changes to take place in the newer creoles (e.g. Tok Pisin and Sango), as they come to be more widely spoken. The first thing we might predict is that the use of resumptive pronouns in subject and direct object position would die out. This may represent a first step on the way to developing relativization as a distinct syntactic category; in all four creoles relativization sometimes merges with conjunction (or adjunction), especially when there is no relative marker, i.e. deletion. Thus, we would also expect some constraints on deletion to be imposed as time went on (cf. Bickerton and Odo 1976; Bickerton 1977).

Here we may return again to O'Neil's argument that the development of embedding is connected with the advent of literacy among the speakers of Germanic languages. I think the crucial factor involved in the creation of relativization as a distinct syntactic category is not literacy per se, but stylistic expansion or elaboration (which may of course involve literacy, but needn't). In functional terms the absence of embedding mechanisms in a language means the loss of a powerful focussing tool for manipulating discourse (cf. e.g. Keenan 1972). This at any rate seems more plausible than arguments based on perceptual strategies, or purely syntactic principles.

3.4 The early modern English period

Returning now to specific developments in the English relative system, we observe that the use of the three available relatives, *who*, *which*, *that*, did not parallel in all respects that of present-day English until the end of the early modern English period (ca. the end of the seventeenth century). In the early seventeenth century *who* still had not entirely taken over the place of *which* as the relative with animate/personal antecedents. Writers of this period fluctuate in their use of these three pronouns, although there is an increasing tendency from late Middle English onwards to confine the use of *that* to restrictive relative clauses. Bately (1965: 245–9) says that the majority of grammarians of this period put restrictions only on the form *who*; otherwise, they seemed to think that *which* as well as *that* could be used with antecedents of all genders. Wallis, she says, was the only grammarian in the seventeenth century to restrict *which* to non-personal antecedents. But it was not until the end of the first decade of the eighteenth century that its pronominal use with personal antecedents became actually proscribed in grammars. (I examine prescriptive grammar and the use of the relatives in 5.5.)

3.5 Relative markers in Middle Scots

Since I will be dealing with the modern English system of relatives in some detail in the next chapter, where I describe the linguistic factors affecting the choice of particular relatives, I turn now to northern English developments, and in particular to the situation which obtained in Middle Scots.

There are several differences in the northern English relative system which are worth noting: 1. the existence of *at* alongside *that*; and 2. the northern *quh-* forms of the relative, which are later supplanted by the English *wh-* forms. In northern Middle English *at* was used as a relative pronoun fairly frequently, mostly in restrictive clauses, but also in non-restrictive ones during the fourteenth–fifteenth centuries. It is possible that it was adopted from the Old Norse *at* since its use with the infinitive, a commonly used construction in Old Norse, is found in northern English from 1280 to 1470. As Caldwell (1974: 31) is careful to point out, however, this probably has nothing to do with the reduced form of the relative or conjunction *that*, which occurs widely not only in modern spoken Scots and northern English dialects, but also probably to some extent in most forms of modern spoken English as part of general phonetic reduction which occurs in unstressed syllables. It seems more likely that the form today results from this more general process of simplification which affects initial /ð/ in unstressed position rather than the reflex of Old Norse *at* which survived in the modern language. If the same source is to be cited for both however, then Caldwell suggests that they coalesced quite early. In any event, it becomes rare after 1500, and Girvan (1939) suggests that the disuse of *at*, whatever its origin, can be explained by the fact that it came to be identified as a reduced or colloquial use of *that* and was abandoned on that account, especially in print.

The *quh-* forms of the relative were the native northern English forms, and these began to encroach upon *that* in a way similar to that described in 3.3 for Middle English as a whole. Variation between the native forms and the English *wh-* forms occurred in the written language of the sixteenth century until gradually the English spelling options came to be increasingly preferred over the native Scottish ones, and the *wh-* forms of the relative pronouns replaced the Scottish *quh-* ones.

Caldwell (1974), who studied the relative pronoun in Early Scots from ca. 1375 to 1500, doubts that the form *quhilk* as a relative pronoun (but not as an interrogative) was an integrated part of the spoken language. In the texts which she examined (literary prose and official/record prose) there is, she says, a correspondence between the type of text and the form of the relative pronoun. In native vernacular verse *that* remains the most frequently used relative, both restrictively and non-restrictively. She reports a gradual (but still very limited) encroachment of *quhilk* on *that*, which reaches its peak about the time of Henryson (ca. late sixteenth century). In literary and record prose, which correspond closely in their use of the relative pronoun forms, she reports that *that* is the most frequently used relative in restrictive function, while *quhilk* is the most frequent form found in non-restrictive clauses. Overall, the encroachment of *quhilk* on *that* is greater in prose than verse. There is, however, no real basis, I think, for concluding from the evidence that Caldwell presents that the *quh-* or *wh-* forms of the relative were any less integrated into the spoken language then than the WH forms are today.

I submit that a survey of certain types of stylistically differentiated texts in modern English and different styles of modern spoken language would reveal essentially the same facts about the use of the relatives today as it would have done in the period in question (i.e. early sixteenth century); namely, that WH forms occur more frequently in more formal styles, whether written or spoken, and that *that* and Ø occur in the least formal styles of speaking and writing. The only thing which has changed since the introduction of the complete relative paradigm into English, i.e. *who, which, that*, is the relative level of frequency with which the observed variation takes place. The difference is in other words quantitative rather than qualitative. I hope to demonstrate this in Chapter 7, where I give some evidence from the modern spoken and written language for comparison with the historical material.

It remains now only to mention that what was said above applies to both the singular and plural inflected forms; the latter, *quhilkis*, is limited to Scots and does not occur in English at all, as well as to forms of the type *the quhilk(is)*, which have been omitted from the discussion so far. The origin of *the quhilk* and its English variant *the which*, is disputed. The form occurs first in the north, and Curme (1912) believes it is of native origin and not a loan translation of the French *liquels*. Those who argue for a native source (cf. also Reuter 1937, 1939) point to its origin in the Old English use of the relative particle *þe* with the Old English demonstrative *se*, as in *seþe* with the relative being replaced by *which* later in the Middle English period.[19]

Mustanoja (1960: 198) says that it is probably the case that this pattern in French strengthened the native English one as there are many cases where an obvious parallelism between English and French usage strengthened the position of a native English construction. (I have already cited above the

19. Traugott (1972: 156) has commented that this usage should hardly be surprising since definiteness is essential to relativization. What is more surprising, she says, is that only *which* seems to take this construction. She has also pointed out that the usage of *which* + noun (where the noun may have semantic but not formal identity with an NP occurring previously in the discourse) suggests that relative subordinates are not necessarily always pronouns substituting for a noun. They may also be referential subordinators attached to rather than substituting for a noun and indicating identity with the head noun.

possible influence of Latin in the expansion of the relative paradigm with respect to the adoption of the interrogative forms as relatives.) Caldwell's study, however, turns up some support for the native origin theory since she finds that *the quhilk(is)* appears in considerable proportions only in prose (and in non-restrictive function) and hardly at all in verse. The latter fact is hardly surprising if we consider verse as the representative of native vernacular tradition.

To complete the picture in Middle Scots, it can be noted that *quha* is not established as a true relative in the nominative during the early period that Caldwell studied. She found that it behaved like its English counterpart *who* in that it was used as an indefinite or generalizing relative and also in epistolary formulas. The oblique forms, *quham* and *quhom*, on the other hand, were used fairly extensively when the relative was dependent on a preposition. *Quhais* and *quhois* are comparatively rare in early literary use since possessive relative clauses seem to be on the whole rather infrequently used in early Scots (cf. Caldwell 1974: 58). Other constructions were employed to avoid forming possessive relatives (these strategies will be discussed in 4.3.4 and 4.5).

Caldwell (1974: 78) cites the following factors which favored the spread of *quha* as the nominative relative: 1. the oblique forms were already present; and 2. there was a tendency to use *that* as a restrictive relative and (*the*) *quhilk*(*is*) for non-personal antecedents. The non-personal use of *quham* was being lost so *quha* was available to fill the personal function that (*the*) *quhilk*(*is*) was losing. This tendency was not however rigidly observed, i.e. there were cases in which *that* was used non-restrictively and (*the*) *quhilk*(*is*) occurred with personal antecedents.

3.6 The case of relative marker deletion/omission

Before discussing the specific problem of relative marker deletion/omission, I will briefly refer again to some of the terminology mentioned in 3.1, in particular *asyndetic hypotaxis* (*parataxis*); and I will introduce some new terms, e.g. ἀπὸ κοινοῦ, *ellipsis* and *contact clause*, all of which have appeared in discussions of the relative pronoun but have not been used in the same sense by all scholars.

The term ἀπὸ κοινοῦ is the broadest of these and has been used to refer to alleged cases of relative pronoun deletion. Meritt (1938: 16), who has done a comparative study of the phenomenon in the Germanic languages, has defined it as a:

syntactical construction in which a word or closely related group of words, occurring between two portions of discourse, contains an idea which completes the thought of the first part, to which it is grammatically related, at once supplies the thought essential to the following part, to which it may also be grammatically related, and is not felt to belong more closely with the first part than with the second.

It is clear from the phrasing of the definition that it could take in a number of syntactic phenomena. It would include relative clauses from the early stages of the English language, where there was no hard and fast rule for deciding in all cases whether a demonstrative was being used with relative force or whether the element in question belonged to the first or second, or indeed, both parts of the construction. It could also be used to refer to instances in later stages of the language where clear cases of deletion/omission can be cited. This will depend upon how Meritt's phrase, 'is not *felt* to belong more closely with the first part than with the second', is interpreted by the individual scholar. There has been little attempt apart from Meritt's work to use the term discriminatively, and it has often been applied to many constructions which are not very similar.

Meritt (1938: 110) believes that ἀπὸ κοινοῦ had its origin in the Germanic languages in constructions of asyndetic parataxis in which two clauses were conjoined which were approximately of equal importance, i.e. one was not subordinate to the other, by means of a connective. There was usually a noun falling between the two verbs which was both grammatically and contextually attracted to both. In Old English it was customary to join successive sentences by conjunctions as in:

(9) Her fordferðe Hardnacnut cyng æt Lambhyðe on VI Idus Iun ond he wæs cyng over all Englaland. (*Anglo-Saxon Chronicle* 1042)
(Here passed away Hardnacnut King at Lambhyðe on 8 June and he was king over all England.)

There are also instances where sentences follow one another without conjunctions, i.e. asyndetic parataxis, as well as cases which have been called *asyndetic hypotaxis*, i.e. where the second of two sentences is dependent on the first. But how one decides in historical texts when part of a sentence becomes subordinate without some formal marker to indicate that such a relationship is intended remains unclear.

Bender (1912) says that ἀπὸ κοινοῦ originally resulted from subordination without relative pronouns; this usage, he concludes, was characteristic of a transitional period from parataxis to hypotaxis (although the construction could also result from the omission of a relative pronoun).

Meritt holds the view that although this kind of clause construction might be due in some instances to the omission of the relative pronoun, it might also be a continuation of an earlier asyndetic means of joining sentences before the use of the true relatives. The construction was always one of hypotaxis, he says, and was therefore distinguished from asyndetic parataxis, which bears some similarity to ἀπὸ κοινοῦ. It seems, however, from what has been said that this distinction rests either on a process of very fine discrimination on Meritt's part or is a matter of some subjective interpretation. In any case it is easy to see why the term ἀπὸ κοινοῦ has been applied to these types of relative constructions.

The predominant opinion about the origin of Ø relatives is like that of ἀπὸ κοινοῦ, i.e. that it is an indication of the colloquial language of the period (cf. e.g. Poutsma 1904). It was believed to have had its origin in the colloquial use of Old English and to have continued into Middle English, where during the later part of the Middle English period its use increases. The fact that it so rarely occurred earlier was believed to be the result of Latin influence, which suppressed native syntactic tendencies. Regardless of its status as a colloquialism in Middle English, or thereafter, relative pronoun omission (or ellipsis) does not seem to be a concept which can be applied to the Old English period, or even in the early Middle English period, where the exact degree of subordination or the intention of the author can only be guessed at (cf. Mustanoja 1960: 204 in support of this). These non-introduced relative clauses make their appearance in the second half of the fourteenth century. Since the earliest Scots texts with one exception go back only to 1375, and there is evidence that true relativization occurs at this time, deletion of the relative is a meaningful concept which can be applied to Middle Scots texts of the first half of the sixteenth century. At this time Ø clearly exists in opposition to *that* and *quhilk*.

Einenkel (1891–2, 1906) suggests that relative pronoun omission is due to the influence of French syntax on the language, while Jespersen cites Scandinavian (Danish) influence. There were, however, certain types of constructions in use in late Old English and in Middle English which could have paved the way for more Ø clauses to be used in the language; and again we may have another instance of foreign influence strengthening an existing pattern. Jespersen (1968: 81,133), for example, has suggested that what he has called *contact clauses* of the following type provided a pattern.

(10) There is a man wants to see you.

This type of construction occurred rarely in early Middle English prose, but more often in poetry, which led Mustanoja to suspect that such contact clauses were used for metrical purposes. By the end of the sixteenth century these clauses (in this particular case we are dealing with omission of the subject relative, since the place where a relative could be inserted is that of subject of the relative clause) became quite common in literary prose, and are quite frequent in Shakespeare, for example. Many of these cases could, however, equally well be taken as non-expression of the personal pronoun, especially in non-restrictive relative clauses where the paraphrase, *and he*, exists as an option. A distinction can of course be made between omission of the relative and the personal pronoun where a coordinating element or conjunction is retained. Instances in which it is clear that we are dealing with personal pronoun omission will be excluded from this study.

Contact clause constructions, either with existential or locative, *there is/are*, or in combination with the verb *haten* 'to be called or named', have also been referred to as instances of ἀπὸ κοινοῦ (cf. Visser 1963: § 18; and Kellner 1892, who discusses the comparable *hiez* construction common in Old High German). Since it occurs only with a limited number of verbs, it is probably not appropriate to cite this construction as an example of relative omission; nevertheless, the existence of these patterns in the language may have helped the expansion of ∅ in other syntactic positions.[20]

Another pattern which may have exerted some influence was the double *that* construction. In Old English there are instances in which a clause introduced by *þæt* does not occur without having been 'heralded' first (cf. Visser 1963: §§ 501–26) by a previous occurrence of *that* as in:

(11) Ic ðæt gehyre ðæt ðis is hold weorod (*Beowulf* 290; cited by Visser 1963: 460)
(I that hear that this is loyal troop.)
'I hear that this is a loyal troop.'

Even though word order was relatively free in Old English (although in verse especially there was a tendency towards OV order), the heralding *þæt* was almost always placed before the verb so that it did not occur next to the element which was identical to it in form and followed it. Visser furthermore says that this was not the case with *ðis*, which was also used as a heralding object. It appears that there was some avoidance of two successive *that*s, perhaps for reasons of stylistic inelegance or ambiguity.

In Middle English and later periods, when the loss of inflectional endings made certain constraints on word order inevitable, the only way to avoid

20. These might be better viewed as instances of relative reduction, with or without deletion of rel + *be*, i.e. 'whiz' deletion.

two successive *that*s was to delete one of them. When this happened in a relative construction containing *that*, it is not possible to identify with certainty *that* as a demonstrative pronoun or as a relative (see (12) below). This has also been called an instance of ἀπὸ κοινοῦ, since *that* can be interpreted as belonging to both the first and second clause. Where two *that*s do occur in succession, this may be for metrical reasons as in (13).[21]

(12) He bad thai suld him say quhat toune wes that he in lay. (Barbour's *Brus* IV. 201–2)
(He asked they should tell him what town was that he lay in.)

(13) Quha is that that cryis for me sa fast? (Lindsay, *Ane Satyre* 636–7)
(Who is that who cries for me so vigorously?)

It may of course be argued that in (12) the only possible deletion is that of complementizer *that* after *bad*, and that this construction represents the normal or unmarked form of reporting indirect questions in discourse since these constructions are very common during the later part of the Middle English period. Compare modern BEV indirect questions without *if* or *whether* and inverted word order as in (14). At best such cases are examples of ambiguous deletion.

(14) He asked Johnny's mother could Johnny come out to play. (BEV)
He asked Johnny's mother if/whether Johnny could come out to play. (standard English)

Instances of object pronoun deletion/omission, i.e. where a relative, if it were present, would be the object of the verb of the relative clause, are rarer than subject pronoun omissions. Mustanoja (1960) says that this usage has not been attested in Old English and appears towards the end of the fourteenth century when the first clear-cut cases of subject relative omission begin to occur. The reverse appears to be true today; namely, that subject relative omission is rare and is nearly always confined to existential/locative constructions of the *there is* type, while object relative deletion tends to be much more frequent. This is an area of English grammar which has been characterized by fluctuation for several centuries. This can be seen in a number of studies which have been concerned with counting the number of relative pronoun omissions in various texts from the Old English period onwards (cf. Mustanoja 1960: 205–6 for a list of some of these).

The fact that relative omission in subject position has become rarer is probably the combined result of a number of factors. For one thing, prescriptive statements, which I examine in Chapter 5, undoubtedly had

21. Skeat (1894) however emends (12) to read: 'quhat toune wes that that he lay in'.

some effect in promoting the use of *which* over *that*, and in discouraging Ø forms (at least in the written language). There is also the possibility that Ø forms might sometimes be potentially ambiguous, for example in subject position, as a number of people have suggested.[22] This may be one reason why this once popular usage is no longer so frequent today; at any rate, this seems to be the opinion of Bever and Langendoen (1972). The omission of a subject relative pronoun makes a statement difficult to interpret since it is not always clear whether we are dealing with a simple statement involving complementation or relativization. In the following sentence it is difficult to decide how the element which has been deleted is to be recovered, i.e. either as relative or complementizer *that*.

(15) I know (Ø) a man (Ø) wants to see you.

Object pronoun omission, on the other hand, leaves behind a nominal or some constituent other than the finite verb, so that the statement is not ambiguous. It is not clear why this possibility, which has since come to be so firmly established in modern colloquial usage, was not exploited more often in the earlier stages of the language. According to Visser, most of the cases of omission of the object relative pronoun in early modern English occur when the relative clause begins with an unstressed pronoun and not a full nominal (cf. Visser 1963: 629), so that the first of the two examples which follow is more likely to occur than the second.

(16) The man she knew.

(17) The man the woman knew.

Although Bever and Langendoen (1971: 442–3) do not share this view, Visser suggests that rhythmical pattern may have led to the selection of the Ø clause in this instance. It is also likely that there was a constraint on the occurrence of the Ø clause with a full nominal directly in contact with another full nominal. This double nominal construction may have been difficult to interpret, if not otherwise rejected for its possible stylistic inelegance. Two nominals do not normally occur in English without some intervening constituent, usually a verb, between them. This construction would have presented no problem in earlier stages of the language when the two nominals need not have followed each other directly; and even if they did, inflectional endings (except in the case of neuter *a-* stems) would have been available to disambiguate them.

Bever and Langendoen (1971: 444–5) have viewed the loss of inflectional

22. Lohmann (1880) associates the change in the ruies for deletion with the OV to VO word order change. And Flebbe (1878) notes that all the Germanic languages have permitted ellipsis under various conditions, but today only Danish, English and Swedish do (cf. n. 14 above).

endings with the concomitant restrictions on word order, and the appearance of restrictions on the absence of relative markers in clauses modifying non-initial nouns, as related trends in the history of English. They think that the loss of inflections had a great effect on the marking of subordinate and superordinate clause relations in general, and in particular on the relationship of a relative clause to its head noun. When inflectional endings were lost, so was a great deal of information about sentence-internal relations; consequently, word order became a crucial clue to interpretation. Relative clause constructions with no subject pronoun became 'perceptually complex'. At no stage in the English language does relativization occur on a nominal preceding the verb in its own clause resulting in a clause beginning in a finite verb. Sentence 18 is potentially triply ambiguous as indicated in the three possible glosses, a, b, and c.

(18) The girl knew the man became sick.
  a. The girl (who, that, ∅) knew the man became sick.
  b. The girl knew the man (who, that, ∅) became sick.
  c. The girl knew (that, ∅) the man became sick.

In modern English, (c) is the most likely interpretation for most speakers, although (b) existed as a possibility earlier in the language when a relative clause which modified a noun following a verb in its own clause could begin with a finite verb. In modern English, according to Bever and Langendoen, the subject relative can normally be omitted only in existential/locative sentences, cleft sentences and cleft sentences with WH questions.[23]

Bever and Langendoen claim that this development in constraints on the deletion of relatives in certain positions represents an example of how perceptual strategies can affect formal rules in the grammar. In other words, they claim that in this case the rules have changed by dint of the demand of perceptual or cognitive strategies. Plausible though this argument may seem, there are at least two problems with it: 1. The potential ambiguity which results from the lack of relative markers is really only a problem in the written language. In the spoken language tonic placement would probably disambiguate most doubtful cases, e.g. (15) and (18). 2. The ambiguity argument does not explain why subject pronoun deletion is prohibited now, but was not, for example, in Shakespeare's time when

23. Bever and Langendoen (1971: 441) note two counter-examples from Shakespeare where a relative clause has been formed on a nominal preceding the verb in its own clause. Hamp (1975) has argued that the changes discussed by Bever and Langendoen might be explained not by general perceptual mechanisms but by borrowing from Welsh.

largely the same constraints on word order operated (unless of course, this usage was for metrical reasons, but cf. the appendix to Chapter 6).

These are perhaps sufficient reasons for abandoning the perceptual argument, but the crucial counter-example comes from the modern spoken language. The real difficulty in invoking such perceptual explanations is the fact that subject pronoun deletion does occur in some dialects of English; and, as I argue in Chapter 7, there is no reason to believe it is any less frequent now than it was centuries ago. If this is the case, then must we posit different perceptual strategies for those speakers who can delete subject relatives (cf. Romaine 1981b)?

Alternatively, one might try to account for changes in the relative system in terms of purely syntactic principles, as Lightfoot (1979: 333–6) has done. He ascribes some of these changes to analogical levelling of surface structure patterns and the effects of the Transparency Principle. As a result of levelling, the new nominative singular of the demonstrative (which at the same time was being extended to serve a new function as definite article), was homophonous with the complementizer *þe*. Lightfoot argues that it would have been unclear whether *þe* was a nominative demonstrative, an article or a complementizer. This ambiguity would then create parsing difficulties and a lack of transparency. One solution to this problem was the development of WH pronouns from the interrogative system.

Again, I think this problem is a pseudo one, i.e. the ambiguity in question was probably resolved by context and cues in the spoken language. Lightfoot (1979: 335–6) furthermore claims that the differential introduction of WH relative pronouns into various syntactic positions is consistent with the operation of the Transparency Principle. The latter, according to Lightfoot, is an independent principle in the theory of grammar which explains, i.e. causes, syntactic change. It is capable of characterizing independently the limits to the degree of exceptionality or derivational complexity, so that when a grammar approaches the limit, some kind of therapeutic re-analysis will take place to eliminate the offending opacity. In the case of the relative pronouns in English, Lightfoot maintains that the lateness of *who* can be explained by the fact that its environment (i.e. a subject NP) was the least ambiguous. That is, a relative clause introduced by *that* and a deleted subject NP would present no parsing difficulties and permit a less opaque analysis.

It is difficult to see how Lightfoot can claim independent status for the Transparency Principle. If the principle is not motivated by purely syntactic constraints (as I have claimed elsewhere, cf. Romaine, forthcoming d, e), then it must make reference to speakers and their perceptual processing strategies and cognitive abilities. Thus the 'explanation' is similar to Bever and Langendoen's in that it makes appeal to mentalism. I hope to show here that this particular change cannot be plausibly viewed as solely structurally induced and that an equally interesting and plausible account of developments in the English relative system can be provided by appealing to social and stylistic, i.e. external, factors. In fact, the very nature of the mechanism of change in this case, i.e. its gradualness and variability, argues against Lightfoot's interpretation based on the Transparency Principle (cf. Romaine, forthcoming d, e).

4 *The linguistic variables*

In this chapter I will examine a number of possible linguistic factors which affect the realization of the relative marker (i.e. either as WH, TH or Ø):

1. type of clause – restrictive or non-restrictive
2. features or characteristics of the antecedent/head NP – animateness, definiteness, type of noun modification structure, e.g. determiner, quantifier, superlative
3. syntactic position/grammatical function of the relative in S_2, the relative clause – subject, object, indirect object, predicate nominative, temporal, locative, stranded and shifted prepositions and genitive

4.1 Type of clause

Most grammars of English, whether prescriptive or descriptive, recognize at least two types of relative clauses: restrictive and non-restrictive. This distinction is made on the basis of the way in which the head NP or antecedent is modified by the relative clause. A restrictive clause further limits the head NP's reference, while a non-restrictive clause adds only additional information to a head which is already independently identified, or is unique in its reference and has no need of further modification to identify its referent. Classic examples of each type are:

(1) The girl who lives next door to me. (restrictive)
(2) Mary Smith, who lives next door to me. (non-restrictive)

Proper names constitute a class of unique referents because their identity is the same no matter what else may follow after. In the case of possible 'mistaken identity' though, proper names may occur with restrictive clauses, e.g. where there is clearly more than one person with the same name. In the following example, the use of the definite article also adds to this interpretation (cf. also Lyons 1977: ch. 7).

(3) The Mary Smith that I know lives next door.

In addition to context cues, restrictive and non-restrictive clauses are further distinguished by intonation and juncture in the spoken language, and by comma punctuation in the written language. Restrictive clauses are generally linked to their antecedents by unity of intonation contour and continuity of the degree of loudness, while non-restrictive clauses tend to show a fresh intonation contour and a change in the degree of loudness.[1]

In this study, since I am dealing with written material of an older period when punctuation is neither reliable nor systematic, I have to rely on an examination of the linguistic environment to decide whether a clause is being used restrictively or non-restrictively. In many cases this can be determined only by reference to a unit of previous discourse larger than the sentence. It is possible, therefore, that some ambiguities in classification will remain since two of the possible criteria for classification (phonetic, graphic and semantic) are not recoverable.[2]

The examples I have already given are what might be called classic or 'ideal' types; their classification as either restrictive or non-restrictive is relatively unproblematic. Jacobsen (1965) has suggested that the two categories, restrictive and non-restrictive, are not always mutually exclusive, but are better thought of as two end points on a continuous scale; thus, some relative clauses are restrictive or non-restrictive to a greater or lesser degree than others. The major difficulty seems to be with non-restrictive clauses. The problem here is twofold: 1. What is their relation to their antecedents? And 2. What is their relation to other structures in the grammar, e.g. conjunction, complementation and subordination? The first 'relation' is one of anaphora; it is syntagmatic and text-centered. The second 'relation', while not paradigmatic, strictly speaking, is structural.

Chomsky (1965: 217), among others, has suggested that there are several reasons for supposing that non-restrictive clauses are complements of the full NP or of a sentence. Thorne (1972) has also argued that non-restrictive relatives arise from independent sentences because they have their own performative verb. Non-restrictive clauses happen to have a coreferent in

1. Since in the spoken language the difference between restrictive and non-restrictive depends on intonation, we might say that, in this context, certain intonation contours are the functional equivalents of the identification, focussing and de-stressing processes involved in relativization. It follows then that whatever is most important semantically should receive the most intonational prominence. Anaphoric material is not new and will therefore generally be de-stressed because the reference is understood from either previous reference or common focus. In this instance the functions of separation, focus and identification are duplicated on two levels.
2. Purely phonetic criteria also seem to be ambiguous, so that no single criterion seems to provide a satisfactory basis for dividing clauses into restrictive and non-restrictive. Phonetic criteria do not always produce a division which corresponds to a semantic or grammatical one. A clause may be semantically restrictive, but be separated from its antecedent by a tone group boundary (cf. e.g. Hill 1958; Taglicht 1973).

the main clause, but the message is contained in the main clause. We could argue on this basis for different phrase markers for restrictive and non-restrictive clauses. Although an analysis of relativization which describes restrictive clauses as derivative of sentential embedding and non-restrictives as derivative of conjuncts may seem inelegant for some languages, like English, the distinction seems useful in a wider sense; for example, in languages which lack either one type or the other.[3] The results I present in Chapter 6 (cf. 6.3) could also be used to argue for different analyses for the two types of clauses.

It has often been noted that many non-restrictive relative clauses in English are either substitutable for or paraphrasable by coordinate structures (cf. Quirk 1958),[4] as in the following examples:

(4) This monument, which was partially destroyed in 1872, was erected to commemorate his birth.

(4′) This monument was erected to commemorate his birth and it was partially destroyed in 1872.

Such examples as these have led some to subdivide the category of non-restrictive clauses into two main types: 1. simple or descriptive clauses, which add further information about the antecedent without furthering the discourse; and 2. resumptive or continuative clauses which advance the discourse by adding new information. These continuative clauses in many cases give information about an antecedent which is further back in the discourse, i.e. not next to the relative marker. Compare (5) and (6):

(5) The red handbag given to me for Christmas, which I never really liked, got stolen.

(6) Bill, who was John and Mary's only child, just got married.

In continuative clauses the shared referent may be repeated. This repetition is very common during the late Middle English period, but is rare in earlier stages of the language. When the relative system was expanded by the introduction of WH forms, we find that the WH forms are often used with nominals which shared either formal or semantic identity with a

3. In the Australian languages a continuum is represented from adjoined to embedded relative structures via languages that have both types; the continuum may also be reflected in a single language, as in Yidiɲ, where the relative clause combines features of both types in a single construction, thus representing an adjoined–embedded squish (cf. Hale 1976: 78–105).

4. This is also the case with many restrictive clauses in languages where relativization strategies undergo promotion in certain syntactic positions (cf. 4.5), as well as in languages which are either dying or undergoing some functional restriction with respect to the use of subordination structures. In a case where both these conditions exist, East Sutherland Gaelic, one way out of difficult relatives is by a coordinate paraphrase, as in *The woman in whose house it happened* which becomes *The woman and it happened in her house* (Dorian, pers. comm.).

previous unit; this unit could be separated from the relative clause or occur immediately before it as in:

(7) The quhilk day *Robert Ryngane & margaret cristeson* his spouse Ilkane of thame in amerciament of court as thai that wes lauchfully summond thairto be ane precept as in the samyn is contenit for blud drawine & hurting of [blank in manuscript] *quhilkis personis* non comperand dome wes tharupone gevine. (*Sheriff Court Book of Fife* 58v)

(8) The lard of Cesfurd hes unvorthely takin *ane hous* of my lord Bothuellis in Tyvedale callit Ancrum *quhilk hous* nocht beand haiste-ly deliverit my lord governour with all his cumpany wil pas to the recoverance therof. (*The Scottish Correspondence of Mary of Lorraine* XLVII)

(9) . . . *henry sibbald Johne squyer & thomas berwyk* sergeandis of the said schirefdome *quhilkis personis* deponit be thar aithis to exerce the saidis offices . . . (*Sheriff Court Book of Fife* 64r)

The availability of WH forms to make reference at a distance in this way probably also contributed to the specialization of *that* to restrictive clauses and *which* to non-restrictive clauses, which exists in the modern language today.[5] The types of constructions exemplified above do not seem to be very common in the modern language, except perhaps in legal registers and 'quantitative' relative constructions of the type given in (10).

(10) apples, oranges and pears, all *of which* are good to eat.

Reuter (1938: 37) reports that in the fifteenth century the continuative clause constructions were widespread among all authors and all types of literature; the usage seems to have reached a high point in the sixteenth century. During the seventeenth century, however, it begins to decrease. Reuter cites its proliferation in the literary language as well as in the *Paston Letters* as evidence that the construction had also penetrated into the ordinary, everyday spoken language. He says it is also quite common in the popular novels of the Elizabethan and later periods.

There is also a use of *which* that is common in the modern spoken language which Reuter suggests may have its origin in certain types of continuative clauses with so-called 'sentential' antecedents. (I say 'so-called' because in many cases a whole sentence does not serve as the unit of discourse being referred to.) This use of *which* is described by Reuter as an

5. Jacobsson (1963) reports that the use of *that* in non-restrictive clauses is more common in the modern written language than expected from the accounts given in descriptive grammars.

instance of *which* without relative force. Compare (11) and (12); in (11), *which* might be said to have a sentential antecedent, while in (12) it is not clear what is being referred to in the previous discourse:

(11) I hard it murmurit in Strewelyn that thai wald stop it *quhilk* causit me to wryt to the Lord of Kilmawaris ... (*The Scottish Correspondence of Mary of Lorraine* XI)

(12) I hawe rasavit your gentil letter vraytin with your awne hande quiche promittis to me ane thousant crownis in pension for my service, *quiche* I hawe nocht dissarvit so gret revarde. (*Scottish Correspondence of Mary of Lorraine* LXXXV)

I have given examples of these types of constructions from Middle Scots to show that these 'sentential' clauses were in use then also. Here again, it can be seen that there is a problem in defining coreference. We might use examples of this type as another argument for treating non-restrictive relative clauses as different syntactic structures from restrictive ones. A strict notion of coreference cannot, it seems, be 'forced' onto every instance of *which*. In (11) it is difficult to say how much of the previous text is being referred to, while in (12) *which* seems to 'blend' the grammatical functions of deixis and conjunction. In these types of clauses very often 'coreference' may involve a VP rather than a whole sentence, or something which is not even a constituent in the previous sentence.

Ross (1969) used 'VP *which*' in support of this argument that every verb of action is embedded in the object complement of a two-place predicate whose subject is the same as the action verb. Although Ross was among the first generative grammarians to observe that *which* could obey 'sloppy identity' conditions, he nevertheless argued that the antecedent of a pronoun must be a constituent. He also cited the NP status of *which* in its own clause as evidence that whatever stood for *which* must also be an NP. He claimed that adjectives were NPs in the underlying structure on the basis of sentences like (13):

(13) John thinks that Sheila is beautiful, *which* she is (i.e. beautiful).

However, examples such as those under discussion here, in which the pronoun refers to something which is not a constituent at any point in the derivation, provide evidence against Ross' interpretation. It was also at this time that Ross began to formulate the notion of non-discrete, i.e. 'squishy', categories. In this case, *which* appears to function in part as a conjunction (i.e. as a subordinator and means of linkage between two propositions), and also in part as a pronoun in relating parts/constituents of two sentences (cf. Greene 1977: 106). When the pronominal function is not in evidence by virtue of the syntax of the *which* clause (i.e. when *which* does not have an NP role in the clause it introduces), one can assume that the pronominal function has become opaque or lost and it is being used primarily as a conjunction. In other words, this syntactic analysis can be seen as an instance of category change brought about by virtue of fuzzy category membership (cf. Lightfoot 1979 for a discussion of syntactic re-analysis by category change in the English modal verbs). At least one language historian, Earle (1871: 450), claimed that just as English had imitated French in expanding the function of the interrogative pronouns in a relativizing function, so it followed that these pronouns also came to be used as conjunctions just like French *qui* and *que*. Poutsma (1904: 969) has also cited the 'vulgar' use of *which* as a conjunction.

Compare the following two sentences from Middle Scots (cf. also the discussion in Chapter 3):

(14) . . . and fordar I have the princes letres and ane decreit of the lordis of our counsell to enter me to my ane: *quhilk* he objekit and wald nocht do as yit one na wys, *quhilk* is grit hurt and skayth to me the want therof. (*The Scottish Correspondence of Mary of Lorraine* LXV)

(15) All the poyntis forsad was of veritie except the departing of Georg Douglas, bot at the writing of my sad first byll sic word come of his departing *quhilk* was nocht of verate; Georg is remanyt still. (*The Scottish Correspondence of Mary of Lorraine* XLVI)

When the surface structure preceding *which* (*quhilk*) contains two or more levels of underlying sentences, the antecedent can be anywhere from the least to most inclusive of the entire surface structure. These sentences raise queries about the level of structure *which* is derived from and about the syntactio relationship of the *which* clause to the main clause. Pragmatic considerations are relevant also, for if there are two or more syntactic entities which, with respect to structure alone, could be the antecedent, how does pragmatic information resolve potential ambiguity? Although Greene (1977: 118) noticed a trend in middle class American spoken English to make *which* stand for an NP (even at the expense of the structural effectiveness of the sentence), it appeared that for many speakers *which* had become semantically empty. That is, *which* was being used as a dummy marker to introduce clauses. If this is the case, then we may have a chain of grammaticalization in progress, which involves a shift from the propositional component of the grammar to the textual (i.e. discourse). In other words, a grammatical marker whose prime function was propositional became a textual marker (i.e. anaphoric marker), then ended up as a dummy syn-

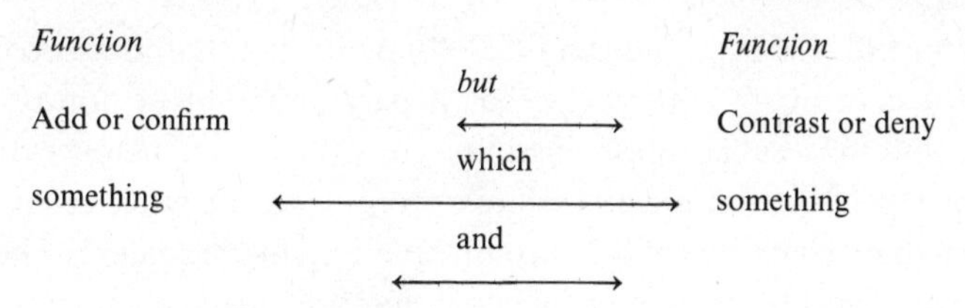

Figure 7

tactic marker (cf. Traugott 1979 for further discussion of the pragmatic – semantic aspects of grammaticalization).

Greene (1977: 108–9) also conducted a test in which she asked speakers to substitute *but*, *and* or *which* in clauses which originally contained *which*. The results indicated an overlap between *which* and the two conjunctions (see Figure 7). Her findings could also be used to argue against the postulation of an underlying conjunction analysis (cf. Thompson 1971) because one would expect speakers to select *and* instead of *but* as a substitute for *which*, if non-restrictive relative clauses have paraphrases in sentences conjoined by *and*.

Reuter has cited similar usages from Dickens' novels where *which* seems to be used more or less as a connecting particle, as in:

(16) '*Which* you are right my dear,' said Mrs. Harris. (*Bleak House*)

Reuter observes that this sort of usage in certain types of dialogue may indicate that it was some kind of hypercorrection, since *which* began to acquire a connotation of formality in the seventeenth century; its overuse in colloquial speech could have served the function of lending an air of syntactic elaboration. Reuter distinguishes sentences of the type in (16) from those in which the relative refers to the whole sentence as a kind of comment or afterthought, as in (17):

(17) She spent all day cleaning the house, *which* surprised me.

The dividing line between all these types of non-restrictive relative clauses is not always clear, and I do not propose to keep all these categories separate here. In the initial tabulation I have distinguished between restrictive and non-restrictive clauses; within the latter category I have made a distinction between non-restrictive clauses with or without sentential antecedents.

I did this to see if there was any correlation between the types of clauses which occur most frequently and the type of text or style within a text. It may be expected that the use of a non-restrictive clause as opposed to a coordinate structure, for example, represents a meaningful stylistic choice.

In support of this idea, Quirk (1958: 40) has noted that most people will accept a coordinate construction as a paraphrase for a non-restrictive clause; but this substitution involves consequential differences in tone pattern, stress distribution and relative prominence. For this reason, he has claimed that an analysis of the two constructions in the contexts where they occur will reveal that a significant choice has been made; in other words, at some level of analysis, they mean something different. I give all the frequency data for the distribution of types of clauses (restrictive, non-restrictive and sentential) in the Middle Scots texts in Chapter 6.

4.2 Features of the antecedent or head NP

Among the features which I will examine for possible conditioning effects on the realization of relative markers are animacy and definiteness of the antecedent. If the antecedent is determined, then I have further categorized it according to the type of modification structure, i.e. simple determiner, quantifier or superlative, with which it occurs. More distinctions could of course have been made on the basis of the elements which may occur before the head noun; I could have chosen, for example, to count ordinal numbers as a separate class since they may occur between determiners and quantifiers, or I could have classified open and closed class quantifiers separately (cf. Quirk et al. 1972: 144–5), but I decided that this would have refined the system too much for my purposes.

Nothing in fact is gained by increasing the number of cells since the number of tokens representing each category becomes smaller each time a further subcategorization is made, until finally the numbers become too small to draw meaningful conclusions. This statement is one which requires some justification; but since it raises issues which relate more directly to my discussion of sampling procedures (cf. 5.1), I have postponed dealing with it in detail here. For the moment, I will just comment that there is evidence that the distribution of noun phrase types in modern English as well as the occurrence of relative clauses in certain syntactic positions in a number of languages is not random; in each case stylistic and linguistic constraints are involved (cf. e.g. Aarts 1971; Keenan 1975). This means that a number of my cells will be very small and others quite large, but this does not reflect a 'sampling error'.

4.2.1 Animacy of the antecedent. In modern English the relative marker is capable of showing agreement with its antecedent in terms of a two-way gender distinction, so that humans (and sometimes other animate beings such as pets), generally require *who*; and non-personal or inanimate antecedents generally take *that* or *which*. As I mentioned earlier in the preceding chapter, this distinction was not strictly adhered to during the period under study here; in fact, as late as the early seventeenth century *which* can still be found with human antecedents, e.g. in the Lord's Prayer. Caldwell (1974) reports that in early Scots both *that* and *quhilk* were in frequent use with personal antecedents. This also seems to be the case during the first half of the sixteenth century; unfortunately Caldwell does not present any figures for comparison with the ones I report in Chapter 6. The examples below illustrate this usage.

(18) ... my intent
Is for till be to God obedient, –
Quhilk dois forbid men to be lecherous: (Lindsay, *Ane Satyre* 217–9)

(19) And his Sone, our Saviour, scheild in necessitie, – *That* bocht ȝow from baillis ranson rude, (Lindsay, *Ane Satyre* 3–4)

4.2.2 Types of noun modification structures. I will discuss the next four features of the antecedent, definite, determiner, quantifier and superlative, together since they represent different types of NP structures which may occur as antecedents of relatives. Not every type of noun phrase may accept a relative clause of course, and those which accept relative clauses do not always accept both restrictive and non-restrictive clauses.

Clearly what some syntacticians have referred to as 'definitivization' has some relevance to relativization. Dean (1967), for example, has suggested that the definite article in sentences with relative clauses can be predicted on purely syntactic grounds. I mentioned briefly in Chapter 2, where I presented various transformational analyses for the derivation of relative clauses, that definitivization is a concept which must apply somewhere in the relative clause transformation to both the matrix and constituent NP (cf. Bickerton 1977: 125–8).

Kuroda (1969) has said that the Art to which WH is attached must have the feature specification [+ def] before pronominalization occurs to ensure that the result is a definite relative pronoun. Although all four possible combinations of definite and indefinite articles may occur, i.e. [+ +], [– –], [+ –] and [– +] (where the first member of each set represents the article of the matrix NP and the second member, the article of the constituent or embedded NP), a definitivization transformation applies when the Art of the constituent NP has the feature [– def]. Where both Arts have the feature [+ def], the relative clause is non-restrictive; if they are both [− def], then the result is a generic 'whoever' relative. When the two articles have opposite values however, a restrictive relative is the result and the matrix Art keeps its original value. As noted in Chapter 2, a conjunction analysis of the relative clause avoids this problem altogether since the specifications of definiteness or indefiniteness are not assigned by the grammar, but by the interpretation of the individual speaker.

The concept 'determiner' has been used to cover a variable range of phenomena depending on which grammatical description one consults. Smith (1964), for example, divides the class of determiners into three groups on the basis of their co-occurrence with different types of relative clauses:

1. indefinite determiners, e.g. *any*, *a*, *every*, which attract restrictive clauses
2. specified determiners, e.g. *a*, *the*, which attract both restrictive and non-restrictive clauses
3. unique determiners, e.g. ∅, proper names, which attract non-restrictive clauses

It is evident that these three categories are not mutually exclusive; no purely distributional properties can distinguish them. The determiners can also behave generically and generics can also be pronominalized by the definite pronoun. A great deal remains to be explained about the behavior of different types of determiners; and it has not been agreed by all syntacticians that the class of determiners should be distinguished solely on the grounds of the interaction of its members with relative clauses (cf. Stockwell et al. 1973 in support of this).

I recognize here that the use of the articles is not the only possibility for determining nouns, but I have decided to exclude certain words from the category of determiner and include them with quantifiers. In this study, then, the class of determiners will include the demonstratives (*this*, *that*, etc.), the possessive and personal pronouns, the definite article, and the interrogative adjectives (*what*, *which*). This class contains some of the possibilities for contributing definite reference to a noun phrase, i.e. those elements which have a determiner function. Proper names will also be included in this category since proper names and definite descriptions have similar semantic properties in that both may constitute complete reference. Quirk et al. (1972) refer to this set (although they include some quantifiers in it also) as a closed system because the items belonging to the system are mutually exclusive with each other, i.e. a choice must be made among them so that not more than one occurs before the head noun. This is true in my system of classification also, with the exception that sometimes proper nouns may be further determined by the use of demonstratives or definite articles. This usage seems to be very common in legal and official texts, although it may also occur elsewhere.

The class of quantifiers in this study includes words which may modify or restrict the reference of the NP in a 'quantitative' sense. This category includes, for example, quantitative determiners such as *every*, *each*, *some*, *any*, *neither*, *no*, *many*, *much*, *few*, *several*, *all*, *certain*, etc., as well as quantitative expressions such as *a few*, *a little*, etc., which seem better analyzed as quantitative rather than componentially as indefinite + quantifier, and compounds formed with some of these elements, e.g. *anybody*, *everyone*. Numerical expressions are also included here, e.g. *five*, *fifth* (i.e. ordinal and cardinal numbers). Again this classification does not agree entirely with that of Quirk et al. or those of other syntacticians. Quirk et al., for example, distinguish between closed and open class quantifiers. Although comparatives and superlatives could have been included under the heading of quantifiers, I decided to count nouns modified by superlative adjectives as a separate group since impressionistically it appears that these constructions allow more Ø clauses. That is, of course, not an unexpected result since the definite article occurs obligatorily in these cases, e.g. *the nicest person*, to give such expressions unique noun reference.

These categorizations can easily come under attack; and I have made some criticisms of other analyses without offering constructive alternative solutions. In defense of my position I would say that the purpose of my study is not to defend or argue in favor of particular theories about the analysis or derivation of articles, determiners or quantifiers, etc.; a great deal has been written about this already. Clearly these are difficult problems for any descriptive grammar, hence the proliferation of different theories and groupings of these elements.

All that is wanted for this study is a method of classifying types of noun phrases which may be relevant to the realization of relative pronouns. Rydén (1966), for example, in his study of relative constructions in early sixteenth-century English distinguishes a number of different types of antecedents and considers instances of *that* + noun, *those* + noun, *any* + noun, etc. separately. Not surprisingly, few differences occur between *that* + noun and *those* + noun. However, when larger groupings of similar items are made, differences appear, e.g. pronouns, numerals and substantivized adjectives. It is often the case that very simple or gross divisions may show the clearest conditioning effects. This is not to say, of course, that we should group together items which show very disparate patterns or skewed distributions, and thus obscure the pattern by overgeneralizing; it cannot be denied that very often quite subtle and complex conditioning factors may be at work in any given instance of linguistic variation. On the other hand, there is no reason to consider every case a separate case; clearly, some compromise is necessary.

The system which I have adopted here for classifying certain types of NP modification structures may not be the most felicitous, but if the data warrant a revision of these categories, then adjustments can be made after the initial sorting procedure. Such adjustments are often necessary in analyzing sociolinguistic constraints (cf. e.g. Labov 1966; Trudgill 1974). In this case there is the added consideration that we are dealing with Middle Scots; thus, there is no reason to believe that these categories, which appear relevant to modern English, will be applicable in every respect and to the same degree to an earlier stage of the language (cf. 5.3). The categories can be used only as guidelines. I will note for the moment, however, that there were few difficulties in applying this system of classification to the Middle Scots texts used in this study. The most important thing in the preliminary counting stage is to specify unambiguously which items belong to a given category and apply this specification consistently before any revisions are made.

4.3 Syntactic position or function of the relative marker

Another source of variability in the realization of relative markers relates to what can be called the syntactic position or function of the relative; that is to say that the relatives occupy the syntactic position of the coreferential NP which they replace in the relative clause itself. In English it is possible to relativize on NPs in at least the following syntactic positions: subject, direct object, indirect object, possessive, predicate nominative and object of a preposition (both stranded and shifted). There are also in addition certain locative and temporal constructions in which relatives and other WH words may appear in relative-like functions. I will discuss each of these possibilities briefly (cf. Ross 1967: 117–226 for a discussion of constraints on relativizability; Keenan 1975).

4.3.1 Subject relatives. Subject NPs are very frequently relativized in both modern English and Middle Scots. The term 'subject relative' will be used to refer to a relative clause in whose underlying structure the coreferential

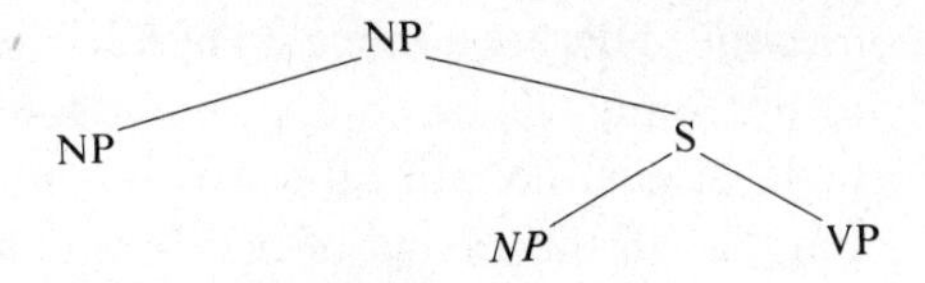

Figure 8 Phrase marker for subject relatives

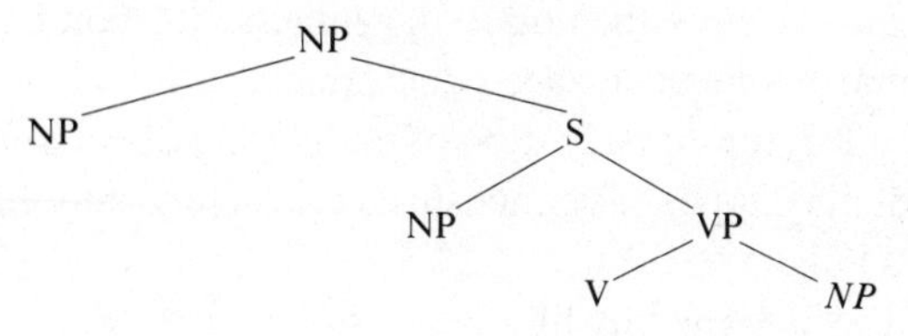

Figure 9 Phrase marker for object relatives

NP is immediately dominated by the S-node that is the sister constituent to the head NP of the clause (if the NP-S analysis is followed, as indicated in Figure 8). The subject relative can indicate a case relation with personal antecedents by using the nominative form *who* in modern English, but this option is much less utilized in Middle Scots of the period in question. Some examples from Middle Scots are given below:

(20) This Frenche man *that* is to cum. (*The Scottish Correspondence of Mary of Lorraine* CXXXII)

(21) Eftir this counsale he slew all the frendis pertenyng to Durstis *quhilkis* wer convenit at his request, and sparit nothir wyffis nor barnis *that* belangit to that blude. (Bellenden's *Boece*, Book 2.Ca.xi; cf. 4.3.2 concerning the inclusion of the first of the relatives in this example under the category of subject relatives)

(22) Thair efter I past forward to Tantallowin to hawe spoken with my lord Angws, *quha* was nocht thair. (*The Scottish Correspondence of Mary of Lorraine* LXXIV)

4.3.2 Object and indirect object relatives. The term 'object relative' will be used to refer to a relative clause in whose underlying structure the co-referential NP is immediately dominated by a VP-node and functions as the direct object of the verb; the S that immediately dominates this VP may be the sister constituent to the head NP of the clause, or it may be embedded in that S at any level. This phrase marker is given in Figure 9.

NPs in direct object position are also very frequently relativized in both modern English and Middle Scots. The indirect object position, i.e.

instances where two consecutive NPs are dominated by a VP, is fairly rare, and the few tokens that were found will be grouped under the category of direct object (although in the original counting the two categories of objects were kept separate). Even though the second of two NPs in a VP can be considered to have a preposition in the deep structure which has been deleted, I decided to group them with direct objects rather than with prepositional relatives, since the notion of syntactic position I am working with here is primarily one of surface structure.

This will also affect the classification of underlying direct objects, which when relativized, may appear as either surface structure subjects or objects as in (23) (cf. (21) in 4.3.1).

(23) a. The ball which the boy hit.
     b. The ball which was hit by the boy.

I am classifying (23a) as a direct object relative and (23b) as a subject relative, even though (23a) could be said to be the underlying structure for (23b). I will return to this when I discuss possible alternatives to relativization on NPs in certain syntactic positions in 4.5.

The following examples of object position relatives in Middle Scots show that the objective form of the relative, *quham*, *quhom*, etc. (modern English *whom*), may be used to indicate case agreement with the coreferential NP which it replaces. The objective-marked forms appear more often during this period than the nominative marked forms.

(24) ... þe barboure pepill *quhom* þai recentlie disconnfist. (Bellenden's *Boece*, Book 6.Ca.xiv)

(25) ... to leif Ingland *quhilk* he had conquest be þe swerd. (Bellenden's *Boece*, Book 9.Ca.ii)

(26) ... the mone *that* I desyr master Jhone till furnis me in Frans ... (*The Scottish Correspondence of Mary of Lorraine* XXI)

4.3.3 Predicate nominal relatives. The term 'predicate nominal' relative will be used to refer to a relative which has the same phrase marker as defined and illustrated above for direct object relatives, except that the verbal element which is the sister constituent of the coreferential NP must be some form of the copula. NPs in this position in both modern English and Middle Scots are infrequently relativized; examples are given below from both:

(27) all *that* he may be. (*The Scottish Correspondence of Mary of Lorraine* CL)

(28) He is the man *that* he seems to be.

Since there are rather few tokens of this type of relative, I have re-grouped the instances of predicate nominal relatives with the object relatives, although I have kept them separate in the original counting.

4.3.4 Genitive or possessive relatives. Possessive relatives are not very frequently found in Middle Scots (or modern Scots for that matter). When they do occur, the form *quhais*, *quhois*, etc. (modern English *whose*) can be used with personal antecedents; in some cases the possessive relative may be used with non-personal antecedents, whether animate or inanimate. Quirk et al. (1972: 863) note that in modern English when the head noun is non-personal, there is some tendency to avoid *whose*, possibly because it is regarded as the genitive form belonging only to *who* and not *which*. The following examples represent possible relative constructions in modern English:

(29) The house *whose* roof was damaged.
(30) The house *that* had *its* roof damaged.
(31) The house the roof *of which* was damaged.
(32) The house *that* they damaged the roof *of*.
(33) The house *that its* roof was damaged.
(34) The house *that's* roof was damaged.

The last two examples would be possible in modern Scots, though, to the best of my knowledge, not for other dialects of English. The infrequency of this construction in Middle Scots as a whole is 'explainable' in part by the fact that there are alternatives such as (30)–(34). In constructions like (31)–(32) the underlying phrase marker is the same as that for relatives in prepositional position (cf. 4.3.6), while in (30) the NP carries the possessive or genitive marker. Another possible alternative would be a stacked relative as in (35):

(35) The house *that* had the roof *that* was damaged.

Caldwell (1974: 59–60) has cited some of the alternatives which were used in Middle Scots. In the examples below an asterisk indicates a possible possessive relative paraphrase which might have occurred (i.e. was grammatical), but did not.

(36) Ther wes nane of sa gret renoun.
 *Ther wes nane quhais renoun was sa gret.
(37) Dame Eme . . . and Rychard wes hyr fadyr name.
 *Dame Eme quhais fadyris name wes Rychard.
(38) Thy father, that I was oratoure and confessoure to.
 *Thy father quhais oratoure and confessoure I was.

(39) Ilk man that his gudis extendis to xx merkis.
* Ilk man quhais gudis extendis to xx merkis. (Note also: * Ilk man that has gudis that extendis to xx merkis.)

Constructions of the type in (39) are very frequently employed in Middle Scots; instead of using the possessive forms of the relative pronoun, the construction *that* + possessive pronoun + noun is used. In legal texts especially, a construction like (40) is common, in which the noun bears the possessive marking and the shared nominal or coreferential NP is not deleted in the relative clause.

(40) Certane utheris personis *quhilkis personis thar namis* eftir followis. (*Sheriff Court Book of Fife*)

The problem of why these relatives with possessive *quhais* were 'avoided' or paraphrased is another question; possibly perceptual factors are involved here too, as was suggested in the last chapter with regard to deletion of relative markers in certain positions (cf. Bever and Langendoen 1971). Such relatives may be too 'difficult' or 'complex' to decode. A similar situation exists today in Scottish Gaelic where possessive relatives involve quite complex structures and are often paraphrased or avoided. This issue will be treated in more detail in 4.5.[6]

4.3.5 Temporal and locative relatives. There seems to be no general agreement on the status of adverbs of time, place and manner. In other words, are adverbs such as *how*, *when*, *where* and *why* to be considered relative markers or kept separate from the other relatives discussed so far? I decided to include *where* and *when* (Middle Scots *quhar* and *quhen*) in this analysis since they participate in the pattern of variation I have been describing; that is to say that a locative or temporal antecedent can take a relative clause which may be introduced by an element taking the form WH (*where*, *when*), TH or ∅ as in:

(41) That was the time (*when*, *that*, ∅) I was born.

(42) All materis hes procedyt in the partis *quhare* we haif bene. (*The Scottish Correspondence of Mary of Lorraine* CXIII)

(43) George Douglas came to my hous of Reidhall that samin nycht *that* I departit fra your grac. (*The Scottish Correspondence of Mary of Lorraine* LXXII)

The other adverbs, *how* and *why*, do not behave similarly. *How*, for example, does not normally occur with either restrictive or non-restrictive

6. Cf. Jespersen's (1894: 320–1) comments on genitive relative paraphrases.

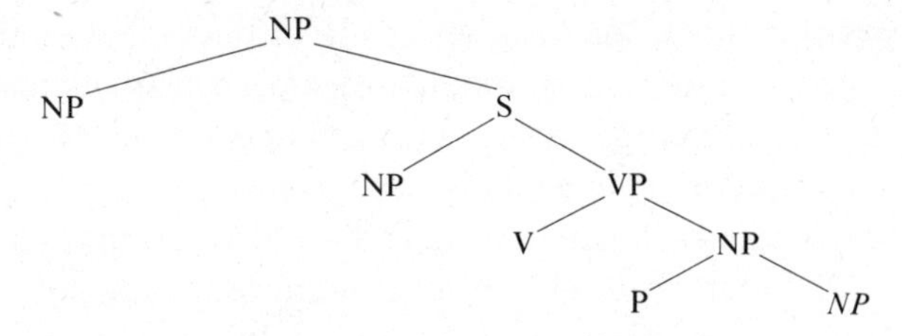

Figure 10 Phrase marker for prepositional/oblique relatives

clauses; and *why* does not occur with non-restrictive clauses, although it is superficially similar to *where* and *when* in that it is a WH form. Certainly, of all these, *where* is more extensively used since a number of *where* compounds, e.g. *wherein*, *whereby*, *whereat*, *wherefor*, etc., were in fairly common use in the earlier periods of the language, although they now survive only in very formal language or registers such as legal language. *When* is used less frequently and did not develop as many extended forms as *where*. I am including cases of temporal and locative relatives in which the antecedent is clearly indicated (examples (41)–(43)), although in some cases the antecedent may not be a temporal or locative expression such as *the time* or *the place*. The antecedent may also be a proper noun or have personal reference. The latter usage is found in the spoken language today, as in (44). Interestingly enough, a possible alternative construction would be a possessive relative as shown in the asterisked form.

(44) These two (children) *where* the father had died.[7]
*These two *whose* father had died.

Sentences without clearly definable antecedents, like (45), will not be included, nor will examples like (46), where it is clear that there is no nominal which is to be understood as coreferential with the temporal or locative marker.[8]

(45) He followed *where* they led.

(46) He followed the soldiers *where* they led.

4.3.6 Prepositional or oblique relatives. The term 'prepositional' or 'oblique' relative will be used to refer to relative clauses in whose underlying structure the coreferential NP functions as the object of a preposition, as indicated in Figure 10.

7. This example is taken from an interview with an elderly woman from Birdsboro, Pennsylvania.
8. These temporal and locative relatives also present problems in establishing coreference. A sentence like (45) might also be interpreted as follows: 'to the place [WH-place] they led to', i.e. the use of a stranded prepositional construction is also a possibility here.

Two types of prepositional relatives can be distinguished: stranded and shifted. The term 'stranded preposition' refers to a construction in which a preposition is separated from its relative marker as in (47). The term 'shifted preposition' refers to a relative clause in which the preposition has been fronted along with the coreferential NP to the beginning of the relative clause as in (48). Preposition shifting or fronting is an optional part of the relative clause transformation, at least according to one analysis (cf. Chapter 2).

(47) ... my relief out of this ward and presone (∅) I am in. (*Scottish Correspondence of Mary of Lorraine* XLI)

(48) Forther the berare will schaw your grace at mayr lenth *quhomto* ye will ples gif credens. (*Scottish Correspondence of Mary of Lorraine* XXII)

A number of constraints operate here to determine which form of the relative is selected as the object of the preposition. The plethora of *where* compounds mentioned above was of course available and used quite frequently in this position. This is particularly the case with non-restrictive clauses with sentential antecedents as in (49). Postposed or stranded prepositional relatives are also frequently found in Middle Scots, although they are possibly less common in the modern written language since this usage came under attack from prescriptive grammarians (cf. e.g. the discussion in Charnley 1958). Nevertheless, it seems to be frequent in the modern spoken language, both Scots and non-Scots.

(49) ... makand mentione that youre grace suld be discontentit with me becaus of the speking with Georg Dowglas *quhartrow* ther is ane murmure of me in your gracis cumpanye ... (*Scottish Correspondence of Mary of Lorraine* XXXIX)

No analysis has been able to account neatly for the fact that there is a restriction which prohibits *that* from occurring with a shifted preposition, thus reducing a three-way opposition among WH, TH and ∅ to a situation in which a categorical rule operates to insert WH forms with shifted prepositions. There is also a 'semi-restriction', primarily a stylistic one, that stranded prepositions tend to be preferred with verbs which occur with prepositions or the so-called 'phrasal verbs' such as *to look at*. There is also a restriction which prevents some prepositions, especially temporal ones, from being stranded as shown in:

(50) *The girl to *that* I gave the book.

(51) The book (*that*) I look at.

(52) ?The meeting *that* I kept falling asleep during.

4.4 Other factors affecting the choice of relative markers

There are several other factors that may affect the choice of the relative marker which I have not included. These are: the distance between the relative clause and its antecedent; and the complexity of the head NP, i.e. what is the effect of antecedents with extended premodification? Quirk (1958) has suggested that in the first case there is a preference for *which*, since it has greater 'carrying power'; in the second instance, *that* is preferred.

Both these factors probably intersect with stylistic ones, so that, for example, we might expect prose as opposed to verse to be characterized by greater distance between antecedents and their relative clauses as well as more complex NP structures. Both factors also relate to 'perceptual complexity'. There is, for example, evidence that relative clauses which do not directly follow their antecedents may be more difficult to understand. (I discuss this in the next section and in Chapter 6.)

4.5 Relativization and syntactic complexity

Keenan and Comrie have been investigating relative clause formation strategies in a number of languages with the interesting result that the languages did not vary randomly with respect to the relativizability of certain syntactic positions of the NP (cf. Keenan and Comrie 1972, 1977, 1979; Keenan 1975). On this basis they have postulated the existence of a case (or accessibility) hierarchy which predicts certain constraints on relative clause formation.

The case hierarchy
Subject $\geq$ Direct object $\geq$ Indirect object $\geq$
Oblique $\geq$ Genitive $\geq$ Object of comparison

The case hierarchy has been used to predict the following:

1. The frequency with which NPs in certain syntactic positions are relativized in a language, i.e. subject NPs are most frequently relativized and objects of comparison are least frequently relativized.
2. If a given relative clause formation strategy works on two possible NP positions, then it must work on all intermediate positions between the two. That is to say that a language will not have a relative clause strategy that works in subject and oblique position only; it must apply to the positions in-between these points as well, namely, direct and indirect objects.[9]

9. Chiang (1977) has claimed that relative clauses in Bahasa Indonesia are an exception to this principle,

3. The left-hand position of the hierarchy is the easiest position to relativize.
4. Impressionistic judgements of the degree of syntactic complexity of written texts will correlate with the frequency with which certain positions in the hierarchy are relativized. In other words, syntactically simple styles will have a greater proportion of their relative clauses near the subject end of the hierarchy, and complex styles will have a greater proportion near the other end.

All of these predictions seem to work well for English (cf. Keenan 1975), and on an impressionistic basis it seems that they may apply to Middle Scots texts as well. I examine this hypothesis in more detail in Chapter 6 where I present the results. For one thing, syntactic complexity represents an important dimension along which a stylistic continuum might be ordered; in Chapter 6 I have tried to set up such a continuum. Labov (pers. comm.) has suggested that new insights into conditioned syntactic variation can be gained by a closer examination of alternatives, i.e. what forms could have been used instead of a construction, and which of the possible alternatives is more syntactically complex?

Another reason for further consideration of the issue of syntactic complexity in relation to relative clause formation is that it does suggest an 'explanation' for the observations on the possessive relatives in 4.3.4. Keenan and Comrie (1977) think that languages may possess more than one relative clause formation strategy; for example, in Welsh, the primary strategy applies only to the subject and direct object positions.[10] In these instances, post-nominal relative clauses are introduced by the particle *a* with deletion of the shared nominal, while other syntactic positions are relativized by a different post-nominal strategy in which a clause is introduced by the particle *y*, and a personal pronoun in place of the shared nominal. A similar alternative strategy to relativization of the genitive position was used in Middle Scots, as I have already pointed out; instead of using the possessive relative *quhais*, a possessive relative clause was often expressed periphrastically through a construction which contained *that/ quhilk* plus a noun determined by a possessive pronoun (cf. 4.3.4).[11]

since the relative formation strategy applies directly to subjects and genitives, but indirectly to direct and indirect objects.

10. Keenan and Comrie collapse the indirect object position with the oblique relatives, since in the deep structure these can be considered the same. Here I have included in the initial counting separate categories for direct and indirect object relatives.
11. The more difficult positions also seem to be the most likely candidates for loss in dying languages. Dorian (pers. comm.) conducted a check for strategies of genitive position relatives with some of her East Sutherland Gaelic informants for me. She reported that for most of her informants subject and

Keenan and Comrie also say that languages may utilize the option of promoting an NP to a higher position in the accessibility hierarchy in order to relativize it. They suggest that where such a strategy exists, it is usually well-developed, commonly used and has a wide syntactic distribution. An instance of this can also be cited in Middle Scots, again in the genitive. Another paraphrase of the possessive relative consists in using the oblique forms, *of quham* or *of quhilk*.

Both of these types of strategies have been observed in a number of different languages. As the case hierarchy is descended there is a greater tendency to use pronoun-retaining relative clause formation strategies, and where a clearly available option exists for promoting a relative clause to a position further up the hierarchy, it is utilized. Keenan and Comrie note, however, that promotion in the case hierarchy in order to relativize may not always be easier or represent a syntactically less complex choice than direct relativization further down the hierarchy. For example, in colloquial English sentence (53) seems to be preferred to (54):

(53) The woman who got her coat stolen.
(54) The woman whose coat was stolen.

These examples however are not alternatives, strictly speaking, since they are arguably not fully synonymous (cf. in particular, Labov 1975b; Labov and Weiner 1977; the discussion in 2.2 above); they are also not fully parallel in that the first is a *get*- and the second a *be*-passive. But even if we change the second of the examples to read:

(54′) The woman whose coat got stolen.

(53) seems to be the more frequently occurring one in colloquial English. Keenan and Comrie account for (53) as a promotion of a genitive to a subject position relative. The passive, however, has generally been assumed to be more complex, syntactically speaking, than the active (cf. e.g. Van den Broeck 1977), so we would not expect to find (and do not, in fact) that underlying objects are transformed into surface subjects to be relativized; although of course they can be (cf. also 4.3.2, examples (23a) and (23b)).

Hawkins and Keenan (1974) cite the experimental result that 10–12 year old children do less well in repetition tests of such 'promoted' constructions involving the passive rather than the active realization further down the hierarchy. For example, (55) below is more difficult to repeat than (56).[12]

object relativization was easy, but possessive relativization was difficult. It is interesting, however, that she reported that her oldest and most conservative informant was able to produce other sentences correctly after she provided the relevant pattern, i.e. explained how it was done.

In general though, experimental work has shown that English-speaking children comprehend relative clauses formed on the subject position better than they do those formed on direct object position (cf. Legum 1975).

(55) The boy who was seen by Mary.

(56) The boy whom Mary saw.

It remains only to say how distance between the relative and its antecedent relates to the notion of syntactic complexity. The relative clause may occur in three positions with respect to its antecedent; it may follow immediately (in which case the highest S of the relative construction immediately follows the head NP); or it may be final (in which case the relative clause is the rightmost constituent of the S that immediately dominates its head NP). Otherwise, if some other constituents intervene, i.e. another relative clause, prepositional phrase, or a participial modifier resulting from relative clause reduction, or if the relative has been extraposed to the end of the matrix sentence, then the relative clause can be considered medial. The tree diagrams in Figure 11 illustrate the various possibilities. Note that in examples a and b if the two relative clauses are regarded as stacked, then the second one immediately follows its head NP, but if the two clauses are regarded as coordinate, as in b, then the second clause does not.

It seems that the ordinary or most frequent position for relative clauses is immediately following the head NP (at least in modern English, cf. e.g. Quirk 1957; Cofer 1972). Most relative clauses in other words have the following phrase structure.

I. NP_1 V [NP_2 – NP_3] V NP_4 (OS)
object subject

In this case the relative marker functions as the subject; it immediately follows the head NP which has the function of direct object in the matrix clause. This type of phrase structure can be referred to as OS, i.e. object-subject.

A medial relative clause has a phrase structure of the type given in II. In this case the relative clause is formed in subject position but does not follow immediately after the head NP which also serves as the subject of the matrix clause. This type of medial clause can be referred to as SS, i.e. subject-subject.

12. The connection between repeatability and complexity is not uncontroversial. The first sentence in this case is longer and would take up more storage space in short term memory than the second, apart from the supposedly greater complexity involved in deriving a passive.

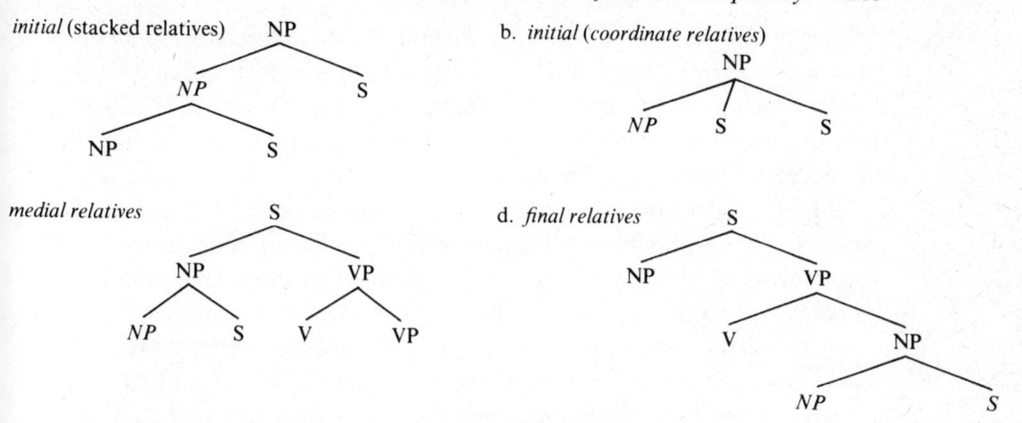

Figure 11 Phrase markers for initial, medial and final relative clauses

II. $[NP_1]$ V NP_2 – $[NP_3]$ V NP_4 (SS)
subject subject

Phrase structure markers are given for two types of final relative clauses in III and IV below. In these cases the relative marker functions as an object, but in III the head NP is the object of the matrix sentence and is closer to its relative marker than in IV, where the head NP is the subject of the matrix S.

III. NP_1 V $[NP_2]$ – NP_3 V $[NP_4]$ (OO)
object object

IV. $[NP_1]$ V NP_2 – NP_3 V $[NP_4]$ (SO)
subject object

Type III can be called OO, i.e. object-object, and type IV SO, i.e. subject-object. It has been suggested that in addition to perceptual difficulty there is a trend of developmental complexity involved here, so that OS relatives are more easily decoded than SS, and SS more so than OO, and OO more so than SO, and that children acquire structures in this order (cf. e.g. Noizet, et al. 1972; Offir 1973; Schachter 1973; Sheldon 1973). This 'perceptual hierarchy' is shown below.

Perceptual hierarchy

OS > SS > OO > SO

It is illuminating to compare this acquisitional continuum with the developmental continuum resulting from the process of creolization. Bickerton and Odo (1976: 274–9) have observed that the few Hawaiian Pidgin English speakers who do produce relative clauses, relativize on the object noun of the matrix sentence far oftener than on the subject noun. We can see that in both the OS and OO types the head NP is closer to the relative marker than in the SO type. They speculate that relativization on the object noun is easier than subject relativization because it still entails (in terms of surface structure) only paratactic conjunction of sentences, rather than the insertion of one within the other (i.e. embedding), as in the case of subject relativization, e.g. SS and SO.

Although a plausible explanation can be based on perceptual factors, it may actually be more reasonable to refer to the influence of discourse, i.e. new information nouns tend to be located in object position. Thus, the high percentage of object relatives is a reflection of this fact. During the course of acquisition it may be that speakers switch from a discourse-oriented system to a purely syntactically motivated one; this notion is behind Sankoff and Brown's (1976) hypothesis concerning the origins of syntax in discourse. This change-over may help to explain Sankoff and Brown's finding that the case hierarchy does not work (i.e. account for the frequency of distribution of relative clauses in various syntactic positions) in Tok Pisin. Bickerton (1977: 284) also finds that in Hawaiian English Creole the rate of insertion of relative markers in OS sentences is at least twice that for OO types. This fits in well with Bever and Langendoen's (1972) hypothesis about perceptual strategies governing deletion. However, we would then expect the same constraints to apply to SS sentences; but Bickerton finds a considerably lower rate of insertion. There is no marking in 70 percent of SS sentences, while half the OS types are marked. This may indicate a crucial discrepancy between developmental (i.e. acquisitional) and synchronic/diachronic continua with respect to relativization. That is, the hierarchy may apply just in case a language has relative clauses and is not in the process of developing them. A similar interpretation based on a switch from discourse to grammatical strategies may also not be too far-fetched in the history of English, where data on the deletion of relative markers indicate there was an increase in the deletion of object relatives from Old English to Middle English, but a decrease in subject deletion (cf. Romaine 1980a, forthcoming f). In other words, the differential rates of deletion may reflect the working out of this change-over in strategies. This fits in well with O'Neil's (1976: 207) opinion that a change from adjunction to embedding (i.e. a syntactic strategy for the incorporation of sentences into sentences) took place between the Old and Middle English periods (cf. 3.3).

5 *The extralinguistic variables: methods for the reconstruction of language in its social context*

> [Historical] records do not, by themselves, produce a unique solution to our problems. But who has ever assumed that they do? Historical records do not produce a unique solution for historical problems either, and yet nobody suggests that they be neglected ... The question is how they should be used.
>
> Paul Feyerabend (1978: 253)

In this chapter I discuss the extralinguistic factors which may affect the choice of relative markers, and a method for taking such factors into account in my study. I take it that it is also within the scope of this discussion to provide a critical review of some current methodological principles which relate to my investigation of the relative markers in Middle Scots, for example, sampling procedures and the problem of defining style and isolating contextual styles within texts. I will be particularly concerned with examining the extent to which the nature of my data allows the transfer or necessitates modification of sociolinguistic methods which have been used in dealing with synchronic speech data (cf. also Chapter 2). Although I am treating specifically one particular set of Middle Scots data, the problem I face is a more general one, which might be called the 'reconstruction of language in its social context'. The question of whether such reconstruction is in principle possible is fundamental to the larger issue my work raises, namely, the status of socio-historical linguistic theory.

5.1 The problem of sampling

There are a number of ways in which a sample of data suitable for sociolinguistic analysis might be obtained. Currently the most fashionable one consists of interviewing individuals and groups both formally and informally. The corpus of possible data for the present study is much more limited than that of most sociolinguistic studies being undertaken today since the language no longer exists in spoken form; it is even further reduced by being limited to Middle Scots texts from the central Scots area written approximately during the period 1530–50. Even so, we must be concerned with the problem of sampling, unless we decide that all texts which fall into this category are to be included.

For the purposes of this study, it is neither desirable nor necessary, judging from what is known about sampling procedures and the regularity of linguistic patterns, to include all instances of the relative which occurred during this period.[1] The notion of 'sampling' as a means of investigating language is implicit in Saussure's dichotomy between *langue* and *parole*. Saussure (1966) speaks of *langue* as a system which has potential existence in the brain of the individual, but is not complete in any speaker; it exists perfectly, i.e. in its totality, within the collectivity or the group. However, the only way we have of getting at this system is through observation or sampling of individual linguistic behavior, i.e. through *parole*.

Labov (1969) and in particular, Sankoff (1974) have reinterpreted and elaborated these notions in what Sankoff has called the 'quantitative paradigm' (cf. Cedergren and Sankoff 1974). Labov, for example, has identified *parole* with the individual aspect of language and *langue* with the social; in order to investigate the social aspect of language we must sample idiolects. Sankoff's interpretation of *langue/parole* (and also competence/performance) in the quantitative paradigm represents a more radical departure from the original definitions of these concepts. For Sankoff, *la langue* is the total of the linguistic forms shared by the members of a speech community together with their probabilities of occurrence. *La parole*, on the other hand, represents random samples of that population.[2] Furthermore, Sankoff has taken performance to be understood as a statistical reflection of competence (cf. also Chapter 7). This suggests sampling at two levels: 1. a sample of individuals/groups (or in this case, texts) needs to be chosen; and 2. samples of linguistic behavior from the first sample need to be obtained. This raises the problem of sampling methods and claims of representativeness.

1. It would of course be possible to do this, although the time involved would be considerable; even if a computer did the initial scanning of all the texts, a linguist would still have to edit the results and sift through the texts for instances of Ø.
2. I am not arguing that *langue* and *parole* can be equated with the competence/performance distinction of Chomsky. In particular, Sankoff's use of the latter is not compatible with Chomsky's view (cf. also Labov 1969 and Chapters 2 and 9). The identification of *langue* with the social aspect of language and *parole* with the individual aspect is also in some respects misleading, since some variationists would claim that within a given speech community individuals can be distinguished not only by differences in language use, but also by differences in the underlying system they have acquired. I discuss the problem of isomorphism (or lack of it) between individual and group grammars in the final chapter.

5.1.1 'Random' sampling and the problem of sample size. One of the alleged methodological advances in sociolinguistics has been the adoption of procedures from the social sciences in the investigation and analysis of the sociolinguistic structure of urban speech communities. Perhaps the most important of these methods is random (or quasi-random) sampling as a means of selecting informants. I will argue here, however, that the term 'random' sampling is being used in a different way in sociolinguistics from its intended statistical use in the social sciences. Furthermore, due to the specific linguistic as well as other requirements which must typically be met in sociolinguistic research, I doubt that random sampling is even a possible, let alone realistic, goal.

This does not mean that we should not pay careful attention to the methods used in the selection of informants (or in my case, texts); however, as a matter of principle, I do not think sociolinguists have anything to gain by 'pretending' to use random samples, when they either do not or cannot. The issue of random sampling also relates to another sociolingustic practice which has been largely accepted since Labov claimed to have demonstrated its validity in New York City in 1966. I refer here to the claim that the number of informants and tokens needed to produce results representative of the linguistic behavior of a speech community is much smaller than that required for other forms of social behavior.

I should perhaps say at the outset that I think Labov is more or less right about the latter claim, though, as I hope to demonstrate, for the wrong reasons, i.e. his argument is circular. The problem of random sampling is, however, a more serious one; and neither Labov nor Trudgill can claim, in my opinion, to have used random or quasi-random samples. Yet I will argue that this does not really matter in the end anyway, because there is an important sense in which language data might already be considered random.[3]

Labov's (1966) study was based on a previously conducted random sample of 988 households. From this sample Labov eventually obtained 122 (or 12 percent of the original 988) interviews. Linguistic requirements immediately reduced the original sample because not everyone was born in New York City or had lived there long enough to be considered a native New Yorker (i.e. resided in NYC since the age of 8). This requirement alone reduced the number of informants from the original 988 to 312; in addition, 35 percent of the population had moved in the two years between the

3. I have argued both these points elsewhere (cf. Romaine 1975 for a more detailed discussion of sampling practices in sociolinguistic research; and Romaine 1978b on the notion of random sampling).

original sample and Labov's study. Thus, Labov's work was based on 122 interviews from the 195 informants left in the original sample (i.e. 63 percent).

In the reduction from 195 to 122, practical or uncontrollable factors enter into the picture. Some informants either could not be contacted, refused to be interviewed, or had died. These problems of course occur in any type of social research. Labov presented data to assess to what extent losses from the original sample affected the representativeness of his sample in comparison with the Lower East Side and the city as a whole (as does Trudgill for his sample in relation to Norwich as a whole), but there is no indication of what differences are likely to be significant. This problem could have been approached with more statistical sophistication, as is normally the case in social surveys where claims are made about randomness and representativeness of samples with respect to larger populations; but neither Labov nor Trudgill has done this.[4] Most importantly, however, no prior thought had been given to the degree of precision (defined statistically in terms of standard error) which would be required for the results. This, as I point out in the following discussion, is considered only post hoc in arguments about the regularity and uniformity of linguistic behavior.

Within the tradition of structuralism and regional dialectology, the assumption that the speech of one informant was sufficient to represent a linguistic system was a working principle. It was also legitimate for the linguist to be his own informant. The reliance on one's own intuition in linguistic matters has also occupied an important place in both British and American linguistics; native speaker intuition figures prominently in Chomsky's works; and Firth, for example, believed that the only reliable observations were those of the trained phonetician on himself. Many sociolinguists, while rejecting these notions, have not considered the question of the optimal sample size sufficient to reveal the sociolinguistic structure of a speech community, but have accepted Labov's assumptions about the relative homogeneity of linguistic behavior.

Labov (1966: 180) has made the comment that 'linguistic behavior is far more general and compelling than many social attitudes or survey responses'. Since it is to be expected that the size of a sample is dependent

4. If cost or other practical limitations are not considered, there are statistical procedures for determining the sample size in terms of an acceptable level of standard error of a proportion (cf. Moser and Kalton 1971). This is determined by the investigator in view of the purposes of the study, the type of analysis to be performed on the results, etc. The statistics which would be needed in Labov's or Trudgill's case are estimates of the variability of each of the strata of the population incorporated in the sample. With this information, the numbers required in the individual strata, and thus in the whole sample, to bring the sample to the previously agreed level of precision desirable can be ascertained.

on the expected homogeneity of the behavior to be observed, it has been assumed that reliable samples might be obtained by using much smaller numbers of informants in sociolinguistic research than in sociological surveys (which typically involve hundreds or thousands of subjects).

Labov (1966: 638) concluded from the results of the New York study that:

> if the previous studies of New York City had followed a systematic method of selecting informants, the 25 or 30 cases described would have been sufficient to show the outlines of a systematic structure of stylistic and social variation. We may conclude that the structure of social and stylistic variation of language can be studied through samples considerably smaller than those required for the study of other forms of social behavior.

This remark is not only circular in its reasoning, but has also set a dangerous precedent for sociolinguistic research. To take the most obvious problem with Labov's statement first, the only way that he could reach this conclusion was by sampling the linguistic behavior of a larger number of New Yorkers first to determine the most relevant conditioning factors, and then compare the behavior of a small subset who reflect these factors with the larger sample. From this extrapolation it is a large and unjustified leap to the conclusion that the social and stylistic structure of 'language' can be studied through such small samples. The rest of the world is not necessarily like New York City (cf. Romaine 1980b).

A different, but equally serious, objection to this line of argumentation can, I think, be made to the implied methodological contradiction. Labov assumes that the speech of one individual is not sufficiently consistent to produce an interpretable pattern apart from the larger social group to which a speaker belongs; therefore, sampling a larger number of speakers is necessary to reveal the larger structure of which the individual is a part. Then, having obtained the larger structure, Labov concludes that one or two speakers who represent a particular category of age, sex, social class, etc. are sufficient to reveal the structure after all.[5]

In fact, if we look closely at the number of informants representing a given cell, about whom a sociolinguistic generalization is made, more often than not, no more than a few informants are involved. For example, in both

5. Le Page (1975: 7) comments:

> the linguist ... jumps very easily from observations on an individual's usage to the creation of an abstraction for which he can write a grammar, and then back again to the individual seen now not as the source of his data but as an exemplar, sometimes unreliable, of the grammar of the dialect the linguist has created.

Cf. also Wunderlich (1974: 138–9).

the Detroit dialect survey (cf. Wolfram 1969) and Macaulay's (1973) study of Glasgow, two speakers are representative of a particular cell, so that Macaulay's conclusions about 'working class Glasgow women', for example, are based on the data from two women. Similarly, when the informants in Labov's (1966) study of New York City and Trudgill's (1974) study of Norwich are distributed among the parameters of age, sex, social class, etc., fewer than four informants are often involved.

Le Page (1975) has also commented on the smallness of most sociolinguistic samples. He suggests that five informants should represent each cell, although there is no evidence to suggest that this number would provide more reasonable or representative results. Intuitively, this seems likely; but any such claim would have to be made on the basis of more sophisticated statistical operations than sociolinguists typically indulge in. An increase in sample size will not eliminate or reduce any bias already present in the selection procedure.

I am not advocating the use of highly complex statistics in sociolinguistics; nor am I arguing against it. I do think, however, that we must recognize Labov's assumption about the homogeneity of linguistic behavior for what it is; namely, a convenient post hoc justification for the limitations of time, money and manpower, which affect most sociolinguistic research (cf. also Le Page 1975: 29). The fact is that the amount and type of work involved in studying the sociolinguistic structure of a large community is, of course, often very different from that encountered in most social science research, since detailed phonetic transcription is generally required.

Labov's observations about the amount of linguistic data needed from an individual or group to reveal consistent patterning, which follow from his 'homogeneity of linguistic behavior' hypothesis, also seem to have been accepted without much question. Labov (1966: 181) says:

> we found that from 10–20 instances of a given variable were sufficient to assign a value that fits into a complete matrix of stylistic variation ... Thus we see that numbers which might be totally inadequate for the study of attitudes, say towards racial segregation, with the associated reluctance to give a straightforward personal response, are quite adequate for the study of phonological variables.

Here again, the conclusion is post hoc and overgeneralized. To my knowledge, this issue has received systematic discussion in only two places in the sociolinguistic literature (Albo 1970; Guy 1974). Of the two, Albo has given more detailed consideration to this problem than Guy, who has discussed only t/d deletion. Nevertheless, Guy's data showed that most of the individual deviations from majority patterns occurred when there were fewer than 10 tokens; above this number, there was 90 percent conformity with the expected pattern. Above 35 tokens, there was 100 percent (cf. Naro 1981).

Albo (1970) examined the patterns of a number of different variables in Cochabamba Quechua and concluded that the sensitivity of the variables to sample size was not constant. The patterns of two of his variables suggested that even a single or very few occurrences of a variant were sufficient to reveal the pattern of the individual. In the analysis of more complex variables however, which contained a number of variants or subsets of variants, a much larger number of occurrences was needed to produce reliable results.

In one case Albo divided the data from one speaker into two parts, one of which contained three-quarters of the speaker's output and the other a quarter. He found that in the smaller sample, three of the variables occurred only once, and four of the variables did not occur at all. This reflects the frequency of occurrence of the variables. Higher frequency types are more likely to occur even in small samples; therefore, smaller samples will tend to emphasize those variables and variants which are more commonly used by the speaker. Albo concluded that there was no single criterion to determine the number of occurrences necessary to produce representative results for a given variable for an individual speaker. In some cases more than 100 occurrences may not be enough, while in others fewer than 10, and even 2 occurrences might show contrastive patterns of usage.

The implication of my argument is that the term 'random' sampling takes on a different meaning within sociolinguistic research than it has within statistics and the social sciences. This does not mean that we should go back to hand-picking informants in the way regional dialectologists sometimes do, or that we have to use larger samples of informants. My argument is that we should recognize the difference between linguistic and other samples of data; and, most importantly, we should not try to justify the results and methods of sampling that we do use by statistical standards which cannot be applied in their strictest sense to linguistic data (cf. Romaine 1980c).

5.1.2 On the random nature of linguistic data. The fact that certain types of linguistic behavior do seem to manifest themselves so pervasively in consistent patterns has, however, some important implications. It follows from this observation that, provided the method of sampling is independent of the characteristic which is being sampled (which is the essential principle underlying the theory of random sampling), it does not matter how regular or systematic the procedure is by which the individual samples are selected. Herdan (1960: 115) has expressed the view that:

> the linear sequences of linguistic forms in written texts or speech are random series with respect to certain quantitative characteristics and any sampling procedure, be it by disconnected linguistic units, or by continuous pieces of texts or by chapters etc. will give a random sample of such a quantitative characteristic, provided only that the sampling method is in no way connected with that characteristic; that is, provided that it does not consist in a direct or indirect selection of just the characteristic one is sampling for.

There are of course critics both of random sampling per se and of any statistical procedure or analogy applied to linguistic behavior. For example, Kendall and Babington Smith (1938) note the claim that there is no such thing as a random method of selection considered apart from the universe whose members are being selected; and, more importantly perhaps, within the same universe a method which is random with respect to one characteristic is not necessarily random with respect to another. More specifically, it has been said that linguistic expression is too much a matter of conscious choice for it to be amenable to pure chance consideration.

Up to this point I have been considering language as a whole. It is clear however that we will want to be able to talk about randomness with respect to different levels in the organization of linguistic material. All of these are not governed in the same way by laws of chance. Herdan (1960: 293) has suggested that language data are somewhat peculiar in that they show a gradual transition from those types of characteristics which are purely random to those which are governed by both chance and choice. The place of a given type of linguistic form along this cline will determine the size of the sample which will be needed to produce the desired result; namely, a corpus which represents in a random way the features of the population as a whole.

At one end of the scale are certain characteristics of language which are on the whole fairly independent of style, and hence language-conditioned, e.g. syllables, letters and phonemes. The occurrence of these types of characteristics will be, by and large, already random; therefore, there is much less need to superimpose a sophisticated scheme of random sampling on them. At the other end of the scale, however, there are qualitative characteristics, such as vocabulary and sentence length, which are not solely language-conditioned, but are to a great extent style-conditioned. These features may show significant variation with individual style if the field of observation is sufficiently extended. In this case the probability that such features will occur is not strictly constant throughout the universe. Therefore, these features need to be sampled differently from those which have a constant probability of occurrence independent of text samples.

It follows from this that the more language-conditioned a linguistic characteristic is, the smaller the sample which is needed to be considered representative of the statistical population. For example, Wang and Crawford (1960) came to the conclusion that the relative frequency of consonants in English is not seriously affected by the types of literary content, or by the dialect of the sample, so that even a relatively small sample yielded typical results. Just to what extent a given feature of language is language-conditioned or style-conditioned is open to empirical investigation.

The grammar and syntax of a language, according to Herdan, occupy a median position on the scale ranging from language- to style-conditioned. Impressionistically speaking, a feature such as the occurrence of relative markers is governed both by rules of the language (which have been discussed in detail in Chapter 4) and 'rules' of style or extralinguistic considerations (which will be discussed later in this chapter). Here choice and the laws of chance intersect.[6]

The above discussion indicates that a representative corpus of relative markers in Middle Scots within the time and geographical limitations imposed needs to be fairly large and reasonably varied with regard to style or type of text. The sample which I have selected here contains approximately 6,300 relative tokens taken from seven different texts which span a stylistic continuum ranging from legal prose to verse (cf. Chapter 6 for exact figures).

This sample constitutes, in statistical terms, what might be called a 'quota stratified sample'. In other words, the sample might be referred to as stratified in the sense that the corpus is stratified by text type or genre. Each text is part of a stratum (e.g. legal prose) from which various samples will be drawn. There is also a sense in which each individual text in a given stratum can be considered to constitute a universe in its own right, in the same way that an idiolect might be regarded as a universe. The sample is also a quota

6. There is some sociolinguistic evidence (cf. Chapter 2) to suggest that phonological variation intersects with extralinguistic parameters in a different way from syntactic variation (cf. Van den Broeck 1977; Lavandera 1978; Naro 1981).

sample in the sense that a limit has been placed on the number of occurrences of the variable to be taken from the lengthier texts, e.g. certain legal and official records which run continuously over a large number of years. Once that number has been reached, then counting is stopped and the quota is considered to be filled or adequately represented. In cases where a portion of a text does not contain the quota, then the whole text will be used.

5.2 Type of text

I have divided the external variables into two main categories: type of text and style. As indicated above, it is evident that each individual text could be considered as a separate sample, and as such can be expected to reveal fluctuating levels of relative marker usage. It might also be expected that some texts may be more internally homogeneous than others, e.g. legal prose vs. epistolary prose. This is certainly a hypothesis which can be tested. Another hypothesis is that similar genres of texts will pattern together on the basis of their usage of relative markers, and that the incidence of ∅ will be an important diagnostic variable or predictor of stylistic level.

I have set up the divisions indicated below as a starting point to group the texts. In the initial coding of the texts I have considered each text both as an individual and as a member of each of these more general categories (in the case where a category is represented by more than one member). For example, *The Bannatyne Manuscript* can be considered as a whole to be representative of the category of verse, while parts of it can also be taken to be exponents of particular types of verse, e.g. comic, moralizing, etc.; the same is true of Lindsay's *Satyre*.

Sample of Middle Scots texts

1. Prose	Official and legal prose	*Acts of the Lords of Council in Public Affairs*
		Sheriff Court Book of Fife
		Burgh Records (Edinburgh)
	Literary (narrative) prose	Bellenden's *Boece*
	Epistolary prose	*The Scottish Correspondence of Mary of Lorraine*
2. Verse	Courtly or serious verse	*Ane Satyre of the Thrie Estaitis*
	Moralizing or religious verse	
	Comic verse	*The Bannatyne Manuscript*

5.2.1 Sociolinguistic definitions of style. All of the so-called external or social variables which will be considered could of course be called 'stylistic' factors, depending on what definition of 'style' is used. There have been many different definitions of this concept ranging from the purely impressionistic to statistical. For example, there are those who have claimed that style is an isolable and separate component of a text, as well as those who have claimed that it is an inherent, integral part of every text. A number of approaches to the problem will be considered here with a view to examining in particular what contributions, if any, sociolinguistics has made towards a definition of style, and how such a definition might be applied here to investigate stylistic factors within texts.

It will become clear, I think, in the following discussion that the notion of style as an absolute and isolable element of language will have to be abandoned in favor of a definition founded on comparison. The notion lacks meaning when applied to a single text, and it is only when we begin to compare one text with another or with what it might have been, i.e. in terms of alternative ways of saying the same thing, against the larger background of the language as a whole, that we can begin to talk about style in a meaningful way. McIntosh (1963: 20) comments on this contrastive aspect of style: 'Style we might almost say is a matter of the selection of particular grammatical patterns and sequences of patterns and of particular items of vocabulary and sequences of items and of course (by implication) the avoidance of others.'

It is easy to see how statistics, originally in the form of simple counting, entered into the study of stylistics as a means of quantifying impressionistic observations. Most of the early statistical work seized on easily accessible items such as vocabulary, mean sentence length, etc. to form statistical profiles of various authors/texts in order to settle largely non-statistical questions, e.g. disputed authorship or chronological ordering of texts. Problems of syntax have, however, rarely and only recently been subjected to similar systematic quantitative treatment (cf., in particular, Winter 1961; Posner 1963; Sankoff 1973; Rickford 1975).

Some generative grammarians have, however, considered how dialectal or stylistic variation might be incorporated into a theory of syntax (cf. e.g. Thorne 1965; Klima 1969; Carden 1972). Such differences are generally ascribed to the existence of different rules or different rule orderings; here the emphasis has been on establishing a formal means of describing the relationship which exists between related or coexistent grammatical systems. One might think of the different styles of a speaker as coexistent systems. Klima (1969: 233–4), for example, has suggested that there is a relationship between simple declarative sentences with complementizer *that*, relative clauses and indirect questions (interrogative clauses); they are all structures which are described by the rules of embedding. The difference between them can be accounted for in grammatical terms by ordering the transformational rule that describes declaratives with complementizer clauses before the rules for WH attachment, and by ordering the transformational rules describing relative and interrogative clauses after the WH attachment rule, in that order. This ordering would also permit the use of the same *that* deletion rule to delete complementizers and relatives (cf. Chapter 2). There has, however, been no attempt to incorporate quantitative information of the type found in variable rules in an orthodox generative grammar. Either the rules apply or they do not, without reference to external factors.

I have used the word 'definitions' in the plural in the title of this section to indicate that there is no single accepted sociolinguistic definition of style. An examination of recent sociolinguistic literature will reveal that the word has been applied in a very restricted, mechanistic manner (e.g. Labov 1966), as well as in a very loose, broad manner (e.g. Hymes 1974b; Lomax 1977).

Sociolinguists who have worked with Labovian models of variation have defined style quantitatively, i.e. as a relative frequency of features or style markers. Labov has said (1966: 129–30), for example, that 'whether we consider stylistic variation to be a continuum of expressive behavior, or a subtle type of discrete alternation, it is clear that it must be approached through quantitative methods'.

Breaks in the stylistic continuum of frequency levels of linguistic features would then serve to demarcate styles. This approach has been criticized as being overly simplistic and mechanistic, but at the same time it has opened up whole new avenues of insight into language variation. For example, sociolinguists are able to talk in terms of objectively measurable differences in linguistic elements which may characterize the speech of individuals or groups in a way not attempted by purely descriptive and generative grammarians. Certainly one of the most important findings based on a definition of style in terms of frequency is the social dimension of stylistic variation, i.e. some features show movement on a continuum from casual to formal as well as on a social continuum from working to upper class.

Labov (1966: 113) has maintained, in favor of this approach, that the only alternative would be to return to the notion of the idiolect, with each manifestation of a style considered as a distinct idiolect. Bloch's (1948: 7–9) definition of an idiolect as the speech of one speaker speaking in one style to the same person is an example of the alternative Labov suggests.

This definition of style can apply at a higher level than the idiolect, because if contrasting levels are characterized or distinguished from one another by quantitative patterns of recurrent selections of optional features of a language, then this is a property that styles share with dialects. In other words, stylistic variation is not different in kind from social dialect variation. Labov's work has demonstrated that the differences which exist between social dialects in American English are largely differences of degree and not kind, i.e. they are quantitative and not qualitative. Winter (1964) has made a similar point. He says that the identification of different styles can be undertaken in much the same way as the identification of different dialects of a language; namely, the boundaries of both dialects and styles can be established on the basis of isoglosses or bundles of isoglosses, either lexical, phonological, or syntactic. These styles may or may not correspond with individual idiolects. One of the hypotheses I am testing here is whether the use of the relative markers can be considered one such isogloss which will serve to distinguish different texts, i.e. idiolects or 'idiotexts', as well as different genres of texts, e.g. legal vs. epistolary prose.

Going beyond this quantitative definition, Hymes (1974b) has suggested a more general use of the term 'style' to mean a way of doing something. This, he maintains, would enable us to transcend the traditional notion of grammar as a descriptive framework for dealing with speech communities. In Hymes' terms, then, a speech community would comprise a set of styles. I pointed out in Chapter 1 how Lomax's system of cantometrics and parlametrics might be seen as an illustration of this. It is important to note that in Hymes' view speech styles would not be mechanical correlations of features of speech with each other and with contexts, but would be available for use outside their defining context. Lomax's application of Hymes' idea points beyond Winter's conception of 'styles as dialects' to the much broader notion of 'languages or speech communities as styles' (cf. e.g. Kanngiesser 1972a). (I return to this issue in the final chapter.)

Hymes has furthermore advocated the adoption of Ervin-Tripp's (1972) more general terms, 'rules of co-occurrence' and 'rules of alternation', as a point of departure for dealing with the problem of style. Rules of co-occurrence can be used to identify a style of speech, and rules of alternation can characterize the choice which may exist among styles, and hence free the resulting styles from a mechanical connection with a particular defining situation.

5.2.2 The isolation of contextual styles. I will now consider in some detail the question of how to go beyond the constraints of regarding each text or group of texts, i.e. genre, as an idiolect or style, and enter into the area of rules of alternation. This strikes me as being similar to Labov's problem in trying to isolate different styles within the single context of the linguistic interview. His views have some relevance here (cf. also Joos 1967).

Labov (1966) has commented that the notion of the existence of different styles within the linguistic interview presented a paradox, since the nature of the interview itself, i.e. a face-to-face interaction between strangers being recorded on tape, defined a context in which only one speaking style occurred, i.e. formal speech. Labov nevertheless claimed to have isolated five styles within the interview which contrasted with each other in terms of the frequency of occurrence of some of the linguistic variables under investigation; and the results in fact showed that these frequencies contrasted regularly in the different styles of one speaker, and that the frequencies of speakers in the same styles could contrast one group with another.

Despite this 'successful' result (successful in the sense that it produced the result Labov hoped for), the way in which Labov divided the interview into a set of styles has come under some attack. Labov postulated the existence of a stylistic continuum ranging from formal or careful to informal or casual speech, in which the degree of formality of the style was seen as contingent upon the amount of attention which was paid to speech.

On this basis Labov isolated the following styles:

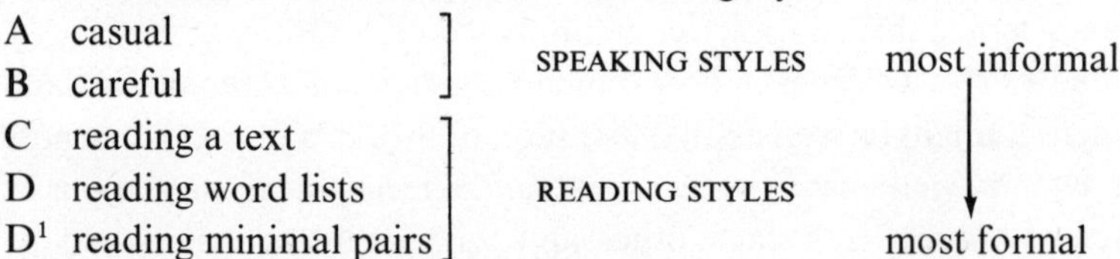

Casual speech was further delineated by defining it in terms of its co-occurrence both with contextual conditions, e.g. speech outside the context of the interview, on the telephone, or to another person, etc., and with topical conditions, e.g. in response to a question about childhood rhymes or danger of death, as well as with certain channel cues, e.g. changes in pitch, volume, tempo, etc.

Although this continuum seemed to operate in New York City, and its existence has been largely taken for granted since then (cf. e.g. Trudgill 1974), there have, as I indicated above, been a number of difficulties and some dissatisfaction with its application elsewhere (cf. e.g. Macaulay 1973; Romaine 1975, 1978c; Milroy and Milroy 1977).

For one thing, a number of sociolinguists have objected to the inclusion of both reading and speaking in the same continuum. Macaulay (1973: 25) disputed Labov's claim that these five styles are on a single continuum, since there is a gap between reading and speaking which may involve more than one step, and other work has concluded that reading and speaking are best regarded as two separate activities (cf. Milroy and Milroy 1977; Romaine 1978c). Macaulay has been particularly critical of Wolfram's study of Detroit speech in which the single interview style was compared with that of the reading passage. Macaulay (1970: 768) claimed that the clearly marked 'stylistic' difference between the two samples of speech was an artifact of the reading passage; the opposite results could have been obtained by asking informants to read a passage containing non-standard variants instead.

My own work in Scotland (cf. especially Romaine 1975) and the Milroys' in Belfast support his claim. It is true in both Scotland and Belfast (owing to the sociolinguistic complexities of the respective linguistic communities) that a number of common vernacular pronunciations which vary in accordance with situational constraints never occur in reading styles.[7] In general, it may be said that the range of variation appropriate to reading is very narrow. In Scotland such vernacular pronunciations may only be used outside the social context of working class speech in a formulaic way, e.g. in proverbial sayings or in Burns readings, etc., or to achieve a special effect. In both cases, in Scotland and Northern Ireland, reading out loud proved to be an intimidating task for some speakers. This fact, together with the failure of certain significant or socially diagnostic variables to pattern along a continuum from least formal (spoken) to most formal (reading), was taken as sufficient justification for regarding conversational and reading styles as separate parts of the linguistic continuum (for further evidence from language evaluation tests, cf. Romaine 1978c, 1980d).

Another problem with the stylistic continuum is the virtual impossibility of incorporating Labov's notion of channel cues elsewhere, since the assessment of the degree of change in these which is sufficient or necessary to signal a shift from one style to another is both subjective and arbitrary; in other words, this will vary with the investigator. The same channel cues, e.g. laughter, may also be interpreted in several different ways; and other cues may be difficult to demarcate, i.e. where do they begin and end? The

7. I have discussed some of the methodological challenges and problems of analysis which such complex communities present to the Labovian model of sociolinguistics in Romaine 1978b, c, 1979c, 1980b.

channel cues do not seem to be really independent of the measurement of the linguistic variables.

Wolfson (1976: 203) has recently criticized the assumption that there is a monotonic and unidirectional relationship between audio-monitoring, i.e. the amount of attention that a speaker pays to his own speech, and style. She suggests that it is reasonable to expect that if some people monitor their speech in order to produce what they regard as formal speech, then it can also happen that some people are attending most carefully to their speech when making an effort to be colloquial. Although Wolfson does not cite a specific example to prove her point, the latter case is not uncommon in Scotland, i.e. there are people who habitually and deliberately use marked Scotticisms against a background of largely middle class speech. In doing so, they are, no doubt, paying a great deal of attention to their speech since speech forms are being selected and removed from their defining context, i.e. primarily lower class speech, into another one to achieve a special effect.

The problem seems to be, then, not so much whether a stylistic continuum exists (if defined in terms of contrasting levels of frequencies with which certain items occur), but rather what it corresponds to, since similar results could be obtained by subdividing the interview in other ways. In other words, the results seem to be the only justification for the method. Nevertheless, Labov's results have some important consequences when they are considered in the wider context of sociolinguistic theory.

If Labov's criteria, i.e. amount of attention paid to speech or phonological cues such as tempo change, cannot be used objectively to delimit styles, then we are back to the notion of frequency. Since a continuum can be constructed solely on the basis of frequency of occurrence of linguistic items, we could look for breaks in the continuum; or we could provisionally group the linguistic data in accordance with some external criteria, as Labov does, e.g. situation, interlocutor, topic or function of the communication, etc. Then we could put the categories in rank order according to the frequency of a given linguistic variable. Either procedure can apply equally well to the written language, where, in any event, there are no phonological cues which could serve as external defining criteria. In other words, divisions could be made in the individual texts according to topic or subject matter, e.g. serious vs. comic verse; interlocutor, e.g. high vs. lowly characters; and function of the communication, i.e. entertainment, didactic, etc. These subsections could then be arranged on a stylistic continuum based on the frequency of usage of relative markers. We could then look for external reasons for this ordering; or, alternatively, the texts could be ordered in a stylistic continuum solely on the basis of internal considerations, such as syntactic complexity as determined by the frequency of relativization on NPs in certain syntactic positions (cf. 4.5). Then we could examine to what extent these findings corroborated the original hypothesis about the correlation between relative marker usage and stylistic level, i.e. formality vs. informality. A very important consideration is the predictive power of the results. In other words, what do the results say about other texts? Can relative marker usage be taken as an independent variable in future work on Middle Scots texts, i.e. is a particular pattern of relative marker usage diagnostic of a particular stylistic level so that when the pattern is observed elsewhere, i.e. outside its defining context, it can be predicted that the text in question has certain properties? Beyond this specific question there is of course the larger theoretical issue of the 'explanatory' and predictive power of a sociolinguistic theory with reference to historical data. Labov has discussed how the present might be used to 'explain' the past (cf. e.g. Labov et al. 1972), but we might well ask here: how can the past be used to 'explain' the present?

5.3 Reconstructing language in its social context

The possibility of reconstruction within a sociolinguistic theory depends on the recovery of past events, as all forms of historical enquiry do. In other words, we attempt to reconstruct information that is not directly available or has been lost. The primary evidence for the past is the same, whether the historical linguist regards himself as a sociolinguist or not; namely, the texts which survive.[8] The special problem for the sociolinguist, however, is that of interpreting or taking into account context in a systematic way. There are of course numerous handbooks on reconstruction (cf. e.g. Hoenigswald 1960), which provide methodological guidelines for recovering linguistic form; I will not discuss these here. My job will be to show how social context impinges on and contributes to a theory of historical change; one outcome should be the provision of historical linguistics with a coherent framework for dealing with the development of social dialects.

My own assessment of the difficulties involved in reconstructing a 'social context' in the historical record of a language does not fit in with Labov's views about the nature of historical data and its relationship (and indeed its relevance) to sociolinguistics. Labov's (1972b: 100) opinion of the place or

8. Cf. Lass (1980) for a more detailed discussion of the constraints on historical reconstruction, especially the appendix to Chapter 2.

value of historical data is in some respects very limited, at least in the following comment:

> The fundamental methodological fact that historical linguists have to face is that they have no control over their data; texts are produced by a series of historical accidents ... the great art of the historical linguist is to make the best of this bad data – 'bad' in the sense that it may be fragmentary, corrupted or many times removed from the actual productions of native speakers.

I have already indicated in Chapter 1 that I do not share Labov's views about the relationship between the written and spoken language. I also do not accept the view that historical data can be bad in the last sense mentioned by Labov.[9] Although historical data, of course, may be fragmentary and hence bad in the sense of incomplete, the only way in which they can be bad in the other sense intended by Labov is by invidious or inappropriate comparison with the spoken language. Historical data can be valid in their own right (as can other instances of the written language) regardless of the extent to which they reflect or are removed from the productions of native speakers. This is not an empirical issue; and it need not hinder sociolinguistic study of the written language, either synchronically or diachronically. If we accept Labov's view (1972b: 109), i.e. that texts can be understood only in terms of their relation to the spoken language and that the only worthwhile linguistic theories are about the language that ordinary people use on the street, then we must content ourselves with a sociolinguistic theory which is very restricted in scope and application. And I would add that such a sociolinguistic theory could not make any serious claims about being a theory of 'language'. I take it that the point of varying our observations, i.e. extending them from synchronic speech data to diachronic written data, is to 'discover' the scope of the theory.

The working principle of sociolinguistic reconstruction must be the 'uniformitarian principle'. In other words, we accept that the linguistic forces which operate today and are observable around us are not unlike those which have operated in the past.[10] Sociolinguistically speaking, this

9. It may of course happen that the copyist is not a native speaker of the variety/language of the text he is copying. In this case, the text could not be taken as representative of the written language of any speaker or community. This is one important constraint on reconstruction which bears on the problem of representativeness. A parallel obtains in the case of the study of language death; namely, can one use the last generation of native speakers of a language as exemplars of the community to reconstruct earlier stages of the language (cf. Dorian 1981)?
10. The assumption of a uniformitarian principle is not without problems; although we may seem to have good empirical grounds for believing in the uniformity of nature, there is no real basis for believing that the future will be like the past (cf. e.g. Popper 1972: 97–9).

Social class	Informal	Formal
working class	High	Mid
middle class	Mid	Low

Style ↓

Figure 12 The relationship between social and stylistic variation (formal and informal represent two ends of the stylistic continuum; and mid, high, and low refer to the frequency with which a given linguistic feature occurs)

means that there is no reason for claiming that language did not vary in the same patterned ways in the past as it has been observed to do today. It is in fact largely due to Labov's work that we have a great deal of information about the sociolinguistic patterning of language to draw on, which will be useful for historical studies.

One of the most important findings which has emerged from Labovian sociolinguistic work is the relationship between the social class continuum and the stylistic continuum. Labov claims that linguistic features which pattern significantly along the social class continuum will exhibit parallel behavior along a stylistic continuum, so that if a feature is found to be more common in the lower than in the upper class, it will also be more common in less formal than in more formal styles for all speakers (see Figure 12, where the relationship is sketched out very simply).

A regular structure of this type gives the theory great predictive power; in other words, if one of the elements is missing in the array, it can be provisionally filled in or predicted in the absence of data (cf. Labov's (1966: 113f.) comments on structural arrays). We can then look for data which will provide tests for our predictions. If, for example, it is true that variables which are socially diagnostic are also stylistically diagnostic, is the converse also true? In other words, if we can establish that a variable is stylistically diagnostic, can we predict or conclude that it will also be socially diagnostic? This is one testable subhypothesis suggested by Labov's work.[11] If linguistic variants are assumed to be embedded in both social and stylistic continua in a predictable way, then a framework which explicates this imbrication represents a means of uncovering social context in historical records; assuming, of course, that we can reconstruct a fully elaborated stylistic continuum, then we can speculate about its likely connections with

11. Although Labov's own work does not provide counter-examples, the work of Fishman, Cooper, Ma et al. (1971) confirms the existence of markers which are stylistically diagnostic, but not socially diagnostic within the community.

the social continuum, and thus 'reconstruct social context' by a process of extrapolation.

One particular problem which will have to be explored by a socio-historical linguistic methodology is the historical development of social class hierarchies and their relation to linguistic features. For example, if one establishes a linear progression of certain linguistic variables through a social class hierarchy in the present state of a language, is one then justified in reconstructing a similar unidirectional relationship between social and linguistic variables in an earlier state of the same language? The complexity of this problem will of course vary from society to society, and its solution will depend on the availability of records from social historians. Much could be learned from a careful monitoring of situations in which the 'same' language is used in two different nations with different socio-political structure, e.g. German in the Federal Republic of Germany and in the German Democratic Republic.

Friedrich (1972), for example, has documented the process by which changes in the basic social institutions in the Soviet Union between 1850 and 1950 are reflected in modern Russian kinship terms and pronominal usage. And Paulston (1976: 359) has discussed the social class semantics of the pronouns of address in Swedish. One important area of investigation which socio-historical linguistics will have to pursue is socially motivated changes in systems of pronominal address. Because of the social significance of personal reference, personal pronouns are particularly susceptible to modification in response to social and ideological change. Such changes may provide important clues to the social class hierarchy and the attachment of social values to certain linguistic forms (cf. Bodine 1975). Haugen (1975: 333), for example, argues that due to Iceland's remoteness and late development of sophisticated class structure, the dual survived beyond its time into a period where the dual and singular pronominal usage overlapped (cf. Guðmundsson 1972 for a treatment of developments in other Germanic languages).

I wish to stress at this stage that there is a great deal to be done before one can construct a viable model of the interaction between social life and language history. As Brown and Levinson (1979: 305) have suggested, the kinds of sociolinguistic variables isolated by Labov and others may be a very general phenomenon, but they do not seem to be universally associated with stratified speech communities. One must therefore be careful in extrapolating from the not very exiguous existing data on sociolinguistic variation, which at present comes largely from English-speaking communities (cf. however, the papers in Romaine forthcoming b).

To take one case cited by Brown and Levinson (1979: 305), one might easily suppose that lack of absolute markers of speaker's group identity in Europe was a correlate of the continuously graded stratification of western class systems and their associated social mobility. One might then expect (erroneously) to find absolute markers of caste status correlated with the rigid hierarchies of Indian communities. This is however not the case; a speaker cannot be assigned to a social group (e.g. caste or subcaste) simply by reference to his speech. Brown and Levinson claim that members of some local communities of twenty or more castes can be divided into two or three gross categories on the basis of phonological or syntactic variation.

Even in cases where one can reconstruct fairly full social and stylistic continua, one would have to obtain information about who had access to which channels, genres and styles which are reconstructable. Control of part of the linguistic repertoire in existence in a community at any given time may be importantly linked to social class structure. Is it the case that in rigidly hierarchical societies not everyone controls specific genres of speaking equally? Albert (1972), for instance, reports that in Burundi only the top-ranking ethnic group is educated in oratory and related verbal skills; lower status persons have to display bumbling and hesitant behavior (cf. Brown and Levinson 1979: 310, who mention that a similar situation obtains in South India). Irvine (1978) observes that it is the griots in Wolof society who retain control of elaborate and conservative modes of speaking, while the nobility remain silent and hesitant to display verbal skills.

One cannot of course claim that through the isolation of stylistic relationships in and among texts, say in Middle Scots where we have a fully elaborated stylistic continuum, we can arrive at the 'vernacular' or 'colloquial working class' Middle Scots, if there was such a thing. But then this should not be the goal of a sociolinguistic theory with reference to historical linguistics. Even if we examine quoted or indirect speech in prose and verse texts (as I do in Chapter 6), which may be assumed to approximate speech to some extent, this is not speech. Furthermore, there is nothing observable to compare the written record with. There is also the additional consideration that the norms for reporting speech in discourse or verse may have been different then or could have varied according to genre. For example, even though there may be a contrast in the use of features between the narrative and quoted speech in one text, or between comic and serious characters, different genres may set bounds on the depth of 'linguistic descent' allowable. Thus we might find a particular feature associated with lowly characters, but we would have no basis for concluding from this observation that such a feature was a common property of speakers belonging to that echelon in the society; the feature in question might still have been characteristic of the usage of highly literate authors.

I suggest, however, that modern sociolinguistic work on the spoken language operates with a similar constraint on observability. Labov (1972b) has discussed the implications of the 'observer's paradox' for sociolinguistic research at great length; and indeed, much of his contribution to methodology has consisted of developing strategies to overcome its limitations. The problem of the observer's paradox is that in order to find the most useful data for sociolinguistic research, we must find out how people speak when they are not being observed. We can of course resort to surreptitious recording (cf. Bickerton 1971: 467), or confine ourselves to anonymous department store surveys; but by and large the bulk of the data for sociolinguistic theory has been obtained from linguistic interviews; and this poses an interesting methodological problem.

Even though the speech obtained in the context of the linguistic interview may resemble what people do elsewhere (and we must, I think, assume that it does, or consider a large part of sociolinguistic theory and methodology irrelevant), it is *not* an *instance* of what people do elsewhere (cf. Wolfson 1976 for a discussion of the linguistic interview as a type of speech event). In this respect then, both in the case of the diachronic evidence from written records and the synchronic data in the linguistic interview, our access to language can be considered indirect. In other words, there is a sense in which the analysis of linguistic variation, whether approached through the standard sociolinguistic interview or through the extant written texts of a language no longer spoken, involves a similar problem of reconstruction. There are of course controls on synchronic research, i.e. native speakers; but both synchronic and diachronic sociolinguistics raise the same question: what claims about representativeness can we make on the basis of the data to which we have access?[12]

5.4 The intersection of stylistic and linguistic factors in the use of relative markers

One of the repeated findings of sociolinguistics is that linguistic and social factors interact in variation; in other words, there are both internal and

12. The 'observer's paradox' is not just a linguistic problem; quantum mechanics (which bears a great deal of similarity to the quantitative paradigm, as I point out in the final chapter) is also concerned with the problem of taking into account the effect of the observer on the behavior of particles. The Milroys (1977) have suggested another way of 'overcoming' the observer's paradox by taking into account in a systematic way the relationship between the informant and the fieldworker.

external controls on many cases of language variation. This principle had been repeatedly demonstrated by other linguists before Labov's (1966) study of New York City. For example, Quirk's (1957) study, which is relevant here because it illustrates the combination of linguistic and stylistic factors which operate to determine the usage of relative markers in modern English, could be considered sociolinguistic. Quirk (1958) also argued against the use of intuitions and impressionistic judgements (cf. Labov 1972d) in the analysis of linguistic variability; he advocated instead the use of frequency analysis. Winter (1961) discussed the possibility of demarcating styles with syntactic markers in a way similar to marking dialect boundaries with phonological isoglosses. Although these studies are highly suggestive of recent findings in sociolinguistics, and rely on what would certainly be called sociolinguistic methodology today, they do not receive much mention in the Labovian sociolinguistic literature. The research done by Quirk especially is worth examining in more detail.

It follows from the acceptance of the uniformitarian principle that an analysis of relative markers in modern English, such as Quirk's, will have some relevance to a historical study, since it would seem likely that the use of relative markers was embedded in both a social and linguistic context as seems to be the case today. This is not to say that the conditioning factors will be the same, but merely that the kinds or types of factors which influence the situation today show us what kinds of things to look for in the past, and offer insight in that sense; conversely, an examination of an earlier stage in the development of the language may offer some understanding of the forces which operated in the language to bring about the present situation.

Of course none of this discussion claims that the *same feature* will always have been a variable, e.g. the use of the definite article in modern Yorkshire dialects is a social variable, but it is not in other dialects of English. Furthermore, it may never have been so in the past, and may never again be so. One goal or task of a historically oriented sociolinguistic investigation would be to examine the genesis and life cycles of social and stylistic variables. As far as the written language is concerned, the whole process of stylistic change needs to be documented (cf. Hymes 1974b: 444). One aspect of stylistic change would be the narrowing or expansion of contextual constraints on the distribution of a feature, e.g. the creation of new genres of discourse, development of literacy, etc.

Caldwell's (1974) study of relatives in early Scots (before 1550) indicates that some of the same factors were also relevant in Middle Scots; in her data and the data I present here, we can see the emergence of the conditioning factors which later become important. Statistical data on earlier states of the language will be useful not only in documenting the history of competing forms, e.g. the encroachment of WH on TH forms, but also in understanding what changes have taken place in relative marker usage in specific environments, in particular, those which favor or inhibit deletion. Presumably, the variants of the relative may undergo gradual changes in their frequency of use in particular environments prior to their disappearance, functional restriction or specialization. Some of the differences between my study and Caldwell's will be discussed in 5.4.2.

5.4.1 Quirk's study of relative pronouns in modern educated English. The principle of 'frequency surveying' underlies Quirk's analysis; of this notion he says (1958: 42):

> The survey is also a sure way of determining and ranking the features that condition variation in grammatical structure instead of relying only upon subjective judgement of the 'feel' involved (which is notoriously treacherous) and in any case difficult to verify or make public. One can make formal and satisfying discriminations at a complex syntactic level by observing, comparing – as it were 'screening' – the variant features, segmental and otherwise, in as much of the wider linguistic context as proves relevant.

Quirk (1957) describes the system governing the selection of relative markers from a corpus of tape-recordings of fifty university-educated adult speakers. The factors which he considers relevant are similar to the ones outlined in Chapter 4. He does not use as many categories for the syntactic position of the relative in the relative clause, but he does allow for the factor of distancing, which I mentioned as a possible additional factor (cf. 4.4). For example, Quirk finds that there is a tendency to avoid separating the antecedent from the relative clause, and that the relative clause normally modifies the object or objective complement rather than the subject of the main verb. Furthermore, he notes that the substitution of WH by TH seems impossible when the antecedent is a whole clause. This illustrates the general tendency for WH to operate under conditions of distance. On the other hand, Ø tends to occur in short clauses and in medially embedded relative clauses as a replacement for *that*.

In a very useful diagram (Figure 13) Quirk et al. (1972: 867) give a synopsis of the options which are available at different places in the system of restrictive clauses in modern English. The options indicated do not of course give any idea of how these are actually utilized; and this is where the

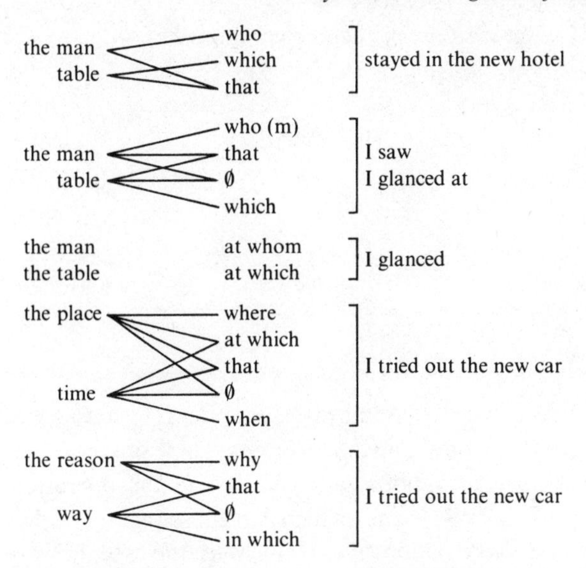

Figure 13 The relative pronoun system in modern English restrictive clauses (from Quirk et al. 1972: 867)

frequency survey is useful. One very interesting result of Quirk's study is the preponderance of WH forms in restrictive clauses. An examination of grammars since at least Sweet (1900) reveals the persistent observation that in spoken English *that* and Ø are preferred to *which*. My results suggest that this trend might have been indicated had Quirk tried to expand his stylistic dimension as well as the social class background of his informants. His results are based on the analysis of the speech of university-educated speakers recorded in three conditions:

1. impromptu conversation which was surreptitiously recorded
2. other recordings of conversation
3. impromptu discussion on a platform before an audience during broadcasting

The performance data from substitution tests revealed that the system of options in Figure 13 is not very helpful in predicting actual patterns of usage and stylistic choice unless it is accompanied by systematic observation of how the system is used. The results of the substitution test (Table 5.1) give the percentage of instances in which informants considered that a particular relative pronoun was capable of being replaced by another in a given instance. The fact that *all* Ø clauses can be replaced by *that* clauses but

Table 5.1. *The substitution of relative pronouns by other relative pronouns (Quirk 1957: 106)*

	Substitution (percent)		
Relative pronoun	WH	TH	∅
WH	—	90	25
TH	95	—	42
∅	80	100	—

few WH clauses can be replaced by ∅ clauses seems to support the view that ∅ clauses come from underlying *that* clauses. These observations seem to fit the standard transformational account, where the operation of a *that* creation rule affects WH forms, which can subsequently be deleted by the application of a *that* deletion rule. If this were the case, however, then we would have expected that all *that*s could be replaced by WH (since all *that*s come from WH derivationally speaking), but the figures indicate that this is not quite the case; *that* can be replaced by *which* 95 percent of the time, and by ∅ 42 percent of the time.

The point is, however, that the data from the substitution test alone do not agree with those from the frequency survey. For example, in the substitution test speakers did not distinguish between *who* and *that* as the subject of a relative clause with a personal antecedent, but in the frequency survey the two were very sharply distinguished; speakers overwhelmingly chose WH. This demonstration brings the 'substitution or commutation test' into doubt as a linguistic procedure. Labov et al. (1972) have also criticized the use of this procedure as a method of deciding which sounds of a language are contrastive or perceived as being the same or different (although Quirk called attention to this more than ten years before). Quirk (1958: 42) says of this procedure that 'The acceptance test with the blanks filled in does not readily distinguish between the merely and marginally possible and actually normal: between what one will accept as a hearer and what one will produce as a speaker.' This statement supports the by now well-attested asymmetry between speech production and perception. Quirk, like Labov, believes that the intricacies of linguistic structure will not be revealed by substitution tests but rather by careful examination of a complex of contextual variables in natural usage.

5.4.2 Caldwell's (1974) study of the relative pronoun in Early Scots. The main difference between my study and Caldwell's is that she has undertaken the examination of a much larger time span, namely 1375–1500. My study, on the other hand, is limited chronologically and geographically to Middle Scots texts from the Central Scots region written during the period between 1530 and 1550 approximately. Caldwell's work then is more in the nature of a survey, while mine is more a case study of a particular period. Caldwell gives only simple percentages for the occurrences of variants of the relatives in a variety of Early Scots texts; and the information she presents is largely linguistic, i.e. the percentages show what linguistic environments are relevant for the presence/absence of relative pronouns. However, she gives little indication of how this linguistic or internally conditioned variation might intersect with social factors such as style. The only non-linguistic factor which she takes into account is a division of the texts into literary vs. non-literary language (with the latter category represented by record and official prose).

Apart from this difference in the treatment of texts, there is also some difference in the linguistic categories which Caldwell uses and those included in my study. She provides figures for subject, direct object, oblique (stranded and shifted prepositions) and possessive relatives. My study includes these syntactic positions plus predicate nominatives and indirect objects, although the instances of relatives in these latter two categories are few. Both studies include temporals and locatives. I am also attempting to form some systematic categorization of types of antecedents on a linguistic basis, while Caldwell speaks in more general terms. Although she makes a subdivision in the category of non-restrictive relative clauses into descriptive and resumptive (or continuative) clauses, not much is made of this distinction. There are no figures given which show contrastive use of the relatives along this dimension; instead, there are a few impressionistic observations.

Caldwell's work is however particularly useful here because it gives my study a comparative base. There are a number of interesting observations which can be made from her data which deserve some mention and further investigation; in particular, there are a number of findings which should be followed up by an examination of data from different sources and later periods. Firstly, a comparison of simple frequency levels should prove instructive. For example, what is the incidence of Ø clauses during the first part of the sixteenth century? What happens to the plural inflected form of *quhilk* (i.e. *quhilkis*), likewise the form *the quhilk*(*is*)? What happens to *quha*? Does its use begin to spread outside epistolary and other formulaic use? If so, how is this transition accomplished, i.e. in what environments? Caldwell suggests that *quhais* passed from prose of a legal and official type into more general prose usage before finally entering general literary use in a manner similar to *the quhilk*. It will be interesting to see in what way the data from my study shed light on these points.

The answers to these questions will depend on a careful examination of both linguistic and extralinguistic constraints, since it is likely that change in the system will be manifested initially in patterned statistical fluctuation in certain relevant environments and spread to others until certain quantitative changes become cumulative, and the resulting system becomes qualitatively different after a sufficient period of time. This model of change is essentially the one postulated in Labov et al. (1972), where the direction and location of certain sound changes in progress were plotted through various phonetic environments, which were found either to inhibit or accelerate change. If this model holds for syntactic change, then we should be able to detect shifts in the constraints on the appearance or omission of relative markers in terms of the categories I have set up here. Two questions are relevant: 1. Where and how does the increasingly greater use of WH forms as opposed to TH forms manifest itself (and what happens to Ø)? Caldwell's data indicate possible early evidence of the tendency for Ø to become much less frequent in subject position in formal literary use (cf. Caldwell 1974: 69). And 2. What is the relationship of these phenomena to register and chronology, i.e. what happens in the early sixteenth century? I maintain that these two questions can be subsumed under one larger one; namely, how is the linguistic variation embedded in context?

5.5 Prescriptive grammar and the relative pronouns[13]

Towards the end of the sixteenth and the beginning of the seventeenth centuries the first English grammars of considerable length begin to appear. With their arrival we can note a rise in linguistic consciousness. It was during this time, when a desire to regulate linguistic matters came to the forefront, that language academies began to be established in Europe,

13. Cf. Cofer (1972: 312–13) for a summary of prescriptive treatment of the relative system in English; and, in particular, Dekeyser (1975: 190–201) on prescriptivism and case marking in pronouns during the nineteenth century.

e.g. the Italian one in 1582, the French one in 1635. The function of these academies was to foster and cultivate the language.

The study of classical grammars was still the cornerstone of education when the vernacular began gradually to have a place in the curriculum. Not surprisingly, grammatical analysis of the vernaculars was carried out according to Greek and Latin models, whose grammatical categories had assumed the status of universals which every 'well-developed' language ought to possess (cf. Chapter 3). There was a sense in which English as a changing language was regarded as a corrupt and defective dialect; therefore, the purpose of these vernacular grammars was to prescribe the correct use of the English language. The following quotation from Lily's *Latin Grammar*, which was officially prescribed for school use by King Henry VIII in 1540, reveals the attitude which was commonly held during this period (cited in Dykema 1958: 2):

> Grammar is the Sacrist, that bears the key of Knowledge, by whom alone admittance can be had into the Temple of the Muses, and Treasures of Arts; even whatever can enrich the Mind and raise it from the level of a Barbarian and Idiot, to the Dignity of an Intelligence. But this Sacrist is a severe Mistress, who being once contemned, will certainly revenge the Injury, it being evident that no person ever yet despised Grammar, who had not his fault return'd upon him.

Formal English grammar quickly assumed a position of authority in the educational system. At least two factors encouraged this. Firstly, the overwhelming prestige of everything classical ensured that the association of grammar with Greek and Latin literature and culture would enable it to claim a fundamental place in teaching. Secondly, as printing presses made the new vernacular grammars available to the public on a scale not possible with the classical grammars (which were largely the preserve of the educated), grammars came into the hands of the socially aspirant middle classes. The fact that during the sixteenth and seventeenth centuries, schools were seen as a means of furthering social ambitions helped to strengthen the teaching of formal grammar because upward mobility was to some extent dependent upon the acquisition of a socially sanctioned variety of English.

By the time Bishop Lowth's grammar appeared in 1762, many of the prescriptive statements about the use of the relatives were already being advocated in more or less the same form as we know them today. Lowth's *A Short Introduction to English Grammar* was probably the most influential and widely used textbook produced in the eighteenth century; Alston

(1967), the editor of a facsimile reprint, claims that not only was it the basis for numerous other grammars published between 1763 and 1840, but it also had a distinct authority which no other grammar before Webster had.

Lowth's grammar made clear some of the rules for the use of the relatives according to gender and case agreement with the antecedent, and case agreement according to the syntactic function of the relative in its own clause. Lowth says that *who*, *which* and *that* have no gender variation, but that *who* is more appropriate to persons and covers both masculine and feminine antecedents; *which* is neuter and applies only to things. He notes, however, that all three were used indifferently in reference to both persons and things, but states that the pronoun *that* should be confined to use with things only. Söderlind (1964: 123) has commented that Dryden was ostensibly the first one to label the use of *that* with a personal antecedent as incorrect. Lowth also felt that the possessive *whose* should be reserved as the possessive form of *who* only, not *which*, and hence should be used only with personal antecedents.

Lowth also has much to say about the rules for case agreement which affect the relative *who* in the relative clause. He lists a number of incorrect uses of the nominative where the accusative should have been used (cf. e.g. Alston 1967: 99); among the examples cited are some taken from Dryden and Swift. In instances where the relative pronoun is governed by the copula, the nominative and not the objective case should be used. Thus Lowth cites, from the King James Bible, constructions of the following type, as errors.

(1) *Whom* think ye that I am? (*Acts* xiii: 25)

On the other hand, when the relative is the object of the infinitive form of the copula, then it should be in the objective case, as in:

(2) *Whom* do you think me to be?

This is an apparent indication that there was a reaction against possible ambiguity in case relationships, so that where there was some doubt, as in the above examples, a pronouncement had to be made. There also seems to be a reluctance on Lowth's part to accept constructions where the relative might be used to fill two syntactic positions simultaneously, i.e. both as antecedent and relative. The following example contains two ambiguous instances of *that*; it is not clear whether a relative or its antecedent is being omitted, since *that* can be used to cover both positions.

(3) We speak *that* we do know and testify *that* we have seen. (*John* iii: 11)

In the absence of the parallel construction in the first half of the sentence, the second half is potentially ambiguous in another way; it is not clear whether *that* is used as a complementizer or a relative (cf. Chapter 4).

Lowth also suggests that in some cases a pronominal element needs to be either copied or retained in the relative clause to make the syntactic relationships clear. He says that the phrase in example (4) should be replaced by that in (5). Example (5) has a so-called 'shadow pronoun'.

(4) The shewbread *which* is not lawful to eat. (*Mark* ii: 26)

(5) The shewbread ... *which it* is not lawful to eat. (*Luke* vi: 4)

This seems to indicate that it was desirable for every relative to have a clearly specified antecedent, but apparently the converse was not the case, i.e. not every antecedent had to have a relative. There was no injunction against the use of Ø relative clauses; and in Lowth's own prose a number of Ø clauses are used where the relative would have occupied the syntactic position of direct object. Lowth also comments on the use of stranded prepositions with relatives, which he notes are common in speech, but are unsuited for writing or for use in more elevated styles. Again Söderlind observes that Dryden appears to be the first to label this usage of the relative as incorrect. The objection to stranded prepositions is possibly connected with the case distinction between nominative and objective forms of the relative, i.e. when a preposition is stranded from its relative pronoun, there is a greater tendency for the pronoun to occur in the nominative (cf. also Dekeyser 1975: 191).

Not much attention seems to have been paid to the use of *that* and Ø in the earliest grammars; the main area of concern appears to be the establishment of the proper domains of *who* and *which*. Bately (1965: 250) points out that, apart from James Howell in 1662, the first grammarians to limit the use of *that* date from the second half of the eighteenth century.

In view of the fact that Addison's 'Humble petition of *who* and *which*' had appeared in *The Spectator* in 1711, it is surprising that Lowth and others did not make more of an issue out of the use of *that*. Addison's now famous remark, 'We are descended of ancient Families, and kept our Dignity and Honour many Years till the Jacksprat *that* supplanted us' is revealing of the attitude of the period. What is perhaps humorous to us is that Addison is appealing to the doctrine of historical correctness, which is a commonly used puristic argument, i.e. purists often condemn innovations and consider the oldest forms of the language the most pure. Although Addison has the spirit of the argument right, he has the facts wrong.

Jespersen (1968: 120) thinks that Addison's article undoubtedly contributed much to the restriction of *that*, in writing at least. Addison himself took on the task of (hyper-)correcting instances of *that* to *who* and *which*; and this no doubt set a precedent for the elaborated *which* style that is characteristic of much early eighteenth-century writing (cf. Chapter 4).

In Scotland, where linguistic consciousness was further heightened by the existence of Scottish and English options at all linguistic levels of usage, and where *The Spectator* was regarded as the repository of polite English culture, particularly with regard to matters of English usage, it is likely that this prescriptivism made itself strongly felt. During this time anglicization was well under way in Scottish printing, and English options began to be chosen more frequently than the Scottish ones for reasons of prestige (cf. Perry 1970; Romaine, forthcoming a).

The prescriptive statements which are made about the usage of the relatives in the twentieth century do not add much that is new. However, judging from Fowler's (1926) lengthy treatment of them, they were still regarded as a sticky area of usage. He says (1926: 709): 'About *which*, in particular, problems are many, and some of them are complicated; that the reader may not be frightened by an article of too portentous length, the two that require the most space are deferred . . .' Fowler then advises against all of the following:

1. The use of *which* with a sentential antecedent.[14]
   E.g. He went home, *which* was fine with me.
2. The lack of commas when *which* is used.
3. The use of *which* after a superlative.
   E.g. The best *which* I have.
4. The use of *which* with temporal and locative antecedents.
   E.g. The time *which* I spent here.
5. The repetition of *which/that*, i.e. the objection is to one *which* or *that* clause depending on another using the same form of the relative. The solution, he says, is to find another way of expressing the idea in one relative clause or through other syntactic means.

There are a number of other stylistic admonitions; but what is interesting is that Fowler comes out strongly in favor of *that*. He cites the misguided notion of correctness that prompted a publisher to ask him to search out

14. While I am concerned here mainly with the history of prescriptive statements about restrictive relative clauses, it is interesting to observe that recognition of *which* with antecedents other than surface level NPs is not recent (cf. also Chapter 4). Jespersen (1909–49), for example, noted instances of *which* that made reference to something not identical to a surface antecedent. Furthermore, such uses of *which* did not always receive bad publicity from prescriptive grammarians (cf. Greene 1977: 1–3).

instances of *which* and replace them with *that* in all its occurrences. The proper place of *that* is in a restrictive clause, in both speech and writing, according to Fowler. He also claims that the notion that the relative *that* is associated with the colloquial and *which* with the written language is erroneous. He says that the reason why *that* occurs much more frequently in the spoken language is that the kind of clause, i.e. restrictive, which takes *that* is used more in the spoken language (cf., however, Jacobsson 1963).

This, I think, may be a matter of dialect differentiation. Certainly Quirk's study of the use of the relative is not in complete agreement with this observation; and the result of Cofer's (1972) work in Philadelphia is different from Quirk's. My own results for the relative system in modern Scots are different again from both. I discuss these data in Chapters 6 and 7. In any case, there are quite a number of non-restrictive clauses in the modern spoken language where *which* occurs, although these clauses are most often those with sentential antecedents.[15] Example (6), where *which* occurs with a shadow pronoun, is of a type that I have noticed quite often:

(6) I used to see a lot of those, *which* I don't know what *they* are.

Although Fowler has little to say about the use of relatives with stranded prepositions, he has a number of things to say about the use of *who/whom*. The interchangeable use of these, he says, is a terrible solecism. This area of variability in the grammar has given rise to two competing trends in the English interrogative and relative pronoun systems: *whom* avoidance and *whom* hypercorrection. Sapir (1921) predicted at the beginning of this century that *whom* would fall into disuse due to the operation of a principle he called 'whom avoidance'. He maintained that *who* was taking on the function of an invariant form such as the interrogative adverbs, *where*, *when* and *how*, and the relatives, *which* and *that*. This tendency in the system is being reinforced by a word order constraint which places subjects in sentence-initial position. Thus the pattern, '*Who* did you see?' (cf. '*Who* is at the door?'), is becoming strengthened at the expense of the socially approved form, '*Whom* did you see?' The form *whom* may well never become obsolete, at least as far as the written language is concerned. Dekeyser (1975: 201) has observed that unmarked *who* interrogatives were universally used in spoken nineteenth-century English, but *whom* still occurred in the written language. As far as the relatives were concerned, the distinction between subject and object forms was maintained in the written

15. Greene (1977: 4) reports that the use of *which* as a non-restrictive relative marker is an integral part of white middle class American speech.

language, but not in the spoken. Thus, *whom* seems to have been restricted to the written language for some time now.

Since *whom* has the endorsement of grammarians, it appears quite often in hypercorrections where *who* should occur. The easiest solution to the problem is not to use either pronoun, and replace both with *that* and ∅. The net effect of both these trends is to favor the increased use of a neutral option which avoids the confrontation entirely. A person who does not know which form to use can avoid revealing his ignorance, while a person who considers *whom* too pedantic may also avoid using both *who* and *whom*.

6 *Analysis of the data by two socio-linguistic techniques: cross-product analysis and implicational scaling*

6.1 Where to start?

Within sociolinguistic theory there are a number of possible points of departure for analyzing the observed variation, once the decision has been made concerning what linguistic data are to be correlated with what extralinguistic data (cf. Chapters 4 and 5). Basically, the question seems to be whether one starts from extralinguistic categories and relates the linguistic data to these, or whether one postpones any such correlation with social parameters until after a linguistic classification or description has been reached (cf. Chapter 1 for comments on the differences between these two approaches).

I have opted for the latter approach here for several reasons:

1. As a linguist, I view the question of the nature of *linguistic* variation as fundamental; it must be answered before any extralinguistic analysis can begin. In other words, the data must be considered in terms of its linguistic organization before certain linguistic questions can be answered, e.g. what environments are relevant for variation? Where does variation begin? What forms are present in each environment?[1]

2. From a practical viewpoint, the analysis of linguistic data in linguistic terms is a necessary first step before constructing an implicational scale or using the Cedergren–Sankoff variable rule program. Both of these techniques require as input linguistic data which have undergone some preliminary categorization.

1. Cf. similar remarks made by Lavandera (1975: 345). The difference in the way I am approaching the extralinguistic constraints in my analysis reflects my interest in investigating how the use that is made of language affects the incidence and distribution of particular structures in the language, rather than how language affects the structure of the social system which uses it. In the end, I think that the so-called boundary between the sociology of language and sociolinguistics does not matter very much, since one needs two sets of data, social and linguistic, to describe covariation; from there one moves on to 'explain' different things. A description of how language varies may of course also be a description of how it is used. Initially, it might be argued that linguistic categories comprise the more easily and precisely describable set of data, although those beginning from a sociologist's point of view might not agree.

Table 6.1. *Total relative markers in restrictive and non-restrictive clauses in all texts*

	Restrictive		Non-restrictive	
Relative	N	%	N	%
WH	513	18	2781	85
TH	1931	70	499	15
∅	333	12	5	0
N = 6062	2777		3285	

Once this part of the analysis has been completed, extralinguistic constraints on the application of the rules will be considered. And if it can be established that variation in the relatives is a stylistic marker, we can then see what indications there are in the data to suggest that it is a social one as well.

6.2 A linguistic description of the relative markers in Middle Scots (1530–50)

In order to study the effect of linguistic factors, I have considered all the data from all the texts in the aggregate first. The figures in Table 6.1 show the incidence of relatives (WH, TH and ∅) in restrictive and non-restrictive clauses. (Clauses with sentential antecedents are considered separately and are not included in these figures for non-restrictive clauses.) It is evident that the most obvious factor conditioning the occurrence of the variants of the relatives is whether the clause is restrictive or non-restrictive.

The results indicate that, on the whole, WH forms are most common in non-restrictive clauses and fairly infrequent in restrictive clauses; conversely, TH forms are found most frequently in restrictive clauses and rarely in non-restrictive clauses. Zero forms occur almost exclusively in restrictive clauses, and even there they account for only 12 percent of the total number of incidences of the variable in restrictive clauses.

These results are of course not unexpected, since by this time WH forms of the relative are fairly well-integrated into the English non-restrictive system. Caldwell (1974) reports a similar tendency for WH forms to be confined to non-restrictive clauses, and TH and ∅ to restrictive clauses. Table 6.1 and such figures as Caldwell typically presents obscure the locus of the variation; this can only be revealed by looking at the quantitative

Table 6.2. *Types of cells in the restrictive and non-restrictive clause systems in Middle Scots*

	Restrictive		Non-restrictive	
Cell type	N	%	N	%
Filled	46	64	42	58
3-way opposition	16	35	2	5
2-way opposition	11	24	14	33
categorical	19	41	26	62
Empty	26	36	30	42
N = 72				

distribution of each variant in the relevant linguistic environments as indicated in Table 6.2. This shows that variation is not equally distributed throughout the system. For one thing, variability is more characteristic of the restrictive clause system. There are not only fewer empty cells in the restrictive system, but also the cells which are filled are almost twice as frequently variant as invariant. By way of contrast, the non-restrictive clause system is more categorical. There are more empty cells here than in the restrictive clause system; and of the filled cells, only two of these show variation among all three variants. The rest of the filled cells are either categorically represented by WH or allow variation between WH and TH only.

Although the results do not take into account all possible occurrences of relative markers during the period in question, the number of tokens involved (N = 6062), and the variety of texts investigated, means that they can be considered representative of the relative clause system in Middle Scots during the period 1530–50. Further investigation could possibly reveal new findings, but it seems unlikely that any of the empty cells will be filled by more than one or two isolated occurrences. This also applies in the case of categorical cells, or cells in which the variation is binary. In particular in the latter two cases, there is always the possibility that different coding in certain ambiguous cases might alter the results slightly.

There are some similarities between the restrictive and non-restrictive systems. For example, in the non-restrictive system, shifted prepositions must take WH relatives without exception. This is also true in the restrictive system, although three cells are empty. There were no examples of personal or animate temporal or locative relatives in either system. These are fairly

Table 6.3. *The effect of the animacy of the antecedent*

Antecedent		Restrictive N	Restrictive %	Non-restrictive N	Non-restrictive %
Animate	WH	265	19	1468	81
	TH	1080	76	339	19
(N = 1412, 1811)	Ø	67	5	4	0
Inanimate	WH	248	18	1313	89
	TH	851	62	160	11
(N = 1365, 1474)	Ø	266	20	1	0
N = 6062		2777		3285	

rare today in the spoken language, and it is doubtful whether a study of the modern written language would reveal a large number of instances (cf. however, Chapter 4 n.7).

The results can be considered less conclusive for cells where insufficient data exist (i.e. where N = less than 35). This affects the syntactic positions which are less frequently relativized (cf. 4.5), i.e. possessives, temporals, locatives, indirect objects, predicate nominals and prepositionals; although there is a difference in the frequency with which these positions are relativized in the restrictive and non-restrictive system (cf. Table 6.5). The frequency of relativization in certain syntactic positions is also a function of style (cf. 6.5). It can also be observed that determined NPs take relative clauses more frequently than quantified NPs, thus making the conclusions for these and other cells with a large number of tokens slightly more reliable than those which are represented by only a few occurrences.

6.2.1 The effect of the animacy of the antecedent. Table 6.3 shows the percentage of each variant which occurs with animate and inanimate antecedents. The animacy of the antecedent has virtually no effect in determining which form of the relative will occur. There is hardly any difference in the percentage for the different variants except in the case of restrictive clauses with Ø; here zero forms occur more frequently with inanimate antecedents. This is a major difference between the relative clause system of Middle Scots (and late Middle English in general) of this period and that of modern English (cf. Chapters 5 and 7 in particular, where some data from modern English are compared with Middle Scots). Caldwell's data show much the same picture. Some of the texts, however,

Table 6.4. *Occurrences of relative markers in relation to features of their antecedents*

	Restrictive				Non-restrictive			
			+ def				+ def	
N	– def	Det.	Quant.	Supl.	– def	Det.	Quant.	Supl.
WH	20	326	165	2	245	2229	293	14
TH	170	1102	563	96	80	393	24	2
∅	25	196	83	29	0	5	0	0
N =	215	1624	811	127	325	2627	317	16
%								
WH	9	20	20	2	75	85	92	88
TH	79	68	69	76	25	15	8	13
∅	12	12	10	23	0	0	0	0

	All + def (N = 2562)		All + def (N = 2960)	
	N	%	N	%
WH	493	19	2536	86
TH	1761	69	419	14
∅	308	12	5	0
	Total N = 2777		Total N = 3285	

do show some use of personal relatives, i.e. *who*, etc., with personal antecedents, but this usage is still very infrequent.[2]

6.2.2 The effect of different types of antecedents. It can be seen from Table 6.4 that the effect of different types of antecedents (grouped according to certain characteristics or features of the modification structure which precedes the head noun) is in most cases negligible. As mentioned in Chapter 4 (cf. 4.2.2), the figures do not seem to support a division into definite/indefinite as a conditioning factor in the occurrence of relative markers, although the distinction is a major one in determining whether relativization occurs at all. There are only slight differences in the numbers of WH and TH forms of the relative associated with definite as opposed to indefinite antecedents in both the restrictive and non-restrictive clause systems. Within the restrictive system, however, a superlative antecedent seems to favor overwhelmingly the use of TH or ∅. Similarly, quantified

2. Nowhere is this greater than 5 percent.

expressions behave largely in the same fashion as other determined nouns. No comparison can be made with an earlier period since Caldwell does not have comparable figures, but a comparison with modern English will yield much the same results.[3]

6.2.3 The effect of syntactic position. As mentioned at the beginning of this chapter, the syntactic position which the relative marker occupies in the relative clause does have some effect on the occurrences of the different variants. This effect can be seen more clearly in Table 6.5. In particular, it seems that a number of syntactic positions promote the occurrence of *that* and Ø over WH forms in restrictive clauses, e.g. predicate nominals; although in general, except for shifted prepositions, which always take WH, the tendency for WH forms to appear in restrictive clauses is not very great. Zero forms appear most frequently in indirect object, temporal, direct object, stranded preposition and subject relatives in descending order. I make no comments on the non-restrictive system because there is not very much variation.

Caldwell (1974), who takes certain of these syntactic positions into account in her study, groups together subject and direct object relatives so that no exact comparison can be made between her data and these. She also gives very little indication of what number of tokens is represented in her percentages so that the recalculation of her figures which would be required for comparison is not possible in most cases. She does comment that some of the percentages represent a fairly small number of occurrences, although there is not much indication how small these are; she adds (1974: 27–8, 65) that her figures on two texts are based on a 5000-line sample. However, since different texts show differing degrees of syntactic complexity with regard to relativization, it seems preferable to use a quota sample based on a minimally acceptable number of tokens, rather than on a number of pages/lines in a text. Caldwell herself has noted the great discrepancies which arise from such a procedure. She observes (1974: 65) that in the first 5000 lines of the *Brus* there are 570 relative clauses, while in the first 5000 lines of *Wallace* there are only 375; she adds that this reflects a stylistic difference between the two texts; and that the lower incidence of subordination in general, which characterizes *Wallace*, might explain the high proportion of zero clauses in that text. This observation does not seem to be well-founded, when we examine some figures on relativization for the

3. Cf., for example, Cofer (1972: 347), who has studied the incidence of relative deletion in Philadelphia.

Table 6.5. *The occurrence of relative markers in different syntactic positions*

		Restrictive		Non-restrictive	
Syntactic position		N	%	N	%
Subject	WH	247	14	1418	75
	TH	1466	82	462	25
	∅	83	5	4	0
	N =	1796		1884	
Direct object	WH	71	12	289	89
	TH	346	57	33	10
	∅	192	32	1	0
	N =	609		323	
Possessive	WH	15	75	201	100
	TH	5	25	1	0
	∅	0	0	0	0
	N =	20		202	
Indirect object	WH	1	50	—	—
	TH	0	0	—	—
	∅	1	50	—	—
	N =	2		—	
Predicate nominative	WH	0	0	—	—
	TH	9	82	—	—
	∅	2	11	—	—
	N =	11		—	
Temporal	WH	26	20	34	100
	TH	58	45	0	0
	∅	45	35	0	0
	N =	129		34	
Locative	WH	122	99	348	100
	TH	0	0	0	0
	∅	1	1	0	0
	N =	123		348	
Preposition stranded	WH	7	11	22	88
	TH	47	75	3	12
	∅	9	14	0	0
	N =	63		25	
Preposition shifted	WH	24	100	469	100
	TH	0	0	0	0
	∅	0	0	0	0
	N =	24		469	

0 = no tokens for a cell which does have other variants in it
— = no tokens for that cell as a whole

Table 6.6. *Index of relativization and number of deletions*

Text	Index of relativization	Number of deletions
Boece	166	30
The Scottish Correspondence	157	102
The Bannatyne Manuscript	88	122
Ane Satyre	78	23
Sheriff Court Book	75	3
Acts of the Lords of Council	69	41
Burgh Records	60	19

texts in this study; at any rate, the correlation between the number of zero clauses and an index of subordination calculated in terms of the number of relative clauses is not as direct as Caldwell indicates it might be. In Table 6.6 the indices of relativization for each text are compared with the number of zero clauses.

The index of relativization was calculated by counting the total number of relative clauses per 1000-line sample from each text. To prevent bias which might be related to stylistic differences within texts, I sampled systematically, so that in the case of *The Bannatyne Manuscript*, for example, I took samples from each of the five parts of the manuscript. In the case of *The Scottish Correspondence* and *Ane Satyre* I took five samples of 200 lines each from different parts of the text. The sample from Bellenden's *Boece* consists of equal samples from each of the nine books. Since record prose appears as a whole more internally consistent, stylistically speaking, I took the first 1000 lines from the *Sheriff Court Book of Fife*, the *Acts of the Lords of Council in Public Affairs* and the *Burgh Records*.

These figures do not support the notion that a lower incidence of subordination as measured by the index of relativization is found in texts with a higher number of zero clauses.[4] *The Scottish Correspondence* has one of the highest indices of relativization as well as one of the highest numbers of deletions; conversely, *Boece* has the highest index of relativization, but a fairly low number of deletions. The text with the lowest index of relativization, *Burgh Records*, does not have the lowest number of deletions.

There is, however, some validity in this hypothesis if we take a more

4. Cf. e.g. Noizet et al. (1972) for a measure of syntactic complexity which relies on the incidence of relative clauses. Most indices which rely on the concept of subordination or embedding include consideration of the relative clause.

Table 6.7. *Index of relativization and type of relative clause*

Text	Restrictive	Non-restrictive	Sentential	∅
The Scottish Correspondence	59	78	20	102
The Bannatyne Manuscript	51	36	1	122
Ane Satyre	50	23	5	23
Acts of the Lords of Council	39	21	9	41
Boece	35	89	42	30
Burgh Records	28	21	11	19
Sheriff Court Book	21	39	5	2

sophisticated and sensitive measure of subordination and deletion than a simple count of the total numbers of relative clauses and numbers of deletions. We know that there is a difference in the texts in terms of the type of relative clauses (i.e. restrictive vs. non-restrictive), and that ∅ forms rarely occur in non-restrictive clauses. Since this is true, we can expect that texts with relatively high proportions of non-restrictive clauses to restrictive clauses will, in general, be less likely to have large numbers of deletions. Table 6.7 shows the number and types of clauses, and the number of deletions to be found in the texts, and more or less confirms this revised prediction. With the exception of *The Scottish Correspondence* and *Ane Satyre*, texts with smaller proportions of restrictive to non-restrictive clauses also tend to have fewer deletions.

When we look more closely at the incidence of deletion in relation to syntactic position (cf. Table 6.5), the data indicate that on the whole (without consideration of individual texts), more deletion of direct object relatives is characteristic of this period than earlier (based on a comparison with Caldwell's figures). The total incidence of deletion for the period ca. 1530–50 as a whole is not very high (12 percent); this figure is obtained by averaging the differing indices of deletion in all syntactic positions, which range from 0 to 50 percent.

Although no exact figures are available for comparison in all syntactic positions for the occurrences of WH and TH forms, Caldwell lists the percentages of occurrence of zero forms for subject, direct object and prepositional relatives. The percent of deletion ranges from 0 to 46 percent (the latter figure from *Wallace*) in subject position; from 0 to 13 percent in direct object position; and from 0 to 2 percent in prepositional position. The different levels of deletion do not correlate to any extent with the chronological ordering of the texts, thus supporting the hypothesis that the

Table 6.8. *The frequency of relativization in different syntactic positions in restrictive and non-restrictive clauses*

	Restrictive		Non-restrictive	
Syntactic position	N	%	N	%
Subject	1796	65	1884	57
Direct object	609	22	323	10
Temporal	129	5	34	1
Locative	123	4	348	11
Preposition stranded	63	2	25	1
Preposition shifted	24	2	469	14
Genitive	20	0	202	6
Predicate nominative	11	0	0	0
Indirect object	2	0	0	0
	2777		3285	

incidence of deletion does seem to be a question of register rather than chronology. The main trend that can be seen is that after the time of the writing of *Wallace* (1475), the incidence of deletion is very marginal indeed; in subject, direct object and prepositional positions, it is nowhere greater than 6 percent. Before this time, however, it may be difficult to argue for true relative deletion, so that the data should be interpreted with caution.

6.3 Syntactic complexity

Table 6.8 shows the frequency with which NPs in various syntactic positions are relativized in both the restrictive and non-restrictive clause systems. The results indicate that not only are there great differences in the frequency with which NPs in certain syntactic positions are relativized along the lines suggested by Keenan and Comrie's (1977) accessibility hierarchy, but that there are also differences between the restrictive and non-restrictive clause systems with respect to the hierarchical ordering of the frequency of relativization associated with the different syntactic positions.

The frequency of relativization in different syntactic positions in the restrictive clause system agrees with Keenan's (1975) predictions for modern English; that is to say, a hierarchy exists with respect to syntactic positions which are relativized as shown below. The positions which occur towards the top end (i.e. subject) are more frequently relativized in modern English as well as Middle Scots.

Table 6.9. *Case hierarchy for syntactic positions relativized in Middle Scots restrictive clauses* (*N* = *2777*)

	Subj.	Dir. obj.	Temp.	Loc.	Obl.	Gen.
N	1796	620	129	123	89	20
%	65	22	5	4	3	0

The case hierarchy
Subject ≥ Direct object ≥ Indirect object ≥ Oblique ≥ Genitive ≥ Object of comparison

Certain adjustments are made to the hierarchy in accordance with the rules for relative clause formation in English; namely, Keenan has collapsed the indirect object position with the oblique case (i.e. prepositions) NPs, since in English a preposition *to* must be retained in this position, and is either stranded or fronted with the relative. Keenan also includes in the genitive category relativization into *of* complements of NPs, e.g. 'the gate the hinges *of which* were rusty'. These have been grouped here under shifted prepositions. Technically speaking, in terms of Keenan's hierarchy, such structures represent a promotion on the scale of relativizable positions from genitive to oblique, and can therefore be considered as genitive paraphrases or genitive avoidance strategies. No data were available in this study for objects of comparison, as in the example, 'The boys __ Mary is taller than', which is at the bottom of the hierarchy. Although the case hierarchy does not stipulate or make any predictions about the place of temporals and locatives in the scale, Keenan reports that in a sample of 2238 relative clauses, these were found to occur with a frequency intermediate between the genitive and object of comparison positions.

When the figures for Middle Scots restrictive clauses are regrouped so that both stranded and shifted prepositions are considered together, and the figures for indirect object NPs are added to these, and predicate nominals are added to the direct object position figures (since it can be argued that predicate nominals share some positional resemblance to surface direct objects), we get the case hierarchy in Table 6.9.

These results agree with Keenan's predictions for modern English, apart from the discrepancy in the ordering of temporals and locatives. It could of course be argued that temporals and locatives are, strictly speaking, not syntactic positions, and hence should not be included in either this case or Keenan's. One possible reason why my results differ in this respect may

Table 6.10. *Case hierarchy for syntactic positions relativized in Middle Scots non-restrictive clauses* (*N = 3285*)

	Subj.	Obl.	Loc.	Dir. obj.	Gen.	Temp.
N	1884	494	348	323	202	34
%	57	15	11	10	6	1

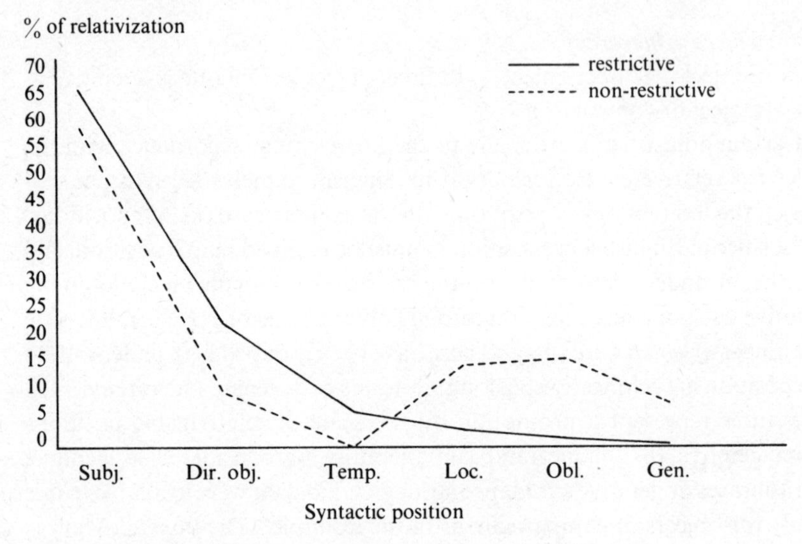

Figure 14 Comparison of restrictive and non-restrictive clauses in terms of frequency of relativization in various syntactic positions

be that my choice of texts is more varied stylistically than Keenan's.

A different ordering obtains in the case of the non-restrictive clauses system, which is given in Table 6.10. This finding, as well as the observation I made earlier in this chapter (namely, that the non-restrictive system is as a whole less variable than the restrictive system), can be taken as further evidence that the restrictive and non-restrictive systems of relative clauses should be considered as syntactic structures which are different in kind; they should therefore be treated differently in the grammar. Although these two types share some formal similarities, they are functionally different in some respects. The fact that the syntactic positions show a different ordering seems to suggest that the non-restrictive system has different strategies for relativizing obliques and locatives than does the restrictive system (cf. Figure 14).

Table 6.11. *Percent of WH forms correlated with syntactic positions in the case hierarchy*

Syntactic position		Restrictive	Non-restrictive
increasing complexity ↓	Subject	14	75
	Direct object	14	89
	Oblique	36	99
	Genitive	75	100

Why this should be so is not immediately obvious. The genitive remains at the low end of the hierarchy, while the oblique and locative positions are ordered before direct object position. The prediction that Keenan's work with the restrictive system in modern English would suggest is that non-restrictive clauses may in some way be more syntactically complex than restrictive ones. To my knowledge, no investigations have taken this point of view, although it is an interesting hypothesis.

It is also very interesting to note that the further one moves down the hierarchy of syntactic positions which are relativizable, the more WH-dominated the system becomes. This can be seen in Table 6.11. This is true of both the restrictive and non-restrictive systems, though at different quantitative levels, since the restrictive system is predominantly TH and the non-restrictive system is predominantly WH (70 and 85 percent respectively).

Locatives do not fit into this progression since they constitute a nearly categorical WH environment. This trend, which does not follow from Keenan's predictions about modern English, suggests that there is a sense in which WH forms might be considered more complex or abstract than either TH or Ø forms of the relative. The standard transformational view of relativization given in Chapter 2 agrees with this interpretation since it posits WH as the more abstract, underlying form, while *that* is introduced transformationally.

This result suggests that it would be worth examining data from other languages where options exist for relativization (cf. Keenan and Comrie 1979). Table 6.12 shows the complementary finding that the incidence of TH and Ø forms is more frequent at the upper end of the relativization hierarchy (and again temporals and locatives are excluded). This reflects the corresponding hypothesis that TH and Ø forms are in some way less abstract or simpler than WH forms. Figure 14 in particular clearly demonstrates the relevance of syntactic position in conditioning not only the

Table 6.12. *Percent of TH and ∅ forms of the relative correlated with syntactic positions in the case hierarchy*

Syntactic position		Restrictive	Non-restrictive
increasing complexity ↓	Subject	89	25
	Direct object	88	10
	Oblique	63	1
	Genitive	25	0

frequency of relativization, but also the frequency with which certain relatives occur in English.[5]

6.4 The measurement of syntactic complexity in individual texts

Having established the fact that the case hierarchy is applicable to the Middle Scots data on relativization, it remains to be seen whether we can develop a quantitative measure of syntactic complexity which will correspond to intuitive or impressionistic judgements. An index of syntactic complexity should allow the confirmation in quantitative terms of statements such as: 'Legal language constitutes a complex register'; or 'The language of certain types of poetry is simpler than that of prose'; etc. These kinds of claims are all too frequently made, and often widely accepted in the absence of data. We would expect of such a measure of syntactic complexity that it would be predictive. In other words, texts of similar types should pattern together if complexity correlates with register. This is a testable hypothesis.[6]

Figure 15 illustrates the frequency with which six syntactic positions are relativized in three Middle Scots texts that can be expected to be different

5. I am not making any claims here about the ontological status of 'abstractness' in grammatical description and perception, i.e. is abstractness the same thing in both cases? My findings presumably reflect the fact that the relative system in modern English is a conflation of two strategies or systems (and this is true also of Middle Scots during the period in question). The WH one seems to be taken as the primary strategy if we consult prescriptive grammars or Quirk's (1957) study; the historically primary system, i.e. TH, might be seen to be a secondary strategy. The picture which Table 6.11 presents appears to be the entrance of WH into the system 'by the back door', since it enters the most complex and least frequently occurring positions in the case hierarchy (cf. Naro and Lemle 1977 for a discussion of perceptual saliency as a factor in syntactic diffusion). The standard transformational view, however, is that all relative clauses, whether introduced by WH or TH, are produced by one basic strategy.
6. This hypothesis is dependent on another one, which I have assumed to be valid; namely, that registers are homogeneous. If my index of syntactic complexity had not performed according to my predictions, its failure might have been due to inadequate genre definitions rather than to any defects in the measure.

Table 6.13. *Frequency of relativization in six syntactic positions in seven Middle Scots texts (percent)*

Text	Total N	Subj.	Dir. obj.	Temp.	Loc.	Obl.	Gen.
Ane Satyre	187	71	22	6	0	1	0
Boece	557	65	18	4	11	2	0
The Bannatyne Manuscript	1169	69	22	3	3	3	0
The Scottish Correspondence	337	49	41	4	1	6	0
Burgh Records	176	71	11	8	3	3	4
Sheriff Court Book	72	83	4	4	1	6	1
Acts of the Lords of Council	279	53	22	10	8	7	1

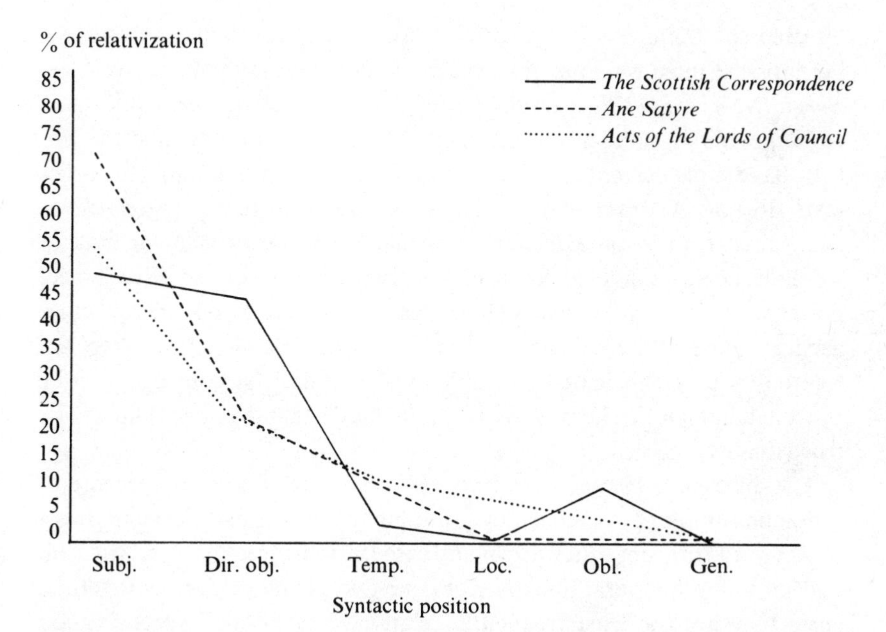

Figure 15 Frequency of relativization in six syntactic positions in three Middle Scots texts

from one another in terms of stylistic complexity: *The Scottish Correspondence of Mary of Lorraine* (epistolary prose); *Acts of the Lords of Council in Public Affairs* (official prose); and *Ane Satyre of the Thrie Estaitis* (verse). The relevant figures for comparison are given in Table 6.13.

The arrangement of the figures in Table 6.13 is not particularly revealing; although it can be seen at a glance that the different texts are characterized

Table 6.14. *Regrouping of relative clauses into upper and lower ends of the case hierarchy of syntactic positions relativized*

Text	Upper (Subj., Dir. obj.)	Lower (Temp., Loc., Obl., Gen.)
Ane Satyre	93	7
The Bannatyne Manuscript	91	9
The Scottish Correspondence	90	11
Sheriff Court Book	87	12
Boece	83	17
Burgh Records	82	18
Acts of the Lords of Council	75	26

by different frequencies of relativization in the six syntactic positions. Perhaps the most obvious observation is that the three official texts, i.e. *Burgh Records*, *Sheriff Court Book of Fife* and *Acts of the Lords of Council in Public Affairs*, stand apart from the other texts in that they characteristically have some percentage of relativization in the genitive, while the other texts do not. Another observation is that *The Scottish Correspondence* again appears to be quite different from all the other texts in having most of its relative clauses divided nearly equally between subject and direct object position. This could reflect two things: 1. the letters do mirror more accurately the colloquial speech of the time; and 2. some of the letters are written by unsophisticated and unlearned writers.[7] Of course, it can be expected that it is due largely to the second factor that the first is likely to be true (if indeed it is).

The differences between the texts are more revealing if the measure of syntactic complexity is refined by grouping together the subject and direct object positions, since they are in any case the most frequently relativized; and grouping temporal, locative, oblique and genitive relatives together, since they are the least frequently relativized positions. Another good reason for grouping the latter four positions together is that they are underrepresented in terms of total numbers of tokens of relatives with respect to the other two positions at the top of the hierarchy. A grouping of the categories in this way will yield a more reliable count than each category considered individually.

Table 6.14 shows the percentages after regrouping. It can now be seen

7. In a letter dated 9 March 1548 (9?), Lady Home writes to the queen: 'Pardon me that writtis sa hamly to your grac...' This may of course be a polite disclaimer as well as an indication of unfamiliarity with the norms for writing letters.

Table 6.15. *Stylistic categories and the index of syntactic complexity*

	Syntactic position	
Stylistic categories	Simple	Complex
PROSE		
national	75	26
local	85	10
total	81	19
narrative	83	17
epistolary	90	11
total prose	83	19
VERSE	92	8

that as one moves down the list of texts, increasingly fewer relative clauses are formed near the top end of the hierarchy, and that progressively more relative clauses are found at the lower, more complex end of the hierarchy. What is particularly striking about this regrouping is that it provides us with a basis for measuring stylistic or syntactic complexity, which does have some predictive power.

For example, it can be noted that the two verse texts, *Ane Satyre of the Thrie Estaitis* and *The Bannatyne Manuscript*, occur near the top end of the scale, i.e. the simpler end, as hypothesized; conversely, the more difficult texts, stylistically speaking, e.g. official and legal prose, occur at the lower end. This measure also separates poetry from prose as shown in Table 6.15.

Of the prose texts the measure indicates that epistolary prose (represented by *The Scottish Correspondence of Mary of Lorraine* in this sample) is the most simple, stylistically and syntactically speaking; and that legal prose (represented by three official records) is slightly more complex than non-official prose. Furthermore, it seems that local official prose (represented by the *Sheriff Court Book of Fife* and the *Burgh Records*) is slightly less syntactically complex than national record prose (i.e. *Acts of the Lords of Council*). The latter category is the most stylistically and syntactically complex type represented here according to this measure.

These sorts of findings coincide well with the predictions that would be made on an impressionistic basis, i.e. by reading the texts without counting the occurrences of any linguistic features. My results have demonstrated that one of the things which contributes to such impressionistic judgements

Table 6.16. *Index of syntactic complexity for all texts*

Text	% Simple relatives / Complex relatives	Index
Ane Satyre	8	1.6
The Bannatyne Manuscript	10	2.0
The Scottish Correspondence	12	2.4
Sheriff Court Book	15	3.0
Boece	20	4.0
Burgh Records	22	4.4
Acts of the Lords of Council	35	7.0

Table 6.17. *Stylistic categories and syntactic complexity*

Stylistic categories	Index
PROSE	
national	7.0
local official	3.7
total official	5.4
narrative	4.0
epistolary	2.4
total prose	4.2
VERSE	1.8

of syntactic complexity is the percentage of relative clauses formed in various syntactic positions; furthermore, it seems to be the percentage of relative clauses formed at the upper end of the case hierarchy in relation to the percentage formed at the lower end which is the most accurate indicator of syntactic and stylistic complexity.

The latter conclusion is indicated more clearly in Tables 6.16 and 6.17, where I have calculated an index of syntactic complexity by dividing the percentage of simple relatives by the percentage of complex relatives, and then converting this ratio to a 1–7 scale, where 1 represents the lowest degree of syntactic complexity and 7 the highest.

So far I have just been using the percentage of relative clauses formed in different syntactic positions as a measure of syntactic complexity, but it seems reasonable to expect that this index will correlate highly with other independent measures, such as those commonly used in other studies[8] (cf. the appendix to this chapter, where I give a demonstration of this).

I think it is also likely that my index of syntactic complexity will correlate well with a number of syntactic variables, as yet uninvestigated, e.g. complementizer *that* deletion. Friedrich and Redfield (1978) have used the frequency of different features of syntax, discourse, rhetoric and lexicon as a means of describing the speech of an individual, in this case, the character Achilles in the *Iliad.* Some of the measures which they use are the incidence of asyndeton and the number of vocatives, etc. No doubt in this instance, as in others, syntactic complexity will correlate with differences in other subsystems of the grammar as well as with other levels of linguistic organization. In the case of Middle Scots, for example, the texts which display a more fully native lexicon might be expected to be syntactically simpler than those which are more anglicized. However, I leave these questions open for further investigation.[9]

6.5 Syntactic complexity and stylistic differentiation

I demonstrated in the previous section that the index of syntactic complexity I have developed here could be used to distinguish individual texts as well as genres of texts, e.g. prose/verse, legal/non-legal prose, etc. So far I have been assuming that individual texts as well as genres are more or less homogeneous. I will now examine to what extent my index can be used to demarcate stylistic levels within texts. As a first example, I have divided the relative clauses in Bellenden's *Boece* into two groups: those which occur as part of the main discourse; and those which are intended to be part of the

8. Mendelsohn (1977), for example, has used a variety of different measures, some of which were developed by Hunt (1970a, b), such as mean T-unit length, to describe the structure of foreign learners' English. Van den Broeck (1977) discusses the use of a number of different measures of syntactic complexity in a study of the social conditioning of syntactic structure in Maaseik. Van der Geest et al. (1973) have used some of the same measures of syntactic complexity to study developmental differences in children's acquisition of communicative competence (cf. Romaine 1979a; and Bartsch 1973 for a general discussion of such measures).
9. Simplicity' here is strictly a linguistic measure, not a value judgement. It is clear that native Scots writing of this period has a range of styles, from those which are very syntactically complex (as measured by mean T-unit length and the relative clause case hierarchy), e.g. official prose, where a large number of native Scots lexical items will also be found, to those which are syntactically simple, and have a large number of native items. However, given the functional restriction which develops with respect to the use of Scots and English from this time onwards, it can be expected that syntactically elaborated messages will be increasingly allocated to English rather than to Scots. This reflects differential use, rather than potential or ability. MacQueen (1957) has done some interesting work on differential rates of loss of Scotticisms of lexis, grammar, etc. in different types of official documents, which could provide useful data for cross-correlation with syntactic measures of this type.

Table 6.18. *Index of syntactic complexity for narrative and quoted speech in Bellenden's 'Boece'*

Style	Index
Narrative	4.4
Quoted speech	3.6
Whole text	4.0

reported speech of individuals. My hypothesis was that if there were stylistic differences in these two divisions of the narrative, then the index of syntactic complexity should reflect this difference. I furthermore hypothesized that if the author consciously varied certain features in the two parts of the text in an attempt to mirror the spoken language in quoted speeches, then the direction of the shift or change from narrative to quoted speech would be towards simplicity rather than complexity. Thus, syntactic simplicity would serve as a diagnostic marker of quoted speech within a narrative and make it stand out from the discourse in which it is embedded. Both these hypotheses are supported as indicated in Table 6.18.

The difference between quoted speech and narrative as measured by the index of syntactic complexity is not striking. Nevertheless, quoted speech is set off from the rest of the narrative by having more relative clauses in the two most frequently relativized positions in the case hierarchy, and fewer in each of the less frequently relativized positions than the narrative in which it is embedded. Syntactically speaking, then, quoted speech within this text is much more similar to verse than it is to the rest of the prose texts, i.e. it is simpler.

Another example which can be measured in a similar way is *The Bannatyne Manuscript*, which can be expected to be much less homogeneous than *Boece*. I have made initial divisions in the manuscript on the basis of the subject matter of the poetry following those of its compiler: Merry Ballads, Ballads of Love, Religious Ballads and Ballads of Wisdom and Morality. The index of syntactic complexity is given in Table 6.19 for each of these headings in the text.

According to these calculations, the Religious Ballads appear to be the most syntactically complex, and the Merry Ballads the least syntactically complex, with the Ballads of Wisdom and Morality and the Ballads of Love occupying a position intermediate between these two. The fact that the

Table 6.19. *Index of syntactic complexity for different types of poetry in 'The Bannatyne Manuscript'*

Type of poetry	Index
Religious Ballads	3.0
Ballads of Wisdom and Morality	1.8
Ballads of Love	1.8
Merry Ballads	1.6

differences are not great could be an indication that the manuscript is homogeneous with respect to the usage of this syntactic feature; or that another basis for dividing the texts, e.g. by metrical type or verse form, might have been more telling. I explore this hypothesis in the appendix to this chapter.

Although the date for *The Bannatyne Manuscript* is given as 1568, it is an anthology of verse of all types. Some of the poems are by Henryson, Douglas and Dunbar, while others are anonymous. My choice of the manuscript raises some problems concerning the status of verse as a genre; this does not, however, affect my conclusions about these particular texts, but it does limit the generalizability of my predictions. For example, I would not necessarily expect it to be the case that my measure of syntactic complexity always distinguished prose from verse. There is also the problem that genres may have typical subject matter, and this as much as style may affect their patterns of relativization. To test this, however, i.e. to isolate the stylistic norms of a genre, I would need to hold subject matter constant.

The Bannatyne Manuscript also presents a problem for my chronological limitation of the sample to ca. 1530–50, since it includes poetry from an earlier as well as a later period. Despite the difficulties involved in making comparisons based on the compiler's divisions, the tendencies in the text as a whole (i.e. deletion and syntactic complexity) agree to a great extent with those found in Lindsay's *Satyre*, which presumably is the work of one individual and falls within the time period of my study. Of the other texts I have used in this study, *The Scottish Correspondence* might be expected to be less homogeneous than other prose texts since the letters of different individuals are included in my sample. As far as I know, however, there is no real problem with chronology in the latter case.

For the moment I merely note that the results in Table 6.19 are not what one would expect from Aitken's categorization of stylistic levels in Middle

Scots (cf. Chapter 1).[10] He says that the courtly poetry and comic verse represent two opposite extremes of the stylistic continuum in Middle Scots, and that moralizing verse occupies an intermediate position between these two. Since Aitken's categories were formed on an impressionistic basis, and were based primarily on considerations of verse form and vocabulary, it should not be surprising that quantitative measurement of the incidence of a syntactic marker has turned out a somewhat, but not very, different ordering. And Aitken of course makes no predictions about syntactic complexity.

No one has attempted to classify Older Scots texts on the basis of syntactic markers, so that my study can be seen as a first step in that direction. It is interesting that in this case the biggest gap occurs between the Religious Ballads and the other three types of ballads. This suggests that syntactic markers may not serve to demarcate stylistic levels to the same extent as other linguistic features, e.g. vocabulary. A more detailed examination of a number of different syntactic variables in relation to other types of linguistic variables would be necessary to confirm this. In the next section I examine the possibility that the incidence of deletion might be one such syntactic variable which correlates with stylistic levels and syntactic complexity (cf. also the appendix to this chapter).

6.6 Index of relative marker deletion

Since Aitken and Caldwell have both suggested that deletion of relative markers is one feature of syntax that seems to correlate impressionistically with stylistic level, I now compare the texts on this basis. From the figures I have presented so far, particularly in Tables 6.6 and 6.7, on the relationship (or lack of it) between the index of relativization and numbers of deletions, it should be clear that an index of relative deletion will need to be devised which takes into account the observation that some environments favor variation and, in particular, deletion, while some behave categorically or inhibit deletion.

The decision of what to count or include in this index is very important, and cannot be based on the gross numbers of deletions to be found in all the

10. An alternative to using the divisions of the compiler would have been to contrast the works of one author with another, but since relativization is much more frequent in poetry than in prose, this would have reduced my sample size too much. Another possibility would be to compare the works of one author which fall into opposite ends of the stylistic spectrum. This avoids the chronology problem, but not the difficulty in obtaining sufficient data (cf. my remarks in the appendix to this chapter).

Table 6.20. *Deletion in restrictive clauses in Middle Scots*

Syntactic environment	Deletions N	Deletions %	Retentions (WH + TH) N	Retentions (WH + TH) %	Total N
Superlative	28	22	98	78	126
Temporal	44	34	84	66	128
Dir. object	120	21	451	79	571
Preposition	9	14	54	86	63
Subject	83	5	1639	95	1722
Total	284	11	2326	89	2610

texts. Labov (1969: 728) has commented that the final decision as to what to count is actually the solution to the problem at hand. If all the environments in which relative clauses occurred were to be given equal weight in the deletion index, the frequency of deletion would appear to be much lower than it actually is; and a number of important constraints on deletion would be obscured, since they would appear to apply to only a small portion of the relevant cases. In addition, the distinction between categorical and variable environments made in the beginning of this chapter would be lost.

The following environments can be excluded at the outset because they are categorical or do not allow deletion: shifted prepositions, possessives, locatives, and the system of non-restrictive clauses. In the latter two instances, the few tokens of zero relatives were not sufficient in relation to the total number of tokens of relatives to be significant. On the other hand, the following environments appear to favor deletion: superlative antecedents, objects, temporals, indirect objects, stranded prepositions and predicate nominals. This can be seen in Table 6.20, which shows the amount of deletion in these environments for all the texts. Only restrictive clauses are included; and the figures for predicate nominals have been included in those for direct objects, and those for indirect objects in those for stranded prepositions.

In Table 6.21 I give the percentage of deletion in each of these environments in relation to the total numbers of deletions in all the texts. According to Table 6.20, temporals show the greatest tendency towards deletion, with superlative antecedents and direct object relatives following close behind. Fewer deletions were observed with stranded prepositions, and the fewest deletions were found in subject position. Table 6.21, however, reveals that direct objects account for nearly half of the total cases of

Table 6.21. *Deletion in relation to total numbers of deletion in all texts*

Syntactic environment	Number of deletions	%
Direct objects	120	42
Subjects	83	29
Temporals	44	16
Superlatives	28	10
Prepositions	9	3

Table 6.22. *Index of deletion for seven Middle Scots texts*

Text	Index of deletion (%)
The Scottish Correspondence	25
The Bannatyne Manuscript	9
Acts of the Lords of Council	9
Ane Satyre	8
Burgh Records	6
Boece	3
Sheriff Court Book	2

deletion, followed by subjects, temporals, superlatives, and stranded prepositions.

With the figures from Table 6.20 in mind I constructed an index of deletion which would compensate for the fact that certain environments favored deletion more than others, and that certain texts had larger numbers of tokens of Ø in some syntactic positions than others. I calculated the index of deletion by counting every third instance of deletion in temporal position, every second instance of superlative and direct object deletion, and every instance of deletion in subject and prepositional relatives, divided by the total number of non-deleted forms in each text. The results are given in Table 6.22. For the moment I have chosen an index of deletion which conflates the output of different syntactic environments, rather than one which conflates the outputs of the individual texts, since I am interested in the differences between texts. This is of course not the only way I could have devised this measure. I comment later in this chapter on the consequences of this operation in terms of the amount of observed variation and the locus of variability.[11]

11. Cf. also Chapter 9 where I discuss the differences between the quantitative and dynamic paradigms, and Bickerton's (1973c) re-analysis of Sankoff's (1973) complementizer *que* deletion data.

Table 6.23. *Index of deletion and stylistic categories*

Stylistic category	Index of deletion
PROSE	
national	9
local official	5
total official	5
epistolary	25
narrative	3
total prose	9 (revised 5)
VERSE	9

Table 6.23 shows the figures for deletion in relation to the stylistic categories established so far. *The Scottish Correspondence* clearly stands apart from all the other texts on the basis of its high index of deletion; and within the category of prose, it is very different from all other types of prose included in this sample. In a similar way, it stands out from the other texts in terms of its index of syntactic complexity (cf. Table 6.17). What is perhaps an unexpected result is that the *Acts of the Lords of Council* has such a high index of deletion compared to local official prose and non-official prose. Not surprisingly, when *The Scottish Correspondence* is included in the total index of deletion for the prose texts, there is a difference between prose and poetry in terms of the index of deletion. Therefore, I have given a revised prose index which excludes this text. When this is done, then a basic division of the corpus into prose and verse is well supported on the basis of the index of deletion, with higher indices of deletion being more characteristic of verse texts.

Again, the results invite the interpretation that the relationship between syntactic complexity and deletion is not completely straightforward; in other words, we cannot say that those texts which are the most syntactically complex will also show the lowest index of deletion (cf. Tables 6.6 and 6.7). One reason for this may be that there are other stylistic constraints which are interacting with these linguistic measures. For example, it is possible that metrical type may have an effect both on syntactic complexity and deletion. However, the fact that epistolary prose has an even higher index of deletion than verse indicates that it is not just metrical type which has an effect on deletion. Another possible extralinguistic factor concerns the source of the texts: in particular, my choice of *Boece* as representative of narrative or non-official prose. Since prose developed later than verse as a literary medium in Scots, the first works were Latin translations. Bellenden's translation of *Boece* no doubt reflects its non-native origin.[12] I pursue this consideration of extralinguistic factors and their effect on syntactic complexity and deletion in the appendix to this chapter.

Another reason for my results may be my choice of deletion as a syntactic marker. I suggest that my findings indicate that it is not just deletion which serves as a diagnostic indicator of stylistic level. This becomes evident if we examine what happens when the index of deletion increases or decreases. The result is a change in the levels of *both* WH and TH, so that an increased use of zero forms correlates with the incidence of both WH and TH forms. This indicates that an index which takes into account all three forms might be a more accurate measure of stylistic level than any one of the three on its own.

One way in which this could be done is to construct a variable scale index, where each variant is assumed to correlate with a linguistic as well as an extralinguistic dimension, and is assigned a particular value on a continuous scale (cf. Labov 1966: 15).[13] In this case I devised a variable index, which I will refer to as the variable (relpro), by assigning three points to each occurrence of WH, two points to each occurrence of TH and one point to each occurrence of Ø.

Although I have perhaps distorted the situation somewhat by converting a situation of discontinuous or discrete variation to a continuous one (cf. Chapter 2), I will argue at this stage that what I have done does fit in with the standard transformational account of the deletion of relatives. In other words, WH forms are at one end of the scale, i.e. they are the underlying, more abstract forms (and also, it seems, the most complex), while Ø forms are at the other, i.e. they are the result of the application of two rules. The

12. Lewis (1954: 116) makes the following comment about Bellenden's lack of skill in translating vernacular history:

> He is not one of the great translators and does not quite succeed in getting rid of the idiom of the original. Tell-tale absolute constructions, historic presents, and excessive linking of sentences abound.

Still there is the possibility that subject matter as much as non-native origin may be affecting syntactic complexity in this case. In Table 6.13 it can be seen that *Boece* has the largest number of locative relatives; since narrative typically recounts the unfolding of action in time and space, it is likely to be interested in defining spatial relations between the objects it makes reference to. And a large number of locative relatives increases the syntactic complexity of the text, at least according to my index of syntactic complexity (I owe this observation to Sylvia Woolford).

13. There are of course a number of objections which can be made to these types of variable scales which Labov and others have used to quantify phonological and syntactic variables. I raised this issue in Chapter 2 and return to it in Chapter 8 (cf. also Romaine 1978a and 1979c; and also Lavandera 1978). For the sake of the argument I am assuming at the moment that the procedure is a valid one.

Table 6.24. (*Relpro*) *index for all texts*

Text	(Relpro) index
The Scottish Correspondence	180
Ane Satyre	193
The Bannatyne Manuscript	198
Acts of the Lords of Council	203
Sheriff Court Book	206
Burgh Records	207
Boece	248

Table 6.25. *The* (*relpro*) *index and stylistic categories*

Stylistic categories	(Relpro) index
PROSE	
official	205
non-official	248
epistolary	180
total prose	205
VERSE	196

TH forms are intermediate between these two. The scale is given below:

Variable scale for (*relpro*)
(relpro–1) WH
(relpro–2) TH
(relpro–3) ∅

According to this scale the values for the (relpro) index will range from 100–300. Texts which have a higher incidence of deletion would show a lower (relpro) index than those which have lower incidences of deletion. Table 6.24 shows the (relpro) indices for all the texts.

The variable index suggests four divisions in the texts. *The Scottish Correspondence* again stands out as very different from the other prose texts, as does *Boece*. The official prose and verse categories comprise the other two groups. Table 6.25 shows the indices for these four groups.

6.7 The isolation of contextual styles and the language of individuals

Thus far my results have demonstrated that the index of syntactic complexity and the (relpro) index can be used to stratify the seven Middle Scots

Table 6.26. *The (relpro) index for three groups of characters in Lindsay's 'Ane Satyre of the Thrie Estaitis'*

Group	(Relpro) index
1 Virtues	210
2 Vices	182
3 Low status	182

texts into stylistic levels. This supports another hypothesis of my study; namely, that (relpro) usage is stylistically diagnostic. I would now like to discuss in more detail what indications there are in the data to suggest that the use of the variable (relpro) is socially diagnostic as well, i.e. indicative of social levels.

As I mentioned in Chapter 5, the reconstruction of social information from historical records such as these is by nature only partial, and is of course dependent on the richness and variety of the extant texts. I have already demonstrated that prose and verse texts are well differentiated with respect to their usage of the variable, and that within these categories there are further subdivisions which can be made on the basis of verse form and subject matter. In isolating quoted speech within a body of narrative in *Boece*, I have illustrated that the index of syntactic complexity distinguishes this instance of language as a separate and well-defined register within the context of one text. I would like now to pursue the isolation of contextual styles further by taking a closer look at two texts which presumably approximate the spoken language. My aim in doing this is to explore the connections between the social and stylistic continuum with respect to the use of the relative markers.

6.7.1 Stylistic levels in *Ane Satyre of the Thrie Estaitis*. Since the total number of instances of the variable (relpro) is not large in this text, I have decided to make only three divisions. The figures given in Table 6.26 show the (relpro) index for the speech of three groups of characters in the play. Group 1 is composed of a number of 'high' or serious characters: namely, the Virtues Diligence, Gude Counsall, Veritie, Chastitie and Divine Correctioun. At the other end of the stylistic continuum are Groups 2 and 3. Group 2 is made up of six of the Vices: namely, Wantoness, Placebo, Sensualitie, Flatterie, Falset and Deceit. Group 3 contains eight comic

Table 6.27. *Percentage of variants of (relpro) in three groups of characters in 'Ane Satyre of the Thrie Estaitis'*

Group	WH	TH	Ø	Total (N in parentheses)
1	12	85	2	
	(5)	(35)	(1)	(41)
2	3	77	20	
	(1)	(27)	(7)	(35)
3	3	77	20	
	(1)	(30)	(8)	(39)

characters, or persons of lower status in the play: the Sowtar, the Sowtar's wyfe, the Taylour, the Taylour's wyfe, the Pauper, the Pardoner, Thift and the Parson.

Groups 2 and 3 are clearly differentiated from Group 1 on the basis of their usage of the variable, but not from each other. When these group indices are compared with the (relpro) index for the text as a whole, it can be seen that Group 1 exceeds the average, while Groups 2 and 3 fall below it. The index for the whole text (193) is the result of averaging two stylistically differentiated levels of usage within the text.

If the usage of the three groups is examined in more detail as in Table 6.27, it can be seen that Groups 2 and 3 differ from Group 1 with respect to their usage of each variant of (relpro), but what is especially different about both groups' use of the variable is their much greater use of Ø. Furthermore, there is a difference between Groups 2 and 3 in terms of subject relative deletion. In Group 3, nearly half of the zero relatives occur in subject position; while in Group 2 more than half of the zero relatives occur in temporal relative clauses, with only one deletion in subject position. The one zero form in Group 1 occurs in a temporal clause.

6.7.2 Stylistic levels in *The Scottish Correspondence of Mary of Lorraine*. It is generally felt that letters and diaries are an excellent source of colloquialisms which existed at earlier stages of the English language. Whether this is true is a matter of debate, but it cannot be disputed that, stylistically speaking, *The Scottish Correspondence of Mary of Lorraine* is quite different from all the other texts in terms of its usage of the relative system. It has the lowest (relpro) index of all the texts (180); and although it is not the least syntactically complex of all the texts, it stands apart from all the other

Table 6.28. *Comparison of (relpro) indices in the letters of Methuen, Otterburn and five women from 'The Scottish Correspondence of Mary of Lorraine'*

Author	(Relpro) index
Otterburn	194
Methuen	177
Women	167

prose texts. It also has the highest index of deletion of all the texts, both prose and verse (25). Since the index of deletion for this text is more than twice that of the texts which have the next highest indices, it is also very different from the verse texts in this sample. Whatever its status is as representative of the spoken language of the day, it provides us with an excellent opportunity for examining in some detail the language of individuals, as well as perhaps one of the few instances of the language of women writers.

As a sample of the language of individuals I have analyzed separately the instances of relatives which occur in twenty-four letters of Otterburn, eighteen letters of Methuen and nine letters written by women, which appear in my sample of *The Scottish Correspondence*. Otterburn and Methuen were chosen because they produced some of the largest amounts of correspondence in the sample, and this was all analysed. Unfortunately, the data from the women in my sample had to be considered in the aggregate because no individual produced enough tokens for reliable comparative analysis. These data are taken from four letters by Lady Home, three by the Countess of Moray, and one each from the Countess of Atholl and Catherine Bellenden.

Table 6.28 gives (relpro) indices for Otterburn, Methuen and the women. The indices distinguish both Otterburn's and Methuen's correspondence from each other, as well as both men's correspondence from that of the women. In this case, Methuen's letters are quite close to the (relpro) index for the text as a whole (180), while Otterburn's and the women's letters are above and below it respectively.

Table 6.29 gives more detailed figures on the usage of the variants of (relpro). Again, as in *Ane Satyre of the Thrie Estaitis*, we can observe that each subsample of the text is characterized by different levels of usage of all

Table 6.29. *Percentage of variants of (relpro) in 'The Scottish Correspondence of Mary of Lorraine'*

Author	WH	TH	∅	Total (N in parentheses)
Otterburn	6	82	12	
	(2)	(27)	(4)	(33)
Methuen	9	68	24	
	(3)	(23)	(8)	(34)
Women	8	50	42	
	(2)	(12)	(10)	(24)

three variants. In this instance, however, the three samples are overwhelmingly differentiated with respect to one another in terms of their usage of ∅. Methuen's letters delete twice as often as Otterburn's, while the women's letters delete nearly twice as much again as Methuen's, or nearly four times as frequently as Otterburn's letters. Once more, if the figures for subject relative deletion are examined, it can be seen that only in the women's letters are any instances of subject deletion to be found. The deletions which were recorded in Methuen's and Otterburn's correspondence are all in direct object position.

There are a number of interesting hypotheses which these data from *The Scottish Correspondence* and *Ane Satyre* suggest. For one thing, if we assume for the moment that *The Scottish Correspondence* as a whole *is* representative of more colloquial language of the period, then it can be said that both Lindsay and Bellenden are perceptive stylists in that they both appear to have exploited contrasting usages of the variable (relpro) as a stylistic device to demarcate different registers within their texts. Lindsay, for example, has used this difference as one means of separating the high from the low (or serious from comic) characters.

If we compare for the moment Lindsay's *Satyre* with *The Scottish Correspondence*, Lindsay seems to have been particularly accurate in his attempt to represent the speech of the more common characters by having them use a higher incidence of zero forms of the relative, and moreover, by recording a higher incidence of these in subject position. Although Bellenden's *Boece* can be divided into two distinct styles on the basis of relative usage, which correlate with the division between narrative prose and quoted speech within the narrative, deletion is not used as a stylistic marker.[14] In this respect, it might be said that, stylistically speaking, the quoted speech in *Boece* seems to be rather stilted and artificial by comparison with *Ane Satyre* and *The Scottish Correspondence*.

This should not of course be surprising, considering the difference in genres and the non-native source of *Boece*. The result which is particularly interesting however is this: If deletion of the relative is a social marker as well as a stylistic one, it seems to be subject deletion which is especially stereotyped. This is one conclusion which might be drawn from the finding that it is the one feature shared by the women's letters in *The Scottish Correspondence* and the lowly characters in *Ane Satyre*. The observation that subject deletion is more characteristic of low status characters, and hence presumably closer to vernacular norms, is not contradicted by its presence in the usage of women, since at that time it can be expected that women would be on the whole more isolated (i.e. regardless of their social status) from the norms of the written language than men.

6.8 Analysis of the data by implicational scaling

The working assumption which is implicit in implicational scaling is that the scale consists of a series of ranked isolects. Each isolect is the output of a grammar (which is part of a polylectal grammar), is invariant, and differs from the one immediately next to it with respect to a single feature or rule in the panlectal grid (cf. Bickerton 1973a). The panlectal grid consists of the totality of possible sets of rules for an arbitrarily limited area in space and/or time. The results of the implicational scale are used as a means of checking data against the predictions of a Baileyan wave model (cf. Bailey 1973). The assumption is that if the data scale to an acceptable degree, then they can do so by virtue of the fact that a succession (or wave) of rule changes has spread evenly through the grammar of a community.

In Table 6.30 I have presented an ideal implicational scale for the deletion of relatives. Each text can be considered an isolect, these all appear on the vertical axis, and all the relevant linguistic environments for deletion are on the horizontal axis. The symbols 0, X and 1 are used here to indicate no deletion, variable deletion and categorical deletion respectively.

14. The (relpro) index for the narrative in Bellenden's *Boece* is 250, while that for quoted speech in the narrative is 237. This difference is largely due to the fact that the quoted speech sample contains a greater proportion of TH to WH forms than does the narrative sample, rather than to a difference in deletion. The (relpro) indices for *The Bannatyne Manuscript* are as follows: Merry Ballads – 203; *Fables of Aesop* (Henryson) – 200; Religious Ballads – 199; Ballads of Wisdom and Morality – 199; and Ballads of Love – 191.

Table 6.30. *Model implicational scale for relative deletion*

Environment	Syntactic position of the relative				
	A	B	C	D	Text
	1	1	1	1	1
	1	1	1	X	2
	1	1	X	X	3
	1	X	X	X	4
	X	X	X	X	5
	X	X	X	0	6
	X	X	0	0	7
	X	0	0	0	8
	0	0	0	0	9

Table 6.31. *Implicational scale for relative deletion in Middle Scots texts (deviations ringed; scalability = 92.3 percent, cf. Excursus for explanation)*

Text	Syntactic position of deleted relative			
	Temp.	Dir. obj.	Prep.	Subj.
The Scottish Correspondence	1	1	1	X
Ane Satyre	1	1	1	X
The Bannatyne Manuscript	1	1	X	X
Acts of the Lords of Council	1	1	X	0
Burgh Records	1	1	①	0
Boece	X	X	X	0
Sheriff Court Book	①	0	0	0

The model predicts that a change moves through the grammar (in this case, a rule which allows the deletion of relative markers in certain syntactic positions), affecting one environment in one isolect at a time. The environments which always or never allow deletion become variable, and then re-establish themselves as categorical. Since isolects are located in both time and space in such a model, they participate differentially (i.e. earlier or later) in an incipient rule change at any given point in the spatiotemporal continuum. Bailey also makes certain predictions about the direction of rule spread. For example, he claims that the farther a rule travels from its origin, the fewer will be the environments above it on an implicational scale. Change begins in the most heavily weighted environment and works its way through the grammar by spreading through successively less heavily weighted environments. This pattern of spread has the consequence that rules generalize in time, but seem to become less general in space because the temporally earlier changes move farther than the later ones.

Table 6.31 shows the actual data for relative deletion arranged in an implicational scale. In constructing this scale I have decided to set thresholds for 0, X and 1, so that 0 = 5 percent or less deletion; X = 5–25 percent deletion; and 1 = 25 percent or more deletion. These levels were arbitrarily set in order to reduce variant cells to more categorical terms. In this case all the cells were variant except for two cells which were empty.[15]

It can be seen that acceptable results can be produced for these data using the implicational scaling technique. These results coincide largely with the results of the frequency analysis in that the ordering of the environments is the same in either case. The results of the frequency analysis reveal the following ordering of syntactic environments.

Temporal	42 percent
Direct object	30 percent
Preposition	20 percent
Subject	4 percent

The ordering of the texts with respect to one another makes sense in terms of the frequency data I have discussed so far. This implicational scale shows the same trend as the quantitative data; namely, that deletion occurs less frequently by syntactic environments which are implicationally ordered with respect to one another. The border between categorical non-deletion and variable deletion of subject relatives is bounded by or coincides with the border between prose and verse texts (except for *The Scottish Correspondence*). It is also the first group of texts in the scale, i.e. verse plus *The Scottish Correspondence*, which is less syntactically complex than the other group of texts.

This scale suggests a number of interesting questions which I will consider in terms of the types of predictions and 'explanations' the Baileyan wave model would put forward on the basis of the ordering of the linguistic environments. I stress at this point that, according to Bailey, it is the internal ordering of linguistic differentiation that counts and not extralinguistic constraints. In other words, Bailey argues that since grammars are ongoing

15. I cite Stolz and Bills (1968) as an example of this type of 'threshold' scaling (cf. the Excursus to this chapter for further comments on this procedure).

entities in time, time accounts not only for spatial patterns of variation, but also for age, social class and stylistic patterns of variation.[16]

Change enters the grammar at the bottom point of the scale in the lower left-hand corner. This is the most heavily weighted environment for the operation of the rule. (In this case, we will assume for the moment that it is a rule of relative deletion.) It spreads out in time and space from this point affecting more environments in more lects.

If, however, we return to Bever and Langendoen's (1972) account of the changes which have taken place in the history of English, we see that they suggest a perceptual explanation for the ordering of the syntactic environments (cf. Chapter 4). They claim that restrictions were imposed on the deletion of subject relatives in response to a more fixed word order constraint, which made the decoding of sentences with deleted subject relatives difficult. Their account of the change in the relative system is one in which a deletion rule becomes progressively more inhibited in its application as it spreads through the grammar over time.

If we consider the extralinguistic dimension of the change, i.e. stylistic factors, we might say that what seems to be happening is the spread of the inhibition of the rule from the top of the scale to the bottom. Subject position would then be the most heavily weighted environment. The change then has its origin in the most informal style (cf. Labov's 'change from below'). My findings in this chapter suggest that the phenomenon of relative marker deletion needs to be seen within the larger context of the history of the English language as a manifestion of stylistic variation rather than in terms of perceptual constraints as Bever and Langendoen have argued. The reason why subject relative deletion has become more infrequent (if indeed it has, and at any rate only in certain types of English) is that it has become socially and stylistically stereotyped through its association with informal registers and non-standard speech. This seems to me a much more plausible 'explanation' than Bever and Langendoen's, but I will present more data in the next chapter to support my argument.

In the next chapter I will also set up models of variation which can be tested against the predictions of the Cedergren–Sankoff program, which is a variable rule model of variation and change. My reason for doing this will be to see in what way the predictions from Bailey's wave model and variable rule analysis about the locus of variation and the direction of

16. Bailey (1969a: 112) comments that this does not relieve us of the task of specifying the extralinguistic significance of the points on implicational scales, but that the primary concern is to organize linguistic material in terms of intralinguistic principles.

change compare, and, in particular, to see if the variable rule model, which incorporates extralinguistic dimensions, illuminates this process.

The variable rule model of change also incorporates the notion of a hierarchical effect of linguistic (as well as extralinguistic) environments as a mechanism of linguistic change. Labov (1969: 742), for example, has claimed that changes or reweightings in the hierarchy of constraints operating on a rule represent a basic mechanism of linguistic evolution. In one sense, then, we might think of variable rules as creating an implicational scale among the environments by assigning different probability coefficients to factors which promote the rule's application (cf. e.g. Fasold 1970). The variable rule model, however, takes social factors into account, so that the application of a rule may also be affected by a hierarchy of social environments, which may be assigned probability coefficients by the Cedergren–Sankoff program, just as the linguistic constraints are. A rule may, for example, apply differentially in response to the prestige of various social environments.

Appendix

1. Correlation of the index of syntactic complexity based on relativization with mean T-unit length

To test the hypothesis that syntactic complexity in my sample of texts is not only a manifestation of different frequencies of relativization on NPs in certain syntactic positions, I have compared my index of syntactic complexity with a more widely used measure, namely, mean T-unit length. A T-unit is defined by Hunt (1970a) as one main clause plus the subordinate clauses attached to it. I computed mean T-unit length for some of the texts by dividing the total number of words by the total number of T-units in samples of approximately 500 words. I did this for texts from each of the major categories which are at different points on the stylistic continuum.[17]

My prediction is that if my measure of syntactic complexity based on relativization is a good measure of impressionistic judgements of complexity (as I claim), then mean T-unit length should correlate with it and rank the texts in the same order on the stylistic continuum. This can be seen in Table 6.32 which gives the values for mean T-unit length for some of the texts.

If we compare these results with those in Tables 6.16 and 6.17 (6.4), we can see

17. Since my results indicated that *Boece*, *Ane Satyre* and *The Scottish Correspondence* could all be further subdivided into contextual styles, I chose samples from the more complex end of the stylistic continuum. For example, the sample from *Boece* is from the main body of the narrative rather than from quoted speech; the sample from *Ane Satyre* is the opening speech of Diligence (rhymed alliterative verse); and the sample from *The Scottish Correspondence* is from a letter by Otterburn.

Table 6.32. *Mean T-unit length as an index of syntactic complexity*

Text	Mean T-unit length
Ane Satyre (verse)	23.2
The Scottish Correspondence (epistolary prose)	34.6
Boece (narrative prose)	41.0
Acts of the Lords of Council (official prose)	83.6

that either measure of syntactic complexity will yield the same rank ordering of texts in a stylistic continuum, i.e. *Ane Satyre* is the least syntactically complex, and the *Acts of the Lords* is the most syntactically complex. There is a clear split between verse and prose texts. Within the prose category, epistolary prose is the least syntactically complex, official prose is the most, while narrative prose occupies a position intermediate between the two. Official prose is in fact strikingly more complex (and correspondingly much more difficult to read and segment into T-units) than narrative prose. This no doubt reflects the fact that narrative prose is intended for a more general audience and has in this instance a didactic purpose.

These results indicate that the index of syntactic complexity based on relativization which I have developed for this study may be more widely applicable as an independent measure of intuitive judgements; and that the stylistic continuum I have set up here for Middle Scots is not an artifact of this index, i.e. complexity is not just a property of the relative system.

2. The influence of metrical type and verse form on syntactic complexity and the deletion of relative markers

It seems reasonable to suppose that metrical type can influence syntactic complexity and the incidence of deletion, since the constraints on the choice of items which can be used to fill out a line (e.g. in octosyllabic vs. decasyllabic verse) or to form certain types of rhyme will impose certain limits on sentence length. I demonstrated in the previous section that mean T-unit length is lower in verse than prose.

The first hypothesis that I will test is that as the syllable count becomes lower, syntactic complexity as measured by mean T-unit length will decrease, but that the incidence of deletion will increase. I already have good evidence to suggest that this is the case on the basis of my analysis of *Ane Satyre of the Thrie Estaitis* (cf. 6.7.1).

My original division of the text into three groups based on character type (i.e. the Virtues, Vices and low status persons) also coincides with a difference in metrical type. The high characters in the play are distinguished by the use of decasyllabic verse, while the comic or lowly characters are marked by their use of octosyllabic verse in tail rhyme stanzas or short couplets. Sometimes, however, this pairing of characters and verse forms is not one-to-one, and changes in stylistic level are accompanied by changes into a verse form more appropriate to the subject matter, e.g. the Vices sometimes use a mock courtly style of speaking which is accompanied by a change in verse form.

Table 6.33. *The influence of metrical type (octosyllabic vs. decasyllabic verse) on syntactic complexity and deletion*

Metrical type	Mean T-unit length	Index of deletion
Decasyllabic (high characters)	23.2	1
Octosyllabic		
(Vices)	10.3	7
(low status characters)	10.1	8

Table 6.34. *Comparison of verse form and deletion in three poems by Dunbar*

Text	Verse form	Index of deletion
The Flyting of Dunbar and Kennedy	rhymed	0
The Twa Mariit Wemen and the Wedo	unrhymed alliterative	14
The Ballad of Kynd Kittok	rhymed	0

Table 6.33 compares the mean T-unit length and the incidence of deletion for a sample from each of the original three groupings. It can be seen that octosyllabic verse is less syntactically complex than decasyllabic, as predicted; and it is also the former that is characterized by higher levels of deletion. This result also provides more support for my conclusion that it is the deletion of subject relatives, rather than relative deletion per se, which is a social and stylistic stereotype, since it is this feature which distinguishes the Vices from the low status group.

Another hypothesis which might be tested is whether rhymed and alliterative verse differ in terms of deletion. My results here are inconclusive, largely due to lack of sufficient data which contrast in terms of this parameter only. In other words, the contrast between alliterative and rhymed proved difficult to isolate within the limitations of my sample, since verse form interacts with stylistic level, i.e. the opposite ends of the stylistic continuum (comic vs. serious) have their own characteristic verse forms. Table 6.34 gives a comparison of three poems by Dunbar which could all be considered to belong to the category of comic verse.[18]

If we compare some figures from the works of Henryson, we can see that there is also a possibility that non-native source may in fact override the effect of contrast between serious vs. comic in influencing levels of deletion. For example, *Orpheus and Eurydice*, a narrative poem, contains more instances of deletion than *The Twa Myss* (from the *Fables of Aesop*), i.e. 21 percent and 14 percent respectively, which may reflect the fact that the latter is a translation.

18. *The Ballad of Kynd Kittok* has been attributed by some to Dunbar.

Excursus

When I said that the results which I obtained using the technique of implicational scaling were 'acceptable', I meant that the fit between the ideal implicational scale and the observed data obtained to an extent which has been cited as significant by those who rely on this method of analysis. This deserves further comment here. In this case I measured the fit between my data and the model in terms of an 'index of scalability' (92.3 percent). This index (by one method of calculation) is arrived at by dividing the sum of non-deviant cells by the sum of the cells which are filled (i.e. 24/26).

Guttman (1944), who developed the scales, suggests that in practice, 85 percent perfect scales or better can serve as efficient approximations to perfect scales. In sociolinguistic practice, however, scales with much lower indices of scalability are being put forward, depending on what one counts as a deviation, and to what extent the rows and columns can be manipulated. For example, if empty cells do not count as deviations (and in Bickerton's 1975 data for Guyanese creole, they very often do not), and full freedom is given to manipulate rows and columns, then virtually any set of data is scalable to an acceptable level, possibly as high as 90 percent. Bickerton (1973a), interestingly enough, does not accept this criticism.

I will illustrate how this works with my data on relative marker deletion. If the number of non-deviations is divided by the total number of cells (both filled and empty), i.e. 26/28, then scalability is increased to 92.8 percent. If the number of deviations is taken to include empty cells, then scalability is reduced to 85.7 percent. Since this data set is fairly small (and only two cells are empty and only two are deviant), these alternative calculations do not produce very different results. Yet in larger data sets, such as Bickerton (1975) presents, the ramifications of the decision of what counts in the index of scalability are much more considerable. In fact, if only filled cells count and empty ones do not count as errors, high levels of scalability can be reached almost automatically by moving speakers (isolects) who produce little data upwards or downwards on the scale. It would be surprising if most data could not be fitted into this model.

I will now take a number of disturbing examples from Bickerton's work on the copula since his analysis is relevant to some points I will make later about Labov's study of the copula in BEV. To start with Table 6.35 (= Bickerton 1973a: Table 2), which is an implicational scale for copula distribution in Bushlot, we observe that the index of scalability is 95.6 percent. Here Bickerton has obviously not counted empty cells as deviations. The index of scalability is based on the number of deviant cells divided by the number of filled cells (i.e. 65/68). This does not seem so bad, until we consider that the total number of cells involved is 234 (i.e. 26 speakers and 9 environments), and that only 29 percent of these cells are filled. We are therefore being asked to accept that scalability is as high as 95 percent when we have no idea what happened to the copula in nearly three-quarters of the cases where it could or could not have occurred.

This is by no means an isolated example in the literature: it is rarely made clear what the thresholds of significance are for any particular type of implicational

Table 6.35. *Implicational table for copula distribution* (*Bushlot*) (*Bickerton 1973a: Table 2*)

	Environment								
Speaker	*1*	*2*	*3*	*4*	*5*	*6*	*7*	*8*	*9*
23	1						1		
16	1				1			1	
7	1			1					
20		1	1						
24		1							
26	1	1			1	1			
2	1	1				1			
9	1	1			1	1	1	1	
25		1							
4						1			
12						1			
14						1			
6						1			
21						1			
10						1	1		
28	1		1	1		1			
3									2
5	1			1			1	23	
27	1		1		1	13	3	3	
15	1		1	1		13			
17			1		3	3	3	①	
1						3			3
13	1			13				①3	
11	1			3		3	①3		
18							3		
19				4		4			4

1 = *de*/*bin de* in Cols. 1–4; *a*/*bina* in Cols. 5, 7, 8; ∅/*bin* in Col. 6
2 = ∅ except in Col. 6
3 = *iz*/*woz* (no person concord)
4 = *be* with full person concord
Col. 1 = locative; Col. 2 = existential; Col. 3 = time/manner adverbials; Col. 4 = preceding non-finite structures; Col. 5 = cleft Ss; Col. 6 = pred. adj.; Col. 7 = NP complement; Col. 8 = impersonal Ss; Col. 9 = V-*ing*. Scalability = 95.6 percent

scale;[19] nor is it generally mentioned how the index of scalability is to be calculated. I have suggested three ways in which this might be (and seems to have been) done, all of which may produce very different results depending on sample size. The real uncertainty about implicational scales is that very often there is no indication of what numbers stand behind each filled cell for which a claim is made (cf. e.g.

19. Some linguists use percentages (cf. e.g. Day 1972); some use actual numbers of tokens (cf. e.g. Bickerton 1975). Some use binary implications (cf. DeCamp 1971a) or n-ary implications (cf. again Bickerton 1975). Finally, some use a threshold system as I have done here (cf. Stolz and Bills 1968). Strictly speaking, the latter should probably not be allowed at all, unless there are constraints on setting thresholds. Stolz and Bills, for example, set arbitrary and different thresholds for a number of unrelated features in one implicational scale.

Bickerton 1975: 148, Fig. 4.10),[20] and that generally speaking, there are often far too many unfilled cells.[21]

Similar comments apply to Bickerton (1973a: Table 3) and (1972: Tables 1 and 2) especially the first, which shows the mesolectal pattern of copula distribution. I have included these as Tables 6.36, 6.37 and 6.38 to illustrate another point in my argument; namely, that if we have full freedom to manipulate the ordering of speakers and linguistic environments, the credibility of the index of scalability as a measure of significance is correspondingly lessened.

If we consider first the order of the speakers, we can see that in Tables 6.37 and 6.38, which display the introduction of the copula and the spread of zero in the creole, neither the speakers nor their ordering into isolects matches from table to table. If we take a closer look at what happens to one individual (speaker 98) in this shuffle, it seems that he belongs in isolect B in Table 6.37, but in isolect A in Table 6.38. Other speakers move in and out of isolects or disappear altogether for no apparent reason. For example, speaker 43 is added to isolect G in Table 6.38, and speaker 103 from isolect D in Table 6.37 does not turn up at all in the second table (although this is no great loss, since his data filled only two cells anyway). I suspect that this is in fact the reason he was dropped from the second table, since one of the cells this speaker did manage to produce data for, i.e. cleft sentences, is also omitted in Table 6.38.

The manipulation of speakers does not seem to be independent of the manipulation of linguistic environments. Of the seven linguistic environments present in Table 6.37, only four remain in Table 6.38. Similar criticisms also apply to the two tables from Bickerton (1973a). Although nine linguistic environments are given in Table 6.35, only eight appear in Table 6.36; furthermore, there is a reversal in ordering of two environments in Table 6.36 (i.e. NP complements and cleft sentences). Nowhere are we given any explanation for these changes in the ordering or appearance (and disappearance) of speakers and environments.

There is one more problem which relates to the counting of deviations. We might call this (both figuratively and literally) the problem of 'where to draw the line'. For instance in my implicational scale for relative deletion, I drew a line between cells which contained X's and those which contained 1s, since this coincided with a

20. Bickerton (1975: 148) himself invites us to inspect the scalability of this table, which he says is either 64.5 percent or 51.4 percent depending on what counts as a deviation. His purpose in drawing our attention to this particular example is to refute the argument that higher scalability could be obtained by manipulating rows and columns. He comments that 'the difference between the data in this table and those in other implicational scales should be readily apparent'. I am not sure I understand what this means. It seems to me that what we are dealing with here is data which do *not* belong in an implicational scale in the first place. Even if we cannot manipulate these particular data to a higher degree of scalability, this does not damage my argument that some people *are* manipulating data to very high degrees of scalability without justification. As to the difference between Bickerton's Table 4.10 (Bickerton 1975: 148) and one such as 6.39, it seems to be the attitude one takes towards deviations which cannot be manipulated to one's advantage (and hence must be counted), as opposed to empty cells (apparent deviations), which may or may not be deviations. In the latter case, the attitude seems to be, what you don't know can't hurt you (or, at any rate, shouldn't affect your index of scalability); while in the former, it seems to be, do whatever you can do.

21. We get some idea of the numbers involved in Bickerton's (1975) description of his corpus. It contains 250,000 words from 300 speakers. Each informant's contribution ranges from one to two sentences to 2000 words, but we are never given an indication of what each informant's contribution is in a given scale.

Table 6.36. *Copula distribution: the mesolectal pattern* (*Bickerton 1973a: Table 3*)

	Environment							
Speaker	*1*	*2*	*3*	*4*	*5*	*6*	*7*	*8*
120	1			1	1			
126	1	1		1				2
129	1	1			1			2
118	1	1						2
121	1			13	3			2
101				13			2	23
100				2	3		2	23
99				23	3		2	23
119	1			3	3			②
125	123	3	2	3	3	3	23	23
108	23	3		3	3	3	23	23
105	23	3		②3		3	3	3
123	3			②3			②3	②
102	3		3	3	3	3		②3
117				②3	3		②3	3
124	3	3		3			②	3
122	3		3	②3	3	3	3	3

1 = *a*; *de*
2 = ∅
3 = *be* (all forms)
Col. 1 = locative; Col. 2 = existential; Col. 3 = non-finites; Col. 4 = NP complement; Col. 5 = cleft Ss; Col. 6 = impersonal; Col. 7 = *-ing*; Col. 8 = pred. adj. Scalability = 87.90 percent
Note (a) absence of time/manner, (b) reversal of NP complement and cleft S

division in the texts between prose and verse. In doing so, however, I ignored the constraint imposed by Bailey that lects must differ from each other with respect to only one feature, i.e. change proceeds in step-like fashion and not by jumps. Technically speaking, any lect or environment which violates this constraint should be counted as a deviation. In practice, however, this does not seem to be done; one argument in favor of ignoring this requirement is that the data from more speakers would fill out the continuum.

The real difficulty is in drawing the line and what one does afterwards. For example, if we look at Table 6.36, we see that Bickerton has drawn a line separating the speakers who categorically use *a*, *de* forms (1) for the copula from those who use the English *be* forms (3). The problem here is how to draw the line in the absence of data on both sides of it. Bickerton solves this by using a dashed line. Why the line is important has again to do with the index of scalability. Typically, only deviations 'under the line' count. Bickerton has drawn the line through Speaker 125 in environment 1; this environment seems to be a deviation any way we look at it. It violates Bailey's 'one feature at a time' constraint by having all three forms simultaneously; if the line is drawn above this environment or below it, it is still a

Table 6.37. *Introduction of English copula* (*Bickerton 1972: Table 1*)

	Environment							
Isolects	1	2	3	4	5	6	7	Speakers
A	0	1	1		1	1	1	120, 121
B	1	1	1		1	13		98
C	1	1	1	1	13	23	3	27, 99
D	1			13				103
E		1	1	3	3	3	1	11, 17, 119
F	1	1	13		3	3		15, 101
G	1	12	13	3	3	3	13	13, 160
H	13	123	13	3	3	3	3	125, 192, 236

Col. 1 = continuative verbal
Col. 2 = locative and existential
Col. 3 = 'predicate adjective' present
Col. 4 = cleft sentence
Col. 5 = 'predicate adjective' past
Col. 6 = noun phrase
Col. 7 = impersonal expressions
0 = continuative *a* + V
1 = V*ing* without aux. in Col. 1; *de* in Col. 2; V(+ att) in Col. 3; equative *a* in Cols. 4, 6 and 7; *bin* in Col. 5
2 = ∅
3 = *iz*/*waz* (*waz* only in Col. 5)
Scalability = 95.5 percent

deviation, since 3s should be bounded by 1s (and not 2s). Drawing the line through the environment is an ad hoc solution.

Since everything depends on the correct ordering of the rows and columns in implicational scaling, there should be some explicit constraints on the mobility of these; otherwise, the device is far too powerful. I could, for example, have scaled my data on relative deletion to more or less the same degree of scalability by ordering the texts and environments in another way, as indicated in Table 6.39.

What conclusions can be drawn from this? One is that perhaps only subject and prepositional relative deletion are ordered implicationally with respect to each other. In any event, it would be hard to argue for an explanation which was entirely dependent on one or the other ordering of direct objects in relation to temporals, since neither ordering affects scalability. A number of the 'explanations' in the literature seem to be rather ad hoc in that the data are arranged or manipulated into some order, and then a suitable explanation is found for this ordering. This in itself is not necessarily bad; in fact, it is probably the only way to fit *some* data into such a model. My argument is that there should be some constraints on ordering, more consistency from scale to scale, and an agreement on the threshold of significance for whatever index of scalability one adopts.

The question which seems to be most relevant to the criticism of implicational scaling is not so much whether there are implicational relationships, but rather, as DeCamp (1973) has put it, what the implicational scales imply. The answer to the

Table 6.38. *The spread of zero* (*Bickerton 1972: Table 2*)

	Environment				
Isolects	1	2	3	4	Speakers
A	1	1	1	13	98
B	1	1	1	23	27, 99
C	1	1	1	3	11, 17, 119
D	1	1	13	3	15, 105
		←	*	→	
E	1	12	13	3	13, 160
F	13	12	13	23	41
G	13	123	13	3	43, 125, 192, 236
H	13	13	13	23	196
I	13	3	13	23	122, 157
J	13		3	23	117
K	3	23	3	3	19

Col. 1 = continuative verbal
Col. 2 = locative and existential
Col. 3 = 'predicate adjective'
Col. 4 = nominal
1 = V*ing* without aux. in Col. 1; *de* in Col. 2; V(+ att) (or, ∅ + Adj.) in Col. 3; *a* in Col. 4
2 = ∅
3 = *iz/waz*
* = point from which copula variability disseminates.

Table 6.39. *An alternate implicational scale for relative deletion*

	Syntactic position of the deleted relative			
Text	Dir. obj.	Temp.	Prep.	Subj.
The Scottish Correspondence	1	1	1	X
Ane Satyre	1	1	1	X
The Bannatyne Manuscript	1	1	X	X
Burgh Records	1	1	①	0
Acts of the Lords of Council	1	1	X	0
Boece	X	X	X	0
Sheriff Court Book	①	0	0	0

first question seems to be unquestionably affirmative. Linguistic features, dialects, idiolects, etc. do show implicational relationships. The problem is that some linguists seem to be quite willing to put forward very arbitrary implicational scales without justifying them.[22]

22. DeCamp (1971a), for example, forms implicational scales which arbitrarily cut across phonology, grammar and lexis without explaining how implicational relations might hold within and between these subsystems.

7 *Variable rule analysis of the data*

> Metaphysics and methodology are intertwined in curious ways. Although there may be difficulty converting a metaphysics into a method of research, there seems to be little difficulty involved in converting a methodology into a metaphysics – one can arrive at remarkable discoveries by mistaking a property of the analysis (working assumptions, methods, etc.) for a property of the data.
>
> E.A. Burtt (1924)

In this chapter I discuss the contribution which variable rule analysis makes to my study of the relative system, and show how some hypotheses about the types of rules needed to describe the variation can be tested using the Cedergren–Sankoff variable rule program. I will be particularly concerned with examining the kinds of arguments which have been advanced in favor of the claim that the program (and variable rule analysis) gives new and reliable evidence for judging certain linguistic issues.

Cedergren and Sankoff's (1974) work on the probabilistic component of variable rules has had a major impact on quantitative analysis in sociolinguistics. The ramifications of this shift in emphasis from frequencies to probabilities are enormous; yet, they have scarcely been treated cogently in their relation to the construction of a sociolinguistic theory which claims to have an empirical base. Labov (1975a: 228), for example, has maintained that the 'new tools of probability theory' give us a 'dramatic increase in power and perception'. The claim about increased power is true, though, ironically perhaps, not in the way Labov seems to think (cf. Romaine 1981a).

Probability theories might be considered more powerful with respect to their domain of application because, strictly speaking, they cannot be confirmed or disconfirmed by empirical findings. If probability statements are not falsifiable, then they have no empirical content. Thus, they can have no explanatory or predictive power.[1] Labov (and others), however, assume

1. I am not claiming that probability theories have no place in empirical work, but rather that strict constraints must be imposed on such theories before they can be useful. I have expanded this argument in the final chapter and also in Romaine (1981a).

that the theory (and the program) is more powerful because it allows us to verify hypotheses, and yields correct and unique solutions to abstract issues. My concern here (and in the next chapter) will be with this claim, rather than with the increase in perception which Labov also claims for the program. I assume that this should be interpreted pragmatically (i.e. computer-assisted analysis saves time, handles larger data sets with greater accuracy, etc.), and cannot be intended to refer to an extension of physical sense perceptions (in the way, for example, that a telescope can be considered to extend our vision).[2] If Labov's use of the word 'perception' carries this implication, it is difficult to see how his claim could be supported, since how would we find out whether the program increased our sense perception?[3]

The use which can be made of the program is essentially a heuristic one. Thus, the output of the program can be seen as a suggestion in heuristics which relates to the construction of a theory (i.e. within the context of discovery rather than validation). The problem which I see in Labov's interpretations of the results of the program lies in the assumption of isomorphism between model and theory, as well as between theory and reality. Labov seems to think that certain characteristics of the model correspond to statements in the theory. This can be true, however, only if a model relationship (rather than a looser one of analogy; cf. Rudner 1966: 26–7) obtains between the model and the theory; otherwise, any such transfer from what we are guessing to be a model to a theory is unwarranted.

7.1 The Cedergren–Sankoff variable rule program

Cedergren and Sankoff (1974) have developed the mathematical background for the variable rule concept, which was introduced into sociolinguistic analysis by Labov (1969) to deal with contraction and deletion in the BEV copula. Labov proposed the addition of variable rules

2. I am reminded here of Galileo's arguments about the increased perceptual power of the telescope (cf. Feyerabend 1978: ch. 9). The problem with Galileo's experience with the telescope was that the principles of telescopic vision were initially not well understood. Therefore, the first telescopic observations produced indeterminate and contradictory images which conflicted with phenomena which could be seen with the naked eye. What 'perceptual power' the Cedergren–Sankoff program has is focussed on the variable aspect of language.
3. It is quite possible that Labov *does* intend his comment in this sense, judging from his remarks elsewhere (cf. also Chapter 9 below).

to transformational grammar to account for the fact that the application of optional rules was subject to regular constraints of covariation between linguistic and non-linguistic features. Labov objected to optional rules on the ground that this notion of systematic variation was not captured, i.e. optional rules contained no instructions about when and how often they applied.

Sankoff (1974), who believes that variability is a central aspect of linguistic competence to be accounted for in the grammar, cites Labov's extension of the concept of 'rule of grammar' to include variable rules as the beginning of an important paradigmatic change. This change involves not only altered goals, data sources and theoretical content, but most importantly, analytical techniques. Since its use by Cedergren (1973), the Cedergren–Sankoff variable rule program has become perhaps the single most important tool of sociolinguistic analysis.

Labov first accounted for the probabilistic aspects of the BEV copula by using an additive model, in which the probability that a rule would apply in a given environment was considered to be the sum of the probabilities of the rule's application in each relevant environment as shown below.

Additive model

$$p = p_o + a_i + a_j + a \ldots$$

In this formula a_i is a fixed number which enters into the formula if and only if feature i is present in the environment, and p_o is an input common to all environments. This model was based on the statistical analysis of variance. It is important to note that the effect of a given feature depends only on its presence, and not on the other aspects of the environment.

It is now generally accepted by those using multivariate analysis (cf. e.g. Sankoff 1978) that a multiplicative model (i.e. where the probabilities assigned to the different features are multiplied rather than added), has advantages over the additive model in accounting for linguistic variation. The additive model often predicted application probability values outside the interval between 0 (when the rule never applies), and 1 (when the rule always applies) in certain cases when application frequencies were very different in different environments, or there were a large number of different environments, since the probabilities were added. The multiplicative model can be summarized in the formula below:

Multiplicative model

$$1 - p = (1 - p_o)(1 - p_i)(1 - p_j) \ldots$$

Again, p_o is an input probability common to all environments, and p_i is the probability of feature i, so that factor $(1 - p_i)$ is present or absent from the formula depending on whether feature i is present or absent from the environment. The value of p_i must lie between 0 and 1.

This model provides a means of taking into account whether it is the presence or absence of a particular feature which determines the application or non-application of the rule. This advantage is not introduced without cost, however, since there is a problem in deciding for a given rule whether it is the application or non-application probabilities which follow the multiplicative law. The main advantage of the multiplicative model is, by and large, that it predicts only probabilities between 0 and 1; although Cedergren and Sankoff (1974: 338) have claimed there is some theoretical advantage also. They say that the multiplicative model presents a very simple interpretation of the probabilistic component of linguistic competence. Labov's early work appears to lay a strong claim to the independent nature of variable constraints; and the multiplicative model meets the requirement of probability theory, that for a number of events to be mutually independent, the probability that all of them occur must be exactly equal to the product (rather than the sum) of all their individual occurrence probabilities.

The data from which these estimations of probability are made are of the type commonly used in cross-product analysis, i.e. observations of the frequency of occurrence of a given feature in relation to the total number of cases in which the feature could have occurred in a given environment. The Cedergren–Sankoff program is, therefore, essentially an estimation technique, which calculates the probabilistic aspects of a rule on the basis of frequency data. A maximum likelihood calculation finds the values of the coefficients which maximize the probability that the observed data would be produced by the model. The program also compares maximum likelihood solutions for an additive model as well as both application and non-application multiplicative models.

The use of the computer is a great advantage, since a number of features which might be relevant to a particular rule can be put through the computer and combined in different ways, so that the effects of the same feature can be observed over several different rules. Furthermore, other types of non-linguistic environmental features, such as stylistic ones, can be considered concurrently. The program also incorporates a procedure for assessing the degree of fit between the data and various models by comparing the predicted occurrences of rule applications to the observed occurrences in terms of chi-square.

Some misunderstanding has arisen over the role variable rules should play in the grammar, or in the competence of individuals/groups, owing to a confusion between probability and frequency or, more precisely, rule probabilities and rule frequencies. Some who have argued against variable rules (e.g. Bailey, DeCamp and Macaulay) object to them because it seems unrealistic to expect speakers to keep track of frequencies of rule applications, or children to acquire them etc.[4]

Cedergren and Sankoff attempt to disarm such objections by insisting on a clear distinction between probability and frequency. They accept the statistical definition of frequency as a random variable, i.e. one which cannot be predicted with 100 percent accuracy, and which varies somewhat between performances, and of probability as a fixed number, i.e. not subject to random variation. The Cedergren–Sankoff program estimates these probabilities on the basis of observed frequencies; therefore, Sankoff insists that rule probabilities are part of the competence of speakers and rule frequencies of performance.

Such arguments are counter-productive in the long run, since nothing would seem to be gained by trying to find out whether variable rules (or implicational scales, for that matter, cf. Bailey 1969a: 109) are part of the performance/competence of speakers, or are in the brain, and hence psychologically real.[5] These seem to me pseudo-issues, which detract both from goals of analysis and description as well as from what I consider to be the larger and more important issue, namely, what is the empirical status of sociolinguistics?

The only claim that I am prepared to support is that variable rules may have a place in the description of some aspects of the utterances of individuals/groups; and that the Cedergren–Sankoff program may be a valuable analytical device, which can be used without commitment to all of the claims which the supporters of the quantitative paradigm have put forward for it. Even if there is a mechanical analogue which does all the things the brain (or the competence of speakers) does, the model is not necessarily what the brain is like. In other words, I think that the program may have descriptive uses which do not necessarily entail the belief that

4. Macaulay (1976: 269), for example, says:
   > Something that has always worried me about the evidence uncovered in urban dialect surveys is how a speaker knows how to produce the appropriate percentage of, say glottal stops for his particular station in life.
5. An examination of 'psychological reality' arguments would take me too far afield here, but since they are beginning to appear more and more frequently in sociolinguistic literature (cf. e.g. Fasold 1978), I raise this issue again in the final chapter.

such quantitative relations are, as Labov (1969: 759) has maintained, 'the form of the grammar itself'. Similarly, speakers of a language may behave as if they 'know' the underlying probabilities associated with rules, but this does not demonstrate that such a thing as a variable rule must be a property of language, or even of grammars which describe language. Questions about the reality of theoretical entities confuse the acceptability of theories with the reality of the things that theories describe. The macro-problem which I see here for a sociolinguistic theory is whether we accept the assumption that languages exist in the real world in the same way as physical phenomena do and are therefore amenable to description by a grammar or theory of grammar incorporating probabilistic rules.[6]

7.2 Variable rule analysis of Middle Scots relative clauses[7]

Since the Cedergren–Sankoff variable rule program was originally designed to handle only binary variables, i.e. those with two variants only, some adaptation of the program was necessary to account for the three-way variation among WH, TH and ∅. This can be done by setting up models of variation which contain two rules (cf. Cedergren 1973). I will be using the following two models:

Model 1	Rule 1	WH → TH	/ X__Y
	Rule 2	TH → ∅	/ X__Y
Model 2	Rule 1	WH → ∅	/ X__Y
	Rule 2	WH → TH	/ X__Y

These models test two major issues in the description of variation in the relative system:

1 What is being deleted? WH or TH?
2. What kinds of rules, and how many, are needed to describe this process?

I will discuss briefly how the output of the program can be said to relate to the types of predictions made on the basis of the models I have set up. The data sets which serve as input to the program do not uniquely determine the estimated values of the parameters in the models. They determine only certain relationships among the parameters within the same factor group. The program assigns probability coefficients to each of the factors, which can then be ordered hierarchically in terms of their effect on

6. This issue has not really been discussed by the variationists except as it relates to the competence/performance distinction.
7. I would like to thank Norman Dryden for helping me set up this program at Edinburgh.

the application of a rule. This, then, is the evidence which the program produces, i.e. similarities and differences in the conditioning effects and their ordering from rule to rule in each model which has been proposed. Thus Labov claims to 'decide' what rule schemata are needed to describe certain processes on the basis of the ordering of variable constraints with respect to one another.

More specifically, Labov (1975a: 215) has stated that when a fit is obtained between the data and a proposed linguistic model, 'we can say that the hypothesis on which the model is erected is confirmed, i.e. that the synthesis of the rule schema is justified by the properties of the data itself'. Therefore, in this case, the choice between the two models for the relative system is based on the nature and ordering of the environmental constraints on the occurrence of TH and Ø forms, i.e. are these the same or different?

Model 1, for example, consists of two separate rules, so that two selection processes take place with variable inputs which may be different. Each rule may have the same or different sets of variable constraints governing its frequency of application. I have used the cover symbols X and Y to symbolize the possible conditioning factors; in this case, X refers to features of the antecedent, and Y to the syntactic position of the relative marker in the relative clause. The input to Rule 2 in this model, i.e. the deletion rule, is the output of Rule 1. If the process of deletion is best described as taking place by two steps, one of *that* creation (from underlying WH forms, assuming these are well motivated to begin with), followed by deletion, then we would expect that the program would generate a different set of probabilities for the constraints, and that the constraint hierarchies would not be isomorphic.

Model 2 also takes WH as the 'underlying' form. If two separate rules are involved, then it can be expected that the ordering of the constraints on each rule will be different. If their ordering is isomorphic, then Model 2 can be collapsed into one rule, which has only one variable input and one set of variable constraints. In this case TH and Ø are alternant outputs of the same rule, as shown below:[8]

8. I am assuming in both cases that WH is the underlying form, which is in accordance with the standard transformational account. Emonds (1970: 169f.) has assumed that all relative clauses in English are introduced by *that* and then go through a stage in which the NP coreferential with the head is pronominalized or deleted. In the case of pronominalization, WH-fronting applies, optionally pulling along a preceding preposition and replacing *that* in the relative clause with the relative pronoun WH. In the case of deletion, *that* introduces the surface relative. In both accounts, however, relative clauses are produced by the same basic strategy.

$$\text{WH} \rightarrow \left\{ \begin{matrix} \text{TH} \\ \emptyset \end{matrix} \right\} \Big/ \text{X\_Y}$$

I will also be using the program to study the effect of stylistic or extralinguistic factors on the application of the rules I have set up here. This can be done with the program providing that the linguistic and non-linguistic constraints have independent effects on variable rules. In general this has been the case, although there are exceptions (cf. Cedergren 1973). In this case since I will be using only one set of extralinguistic constraints at a time, rather than a number of factors such as age, sex and social class, etc., it might be considered unlikely that the linguistic and extralinguistic constraints will interact. This is, however, an empirical issue, and one of great relevance. Labov (1975b: 120) has claimed that we can use the program to test the independence of environmental constraints. I will suggest in Chapter 9 that this issue is of fundamental importance, since the assumption of non-interaction imposes a number of constraints on the possibilities for change, which Labov apparently has not considered.

Therefore, in the first instance, I will be using the program to isolate linguistic constraints only in order to see how strong these are before I add various extralinguistic factor groups to the analysis.[9] I will also use the program to analyze some data from two varieties of modern English, Scottish English and American English, for comparison. Finally, I will analyze some of the longer individual texts in more detail. In each case I have made a number of different runs of the data using different combinations of factors and different factor groups to determine which ones are the most relevant for dealing with the variation.[10]

In the first run of the program the data were considered in the aggregate, i.e. all forms of the relative were pooled according to the linguistic environ-

9. There are other methods of multivariate analysis which may be more suitable for handling data sets where interaction between factors is likely to occur. Naro (pers. comm.), for example, has been using multidimensional scaling in the analysis of the social conditioning of syntactic structure, as well as ANOVA (from the Statistical Package for the Social Sciences), which does an analysis of variance (cf., however, Rousseau and Sankoff (1978) who say it is inappropriate for linguistic data). I have not made use of the most recent developments in variable rule analysis here (cf. e.g. Sankoff and Labov 1979), but I do not think that this affects the line of inquiry I am pursuing. My argument has to do with the claim that the Cedergren–Sankoff program (or indeed, any mathematical model which generates probabilities, assuming that these methods are valid in their own right) can provide evidence which can be used to decide linguistic issues.

10. By isolating factors I could test for possible interaction effects among factors. If the linguistic constraints are pervasive, i.e. hold throughout the data, then similar results should obtain in each run of the data.

Table 7.1. *Linguistic constraints on the rules of relativization*

	Antecedent		Syntactic position			
Factors	A	I	S	D	T	O
Model 1						
Rule 1	0.90	1.00	0.99	1.00	0.88	0.97
Rule 2	0.62	1.00	0.08	0.87	1.00	0.58
Model 2						
Rule 1	0.45	1.00	0.08	1.00	0.98	0.68
Rule 2	0.00	0.53	0.78	0.62	0.15	0.74

ment they appeared in without regard to the text from which they were taken. Only two factors were of major importance:

1. the animacy of the antecedent (here coded as A, I); and
2. syntactic position of the relative marker in the relative clause (coded as subject = S, direct object = D, temporal = T, oblique (stranded prepositions) = O). The results are shown in Table 7.1.

In general, the application probabilities multiplicative model fits these data best as measured by the values of chi-square. In each case the values given in the tables are those which produced the best fit between the data and a particular rule of one of the models. In this instance, for example, the application probabilities produced the best fit for the rules of both models with the exception of Rule 2, Model 2, where the non-applications probabilities multiplicative model gave the best fit. In interpreting the results, it is the relative values of the probability coefficients and their ordering with respect to one another which is to be taken into consideration, rather than the absolute values associated with a given feature in a rule.[11]

In this case, since we are dealing with a large amount of data in every cell,[12] it can be expected that the data will converge quickly; and that if the effects of the linguistic constraints are robust enough, the four models, i.e. the two additive models (one which uses a maximum likelihood calculation and one which uses row averages) and the two multiplicative models, will

11. In other words, a factor with a value of 1.00 does not indicate that the rule applies 100 percent of the time (or conversely, a value of 0.00 does not mean the rule never applies), but merely that this factor is the strongest or most heavily weighted. The measure of chi-square is problematic (cf. n.9, this chapter); it is calculated on the basis of differences between expected and observed values. Its use in the program is for the purpose of choosing between models of variation, rather than the statistical significance of the degree of fit between the data and any one model. Therefore, this measure does not give us any absolute indication of the degree of fit.
12. This results from my conflation of the output of the individual texts.

coincide. This is the result I found here, although I have only presented the values for the multiplicative models. All four calculations produce essentially the same results; the factors which promote the application of the rule have the same hierarchy of effect.

For example, the effect of the animacy of the antecedent appears strongly in each rule in both models. In each case, inanimate antecedents favor the application of both rules more than animate ones. The effect is least strong in Rule 1, Model 1. When it comes to the ordering of the effects in a constraint hierarchy of syntactic positions, it can be seen that the results produced by the multivariate analysis support those of the frequency analysis; namely, the ordering of the effect of syntactic position is different for *that* and Ø, but the hierarchies are not inverses or mirror images of each other in Model 1. Model 2 is closer to the frequency analysis.

The two rules of *that* creation, Rule 1, Model 1 and Rule 2, Model 2, show that subject, direct object and oblique positions all favor *that* creation nearly equally. Model 1 shows in addition a fairly strong effect on the application of the rule for temporal deletion, although Model 2 does not. The constraints are quite clear for the deletion rules (Rule 2, Model 1 and Rule 1, Model 2); direct objects and temporals have nearly equal effect in promoting the rule, while oblique shows a slightly less strong effect, and subject position shows the weakest effect. The values in both rules are very similar.

On the basis of the analysis of the linguistic constraints alone, both multivariate and frequency analysis seem to support the notion that there are two separate rules involved, which operate independently to produce *that* and Ø. Although the rules could be collapsed into one on the ground that the *same* constraints apply in each case, the quantitative data do not support this decision, since the ordering of the constraints is *different* in each case. A collapsed rule would have no way of indicating this sort of observation. I will now analyze in more detail the extralinguistic effects on the application of these rules to determine what support they offer to this idea, and to see whether these constraints interact with the linguistic ones.

In the second run of the program I introduced extralinguistic considerations by coding each text as a separate factor. The linguistic constraints, however, remain the same. The following symbols were used to identify the seven texts in the sample:

M *The Scottish Correspondence of Mary of Lorraine*
Y *Ane Satyre of the Thrie Estaitis*
Z *The Bannatyne Manuscript*

Table 7.2. *Constraints on the rule of relativization in seven Middle Scots texts*

	Antecedent		Syntactic position			
Factors	A	I	S	D	T	O
Model 1						
Rule 1	0.00	0.50	0.44	0.27	0.00	0.00
Rule 2	0.65	1.00	0.16	0.90	1.00	0.60
Model 2						
Rule 1	0.54	1.00	0.20	1.00	1.00	0.61
Rule 2	0.00	0.43	0.45	0.20	0.00	0.00

	Stylistic category						
Factors	M	U	V	W	X	Y	Z
Model 1							
Rule 1	0.88	0.00	0.75	0.78	0.83	0.89	0.91
Rule 2	1.00	0.71	0.85	0.49	0.88	0.75	0.61
Model 2							
Rule 1	1.00	0.44	0.77	0.46	0.84	0.76	0.59
Rule 2	0.90	0.00	0.73	0.78	0.81	0.90	0.91

U Bellenden's *Boece*
V *Burgh Records*
W *Sheriff Court Book of Fife*
X *Acts of the Lords of Council in Public Affairs*

Again results are obtained which are acceptable and consistent as measured by chi-square and the coefficients produced for the *that* creation and deletion rules of both models. The best fit for the data is split between two models in this instance; and it is Rule 1 of Model 2 which fits the data best. The results seem to confirm the hypothesis that the linguistic constraints do not appear to interact with the extralinguistic ones. This interpretation is indicated by the fact that the probability coefficients assigned to the linguistic features do not appreciably change when extralinguistic constraints are added. The deletion rules of both models show that relative markers in temporal, direct object and oblique position are more or less equally likely to be deleted in the order T > D > O, while subjects inhibit deletion. In Table 7.1 the animacy of the antecedent appears to have more effect on the deletion rule than on the rule for *that* creation. Both inanimate and animate antecedents are likely to become *that*, with a preference for animate antecedents to favor deletion. Subjects and direct objects favor the rules of *that* creation in both models. The change of effect for temporals and obliques in Table 7.2 can be attributed to the fact that the cells for these data were reduced in size considerably by the addition of the seven extralinguistic factors.

The incorporation of extralinguistic factors into the analysis serves to emphasize the fact that the linguistic constraints remain largely the same for both rules. What changes is the input probability from one text to another (or in the speech community, from one social group to another). In this case all the texts except *Boece* promote the rules of *that* creation to a great extent, although official texts promote the application of the rule to a lesser extent than the verse texts (*Ane Satyre* and *The Bannatyne Manuscript*) and *The Scottish Correspondence*. The multivariate analysis again supports the evidence from the frequency analysis of Chapter 6, that style is an important factor in the usage of the relatives; it affects both the rules of *that* creation and deletion. Interestingly, *Boece* is clearly differentiated from all the other texts by having the least effect on the application of the *that* rule. This corroborates the observation made in the last chapter that Boece stands out from the other texts as stylistically different on the basis of its (relpro) index.

It is worth noting at this stage that, with the exception of *Boece*, the extralinguistic factors affect both rules in the same way, i.e. they promote the application of both rules, unlike the linguistic constraints, which are different for both rules. This suggests that if extralinguistic constraints are to be taken into account when setting up the rule(s) for relativization in English, then the collapsed schema I set up as an alternative to the second model at the beginning of this chapter is more appropriate (cf., however, the discussion in Chapter 8).

What appears to be stylistically diagnostic is the application of the deletion rules of both Models 1 and 2, where both WH → Ø and TH → Ø. In other words, more forms do not necessarily undergo the *that* creation rule, but more forms are deleted, either by the application of Rule 2 of Model 1 or by Rule 1 of Model 2. The feature which is correlated with the extralinguistic constraints in Model 1 is the ratio of deleted to original *that* forms, i.e. Ø/TH + Ø, which is the calculation employed in Rule 2 of Model 1. The fact that it seems to be *both* deletion rules which fit the data best suggests the interpretation that the route WH → TH is not necessary for deletion to occur (cf. also Table 7.4).

In the next run of the data I will attempt to show more conclusively that it

Table 7.3. *The effect of stylistic categories on the rules for relativization*

	Antecedent		Syntactic position			
Factors	A	I	S	D	T	O
Model 1						
Rule 1	0.00	0.50	0.43	0.26	0.00	0.22
Rule 2	0.60	1.00	0.16	0.89	1.00	0.50
Model 2						
Rule 1	0.50	1.00	0.20	1.00	1.00	0.55
Rule 2	0.00	0.44	0.44	0.15	0.00	0.10

	Stylistic category			
Factors	M	U	P	X
Model 1				
Rule 1	0.90	0.00	0.91	0.80
Rule 2	1.00	0.70	0.62	0.82
Model 2				
Rule 1	1.00	0.44	0.60	0.76
Rule 2	0.88	0.00	0.90	0.79

is the frequency of application of the two deletion rules which is stylistically diagnostic by grouping the individual texts into stylistic categories to maximize this effect. In the data which appear in Table 7.3, the linguistic constraints remain the same, while four stylistic factors are introduced. Bellenden's *Boece* and *The Scottish Correspondence* are kept as separate categories of prose texts since *Boece* behaves so differently. The results of this analysis, where the texts are grouped as shown below, are given in Table 7.3.

M *The Scottish Correspondence of Mary of Lorraine*
U Bellenden's *Boece*
P *Ane Satyre* and *The Bannatyne Manuscript*
X *Burgh Records*, *Acts of the Lords of Council* and *Sheriff Court Book*

In this analysis the best fit between the data and the rules exists again in Rule 1 of Model 2 in the applications model. The hypothesis that the application of the deletion rule is stylistically diagnostic also appears to be indicated by the *that* creation rule figures compared with those of the deletion rule. The three stylistic categories which favor *that* creation do so nearly equally, but in the case of the deletion rule, *The Scottish*

Table 7.4. *Constraints on the rules for relativization in quoted speech and narrative in 'Boece'*

	Antecedent		Syntactic position				Stylistic category	
Factors	A	I	S	D	T	O	Q	N
Model 1								
Rule 1	0.59	1.00	0.84	0.82	0.53	1.00	1.00	0.85
Rule 2	0.00	0.04	0.00	0.34	0.28	0.48	0.00	0.00
Model 2								
Rule 1	0.18	1.00	0.05	0.75	0.24	1.00	1.00	1.00
Rule 2	0.00	0.44	0.39	0.18	0.00	0.41	0.23	0.00

Correspondence promotes its application more than do the other two groups of texts.

The data from the analysis of extralinguistic constraints therefore support the conclusion that deletion is the result of the application of a rule zeroing WH and TH; and that this process can be handled by one rule. This, however, presents a dilemma, since the conclusion which is reached on the basis of an analysis of the linguistic constraints supports the distinction between the rules of *that* creation and deletion as two independent processes. This state of affairs seems to occur rather often in sociolinguistic analysis, although it is very frequently not mentioned or ignored; in some cases, it is commented on and then resolved in a manner which is quite contradictory to the data. I will discuss some of these cases in more detail after I have presented further analysis of the extralinguistic constraints on the rules.

In the next run of the data I considered Bellenden's *Boece* in more detail. The linguistic constraints were analyzed in the same way as before, but the text was divided into two parts: quoted speech within the narrative (Q) and narrative (N), which are two stylistic categories suggested by the frequency analysis in the last chapter. As can be seen from Table 7.4, the multivariate analysis supports these stylistic divisions. According to the probabilities in Model 1 the two parts of the text differ in the rate of application of the rule of *that* creation, but not deletion; while, in Model 2, there is a difference in the rate of application of the *that* creation rule, but the deletion rule applies equally for both. The best fit is split between applications and non-applications models, and the best fit occurs in Rule 1 of Model 2.

What is interesting in the analysis of *Boece* as a separate case is the

Table 7.5. *Constraints on the rules of relativization in 'The Bannatyne Manuscript'*

	Antecedent		Syntactic position			
Factor	A	I	S	D	T	O
Model 1						
Rule 1	0.00	0.73	0.95	0.75	0.00	0.75
Rule 2	0.61	1.00	0.27	1.00	0.93	0.36
Model 2						
Rule 1	0.55	1.00	0.28	1.00	0.80	0.38
Rule 2	0.00	0.65	0.95	0.73	0.00	0.75

	Stylistic category				
Factors	F	W	M	R	B
Model 1					
Rule 1	0.28	0.00	0.07	0.00	0.46
Rule 2	0.70	0.87	0.88	0.44	1.00
Model 2					
Rule 1	0.70	0.86	0.81	0.44	1.00
Rule 2	0.33	0.00	0.15	0.00	0.43

apparent violation of the non-interaction of constraints principle. If we examine the hierarchy of the effect of syntactic position, we see that it is the following (for the rules of *that* creation in both models): O > S > D > T; and (for the rules of deletion in both models): O > D > T > S. The ordering of the effects is different for all the positions in both rules except for the position which is lowest in the hierarchy (i.e. has the weakest effect). In other words, despite the difference in ordering of O, S, D in the *that* creation rule, T still has the weakest effect; in the deletion rules S still has the weakest effect. This re-ordering is possibly a reflection of non-native source.

The Bannatyne Manuscript was analyzed in a similar manner using the divisions of the compiler and the same linguistic constraints as before. The divisions in the manuscript are: Ballads of Love (B), Ballads of Wisdom and Morality (W), Merry Ballads (M), Religious Ballads (R) and the *Fables of Aesop* (F). The results are shown in Table 7.5.

In general the applications model provides the best fit for the deletion rules of both models; and the non-applications model provides the best fit for the rules of *that* creation. Rule 2 of Model 1 provides the best fit for

Table 7.6. *Linguistic constraints on the rules of relativization in Philadelphia English*

	Antecedent		Syntactic position			
Factors	A	I	S	D	T	O
Model 1						
Rule 1	0.00	0.61	0.70	0.88	0.00	0.94
Rule 2	0.00	0.01	0.00	0.43	0.64	0.45
Model 2						
Rule 1	0.00	0.04	0.00	0.44	0.35	0.46
Rule 2	0.00	0.47	0.69	0.81	0.00	0.86

Table 7.7. *Linguistic constraints on the rules of relativization in Scottish English*

	Antecedent		Syntactic position			
Factors	A	I	S	D	T	O
Model 1						
Rule 1	0.90	1.00	1.00	1.00	0.89	1.00
Rule 2	0.00	0.04	0.00	0.45	0.90	0.01
Model 2						
Rule 1	0.54	1.00	0.30	0.68	1.00	0.23
Rule 2	1.00	0.50	1.00	1.00	1.00	1.00

these data. What is significantly different about the linguistic constraints which affect the rules of relativization is the probability coefficient associated with subject position (0.27 in Rule 2, Model 1) in comparison with the values in Table 7.1 (0.08). Both models also predict a very high rate of deletion for temporal relatives as well as for direct objects as expected.

7.3 Multivariate analysis of some data from modern English

This section reports the results of variable rule analysis for two sets of relative marker data taken from two varieties of modern English, Philadelphia English and Scottish English.[13] Only linguistic constraints are

13. The data for the Philadelphia sample consist of interviews with twenty speakers from South Philadelphia, Overbrook, King of Prussia and Havertown. The data for the Scottish English sample consist of interviews with teenagers in Tranent and Gracemount, and adults in the South side of Edinburgh. I would like to thank Keith Brown and Karen Currie for permitting me to use their data for the Scottish English sample; they are not responsible for the use I have made of them here.

Table 7.8. *Summary of the ordering of the linguistic constraints on the rules of relativization in Middle and modern Scots and Philadelphia English*

Sample	*That* creation	Deletion
Middle Scots	S > O > D > T	D > T > O > S
Modern Scots	O = D = S ≥ T	T > D > O > S
Philadelphia English	O > D > S > T	T > O > D > S

considered for the moment, although the data in both samples are taken from tape-recorded interviews in which the speech was characteristic of informal conversation.

Tables 7.6 and 7.7 show the results of variable rule analysis for these two samples from modern English. In each case, Rule 2 of Model 1 provides the best fit for the data, although the Philadelphia sample is best handled by the non-applications probabilities, and the Scottish English sample is best handled by the applications model for the rules of *that* creation and by the non-applications probabilities for the deletion rules.

These findings raise a number of interesting questions. What do these two data sets from modern English have in common with the data from Middle Scots, and what do they say about the nature of the rules of relativization in English? Are we able to say that there has been a change in the relative system from Middle Scots to modern Scots? And is there a difference between Scottish English and Philadelphia English? Table 7.8 summarizes the constraints on the rules for all the data analyzed so far.

Comparing for the moment the data from the Philadelphia speakers with those from the Scottish English group, we can see that Philadelphia English maintains a hierarchical ordering of the conditioning effect of syntactic position on the rule for *that* creation. In other words, in Scottish English the effect of syntactic position seems to have become generalized, so that all environments have an equally strong effect in promoting the application of the rule.

If we look at the findings for Middle Scots and both sets of modern data, there is a difference in the weighting of the syntactic positions D, S and O, but not T, with respect to each other in all three cases. The one constraint which seems to be binding for all three is the lesser effect of temporal position on the realization of relatives.

. A comparison of the results for the deletion rules reveals that the inhibiting effect of subject position on the deletion of relatives is the one constraint which is common to all three samples. Otherwise, O, D and T positions are ordered differently in all three. The modern dialects show a reversal of D and O position with respect to each other, while modern and Middle Scots show a reversal of T and D positions.

The results seem to indicate a decomposition of the rules by differential reweighting of the features which promote or inhibit the application of the rules. In the case of modern Scots, the differential effect of syntactic position seems to have become 'lost'. At any rate, this might be one conclusion which could be drawn from a Labovian or Baileyan interpretation of the implication of this pattern of variation, i.e. that linguistic systems change by successive reweightings of the environments in a rule. The problem is now to decide whether this is an adequate representation of change.

7.4 The contribution of extralinguistic constraints to the study of diachronic change

A very dangerous line of argumentation seems to have developed within sociolinguistics, both in the quantitative and dynamic paradigm, with respect to the nature of variation and change. For some, the implicational relationship between the two holds equally well in both directions so that not only does change imply variation, but also variation implies change. Most sociolinguistic studies in recent years are looking for, and usually report, instances of change in progress on the basis of differing rates of variation for age groups, social classes, etc., while relatively few studies have devoted themselves to the analysis of situations in which change does not occur. Cedergren's (1973) work on the aspiration and deletion of /s/ in Panamanian Spanish is a noteworthy counter-example to the general trend.

To some extent the analytical tools of both these paradigms have been responsible for the bias of interest in the direction of language change. Both implicational scaling and the Cedergren–Sankoff program run the risk of exaggerating or imputing dynamic qualities to situations which may well have exhibited stable variability over centuries. One particular problem inherent in the construction of the Cedergren–Sankoff program is its one-sided emphasis on and abstraction from the variable aspect of language. I would also like to suggest that studies which do not take into account stylistic factors (or indeed any extralinguistic dimension which is observed to condition the rate of application of linguistic rules) run this risk. It is

Table 7.9. *Summary of the interaction of extralinguistic factors on the ordering of linguistic constraints on the rules of relativization*

Data set	*That* creation	Deletion
Middle Scots (all texts)	S > O > D > T	D > T > O > S
Four stylistic categories	S > D > O > T	T ≥ D > O > S
Boece	O > S > D > T	O > D > T > S
The Bannatyne Manuscript	S > D ≶ O > T	T > O > D > S
Philadelphia English	O > D > S > T	T > O > D > S
Modern Scots	S = D = O > T	T > D > O > S

within this context that I see the relevance of sociolinguistic theories (but only, I will stress, if these are truly integrative) of language change and variation and the application of quantitative methods to historical linguistics.

Whatever decisive (and I use this term here in Labov's sense) power such quantitative data have lies not so much in the observation of variation, but rather in the similarities and differences in the conditioning effects, and their ordering in relation to one another from speaker to speaker, dialect to dialect and from one time period to another. If we accept Labov's and Bailey's views, then in the case of variation in the relative system we have an instance of linguistic change. Two questions arise: Can linguistic systems change by means other than successive reweightings of linguistic features? And can feature weights fluctuate in the way seen in Table 7.8 without necessitating change in the system? If the answer to either of these questions is yes, then there is no way that the program can 'decide', on the basis of the ordering of linguistic constraints, whether we are dealing with an instance of change.

One possible source of insight is a more careful examination of the extralinguistic constraints, both in Middle Scots and modern English, of the problem posed by interaction, and of the constraints that imposes on a theory of change. The results I have obtained question the assumption that linguistic and social constraints do not interact. If there were no interaction between the constraints, then we would have expected that all the texts in the sample would show the same hierarchy of linguistic conditioning effects. What would differ would be relative probabilities, but not their order with respect to one another. In Table 7.9 I have listed the constraint hierarchies for all the runs of the data to illustrate that the factors S, O and D undergo partial re-ordering from text to text in the *that* creation rule; and

Table 7.10. *Analysis of linguistic and extralinguistic constraints on the rules for relativization in modern English*

	Antecedent		Syntactic position			
Factors	A	I	S	D	T	O
Model 1						
Rule 1	0.88	1.00	0.96	1.00	0.83	0.91
Rule 2	1.00	0.92	0.20	0.74	1.00	0.58
Model 2						
Rule 1	0.95	1.00	0.14	0.86	1.00	0.66
Rule 2	0.83	1.00	1.00	0.93	0.41	1.00

	Stylistic category			
Factors	Q	N	E	P
Model 1				
Rule 1	0.92	0.73	1.00	0.92
Rule 2	0.84	0.41	1.00	0.97
Model 2				
Rule 1	1.00	0.62	0.84	0.32
Rule 2	0.77	0.79	1.00	0.89

the factors D, T and O undergo re-ordering with respect to each other in the deletion rule.

In the first rule what remains unaltered from one data set to another is the ordering of T, and in the second rule, it is the ordering of S. This can be taken to support the conclusion I reached in Chapter 6 on the basis of implicational scaling; namely, that in the deletion rule, there seemed to be no implicational ordering of the texts with respect to temporals and direct object position deletion of relatives. If we can find the same type of fluctuation in samples of modern data, then, I would suggest, there has been no change in the system; and thus, one way in which systems may remain stable is by fluctuation of feature weights in certain environments.

The problem here seems to be the modern Scots data, i.e. why is it different from both Middle Scots and Philadelphia English? One likely possibility, of course, is that I am dealing with a time gap as well as a stylistic one by comparing Middle Scots texts with modern spoken English. In the next tables I have presented some findings from the modern written language.

The data which appear in Table 7.10 are taken from modern Scots, written and spoken, which I have analyzed using the Cedergren–Sankoff

Table 7.11. *Stylistic continuum for the rules of relativization*

Rate of rule application	Is WH → TH > TH → ∅ ?	Is TH → ∅ > WH → ∅ ?
Style of text		
Middle Scots		
epistolary prose	–	=
poetry	+	=
legal prose	+	+
narrative prose	–	+
Modern Language		
modern Scots (spoken)	=	+
Philadelphia English (spoken)	–	+
modern Scots (writing)	+	–
modern Scots (quoted speech)	+	–

= represents more or less equal application; + represents higher; – represents lower

variable rule program. The linguistic constraints are the same ones which have been discussed so far, but the extralinguistic constraints are stylistic. In this case, E represents the data from modern Scots speech, analyzed in the tables above, while N represents a sample from the written language (a novel), and Q is a subsample of N, which contains instances of speech quoted in the novel. The novel in this case is *The House with the Green Shutters*.[14] The data for the Philadelphia sample is coded P and has been included for comparison.

The applications model fits these data best, and the deletion rules of both models produce the best results, although these are somewhat different in each case. In Model 1, modern Scots speech favors the application of the deletion rule most strongly, followed by Philadelphia English, quoted speech in the novel and narrative in the novel. In Model 2, the Philadelphia sample shows the least effect for the deletion rule, while the Scots sample of quoted speech and modern colloquial speech shows the greatest effect on the application of the rule. The modern spoken language also favors *that* creation quite strongly. The results suggest that the system of relative

14. I chose *The House with the Green Shutters* (as well as the other prose texts in my sample from the modern written language) because they make an attempt to portray some of the features of Scots speech in writing. This does seem to be indicated by the results in Table 7.12, where I have included some data from two Scottish newspapers for contrast. The latter are of course not Scots as far as language is concerned (with the possible exception of lexis), but belong to the more general category of formal writing in standard British English.

Table 7.12. *Sample of modern Scots: ordering of constraints for rules of relativization*

Data set	*That* creation	Deletion
1. Formal written		
Scotsman	D > S > O > T	no deletion
Evening News	O > D > S > T	D > O > T > S
2. Narrative in novels		
House with Green Shutters (Brown)	S > O > D > T	T > D > O > S
Sunset Song (Gibbon)	S > D > O > T	O > D > T > S
Boy Who Wanted Peace (Friel)	O > D > S > T	O > D > T > S
3. Quoted speech in novels		
House with Green Shutters	D > S > O > T	T > D > O > S
Sunset Song	S > D > O > T	O > D > T > S
Boy Who Wanted Peace	S > D > O > T	D > T > O > S
4. Spoken Scots	S = D = O ≥ T	T > D > O > S

marker variation and deletion is more complex than can be explained by either model. A stylistic continuum can be set up with respect to the relationship between the rates of applications of three rules, WH → TH, TH → ∅ and WH → ∅, as shown in Table 7.11. I have included both the Middle Scots and the modern data sets for comparison on the same continuum.

Before discussing the nature of the rules which will account for these complexities, I would like to present some more evidence from the modern language which supports my contention that variation in the relative system is an example of stable variation. Both in Middle Scots and the modern language there is fluctuation in the ordering of the constraint hierarchies. This can be seen in Table 7.12.

The conclusion which can be drawn from these results is that we are dealing with variation motivated by stylistic factors, which shows considerable fluctuation, but yet has remained stable for centuries. This suggests that although rule change may begin with an increase or decrease in the probability associated with an environment, which eventually leads to a re-ordering of some of the constraints in a hierarchy, change does not necessarily occur, i.e. variation of this type does not imply change.

If we examine all the results I have presented so far, they indicate that two rules seem to govern the distribution of the variants. One is a variable rule which deletes TH except in subject position. The other is a rule which

Table 7.13. *Summary of distribution of WH, TH and ∅ for all the data*

MIDDLE SCOTS

	Boece	*Acts*	*Burgh Records*	*Sheriff C.B.*	*Bannatyne*	*Satyre*	*Scottish Correspondence*
WH	55	17	18	10	9	5	7
TH	39	68	72	88	82	82	67
∅	6	15	11	3	10	12	27

MODERN ENGLISH

	spoken Phila.	Scots	written *Scotsman*	*E. News*	novels Friel	Brown	Gibbon	quoted F	B	G
WH	18	8	84	79	42	34	21	15	10	16
TH	56	60	16	15	32	44	71	50	49	60
∅	26	32	0	5	26	22	8	35	40	24

inserts WH forms. I have given a summary of the distribution patterns for WH, TH, and ∅ for all the data in Table 7.13.

One 'explanation' for contemporary variation reflects the history of the language. Two rules, or more appropriately perhaps, two strategies for relativization of different antiquity are competing for the same territory. The environments where they are both productive, i.e. overlap, is the area where the greatest variation exists. The primary strategy is a system which marks relative clauses by the subordinator *that*, which may be deleted variably, while the superimposed strategy is one of pronominalization. The historical account which I presented in Chapter 3 suggests that the WH strategy entered into the written language and worked its way down a stylistic continuum ranging from the most to least complex styles.

In fact if we examine Table 7.13 there seems to be a major break in the continuum between *Boece* and the rest of the texts. The boundary reflects native vs. non-native origin. *Boece* is characterized by its predominant use of the WH strategy, while the other native texts make greater use of the TH strategy. If we compare the results from the modern data with these, we can see a similar situation. Formal written language is characterized by its use of the WH strategy, while speech and the three modern Scots novels (with the exception of *The Boy Who Wanted Peace* by Friel) show much greater use of the TH strategy.

Table 7.14. *Variation in the relative system of Appalachian English* (*data from Hackenberg 1972*)

	Men	Women
	(% of variants)	
WH	6	13
TH	64	65
∅	31	22

One interesting question is whether there is a difference between Scots and English with respect to the use of the two relativization strategies. I think the data support the conclusion that the WH strategy never really entered Scots (either Middle or modern) to any great extent. Quirk's (1957) findings for modern spoken English are different from those I have reported here. The greater use of the WH strategy by Quirk's informants may reflect their social and educational background; or, in other words, the stylistic opposition of the two strategies may also be a marker of the social dimension of standard/non-standard.

Hackenberg's (1972) study of relative deletion in Appalachian English gives additional support to this conclusion. He finds that deletion is not diagnostic of social class; and this seems to be the case if we examine the raw data which Hackenberg has included in an appendix. I regrouped his data according to the sex of the informants and found quite a difference in men's and women's usage, which Hackenberg does not seem to have noticed. This can be seen in Table 7.14. If we look at the social backgrounds of both the men and the women who use the WH strategy, we find that they are mostly middle class people; and characteristically, it is only a few individuals out of the whole sample who use WH forms.[15] This is true of both the modern Scots and the Philadelphia sample.

My conclusion is, then, that it seems to be the use of the WH as opposed to the TH strategy which is socially and stylistically diagnostic, even more so perhaps than relative deletion (although it too is diagnostic, especially

15. In Hackenberg's (1972) sample, only one man (a 65 year old lawyer) produced more than several instances of *who* relatives; the other male informants use *which* or *what*, even with personal antecedents; but even these are infrequent by comparison with TH and ∅ forms. It is also interesting in this case that men typically use more ∅ forms than women, which is what we would expect if ∅ is a social and stylistic marker. (Compare my findings in Chapter 6 with regard to *The Scottish Correspondence*.)

subject relative deletion). There does seem to be an indication that Scots as a whole never adopted the secondary WH strategy, since more fully Scots styles of prose writing today are characterized by the use of TH and Ø. Without more data from a comparable stylistic continuum in English I cannot be certain that this is the case. It remains now to be seen how the results from the Cedergren–Sankoff program fit in with this interpretation and what sense they make in terms of Labov's and Bailey's theories.

The Cedergren–Sankoff variable rule analysis involves quite a few problems of interpretation. For one thing, a number of different probabilities may have either 1 or 0 as their total, so that multivariate analysis may conceal as much as it can reveal in some cases. The theoretical ramification of a probabilistic model such as the Cedergren–Sankoff program incorporates is that the variable rule cannot be falsified by observations which do not match its predictions. The only constraint on the power of the theory is the measure of chi-square.

In the case of relative marker variation, the values of chi-square do not argue conclusively for one or the other model of the two I have presented.[16] The best fit between the data and a rule is alternatively between the data and either Rule 2 of Model 1 or Rule 1 of Model 2. These are, of course, the two deletion rules; although in one case, the direct deletion of WH is allowed, while in the other, deletion is allowed only by way of *that*. This suggests the interpretation that the observed variation results from the interaction of two processes; or, in other words, there are two available routes to deletion. I will now try to show that this argument is not as implausible as it might at first sound.

If it is accepted that the route to deletion of relative pronouns follows the standard transformational account, i.e. a two-rule system in which the rules are ordered so that WH → TH and TH → Ø, it is difficult to explain why the data from Middle Scots and the modern language (both Scots and Philadelphia English) behave in a similar way with respect to the two deletion rules. Why does there appear to be some deletion of both WH and TH? It should not be surprising that the Middle Scots data seem not to fit this model of two successively ordered rules; but the fact that the modern data do not fit it either suggests an unaccounted-for change between the sixteenth century and the present day, if the standard model is adhered to.

16. Strictly speaking, of course, there is no justification (other than an arbitrary one) within probability theory for the assumption that a range of frequency statements fits one or another model to a greater extent. In Chapter 9 I discuss the specific use which the Cedergren–Sankoff program makes of the chi-square measure within the context of the implications of probability theories, and criteria for rejection/acceptance of statistical hypotheses.

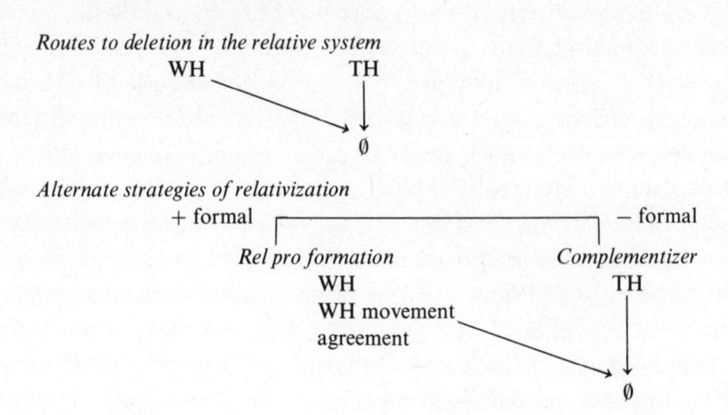

Figure 16

Yet the evidence presented here suggests that the same system of relativization has prevailed for quite some time with only slight fluctuations in the input probabilities of the deletion rules involved, and hence the subsequent relative levels of deletion. Historically speaking, WH was introduced into a system where *that* and ∅ existed in alternation; its effect on this system was to shift the balance of application of the rule TH → ∅ according to stylistic constraints, which are largely the same sorts of constraints that are found to be operating today.

In other words, what determines the direction or route of application as well as rate of application of the rules is a stylistic constraint which affects the treatment of relativization. In formal styles of language, the route to pronominalization may be selected (in which case, the rules of rel pro formation, WH movement, case and animacy agreement, etc. apply); in the other case, however, a factive or complementizer treatment of relativization is chosen so that *that* can then be deleted by the same route which is responsible for complementizer *that* deletion, as indicated in Figure 16.

There is a sense, however, in which it seems counter-productive to speak of deletion at all, particularly in the case of WH. The absence of WH forms in the modern spoken language (with the exception of Quirk's findings) is striking. The addition of the WH relativization strategy seems to have resulted in a 'squish' of two strategies which are opposed in stylistic meaning. In this instance, two strategies are available for doing the same syntactic operation.[17] The descriptive problem involved here is not an

17. Cf. Napoli (1977) for a discussion of a squish in relative clause formation strategies in Italian.

unfamiliar one: are we dealing with coexistent systems? Do we need to write separate grammars?

My results involve difficulties for both Bailey's and Labov's models of change and variation. The variable rule is geared towards the analysis of variation in speech communities where all the social groups use the variable concerned in the same way, though not necessarily to the same extent. Variable rule analysis is compatible with Bailey's wave model in that it produces multivalued scales, but in Bailey's theory no distinction is made between variation and change: all variation implies change.

The coherence of the concept of speech community as a group which shares both rules of grammar and norms for using them hinges upon a unidirectional model of variation. In discussing patterns of style shifting, Labov (1972a) says that each group of speakers shows regular style shifting in the same direction. The groups are different in the sense that they use the variable to differing extents, but they are all moving in the same direction. Even though a higher level group, socially speaking, will be nearer the norm, other groups will shift towards that norm in the same circumstances in which the upper group moves even closer to it. Since the lower groups are further removed from the norm in their ordinary speech, they shift to a much greater extent than the upper social group. This is one reason why greater variability is generally observed among the working than the middle class.[18]

In the next section I will argue that the variable rule model and the Cedergren–Sankoff model produce results which are incompatible with a truly integrative sociolinguistic theory and place arbitrary limitations on change. The latter constraint appears to be an artifact of a methodology which confuses the relationship between model and theory, and inconsistencies on Labov's part.

7.5 The relationship between model and theory

Earlier in this chapter I spoke of model – theory relationships and suggested that the relationship between the Cedergren–Sankoff program and Labov's theory of variation and change was not a true one, although the proponents of the quantitative paradigm seem to have assumed that it is. I am taking as my definition of a true model – theory relationship one which is current in the philosophy of science; namely, two systems which have the

18. I suggest in Chapter 9 that there is also another reason for this finding; namely, most of Labov's studies have focussed on the linguistic behavior of the working rather than the middle class.

same formal structure, i.e. there is a one-to-one correlation between the propositions of the theory and the model (cf. Braithwaite 1960: 90). Although models are of great value as convenient ways of thinking about the structure of theories, there is always the danger of confusing the two. Braithwaite (1960: 94) spells out the difficulties explicitly:

> there is a second danger inherent in the use of models, a danger which is more subtle than that of projecting on to the concepts of the theory some of the empirical features of the objects of the model. This danger is that of transferring the logical necessity of some of the features of the chosen model on to the theory, and thus of supposing, wrongly, that the theory, or parts of the theory, have a logical necessity which is in fact fictitious.

Both the issues that Braithwaite raises are problems here. Labov has argued quite strongly in a number of papers that social factors are operative in linguistic change (cf. Labov 1963 and 1972c especially). Yet the constraint on the non-interaction of linguistic and social factors imposed by the mathematical calculations of the Cedergren–Sankoff program is incompatible with a theory which assumes an integrative view of linguistic change, i.e. it assumes that linguistic and social factors interact to bring about change in the system.

Generally speaking, Labov seems to have tacitly assumed that all speakers of a speech community share the constraints of a variable rule, i.e. a variable rule is a rule of community grammar. Therefore, all speakers who belong to a particular sociolect do not differ in their use of a rule. Yet some of his data clearly show such interactions between social and linguistic constraints from individual to individual and group to group. Labov (1975b: 118–19), for example, has commented:

> The basic t/d constraints appear to be binding on all dialects, motivated by general phonetic and semantic principles. But when there is no clear linguistic motivation for one constraint or another predominating, we have the possibility of dialect differentiation.

Labov is referring here to the observation that the effect of a following pause on the rule of t/d deletion differs from dialect to dialect and, in some cases, from individual to individual. If, however, constraints are re-ordered for one individual or group, then the whole group or community must move in the same way; furthermore, if there is a shift in the feature weight of one context, this brings about a change in other contexts. If change typically begins as an increase in the frequency of application of a rule in one environment, as Labov suggests it does, this involves, as far as the program is concerned, a change in the weighting of other contexts. Therefore, in order for change to take place at all, the community must go through a stage in which it does not share the same constraints on the application of a rule; in this case, then, the grammar of a community cannot be described by one variable rule which all speakers use in the same way.

Kay (1978) has observed that the notion of community grammar is contradicted in a number of places by Labov's own data, and that Labov's conception of the mechanism of linguistic change depends on the interaction of linguistic and social constraints. He has therefore questioned whether variable rules are useful in modelling situations of linguistic heterogeneity in which there is on-going change. I think my results with the relative marker data indicate that Labov's concept of variable rule does not really apply adequately in situations of stable heterogeneity either. I will argue in the next chapter that my results are not atypical; they do, however, reflect a particular type of interaction between social and linguistic factors which is not well handled in a Labovian (or for that matter any unidirectional) framework.

Bailey also assumes that patterns of variation are the result of unidirectional change which begins variably and spreads (though sometimes in the 'wrong' direction according to Bailey's predictions, as I will show in Chapters 8 and 9). Nevertheless, if we are thinking in terms of modelling a socio-historical grammar to account for this particular case of variation in the relative system, the formal representation of the wave model in an implicational scale gives us a good graphic illustration of what is happening. Bickerton (1975) has also used this technique successfully in some cases in dealing with the acquisition of standard features of the acrolect by mesolectal speakers in post-creole continua, even though more than one direction of change may be involved, i.e. change is not always in the direction of the acrolect.

In fact, the analogy with creolization and decreolization, and other types of contact-induced change, is a useful one here.[19] In this case, the original native system, which marked relative clauses with TH or ∅ has been infiltrated by an alternate system. I suggested that the use of the case hierarchy with respect to the frequency with which NPs in certain syntactic

19. I do not wish to push this analogy with creolization as far as Bailey, for example, might. I do not imply by the use of my term 'acrolect' that English (either Middle or modern) is a creole of Neo-Latin, etc. The point I am making is that directionality of change can be a problem in Bailey's as well as Labov's theories (cf. also Chapter 9). A similar reservation applies in the case of my discussion of the similarities between the development of relativization in the post-creole continuum in Hawaii and in Old English. In other words, one need not conclude on the basis of such similarities that Old English was a creole.

positions are relativized as a complexity metric offers some insight into the process (cf. Chapter 6). The situation might best be described as an instance of 'syntactic diffusion'.

I have taken this term from Naro and Lemle's (1977) discussion of an instance of on-going change in Brazilian Portuguese. The particular problem they have studied is variability in subject–verb concord. At earlier stages of the language this rule was categorical; every verb agreed with its subject. In the modern language, however, the rule seems to be on its way out among the lower classes, who show from 10 to 60 percent agreement depending on stylistic factors. Factors which affect the output of the rule are morphological class of verb and surface position of the subject.

Naro and Lemle have suggested that a principle of 'phonic saliency' accounts for the variation. In other words, agreement is less probable precisely in those forms where its absence would be least salient; and it is in the most frequently occurring categories that the lowest probability of agreement is shown. Naro and Lemle claim that this pattern of variation and change is a universal principle determining the implementation of syntactic change. Their conclusion is that syntactic change tends to sneak through a language, manifesting itself most frequently under those circumstances in which it is least noticeable or salient.

They have presented this model of syntactic diffusion as a reasonable candidate for a universal of syntactic change, but have stressed the fact that it is intended to represent the implementation of *natural* syntactic change. They have hypothesized that syntactic change actuated by learned reaction or hypercorrection would work in the opposite way, i.e. would manifest itself first in the most salient environments. This appears to be equivalent to Bailey's view that the direction of natural change is from the most marked to the least marked environment; in creolization the order is reversed.

This interpretation makes some sense here. In Chapter 6 I argued that WH relatives seem to have entered the language in the most complex and least frequently relativized syntactic positions in the case hierarchy (cf. Table 6.11). In Table 7.15 I show in detail how this process of diffusion relates to the stylistic dimension of my study.

This pattern raises an interesting question: is this an instance of natural syntactic change (in Naro and Lemle's terms) or of hypercorrection? The infiltration of WH into the relative system can be seen as completed in the modern written language, at least as far as the more formal styles of writing are concerned; but it has not really affected the spoken language. The entrance of WH by way of the most complex styles of writing and syntactic

Table 7.15. *Implicational scale for the entrance of WH relatives into English*

Text	Syntactic position			
	Gen.	Obl.	Dir. Obj.	Subj.
Scotsman	W	W	W	W
Evening News	W	W	W	W
Boece		W/TH	W/TH	W/TH
Sheriff Court Book	W	W/TH	W/TH	TH
Burgh Records	W	W/TH	W/TH	TH
House with the Green Shutters (N)	W	W/TH	W/TH	TH
Acts of the Lords of Council	W	W/TH	TH	TH
The Bannatyne Manuscript		W/TH	TH	TH
Ane Satyre		W/TH	TH	TH
The Scottish Correspondence		TH	TH	TH
House with the Green Shutters (Q)		TH	TH	TH
Philadelphia English		TH	TH	TH
Scottish English	TH	TH	TH	TH

W = 75% or more WH forms; TH = 75% or more TH forms; W/TH = 25–75% TH forms

positions does suggest a pattern of external prestige borrowing, or 'change from above' in Labov's terms. In this case, even though WH is internal to the system, its use as a relativizer can be thought of as a borrowing from a Romance acrolectal adstratum in Middle English. These results add support to Mustanoja's (1960) belief that French and Latin influence prompted the adoption and strengthening of the use of the WH relatives (cf. also 3.3). They also offer an 'explanation' for the lag of the relative *who* in the nominative; subject position relatives are the most frequently occurring and least syntactically complex, and therefore last to yield to the WH system. Quirk's conclusions about the use of the relative system in modern spoken English reflect the educational background of his informants, who speak standard English and are closer to the norms of the written language; while the data I have presented here from Scots and Philadelphia English are closer to a more colloquial or vernacular norm.

If we examine the data in Table 7.15 more closely, there seem to be at least two important breaks in the continuum. The first is obviously between the first two samples from modern writing and the rest of the continuum; and the second occurs between narrative prose (i.e. *Boece*) and the rest of the texts. The second boundary reflects native vs. non-native origin (cf. Table 7.13). The narrative prose text in the sample is characterized by its predominant use of the WH strategy, i.e. some WH forms appear in all syntactic positions, while the native texts make greater use of the TH strategy.

If we compare the modern data with the Middle Scots data, we can see a similar situation. Formal written language is characterized by its greater use of the WH strategy, while speech and quoted speech within the novel show much greater use of the TH strategy. It is also interesting to note that a third break in the continuum occurs after *Ane Satyre*, as we move closer to the samples from the modern spoken language. Both Middle Scots epistolary prose and quoted speech within a novel are similar to the modern spoken language with respect to their use of relativization strategies. Modern spoken Scots stands out from all the samples by virtue of its predominant use of the TH strategy in *all* syntactic positions, including the genitive, where it preserves the native option of using the primary (i.e. historically older) strategy. What we see in this implicational scale, then, is a process of syntactic diffusion repeating itself in successive stages of the language in response to stylistic constraints. My results suggest that within the larger context of the history of Scots and English we must recognize stylistic stratification as an important factor in both language maintenance and shift.

7.6 Implications for synchronic and socio-historical grammars

Although this case provides a good argument for Labovian sociolinguistics in one respect, i.e. it demonstrates that syntactic change, like phonological change, may manifest itself gradually and variably in response to social and stylistic factors, it is very awkward in other ways. We can see why if we consider how this change would be represented in a formal rule of community grammar.

Generative views on relativization (whether in standard or extended standard theory) are based on the derivation of both WH and TH strategies from the same underlying source. For example, within EST (extended standard theory) they are generated under the node COMP. Now COMP could be deleted in situ (cf. e.g. Bresnan 1977), which would allow for the derivation of the zero marked clauses; or it could be filled by WH or optionally realized as *that* by deletion of WH and *that* insertion (cf. e.g. the account in Chomsky 1977). Thus, the following would constitute an acceptable formal representation of the rule deriving relative clauses.

Rule of WH movement

	NP	$[_S$ COMP	X	rel	Y]		
	1	2	3	4	5	→	
	1	2	3	∅	5	→	deletion in situ
or	1	4	3	∅	5		movement (COMP filled by WH or deletion of WH and *that* insertion)

Emonds similarly (1970: 169) posits a single derivation in which all relative clauses are introduced by *that* and then go through a stage in which the NP coreferential with the head is pronominalized or deleted. Either approach allows for the fact that WH, TH and *for* are now mutually exclusive in surface COMP position, which is due, in Lightfoot's (1979) view, to a reformulation of the WH movement rule in the history of English.

Alternatively, one might adopt an analysis whereby relativization is described as a process of copying and deletion. Schachter (1973), for example, has argued that relativization involves the promotion of material from an embedded into a matrix sentence. Promotion is defined by Schachter as a syntactic process by means of which a constituent of an embedded sentence fills an empty slot or replaces a dummy symbol in a matrix S. This differs from the standard transformational view presented in Chapter 2 in that, in the latter, the matrix S is not considered to have an empty slot. Although in both analyses there is a matrix as well as an embedded S, the standard view does not allow for the promotion of material, and relativization is carried out by meeting identity conditions.

The basic syntactic operation which is necessary in Schachter's analysis is copying, whereby a copy of a constituent of an embedded S is inserted into the matrix where it replaces a dummy symbol. Within the embedded sentence itself then, the constituent that has been copied is either replaced by a relative pronoun or is deleted. This is a much less circuitous procedure than that of inserting a relative pronoun and then deleting it (cf. Lightfoot's remarks on deletion (1979: 328)). In these terms there is no process of relative pronoun deletion, only relative pronoun insertion, or deletion of the constituent after it has been copied. This is similar to trace theory proposals about relativization (cf. e.g. Stockwell 1977), in which relativization is seen as a rule which leaves as its trace a shadow pronoun in the former place of a promoted NP. The pronoun can subsequently be deleted by a rule of shadow deletion.

There is, however, no reason to assume that relatives must be treated as embedded material at all. In the conjunction analysis of relativization which Thompson (1971) has proposed, a similar account to the one above may be provided by claiming that the logical structure of relative clauses is that of coordinate sentences which share a referring expression. If a coordinate focussing rule is applied, then one of the coordinate clauses is shifted to the background with respect to the other one, which then becomes the main predication. This notion is also contained in Schachter's analysis. He suggests that the semantic correlate of the syntactic process of promotion (which is the syntactic common denominator of both focus and relative constructions) is the division of the sentence into two parts which are assigned different degrees of communicative importance: foregrounding, which deals with new information; and backgrounding, which deals with presupposed information.

Scots poses problems for the EST version of the rule in that EST holds strictly to the autonomy thesis, which says that syntactic rules are unaffected by considerations of meaning or use. Thus the rule which deletes either WH or *that* cannot be constrained by the kinds of social and stylistic factors I have discussed here, i.e. the rule should not have to be stated to apply differentially in different syntactic environments in response to stylistic constraints. What determines the rate as well as surface realization of COMP is a variable social and stylistic constraint. If the rule of WH movement applies without constraint, i.e. in conformity with the autonomy thesis, it will generate sentences which are unacceptable. If EST rules are not context-sensitive, and transformations have to apply without exception, one has to appeal to some independent principle to rule out cases of overgeneration, i.e. something outside the formalism or system within which the rule operates (cf. the discussion of a similar problem of overgeneration in Hopi relative clauses by Hale, Jeanne and Platero 1977).

Within the variable rule framework, however, we can allow for precisely this sort of conditioning by adding variable constraints to build in the rate factor for optional rules, which would then handle the surface distribution of the strategies in their appropriate syntactic positions and styles. This is basically a technical solution and ignores the incompatibility of variable rules with generative grammars (cf. Chapter 9 and Romaine 1981a). However, patching up EST by reformulating a categorical rule as an optional, variable one or adding variable constraints does not solve the problem entirely, for there are some speakers of modern Scots who never use the WH strategy of relativization. If that is the case, then why should these speakers have any formal provision for the generation of WH under COMP? Is there a meaningful sense in which we can say that these speakers who do not use the rule share a rule of community grammar with those who do use it? The Scots data argue strongly against a sociolinguistic theory tied too closely to generative grammar and to Labovian notions of the speech community. We cannot account for the use of relative clause formation strategies in terms of a variable rule which is used by the Scots speech community in the same way.

A consideration of my results in the light of the socio-historical context of Scots indicates that we are in fact dealing with coexistent systems. We need at least two rules, one of which adds a WH strategy to the grammars of some speakers. The modern system's complexity reflects the fact that it is a conflation of what were historically two separate systems. This would argue against a formal account of relativization from the same basic strategy; in spite of possible counter-arguments to the effect that a common derivation makes for a simpler and neater description in purely linguistic terms (which I would not deny), I would say that social factors should receive equal consideration with linguistic ones (cf. Romaine 1980a).

8 *The bearing of sociolinguistic data on linguistic hypotheses*

> If you can't prove what you want to prove, demonstrate something else and pretend they are the same thing.
>
> Darrell Huff (1973: 72)

In the preceding chapter I attempted to apply variable rule analysis to a specific test case, variation in the relative marker system, to see if there was any justification for the claim that the Cedergren–Sankoff program can demonstrate a convergence between formal rule schemata and quantitative data. The results of the analysis were indeterminate and difficult to interpret, but they were indicative of problems in Labov's theory of variation and change. My data might be thought to be in some sense atypical and consequently my findings to be atypical also, but I will argue that this is not the case. In this chapter I focus on the empirical and ontological status of some of the so-called decisive solutions which have been proposed in sociolinguistic theory to show that there are indeterminacies as well as inconsistencies in a number of these analyses. I take up first Labov's (1969) analysis of the copula in BEV as a case in point. I mentioned in Chapter 2 that it was in this paper that Labov argued most forcefully for a program of empirical research which would produce decisive and correct solutions. I will demonstrate that the analysis Labov presents is not necessarily the 'right' one based on the quantitative data.

8.1 Labov's analysis of contraction and deletion of the copula in BEV

Labov decided to treat contraction and deletion of the BEV copula as two separate rules which were ordered so that contraction preceded deletion. Two major linguistic constraints were found to be relevant to the application of both rules: 1. preceding environment – either NP or Pro form; and 2. following environment – NP, PA (predicate adjective), LOC (locative), Vb + ing (progressive verb form) and Gn (*going to* verb form).

Table 8.1. *Contraction and deletion of the BEV copula: Labov's Case 1 – contraction followed by deletion; and Case 2 – deletion followed by contraction* (*N in parentheses*)

Environment	__NP	__PA	__LOC	__Vb + ing	__Gn
CASE 1					
1. contraction	63 (235/373)	66 (138/209)	79 (55/70)	92 (84/91)	98 (57/58)
2. deletion	51 (119/235)	54 (75/138)	65 (36/55)	80 (67/84)	95 (54/57)
CASE 2					
1. deletion	32 (119/373)	36 (75/209)	52 (36/70)	74 (67/91)	93 (54/58)
2. contraction	48 (116/244)	47 (63/134)	56 (19/34)	65 (17/26)	76 (3/4)

Labov's claim that contraction and deletion are two separate but similar rules which apply in the order stated is based on two aspects of the variable constraints which affect the rules. Firstly, he observed that the effect of the preceding environment operated differently in the case of contraction and deletion so that a preceding vowel favored contraction and a preceding consonant favored deletion. Secondly, he found that the constraints for the following syntactic environment applied to both contraction and deletion, but were ordered identically, so that deletion was the result of a more exaggerated or double operation of the constraints on contraction.

After deciding to keep these two rules separate, Labov then cites quantitative evidence as the basis for ordering the rules so that deletion applies after contraction. He specifically rejects an analysis in which deletion is ordered before contraction on intuitive grounds. If, however, the data are manipulated to fit different rule orderings, it becomes evident that the quantitative cumulative output of each rule will be the same regardless of the order in which the rules apply. The variable inputs of the individual rules would have different frequency values, but the constraint hierarchies would remain unaltered; and it is the latter fact which is important, at least according to Labov's predictions about change.

Table 8.1 shows Labov's data (1969: 732, Table 2), which gives the percentage of full, contracted and deleted forms of *is* according to the grammatical category of complement which follows. Since Labov does not give the numbers in all cases, and does not consider what would happen if the rules were ordered in reverse fashion, I have calculated the numbers of

Table 8.2. *Comparison of different rule orderings for relativization: Case 1 –* that *creation followed by deletion; and Case 2 – deletion followed by* that *creation (% of rule applications)*

Environment	Temp.	Dir. obj.	Prep.	Subj.
CASE 1				
1. *that* creation	80	89	88	86
2. deletion	44	35	18	5
CASE 2				
1. deletion	35	31	15	5
2. *that* creation	74	83	84	77

tokens behind the percentages for the Jets (one of the groups of teenagers whom Labov studied), and compared these with the figures which obtain when the rules are ordered as Labov claims they are.

It can be seen that the consequence of ordering contraction after deletion is a change of the frequency levels of application of both rules, but that the ordering of the environments in a constraint hierarchy is unaffected. In other words, no matter which rule is applied first, the constraints affect it in the same way, although not to the same degree.

This example shows, I think, that the quantitative data are indeterminate with respect to the issue of rule ordering. In fact, if similar calculations are performed for the relative data, where the rules for *that* creation and deletion are reversed, the net effect of the constraint of syntactic position is unaltered. In this case, the consequence of ordering deletion before the rule for *that* creation is like that of ordering deletion before contraction in Labov's. The cumulative output is the same regardless of the order in which the rules apply (see Table 8.2).

The conclusion which can be drawn from both these examples is the same: the quantitative data of variation argue that the grammar by which they are to be described is one in which the order of application of the rules does not matter. I submit this as evidence against Labov's (1969: 715) claim to have presented a method 'for the decisive solution of abstract questions of rule form and rule relations, based upon the direct study of linguis c behavior'.

There is also good evidence from creole studies to indicate that Labov s rules for contraction and deletion of the copula 'go the wrong way'.

Bickerton's (1975) work on Guyanese creole, for example, supports the theory that speakers sometimes start with the Ø forms and introduce the copula later, i.e. in the mesolect. Only in the mesolect does it make sense to speak of 'copula deletion' (cf. Bickerton 1975: Table 3.5, 1973a: Table 3).[1]

In the implicational scale which Bickerton (1972) presents for the distribution of copula forms in the mesolect, the 'true' copula enters the system in isolect E where *iz/waz* forms are present. Zero forms are thus 'created' in the mesolect through the addition of an opposition which did not exist before in the system. The jump from the basilect into the acrolect or upper mesolect occurs when *iz/waz* are introduced into the grammar in isolect D; zero forms enter there into contrast with *iz/waz*. These data call Labov's analysis of the BEV copula into doubt, since they suggest that perhaps *complication* of the system through the introduction/acquisition of the copula rather than the *simplification* of the grammar through copula deletion may be the more reasonable analysis in both Guyanese creole and BEV (cf. Romaine 1979b).

The problem with Labov's analysis is that he has assumed that the most complex form is the underlying one and then has simplified it by deletion. But if there is no real basis for arguing from the quantitative data to a uniquely ordered set of rules, then there does not seem to be any good counter-argument to adding the full and contracted forms later in the grammar, as a sort of adstratum which the speaker approaches as he acquires the standard forms of the acrolect. Labov, however, is not alone in using the evidence of variable constraints in arguments of this type.

8.2 The use of variable constraints in linguistic argumentation

Wolfram (1975) has discussed both Labov's study of contraction and deletion of the copula, and his own (1973) analysis of post-vocalic/post-consonantal t/d deletion in Puerto Rican English (PRE), in order to illustrate that variable constraints can provide formal motivation for treating linguistic processes as unitary or disparate.

He claims that in each case, if independent tabulations of the two processes show the constraint hierarchies to be isomorphic, then the decision to treat t/d deletion and /d/ devoicing on the one hand, and contraction and deletion of the copula on the other, as part of the same process, is

1. Some of these copula tables are given in the Excursus to Chapter 6.

justified. In other words, the constraint hierarchies should match in both cases for both rules.

I give three rules for t/d deletion for comparison:

1. Post-consonantal t/d deletion (from Shiels 1972: 237)

$$\begin{bmatrix} -\text{voc} \\ +\text{cons} \\ -\text{cont} \\ \alpha\,\text{voice} \end{bmatrix} \rightarrow (\emptyset) \Bigg/ \begin{bmatrix} +\text{cons} \\ \alpha\,\text{voice} \\ \Delta(+\text{cont}) \end{bmatrix} \underline{\Gamma}\,(-\,\#)\,\_\_ \begin{matrix} \text{A}([+\text{cons}]) \\ \\ \text{B}([-\text{seg}]) \end{matrix}$$

2. Post-vocalic t/d deletion (from Wolfram 1973: 146)

$$\begin{bmatrix} -\text{cont} \\ +\text{ant} \\ +\text{cor} \\ -\text{nas} \end{bmatrix} \rightarrow (\emptyset) \Bigg/ \begin{bmatrix} \text{V} \\ \Gamma\text{-stress} \end{bmatrix} \Delta\,\_\_ \begin{bmatrix} \text{B}\,\overline{+\,\text{voice}} \\ \text{E}\,-\,\text{past} \end{bmatrix} \#\#\,\text{A}\_\_\text{V}$$

3. Final t/d deletion (both post-vocalic and post-consonantal, from Labov et al. 1968)

$$[-\,\text{cont}] \rightarrow (\emptyset) / \langle +\,\text{cons} \rangle \langle \emptyset \rangle \,\_\_\, \#\# \langle -\,\text{syll} \rangle$$

The constraints on the application of these rules can be summarized as follows:

1. Shiels
   - i. following consonant
   - ii. following pause
   - iii. preceding non-morpheme boundary
2. Wolfram
   - i. following consonant
   - ii. deletable C is voiced
   - iii. deletable C in unstressed syllable
   - iv. preceding non-morpheme boundary
   - v. deletable C part of a derived adjective
3. Labov et al.
   - i. preceding consonant
   - ii. following consonant
   - iii. preceding non-morpheme boundary

The differences among the three constraint hierarchies are in three areas: 1. the voicing constraint operates on the post-vocalic deletable consonant, but not on post-consonantal consonants; 2. the effect of stress is not mentioned by Shiels or Labov et al.; and 3. the constraint of a preceding non-morpheme boundary is ordered differently depending on the rule. Wolfram takes these differences as sufficient evidence to argue for the separation of the two rules, since the collapsed version, i.e. the more general one of Labov et al., obscures and even fails to note crucial differences in the constraint hierarchies of post-consonantal t/d deletion.

Wolfram suggests then that the decision to collapse or separate rules be based on tabulations of separate hierarchies as I have just illustrated; and if the hierarchies differ, as they do here, then the rules should be considered disjoint. Wolfram's conclusion, however, could only have resulted from some a priori hypothesis or decision as to the possible separateness of the rules, which presumably underlay the separate tabulation in the first place. In other words, this indicates that the decisions of both separation of rules and rule orderings are taken very early in the analysis, i.e. when the decision is taken as to what to count and how to count it.

If this is the case, then the following claim by Labov (1975a: 196) about the decisive power of quantitative data is suspect:[2]

> quantitative synthesis, which follows measurement, can give us the objective justification we need; we can show that our rule synthesis is a property of the data itself, and not the result of habit, ideology, or speculative assumptions about the human brain.

I leave aside for the moment the ontological status of such a claim and turn to the problem of inconsistency in argumentation based on variable constraints. With respect to this issue, both Labov and Wolfram are guilty.

In the same paper on contraction and deletion, Labov (1969) also proposed that copula deletion is derived from a process of /r/ vocalization and subsequent post-vocalic schwa loss, which is also responsible for the presence of forms like /po/ for *poor*, etc. Wolfram, however, justifiably argues that on the basis of the ordering of the variable constraints involved in both instances, which are different, the two processes are disparate in some way, and hence should be kept separate.

My point, however, is this: In one case Labov has claimed that contraction and deletion were separate on the basis of the ordering of the variable constraints, but has then ignored similar evidence in collapsing the rule for deletion with /r/ vocalization in order to show that contraction and de-

2. Even if Labov were methodologically consistent in his use of the evidence from variable constraints as a basis for choosing among competing analyses, I would not accept his claim that any rule synthesis or quantitative representation of sociolinguistic data is a property of the data itself. Variable rules can, of course, be properties of models; but there can be no basis for assuming that hypothetical mechanisms of a model can be candidates for reality in this case. Labov's comment also implies that there can be such a thing as theory-free observation (cf. Chapter 1; Lass 1976c).

letion were manifestations of a more general phonological process, which was responsible for the loss of post-vocalic word-final /r/, even though some of the constraints were different.

Cedergren's (1973) study of a number of variable rules in Panamanian Spanish deserves mention here, since her arguments are, by comparison with Labov's, much more consistent, even if less economical. Cedergren decided to treat variability in Panamanian Spanish /s/ as a two-rule process of aspiration and deletion (largely on the basis of historical considerations), but her analysis reveals that the deletion rule shows a complete reversal of the order of phonological constraints in effect for the rule of aspiration. Later she describes /r/ variation as the result of a similar two-rule process of aspiration and deletion in which /ṙ/ → /h/, and then /h/ → ∅.

She rejects, however, a solution in which only one rule of /h/ deletion is incorporated into the grammar of Panamanian Spanish, applying both to the /h/ generated by the application of the rule /s/ → /h/ and the one from the rule /ṙ/ → /h/. She argues (1973: 113) that not only would one rule of /h/ deletion provide no information about the intricate patterning of linguistic as well as extralinguistic constraints affecting the variable, but also that the relevant environments for both rules are different (cf. Longmire 1976: 141).

The aspiration rules for /s/ and /ṙ/, on the other hand, revealed the same order of phonological and boundary effects, which would support one variable rule of aspiration in Panamanian Spanish. This rule would operate on the general class of coronal, strident continuants. Cedergren rejects this generalization on the grounds that it is doubtful whether this rule clarifies the process either at high levels of linguistic abstraction or in its application in the speech community. Cedergren's decision raises the very important issue of whether extralinguistic constraints are to be given any consideration in setting up rule schemata and relations among them and, if so, how much? This question has also received contradictory treatment in a number of sociolinguistic analyses.

8.3 The role of social factors in linguistic descriptions and argumentation

For sociolinguists working within the quantitative paradigm, the assumption now seems to be that one of the most important questions to be answered is not whether linguistic rules are affected by social constraints, but rather what place social factors have in a linguistic description of change and variation. I will now take up one aspect of this problem;

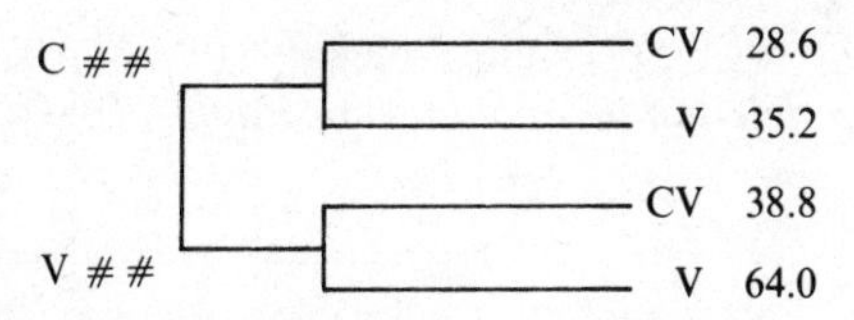

Figure 17 Hierarchy of linguistic constraints on initial unstressed syllable deletion in Appalachian English (figures are %)

namely, to what extent should social information be incorporated into linguistic description?[3]

The thrust of my argument will be that if we accept the strongest possible claim about the degree to which social conditioning factors are operative in linguistic processes, then social as well as linguistic constraints can have a place in linguistic argumentation. This seems to be the position espoused (in principle, at any rate), by Cedergren and Sankoff (1974: 334):

> Once accepted and incorporated into description, variability can be made a function not only of the presence or absence of linguistic elements but also can be constrained by extralinguistic factors, all within the same notational framework.

Wolfram and Christian's (1976) analysis of *a*-prefixing in Appalachian English implies that extralinguistic constraints on the application of rules do not carry any weight. They present the view that *a*-prefixing (a term which the authors use to describe the *a*-prefix that occurs with *-ing* participial forms such as *a-coming*) is the result of a more general phonological process which deletes unstressed syllables. The application of this rule produces such stereotypes as *'maters* – 'tomatoes', as well as other reduced forms such as *'cause* – 'because', *'round* – 'around', etc., which are common to casual styles of speech in most other varieties of English.

An examination of the variable linguistic constraints involved in these two processes, *a*-prefixing and deletion of unstressed syllables, reveals that less *a*-prefixing occurs following a vowel, which is the same linguistic constraint that favors deletion for unstressed syllables (especially in initial V syllables). Figure 17 shows a constraint hierarchy which I have constructed on the basis of the figures Wolfram and Christian (1976: 52) present for the deletion of initial unstressed syllables. (No comparable figures are given for *a*-prefixing.)

Wolfram and Christian then propose the following variable rule to

3. I have presented this argument in a slightly different form in Romaine (1979c).

Table 8.3. *Variable rule analysis of linguistic constraints in* a-*prefixing and initial syllable deletion in Appalachian English* (*non-applications model*)

	Grammatical category		Syllable type			Preceding environment	
				non-ing			
Factors	-ing	non-ing	-ing	V	CV	V	C
	0.72	0.00	0.00	0.13	0.00	0.35	0.00

account for both *a*-prefixing and the deletion of initial unstressed syllables.

$$\begin{bmatrix}+\text{syl}\\-\text{cons}\end{bmatrix} \rightarrow (\emptyset) \Big/ \text{B}\begin{bmatrix}+\text{syl}\\-\text{cons}\end{bmatrix}\underset{[-\text{stress}]}{}\#\#\,\Gamma[+\text{cons}]\;\underline{\quad}\;\begin{Bmatrix}\text{A [Vb + ing]}\\ [+\text{syl}]\\ \text{C}_\text{o}\,[-\text{stress}]\end{Bmatrix}$$

This rule orders the constraints for both processes as follows:
i. grammatical category
ii. preceding environment
iii. syllable type

When the output in Table 8.3 from the Cedergren–Sankoff variable rule program is compared with the rule, we can see that it agrees with the frequencies displayed in Figure 17. The most powerful constraint which affects the application of the rule is the presence or absence of a Vb + ing form; syllable type and the preceding environment are second and third order constraints. The probability coefficients predict that the next most favorable environment for the application of the rule is the presence of a vowel followed by a syllable beginning with an unstressed vowel, e.g. *the electrician*.

Although this rule is not too far-fetched in a strict linguistic sense, it is very striking in its heterogeneity of sociolinguistic relationships. In a sociolinguistic sense, the rule must be considered very unrealistic, since it contains a reversal of the social constraints which govern the application of the rule (even though the linguistic constraints can be ordered isomorphically and collapsed into one schema). In one case, the *presence* of an initial unstressed syllable, as in the *a*- prefixed verb forms, is stereotyped and carries considerable social stigma; while in the other case, it is the *absence* of an initial unstressed syllable which produces socially stigmatized forms, as well as the reduced forms which are characteristic of informal speech. Therefore, an unusual state of affairs obtains in this instance. Both the application and the non-application of the rule have the same *social* outcome, while its application always has the same linguistic outcome of phonological reduction.

In this instance, it is the extralinguistic constraints which are mirror-images of each other, and too different to be accommodated realistically within the same rule. Yet Wolfram has made no comment on this collapsing of two rules into one; he has suggested elsewhere, however, that there may be a universal constraint on mirror-image hierarchies in related rules (cf. Wolfram 1975). The most important basis for deciding when to collapse or separate rules would therefore appear to be the nature of the *linguistic* constraints alone; yet such considerations can be ignored altogether when it is convenient.

Linguistically speaking, of course, this variable rule (like Labov's rule for post-vocalic schwa loss and copula deletion) represents a very economical solution. It accomplishes in one rule what otherwise might have taken two; but it misrepresents the way in which the rule actually operates in the speech community.[4] Accordingly, it might be legitimately questioned in what sense the rule is a *sociolinguistic* rule rather than a linguistic rule, and whether in fact Wolfram and Christian can claim to have presented a *sociolinguistic* analysis of *a*-prefixing and initial unstressed syllable deletion in Appalachian English.

In Table 8.4 I illustrate the indecision in the sociolinguistic literature where the linguistic and extralinguistic constraints vary. Four possible relationships between the nature of the linguistic and extralinguistic constraints may exist for two rules. Two cases are straightforward: ones in which the linguistic and extralinguistic constraints are both the same or both different. In Case 1 the decision to collapse rules is well-motivated on linguistic and extralinguistic grounds; while in Case 2, the decision to

4. Lass (1976b: 140) has commented on the somewhat circular strategy of arguments involving the alleged goodness of fit between linguistic data and formal notation:

> if a notation seems to capture LSG's [i.e. linguistically significant generalizations], then it becomes a procedural imperative for the linguist to seek out examples of the kind of phenomena that the notation fits; and any set of items that can be collapsed with the notation adds to the 'value' of a description. Thus if two rules *can* be conflated with a given notation, they *must* be: failure to engineer such an abbreviation, or to formulate a set of rules so that abbreviation can occur, opens one to the charge of 'missing a generalization'.

This seems to be the problem here. Labov, especially, seems concerned with maintaining the formal notation and organizational principles of generative phonology, even to the point of claiming that his results give independent confirmation of both these (cf. Labov 1969: 761 and my comments in Chapter 2).

Table 8.4. *Ordering of linguistic and extralinguistic constraints in variable rules*

	Constraints			
Case	linguistic	social	No. of rules	Example
1.	same	same	1	
2.	different	different	2	/h/ deletion (Cedergren 1973)
3.	same	different	1–2	aspiration of /s/ and /ṙ/ (Cedergren 1973) *a*-prefixing and initial syllable deletion (Wolfram and Christian 1976)
4.	different	same	1–2	contraction and deletion of BEV copula (Labov 1969) loss of /r/ and copula deletion (Labov 1969)

separate rules is well-motivated. The fuzzy area is where the constraints, either linguistic or extralinguistic, are not isomorphic; and it is here that idiosyncratic choice prevails. I take this as further evidence against Labov's claim that decisions between systems of rules can be conclusive on the basis of a set of quantitative relations of the type used in sociolinguistic analysis. Moreover, it is impossible to see how Labov can realistically maintain this point of view when his own data are full of such contradictions. If sociolinguistics is to become a viable enterprise in its own right, then it must adopt an integrative approach in both theory and description.

8.4 A sociolinguistic analysis of variation in word-final /r/ in Edinburgh: a case for integrative sociolinguistic description

I take my own analysis of variation in word-final /r/ in a variety of Scottish English as an example here, since it represents a case where linguistic variation is best accounted for in terms of both social and linguistic factors. It also illustrates a number of more general problems in methodology, e.g. continuous vs. non-continuous variation and the use of variable scales (cf. Chapter 2). I will argue that the choice of representation of this instance of variation as either continuous or discrete is connected with (and to some extent even obscures) the decision to separate or collapse rules. Thus, the fact that variation can be observed and described by a continuous variable scale with intermediate stages (which are either attested or unattested) does not demonstrate that the variation could not also be accounted for by an underlying discontinuous model. In other words, the identification of steps in a linguistic process and their ordering are not independent of each other.[5]

In my original analysis of word-final /r/ (cf. Romaine 1975, 1978a), I scored the variants of /r/ as three discrete variables rather than as one continuous variable. The variants that were observed include the following: [ɾ], [ɹ] and ∅ (lack of /r/).

The argumentation behind this decision was that although the variants represent a class belonging to (r), the move or choice among these different variants did not have the same gradient character as a vocalic variable like Labov's (eh), for example, where index values can be seen to go up or down in relation to movement along a phonetic dimension.[6] If the decision had been taken to organize the (r) variants on a continuous scale such as the following, then the implication would be that there are intermediate values between the variants, and that [ɹ] is in some way an intermediate step in this process.

Variable scale for (*r*) *in Scottish English*
(r–1) [ɾ]
(r–2) [ɹ]
(r–3) ∅

Phonetically speaking, [ɹ] is a reasonable intermediate stage by which /r/ can be deleted, if the process by which [ɾ] → [ɹ] → ∅ is thought of as a series of steps of successively lesser degrees of approximation between two articulators. In other words, a tap or a trill represents the greatest degree of approximation, i.e. intermittent closure, and the approximant a lesser degree, until finally the segment is vocalized.

There seems to be no agreed way of giving a feature specification for taps

5. Cf. Hoenigswald (1973) and Lass (1978) for a discussion of this problem in historical linguistics and the task of reconstruction.
6. Labov's (1966) treatment of the variable (eh) in NYC is a classic instance of variation organized on a continuous phonetic as well as social dimension. He orders the variants along the following scale:
(eh–1) [ɪ˂:ᵊ]
(eh–2) [e:ˇᵊ]
(eh–3) [æ:ˆ]
(eh–4) [æ:]
(eh–5) [a:]
An individual's score for the use of this variable is calculated by coding each occurrence of the variable in a number of members of the relevant word class from 1–5, depending on its phonetic realization, then taking an average of the numerical values. The resulting index score corresponds with the phonetic dimension of height, and with a social dimension of standard/non-standard; the lower a person's index score is for (eh), the higher the phonetic value of his vowel is, and the closer he is to the non-standard end of the social continuum.

or flaps,[7] but the first step of the process can be described by Rule 1 below, and the final stage by Rule 2, an /r/ vocalization rule, which has been postulated to exist in a number of English dialects.

Rules for final (*r*) *variation in Scottish English*

1.
$$[\text{ɾ}] \rightarrow \left\langle \begin{bmatrix} +\text{voc} \\ +\text{cons} \\ +\text{cont} \\ +\text{son} \\ +\text{central} \end{bmatrix} \right\rangle \Big/ \; [-\text{cons}] \_\_ \; \#\# \; [+\text{cons}]$$

2.
$$\begin{bmatrix} +\text{voc} \\ +\text{cons} \\ +\text{cont} \\ +\text{son} \\ +\text{cent} \end{bmatrix} \rightarrow \langle -\text{cons} \rangle \Big/ \; [-\text{cons}] \_\_ \; \#\# \; [+\text{cons}]$$

Labov (1966) has written the latter rule as:

$$[+\text{cen}] \rightarrow \langle -\text{cons} \rangle \, / \, [-\text{cons}] \_\_ [-\text{syl}]$$

Both Rule 2 and Labov's rule predict that a central segment loses its consonantal value variably in post-vocalic position, if the following element is not a vowel.

Linguistically speaking, there are at least two choices for the formal representation of this process: 1. separate rules of the format given above, with variable inputs to each rule; or 2. one collapsed rule with the same set of environmental constraints, but variable inputs. I will now discuss what type of evidence can be put forward to decide between the two.

Table 8.5 shows the results of the analysis of the data using the Cedergren–Sankoff program to 'test' the model I presented above where two rules are involved in the deletion of word-final /r/. The linguistic constraints are coded as V (following vowel), K (following consonant) and Q (following pause). The major extralinguistic factor which was found to operate on these rules was the sex of the speaker.

It can be seen that a following pause has an effect in promoting the application of Rule 1, while it inhibits the application of 2. The effects of a following consonant and a following vowel are also different in both rules, which argues against treating the process as one rule. The ordering of the social constraints on the application of both rules is also different. Rule 1 applies more often if the speaker is female, while 2 applies more often if the

7. Ladefoged (1975) has suggested that a possible physical value of the rate of movement of an articulator might be used.

Table 8.5. *Variable rule analysis of variation in word-final /r/ in Scottish English*

	Following segment			Sex of the speaker	
Factors	K	V	Q	M	F
Rule 1: [ɾ] → [ɹ]	0.38	0.00	0.50	0.00	0.20
Rule 2: [ɹ] → ∅	0.45	0.46	0.00	1.00	0.26

speaker is male. In this case, then, the decision to separate the rules is well-motivated on the basis of the ordering of both linguistic and extralinguistic constraints.

This decision raises an interesting question. Is Rule 2 the 'same' rule which can be assumed to exist in non-rhotic dialects of English like RP, or variable ones like New York City? If so, then the application of Rule 2 to the output of 1 (which is Scots-specific) carries it one step further, and has the effect of making Scottish English more like non-rhotic dialects of English. In this particular instance, then, we have an example of how a rhotic and (in this respect) more conservative dialect like Scottish English may implement such a change.[8]

If we take a closer look at the ordering of the linguistic constraints in my deletion rule for Scottish English and Labov's rule for /r/ vocalization, there is a difference in the effect of a following pause, which is neglected as a relevant conditioning factor in Labov's rule. There is evidence here (as well as in Labov's own and other sociolinguistic studies) to suggest that it should be included. The effect of a pause in certain phonological processes appears to be an important dialect boundary. For example, in the case of t/d deletion, a pause has a similar effect to a consonant in promoting the application of the rule for black New Yorkers, but it is more similar to a vowel in the speech of white Philadelphians. The effect of a following pause is not just the reflection of a caste boundary between black and white; it also appears to be a regional and ethnic dialect boundary in American English.

8. I am not claiming any particular ontological status for the notion of 'same' here, other than that which I assume it to have in discussions where it is used by others. That is to say, I am thinking in terms of the inventory and kinds of rules one might have in a polylectal or panlectal grammar of English, which one could draw on in the description of a particular dialect. I am not implying by my use of 'same' that speakers of Scots are in any conscious sense aware of what goes on in NYC with respect to the variable pronunciation of post-vocalic /r/ (although Bailey would probably maintain that this was part of the polylectal competence of English speakers). I am also not arguing that the sequence [ɾ] → [ɹ] → ∅ is not a well-motivated historical analysis; I am considering only a synchronic grammar.

Table 8.6. *Variable rule analysis of two rules in Scottish English*

	Following segment			Sex of the speaker	
Factors	K	V	Q	M	F
Rule 1: [ɾ] → [ɹ]	1.00	0.53	0.94	0.54	1.00
Rule 2: [ɾ] → ∅	0.35	0.26	1.00	1.00	0.31

Table 8.7. *Numbers of* [ɹ] *and* ∅ *according to phonetic environment*

	(r) type	
Phonetic environment	[ɹ]	∅
Following consonant	102	23
Following vowel	90	25
Following pause	153	132

The further one moves from Philadelphia towards New York City, the more t/d deletion occurs before a following pause. Of course, it should not be surprising that the ordering of the constraints should be different in Scottish and New York City English even if the two dialects have an /r/ deletion rule in common (especially since New York City English is historically derived from the ancestor of non-rhotic southern English). This is particularly the case if Scottish English is undergoing change, since Labov claims that one of the ways in which a change manifests itself is through reweighting of constraints (cf. Chapter 7).[9]

I would like to argue now that such an interpretation does not fit either the social or linguistic facts as well as an analysis in which there are two rules which both have [ɾ] as their input. In Table 8.6 I have shown the results of variable rule analysis for these two rules using the same linguistic and extralinguistic constraints as before.

In Rule 1 the effect of a consonant and a pause are similar in promoting the application of the rule; furthermore, this rule is marked as being largely a 'female' rule. Rule 2, which deletes [ɾ], is largely a 'male' rule; and this time the effects of a following consonant and a following vowel are nearly equal,

9. I have discussed the possibility of sound change in progress with respect to /r/ in Scottish English in Romaine (1978a).

but much less than that of a following pause in promoting the application of the rule. This account of the variation is not only more in accordance with the linguistic data, as shown in Table 8.7, but is also more in line with the social facts.

Although there are precedents in the literature for ignoring the evidence from the extralinguistic constraints, in this instance, the social information about the use of (r) supports the analysis I have presented. For one thing, the use of the approximant has been noticed for quite some time as a marker of female middle class speech (although my research indicates that it seems to be more commonly used than has generally been observed). Both males and females are innovating or moving away from the Scottish norm of [ɾ] in different directions, males towards ∅ and females towards [ɹ].[10]

What is interesting about the innovation in the case of Scottish English is that the males are innovating in a direction away from the local Scots prestige norm [ɾ], but in adopting r-lessness, their usage happens to coincide with a much larger national norm (i.e. non-rhotic English like RP). I have argued elsewhere (cf. Romaine 1978a: 156, 1979c) that this pattern of sex differentiation suggests that r-lessness is a separate, competing development in Scots, and is not being adopted in conscious imitation of a Southern English prestige model such as RP. If the latter had been the case, then we would have expected the females to lead the shift of the norm in this direction. Thus, I would argue that both linguistic and extralinguistic evidence agree in the suggestion that the rule which deletes word-final /r/ in Scottish English is not the same one which is responsible for the deletion of post-vocalic /r/ in non-rhotic accents of English.

It should now be clear that no principled basis yet exists for taking into account the evidence from social constraints in linguistic decisions; and this shortcoming in my opinion affects the viability of sociolinguistic theory.[11] It is therefore questionable to what extent some of the analyses and

10. I could have captured this observation in another type of variable scale, where the norm occupies the middle position (cf. Nordberg 1975). In such a scale, variable index scores above and below 200 would indicate that a speaker/group was introducing variation in the use of (r) from an assumed norm of [ɾ]. I decided against this, however, because this type of index scale is misleading and conceals the locus of variability (cf. Romaine 1978a: 147). For example, if a speaker has a score of 200, this might be the result of equal use of the variants (r–1) and (r–3) rather than consistent use of (r–2).

    Revised variable scale for (r) in Scottish English
    (r–1) ∅
    (r–2) [ɾ]
    (r–3) [ɹ]

11. Sherzer (1970) has made a case for incorporating social reality into phonological descriptions, but not within the context of variable rules.

explanations suggested by Labov and others really integrate linguistic and social factors in one descriptive framework. Oddly enough, it is Labov, who has argued very strongly (cf. e.g. Labov 1963, 1972a) that social factors must contribute to the explanation of linguistic differentiation and change; yet, as I pointed out in the preceding chapter, his work seems to contradict this hypothesis.

I mentioned earlier (cf. Chapter 7) that a number of Labov's findings appear to be artifacts of a methodology which has only been fully tested in one particular case, namely, New York City. Virtually every study since then which has attempted to implement the Labovian framework on a reasonably large scale elsewhere has run into a number of difficulties, e.g. (and I cite only some of the more recent and on-going sociolinguistic studies in Britain which specifically claim to be modeled on Labov's 1966 work) Macaulay (1973), Milroy and Milroy (1977) and Romaine (1978b).

I have argued that studies of sociolinguistic variation in urban speech communities such as Edinburgh and Belfast, which are characterized by a long and complex history of linguistic and social interplay between dialect and standard, challenge some of the basic principles and explanations which have been assumed, largely without question, from Labov's study of New York City.[12] Some of the difficulties in choosing between competing solutions to linguistic issues are intimately related to the problem of maintaining the speech community as a coherent concept.

8.5 What is a speech community?

It may seem counter-productive to question a concept like 'speech community'. Since Gumperz (1968) defined it as a sociolinguistic entity and fundamental unit of analysis, it has been endlessly referred to in the literature. My point of departure here will be Gumperz's notion of a speech community as a group of speakers (not necessarily of the same language) who share a set of norms and rules for the use of language(s). Thus, Labov (1966: 7) says about New York City:

> That New York City is a speech community, and not a collection of speakers living side by side, borrowing from each other's dialects, may be demonstrated by many kinds of evidence. Native New Yorkers differ in their usage in terms of absolute values of the variables, but the shifts between contrasting styles follow the same pattern in almost every case.

12. Creole studies present a number of challenges to the variable rule model too. I discuss some of these in the next chapter.

This type of speech community goes hand in hand with unidirectional variation organized along a continuous sociolinguistic dimension. Labov's work has concentrated on situations of this sort. To take another illustration, Labov (1963) has argued that centralization of /ay/ and /aw/ on Martha's Vineyard has a social meaning. A speaker who uses the more centralized variants of these diphthongs is asserting local solidarity in a strong way through positive identification with life on the island. The variation in this case can be ordered along a continuous linguistic dimension which represents differing degrees of centralization, as well as a social one which corresponds to the speaker's strength of identity with the local community of fishermen. The implication of this pattern of variation is that speakers vary in their use of /ay/ and /aw/ only to the extent that certain groups carry the change further along than others. What is implied is a relationship of relatively greater or lesser use of the same variable.

It seems reasonable to suppose, however, that in different speech communities social and linguistic factors are linked not only to different degrees, but also in different ways, so that the connection between linguistic and social factors in a particular speech community is a matter for investigation and cannot be taken as given. The conclusion may be unavoidable that speech communities in which sociolinguistic variation is organized in the monotonic and straightforward way that Labov describes must be the exception rather than the rule.[13]

For example, Milroy and Margrain (1978: 25–6) have difficulty in making sense out of the classic definition of speech community, even when trying to describe the behavior of one group of speakers in Belfast:

> These results show that even in a single speech community – and it would be plausible to describe Belfast vernacular speakers in that way – there are many differences in the manner in which speakers take hold of 'pieces' of the language and use them as symbols of community loyalty.

Their conclusion is that 'sociolinguistic structure is woven in a complex way throughout the community, with different phonological elements being associated with various social groups' (Milroy and Margrain 1978: 31).

They do not find their results surprising; nor would most creolists working within the dynamic paradigm, which takes the individual as the starting point of analysis, largely to avoid this problem of defining group

13. Elsewhere I have called these kinds of communities 'prototype variable rule communities' (cf. Romaine 1980b); they are what Le Page (1979) has referred to as 'highly focussed' communities.

boundaries (cf. especially Bickerton 1971: 487–8). In fact, both Milroy (1978) and I (Romaine 1975) have suggested that a number of the most interesting cases of variation, in Belfast and Edinburgh respectively, are those in which variation behaves non-continuously (as for example in the alternation between *hame* and *home* in Scots).[14] This type of variation is often characteristic of diglossic and post-creole continuum situations, which are perhaps better described in terms of coexistent grammars.

It could be argued that I am exaggerating the difficulty in defining a speech community by picking the most awkward examples. It is no doubt quite true that Belfast and Edinburgh are very heterogeneous; but, as it turns out, even fairly homogeneous speech communities display more than one direction of change and variation, and subgroups within the community are characterized by bimodal distributions with respect to the use of the same variable, i.e. they use it in *different* ways.

Guy (1977), for example, reports that within one group of speakers the same constraints on the rule of t/d deletion are not in effect to the same extent. There do not seem to be any extralinguistic factors which will account for the bimodal distribution; for some speakers the most important constraint on the application of the rule is the presence of a monomorphemic form (e.g. *last*), while for others, it is the presence of an irregular past tense verb form (e.g. *told*). This finding is particularly interesting because t/d deletion seems to be a stable process and is not undergoing change.

Once we abandon the assumption that all dialects or lects must have the same underlying forms, or stop describing non-standard varieties in terms of their divergence from an idealized standard, the picture becomes messier. However, as I pointed out in the first part of this chapter, there does not seem to be any reason for assuming that black speakers start out with the full forms of the copula as Labov claims that white middle class speakers do and then delete them. The only justification would be a descriptive one.[15]

14. Wolfram (1969) has suggested that the concept of the linguistic variable can include variants which may be part of coexisting codes. Macaulay's (1973) study of Glasgow runs into trouble by handling one such instance of variation as a continuous dimension rather than as a case of discrete alternation. I refer here to the variation between /au/ and /u/ in *house*, etc. (cf. Romaine 1975 and also Macaulay 1977 for objections to my criticisms of his analysis). This example also illustrates my point that, where two possible analyses are available (i.e. variation can be handled as continuous or discrete), social context should be taken into account.

15. There is another consideration which I hinted at in Chapter 2 (cf. n.8). At the time Labov was working on BEV there was a controversy between the so-called difference/deficit theorists, and a great deal of money was being spent on educational programs which were designed to compensate for the alleged language-poor backgrounds of lower class children. There was thus a decided advantage in de-

It is worth pointing out here that a similar argument applies to t/d deletion. There is growing evidence to indicate that BEV speakers may begin with Ø forms, and then add final t/d later in a sporadic and hypercorrect pattern. Bickerton's (1975) data show that the acquisition of past tense forms in Guyanese creole seems to recapitulate the child's learning process, i.e. first, the child acquires some strong verb forms, then the more general *-ed* principle takes over (cf. Bickerton 1975: 148, Table 4.10). The same phonetic conditioning constraints which I discussed earlier in this chapter do not appear to operate for Guyanese speakers. Presence of *-ed* is rare even in the most favorable environments, where it occurs in only one-third of the cases, as opposed to 83 percent in Fasold's data for black speakers in Detroit (1977: 555). Bickerton, therefore, speaks of the 'insertion' rather than the presence or deletion of *-ed* in this instance, and questions whether phonological processes of deletion are responsible for the absence of English past tense forms.

Bickerton (1975: 84) believes that 'deletion' arguments in the case of creoles are generally counter-intuitive. Firstly, they assume phonological processes which are otherwise often unmotivated; and secondly, they claim that speakers put things in to make their utterances more like English and then take them out to give quite a contrary appearance. The relationships which hold between rules in a grammar depend on the forms one takes to be underlying, rather than on the properties of the data itself.

There does not appear to be anything in the nature of quantitative data which necessarily entails its description as a set of ordered rules in which the most complex forms are the underlying ones.[16] But we should not reject Labov's theory for failing to provide empirical tests for some of its basic assumptions since, pace Labov, a significant portion of the theory is non-empirical anyway. The fact that Labov does not accept the latter view is a problem I deal with in more detail in the next chapter. What we can legitimately demand of a theory, however, is that it should give a satisfac-

monstrating that all speakers shared the same underlying forms, but just used the rules to a greater or lesser extent. For example, Labov (1969: 722) stresses the following relationship between BEV and white English:

> WHEREVER SE [i.e. standard English] CAN CONTRACT, NNE [i.e. non-standard Negro English] CAN DELETE *is* AND *are*, AND VICE VERSA; WHEREVER SE CANNOT CONTRACT, NNE CANNOT DELETE *is* AND *are*, AND VICE VERSA.

16. The reason which is usually advanced in favor of this approach is the criterion of simplicity, which is connected with rule ordering. I do not think that linguists can make a cogent case for accepting the principle of simplicity as a methodological rule. I am not arguing that we should choose a more complex analysis or hypothesis than necessary, but merely point out to those who believe that linguistics is an empirical science that the laws of nature very often turn out to be more complex than we originally thought. Within empirical science then, there does not seem to be any basis for believing in the simplicity of nature. Likewise, I do not see any grounds for thinking that languages are simple.

tory account of the totality of facts as constituted by its own basic concepts (cf. e.g. Feyerabend 1978: 284). In other words, a theory gets into trouble with its own facts by not accounting for them.

If it is true that most theories derive their strength from a few paradigmatic cases and then have to be distorted to cope with the rest, as Feyerabend (1978: 40) has observed, then the relevant question to be raised here is: how much distortion do we tolerate before deciding to reject a theory? In the final chapter I consider the 'facts' and what the status of sociolinguistic data is with respect to a theory of language.

9 *On the epistemological status of sociolinguistic theory*

> To show how a fact is useful is not to explain how it originated or why it is.
>
> Emile Durkheim (1964: 90)

> Controversy is the yeast which keeps science in lively fermentation. But its progress is also beset with pseudo-controversies which appear to reflect differences in opinion, whereas in reality they only reflect differences of emphasis on single aspects of a complex process at the expense of others.
>
> Arthur Koestler (1975: 246)

> Confusion is created by taxonomic principles appearing in the guise of causal mechanisms.
>
> Rom Harré (1972: 203)

Both Labov and Bailey agree that it is the 'facts of variation' which are central to linguistic theory. If a reasonable account of language change depends on the possibility of describing orderly differentiation within language, as they maintain, the problem is to decide which of the competing variationist theories, i.e. the quantitative or dynamic paradigm, is best able to incorporate the facts of variability within a linguistic description. There is, however, disagreement between the two over the set of facts a linguistic theory can properly choose to address, and what a formal model of grammar which incorporates the observation of variability looks like.

Bailey has emphasized in a number of places that linguistics must make dialectology central, but that 'the job of linguists is linguistics' (Bailey 1969a: 118). By this he means (111–12):

> The linguist's task is to describe the linguistic (dialectal) variety with linguistic criteria and, unlike past dialectologists, leave it to the sociologists to explain diachronic origins in terms of migration patterns and the like . . . This will mean that we are organizing linguistic materials on intralinguistic principles. This can be done even in ignorance of past migration routes and all the other things that are so extensively dwelt on in word geographies of the past.

Labov (1972c: 319), on the other hand, says:

> an asocial account [of language change] would be incoherent. The histories that I have outlined would not exist if social differences were abstracted from the grammars involved, for the accounts of change would be vacuous.

The issue can be formulated in the following question: can an autonomous linguistic theory provide an explanatory basis for a theory of language change?[1] In this chapter I will be concerned with how the types of evidence and explanations put forward by Bailey and Labov, and their followers, support their respective theoretical positions about the nature and locus of variability, and the role of social factors in linguistic change and differentiation. I cite some of the important empirical findings from research on variation and change in terms of their relation to predictions in both models.

9.1 On the nature and locus of variability

I will concentrate here on differences in assumptions made by each paradigm with respect to the nature and locus of variability, rather than on the choice of models for the representation of variation and change (cf. 9.2 for the latter). Two questions are relevant to the discussion: 1. Where is variation, i.e. idiolect or sociolect, and are idiolectal and sociolectal grammars isomorphic? And 2. Is variability a matter of competence or performance, or both?

9.1.1 Idiolectal vs. sociolectal grammars. With regard to the question of where variation takes place, Bickerton states the dynamic paradigm's position quite clearly. He claims that the observed variability in the quantitative model results from the grouping of internally homogeneous individual lects in a group. As far as Bickerton is concerned, the concept of inherent variability is an artifact of the quantitative method of analysis; and it is the behavior of the individual which is of linguistic significance. He says (1971: 488):

1. Hjelmslev (1953) maintained that only an autonomous linguistic theory was capable of scientific treatment, while Labov seems to support the opposite point of view. Lass (1980), however, claims that neither an autonomous nor a projectionist one will make any difference in the degree of predictive success for a theory of language change (cf. especially 4.8). His argument is that if languages are autonomous objects, there is no conceivable reason for them to change; change could be introduced into such a system only by an axiom. If language is not autonomous, it is still debatable whether there are reasons for change (cf. 9.2.3, this chapter).

Table 9.1. *Implicational scale using frequency data for deletion of the relative marker in Middle Scots texts (categorical environments circled and deviations italicized; scalability = 77 percent)*

Text	Syntactic position				Total (environments conflated)
	Temp.	Dir. obj.	Obl.	Subj.	
The Scottish Correspondence	25	*48*	18	10	27
Ane Satyre	50	29	(*100*)	3	12
The Bannatyne Manuscript	18	*19*	6	6	9
Acts of the Lords of Council	59	30	13	3	16
Burgh Records	50	30	*80*	1	12
Boece	10	*23*	*40*	1	6
Sheriff Court Book	33	(*0*)	(*0*)	2	3
total (individuals conflated)	42	30	20	4	12

it is my contention that no group exhibits either complete uniformity or complete variability, and moreover that there is no group within a given language-community such that the linguistic behavior of all its members will fall within a certain range, and that of all of its non-members outside it. One can always produce discrete figures by drawing non-linguistic boundaries, averaging performance within those boundaries, and then comparing the averages; if one takes individuals, irrespective of group or class membership, and ranks them along a continuum, one gets a very different picture.

Bickerton (1973c: 29) claims to have demonstrated this by re-analyzing Sankoff's (1973) data on complementizer *que* deletion in Montreal French. When the data for each individual in each relevant environment are kept separate, the amount of variation is 22 percent. However, when environments are conflated, but individuals kept separate, variation increases to 49 percent; the reverse procedure, i.e. keeping environments separate, but grouping individuals together produces 57 percent variation. Thus Bickerton concludes that the very high amounts of variation characteristic of the quantitative paradigm result from such conflations of environments or of the outputs of individual speakers.

In Chapter 6 I mentioned that variation in the relative markers was not equally distributed throughout all the relevant environments (cf. the tables in Chapter 6 and its appendix). I also claimed that the results of the frequency analysis of the data coincided largely with those from the implicational scaling (cf. Table 6.31 in Chapter 6). I now demonstrate in what way my results reflect the fact that I have, in one case, conflated the environments, and, in the other, the output of the individual texts.

In Table 9.1 I give the percentages for deletion of the relative marker in four syntactic positions, which were the basis for the implicational scale I presented in Table 6.31. It can be seen that the overall percent of variation (12 percent) is the average of a range of values from 0 to 100 percent in each individual environment. There are more deviations (i.e. where the implication relationship T > D > O > S is violated) this time compared with Table 6.31, because I have not reduced the variability by setting thresholds as I did previously.

Bickerton has dismissed variable rule analysis as a sophisticated data-displaying device because virtually any set of variable constraints can be manipulated to produce good cross-product data, but will not necessarily reveal anything of interest linguistically. I and a number of others have raised a similar objection to Bickerton's manipulation of isolects and environments in implicational scales (cf. the excursus to Chapter 6).

Sankoff and Rousseau (1974) have suggested a computer method of assessing variable rule and implicational scale analyses of linguistic variation. Their program performs a variable rule analysis of a set of data, sets up an implicational scale, and then uses the probabilities predicted by the variable rule to calculate the errors to be expected in fitting the data into the proposed scale. The comparison is, however, unidirectional, i.e. it predicts whether a variable rule analysis should be rejected in favor of a scale and not whether a scale should be rejected in favor of a variable rule. Using this method with Sankoff's complementizer *que* data, Sankoff and Rousseau concluded that the number of errors in Bickerton's ideal scale is exactly what would have been expected from a variable rule analysis. Therefore, each model was operating with the same error level; and one did not fit the data significantly better or worse than the other. And here again, we have a case where the quantitative data are not decisive, i.e. they do not argue convincingly for a particular analytical solution (cf. Chapter 8).

It is not usually the case, however, that implicational scales and variable rule analysis are applied to the same data; Sankoff's complementizer *que* analysis is an exceptional example in the sociolinguistic literature. More often, linguists working in creole or creole-like situations prefer implicational scales, while those studying urban dialect variation prefer variable rule analysis. It is scarcely surprising that some data fit some models better than others or that quantitative solutions are non-unique (cf. Romaine 1979b).

The nature of variation in a post-creole continuum is different from that found in New York City. Bickerton has argued quite convincingly that some of the Guyanese data could not be adequately handled by variable rules. If we look at some typical implicational scales in Bickerton (1975), or those which I have given for the distribution of the forms of the copula in the mesolect (cf. Excursus, Chapter 6), it can be seen that there is often no item in which all informants show variable behavior. Hence, variable rules would obscure the invariant patterns of some individuals.

Likewise, the social structure of Guyana, and for that matter probably that of most post-creole continua, is such that no unambiguous social lines divide variant behavior from invariant. Therefore, Bickerton has concluded that the basis for the distribution of lectal features is purely linguistic.[2] He does not accept the argument that the addition of a social component to implicational scales can contribute anything to our knowledge of the patterning of linguistic structure, or to an explanation of change (but more on the latter issue in 9.2).

There is also justification for this view in Bickerton's data. There does not seem to be any evidence, for example, that the markers of tense/aspect, or indeed a number of the features which Bickerton has examined, are affected by the types of environments typically specified in variable rules. Whatever model is chosen in a particular case, the fit is not perfect; nor should it be expected to be. In variable rule analysis there are always some individuals who behave categorically with respect to a given environment of the rule. By the same token, some data are more scalable than others, but there are unlikely to be many perfect implicational scales. As I point out in the next section, however, the latter is not really a problem, since implicational scales are assumed to be a model of competence and not performance.

The real issue here is what level of abstraction is relevant to the construction of a grammar (and this has important implications for the types of arguments, explanations and predictions which are relevant to the proposed theories, as I will argue in later sections of this chapter). Labov (1969: 759), for example, has said:

> the construction of complete grammars for 'idiolects', even one's own, is a fruitless and unrewarding task; we now know enough about language in its social context to realize that the grammar of the speech community is more regular and systematic

2. Bickerton generally deals with syntactic variation and Labov with phonological; and this could have a bearing on the findings, since syntactic variables interact in a number of cases in a different way with social structure, if at all (cf. my comments on this in Chapter 2).

than the behavior of any one individual. Unless the speech pattern is studied within the overall system of the community, it will appear as a mosaic of unaccountable and sporadic variation.

Labov's claim, then, is that the locus of language is in the community or group, and that the speech of any social group will be less variable than the speech of any individual. Thus, variable rules are written for groups rather than for individuals; and it is maintained that there is isomorphism between individual and group grammars. In the dynamic paradigm, however, not every member of a community operates with the same set of rules; the result is then that community and individual grammars are not isomorphic.

Ironically, the quantitative paradigm and transformational grammar are more similar to each other in this respect than the latter is to the dynamic paradigm; both Labov's and Chomsky's idealization of the data result in a grammar that does not describe the speech of any particular individual, though for different reasons.

As I have already pointed out, however (cf. especially 7.4 and 8.5), the behavior of individuals in a group is not always isomorphic with that of all its members, but the assumption that it is places a constraint on change in the system by defining transition as impossible. The way out of this dilemma, as I will explain more fully in 9.2, is to obliterate the distinction between origin and propagation of a change (cf. Weinreich et al. 1968: 186–7). Bailey's theory is also incompatible with the existence of individual speakers in the sense that idiolects are not homogeneous, but inherently variable; but Bailey (1973: 137) would claim that the fluctuating statistics of different cells are a matter for performance, and hence do not affect the competence system indicated by the implicational scale.

The variability of individuals, or more precisely their lack of isomorphism with the group, turns out to be more embarrassing to the quantitative paradigm, judging from some of the attempts to 'explain' deviations (cf. e.g. Guy 1974; Romaine 1975: 215–19; Naro 1981). Most of these efforts appear to be carried out in a misunderstanding of the process of abstraction and the nature of the group as a level of abstraction.[3] Naro's (1981: 88) comments about the relationship between individual and group grammars are indicative of the prevailing confusion:

3. Cf. also Kanngiesser (1972b: 37–9) on the consequences of Chomsky's homogeneity hypothesis for diachronic linguistics, and its relation to competence; and also Wunderlich (1974: 139–41, 396).

Given current psycholinguistic theories, according to which linguistic activity is controlled by the individual brain, such collective data [i.e. the data belonging to a sociolect] would seem to be meaningful only in so far as each member of the group behaves in a way similar to the other; otherwise, group data would amount to no more than a meaningless average of disparate behaviors. If this occurred, the group figures would not describe correctly the performance of any individual and could have no psychological reality[4] ... In any comparison of statistics for a group of speakers with the corresponding results for its component members, it is very important to bear in mind the fact that the group always has the advantage of possessing a greater quantity of data; thus accuracy is increased and the chances of noticeable fluctuations in less frequently occurring categories, resulting from probabilistically determined outcomes, is reduced. In this sense, the idea that the group is more regular than the individual is a triviality.

Naro and Guy are concerned with demonstrating that differences between individual and group behavior can be reduced to lack of sufficient data. But the point here is, as Labov (1966: 6) says, that a grammar is not just a collection of idiolects. We cannot therefore describe the properties of the whole as an additive function of the properties of its parts. There are, in other words, certain emergent properties of the group which make it cohere as a group. Such emergent properties are to be understood as characteristics which are not properties of the individuals of which they are a collection. These characteristics need to be explained by reference to the structure as a whole, and not just to the components that enter into the structure (cf. Harré 1976: 140–6). It is therefore important to distinguish between the rules which govern individual behavior and those which guide the behavior of the group as a whole (cf. Koestler 1978: 44–5, 81).

The locus of language and the place of the individual within linguistic theory is a basic but unresolved issue. The dichotomy between the language of the group and the individual can be seen in Saussure's distinction between *langue* and *parole* which, according to Labov (1972a), has the following consequence: if *langue* is a social fact or knowledge shared by every member of the speech community, then the investigation of a single individual is sufficient to provide an account of it. Data on *parole*, on the other hand, can only be obtained by examining the behavior of individuals as they use the language, so that the individual aspect of language can be studied only through observation of language in its social context.

4. There is nothing corresponding to 'group competence', unless it is something like Durkheim's idea of the 'group mind' or collective consciousness (cf. also Saussure, for example). The concept of competence seems to make sense only at the individual level.

The Saussurean framework, however, by definition, excluded from its scope the study of language in its social context, which forms the cornerstone of Labovian sociolinguistics. Likewise, the diachronic analysis of language in its social context is a paradox which cannot be resolved within the confines of Saussurean linguistics. Change could be investigated only diachronically, and the social aspect of language could be investigated only synchronically in the speech of an individual. Thus, Saussure says (1966: 128, 140):

> Synchrony knows only one perspective, that of the speakers, and its whole method consists in gathering their testimony; ... diachronic linguistics, in contrast, will study the relations connecting successive items that are not perceived by a single collective consciousness.

Once the locus of language is shifted from the individual to the speech community, the theory of grammar addresses a set of facts which belong to the domain of cultural objects or events. The ontological status of such facts has important implications for both the goals and methodology of linguistics, as well as the adequacy of its alleged empirical claims. Is language considered to be an entity apart from its speakers?

The empirical status of cultural objects, social events, etc. is the subject of considerable controversy in the philosophy of science.[5] Naro does not seem to take account of the fact that probabilities of the type used in variable rules predict over an aggregate and never in an individual instance; his remarks suggest that somehow the behavior of the group is reducible to that of its individual members. Thus Naro's position, which appears to be representative of a number of advocates of the quantitative paradigm (cf. e.g. Fasold 1978), is one of methodological individualism; in other words, he assumes that social events should be explained by appeal to principles which govern the behavior of participating individuals in certain situations, and that these social facts are reducible to facts about the behavior of individuals and individual human psychology.

Methodological holism, on the other hand, deduces the behavior of individuals from macro-laws which apply to the group as a structural holon (cf. Popper 1961: 76–83 for criticism of the holistic view). The type of grammar which is constructed on the basis of Labov's theory makes predictions about, or describes, speakers' utterances on certain occasions. Thus, the entities which constitute the data for the theory can be said to

5. I expand this discussion in 9.3.3, where I discuss the unity of scientific method (cf. Popper 1961: 130f.).

be observable events which have spatio-temporal location, and thus can count, in Popper's terms, as observation reports against which empirical claims can be tested. Labov's theory deals with cultural reality; the data are such cultural or social facts as tokens in written texts, judgements of individual speakers, occurrences of spoken utterances, etc. It is difficult to see how such a grammar or theory of grammar could generate claims about psychological reality, or how facts such as those which are typically described by variable rules could be provided with psychological explanations (cf. Sanders 1974: 12–13).

A Chomskyan grammar, on the other hand, makes predictions about what speakers know about their language. The predictions and explanations can in this case have no reference to anything which is a part of the spatio-temporal world (cf. e.g. Ringen 1975 on the empirical status of transformational grammar).[6] Claims about such grammars can under certain conditions be tested through observations of linguistic behavior, but the claims are not about human behavior.

9.1.2 Is variability a matter of competence or performance? Some of the advocates of both paradigms have proposed that there is isomorphism between the formal model of grammar and human mental processes or abilities; and furthermore, that there are some empirical tests which support these claims of psychological reality. Bailey (1969a: 109), for example, has argued that 'If the theory that linguistic variation is organized in the brain in terms of implicational scales is correct, then it makes certain predictions which are testable.' He then goes on to explain that it is easy to find a relevant example where the theory predicts that a chaotic arrangement of the data can be reduced to a neat order, if the data turn out to be 85 percent scalable or better. But if this type of example is to be taken as a test of the prediction that variation is organized in the brain in an implicational scale, then what do we do with the counter-examples (which are also easy to find), where data are not scalable to 85 percent or better? In other words, what does the brain do with such instances of variation? (Cf. my comments on scalability in the excursus to Chapter 6.)

Likewise, Wolfram and Fasold (1974: 106) have claimed isomorphism between brain mechanisms and properties of the grammar: 'Taken seri-

6. I will not deal with the growing body of literature on this subject here, since I am concerned with sociolinguistic theory (cf., however, the papers in Cohen 1974 and Cohen and Wirth 1975; and also Linell 1976 for some recent views on the status of transformational grammar and linguistics as an empirical science).

ously, every capability built into a linguistic theory constitutes a claim that the same capacity is built into the language control parts of the human brain and speech mechanism.' Cedergren and Sankoff (1974) suggest that a theory of performance is reducible to a theory of competence in their claim that performance is a statistical reflection of competence (cf. Chapter 7). Labov, on the other hand, has said that he is not sure whether the distinction between competence and performance is a valid one; and that his notion of variable rules entails a revision of what it is to 'know' a language (cf. Labov 1969; Chapter 2, this volume). Labov does not really pursue this issue explicitly in his later writings, where he is more concerned with analytical aspects of variable rules. More recently, however, he has commented (1978: 13):

> There is ample evidence that human linguistic competence includes quantitative constraints as well as discrete ones, and that the recognition of such constraints will allow us to build our grammatical theory on the evidence of production and perception in every-day life.

There has been an on-going debate between the quantitative and dynamic theorists over what it is speakers know about variation in language. Bailey (1969b: 137) says:

> What speakers know is not how frequently they utter this or that, but what relative changes in frequencies – presumably organized in some system in the brain – indicate (socially, stylistically etc.). They look like implicational relationships to me.

The advantage of this position according to Bickerton and Bailey is that it entails no drastic alteration of existing notions of capabilities of the human brain, or of Chomsky's views on rules and competence. The rules of the dynamic paradigm are still categorical rules, although not every member of the community operates with the same set of rules. Community and individual grammars and competences are not isomorphic. Thus Bailey maintains that variability in speakers' judgements about the grammaticality of sentences reflects a difference in underlying structures, rule orderings, etc. (cf. Chapter 2); such a claim is possible only if competence is not homogeneous. Otherwise, the intuitions of all speakers in a speech community would be identical.[7]

The 'cost' of this modification according to Bickerton is that we must

7. Cf. also the discussion in Kanngiesser (1972b: 147–8) on the type of competence which must be described in a sociolinguistic theory, and comments on why a sociolinguistic theory cannot be based solely on a model of performance.

write polylectal grammars; speakers thus have a panlectal or polylectal competence which is formally modelled in the implicational scale. DeCamp's (1971b) suggestion that implicational scaling be included in an extended generative theory is perhaps the most serious proposal for including simple notions of frequency in an account of competence.[8] Most other discussions of variability within generative grammar do not go beyond postulating the optional application of rules as a means of generating variants. In any event, these optional rules are not able to predict variation which does not result from chance applications of the rules; optional rules are accurate predictors only if some rate of application can be defined for them. Bailey, however, has argued that rates of variation are not of interest for grammars because it is not psychologically plausible that children can learn them.

DeCamp has proposed that there are abstract units in the grammar which control style shifting by governing derivations, transformations and lexical selections. These units are arranged in hierarchical order, i.e. they are implicationally ordered from positive to negative values. This view of competence is compatible with a weak mentalist hypothesis put forward recently by Fasold (1978), who claims that variable rules should form part of a theory of human linguistic competence.

Fasold (1978: 88–9) maintains that most of the evidence from variable rule research supports the hypothesis that speakers know the factors associated with a given rule and their hierarchical order of effect in promoting the application of the rule. The evidence he provides is of the type Bailey claims is relevant to the testing of psychological reality hypotheses; namely, the finding that a set of data fits a model to an acceptable degree. In Bailey's case, the claim is made that if the data scale to an acceptable degree, then the brain must somehow be organized in a similar way to yield such patterns. Fasold cites as evidence for his hypothesis the observation that Wolfram's rule for /d/ deletion in Puerto Rican English contains three constraints in a hierarchical order which is supported by frequency. I quote

8. Even though Labov (1969) considers himself to be working within generative grammar, I regard his views as incompatible with it (cf. my comments in Chapter 2). Labov (1972a: 259) has claimed that he does not believe we need a 'new theory of language' at this point, but a 'new way of doing linguistics that will yield decisive solutions' (cf. my criticism in 9.3.1). Even this seemingly more modest statement entails a new conception of what a formal model of grammar which incorporates the observation of variation looks like. In fact, Chomsky (1966: 36) has argued quite strongly against the incorporation of probabilistic rules into the grammar. He says:

> No sense has ever been given to the notion of 'probabilities' or continuum type scales ... in the domain of grammatical descriptions; and every concrete proposal that has been made has been shown to lead to absurdity. Perhaps the time has come for linguists who insist on the importance of such notions to face this simple fact.

at length from his argument (1978: 88–9) since it illustrates very well some of the points I made in the previous section and adds to my methodological discussion:

If the . . . hypothesis were perfectly supported by these data, the percentages would become progressively larger as we move down the chart [i.e. a constraint hierarchy of the type I presented in the last chapter for *a*-prefixing]. The percentages do in fact increase in value from top to bottom, aside from a negligible statistical fluctuation at the bottom of the chart . . . It might be objected that data such as those . . . are group data and that the patterns would not work for individual speakers. Since linguistic competence is related to individual competence, if the relationships in data displays . . . are the result of averaging the data for groups of speakers, they would say nothing about individual linguistic competence. However, there are a number of studies in which it has been shown that the patterns hold for individuals as well as for groups . . . It is reasonably clear that the group patterns hold as well for individuals when enough data are collected from each speaker.

Again, my question would be, what do we say about the cases where individuals do deviate from the group (cf. 8.5), i.e. what kind of knowledge or competence produces a deviation? Here it seems that Fasold might have chosen a more felicitous example, since there are some in the literature. In this instance the hierarchical effect is somewhat 'neutralized' or peters out at the bottom of the hierarchy in 'negligible statistical fluctuation'. He refers here to the frequencies 70.4 percent and 70.3 percent which are associated with the third order constraint. Furthermore, he comments in a footnote (1978: 88) that he has not included all of the constraints which Wolfram says affect the application of the rule; Fasold's reason for this is that 'many of the cells showing the fourth-order constraint are very sparsely populated and the fourth-order constraint appears weakly ordered in any event and may not be an actual factor influencing application of the rule'.

I would maintain the view, however, that probabilities, variable rules and constraint hierarchies say nothing about individual linguistic competence for two reasons, the first of which I have already mentioned; namely, that the principle of methodological individualism is invalid. The alternative to this position within Labov's theory would be to postulate some sort of 'group competence or mind', which would have to be homogeneous. It is doubtful, even if there were something corresponding to a group competence, that this could provide a reasonable basis for a sociolinguistic theory (cf. Kanngiesser 1972b: 147–8). This point is, however, not really an argument, but more in the nature of a personal metaphysical assertion.

The most important reason why variable rules say nothing about individual competence is that the only type of competence which a theory based on probabilistic laws could make reference to is, in my opinion, an uninteresting one, or very limited at any rate. And furthermore, it would be a very different notion of competence than the one embodied in Chomsky's theory. Moreover, I do not think that the former notion could form the basis of a viable sociolinguistic theory either, because it does not offer any explanations of the type of competence I assume a sociolinguistic theory wants to describe, i.e. communicative competence (cf. Hymes 1974a, Le Page 1979).

I agree with DeCamp that it is improper to regard variable rules and implicational scales as rival procedures in this respect because they involve entirely different conceptions of what a linguistic theory should be like and what it should describe. Variable rules make predictions about the likelihood of occurrence of variant utterances. Thus Labov's remark (1969) that the variable rule concept necessitates a revision in the notion of rule of grammar and what it is to know a language is in some respects an extraordinary understatement. To 'know' English, for example, cannot be equated with knowing the probabilities or hierarchy of effect of different environments associated with rules in the grammar. We can formulate statistical laws about the likely occurrence of utterances in a language and yet not be able to understand anything that is said. I do not find myself able to believe that knowledge of the language can be separate from the role it plays in comprehension. I am not claiming that Labov denies the existence of this kind (or part) of competence, but merely that there is nothing in the variable rule concept which would enable us to say interesting things about this aspect of competence (cf. also the discussion in Matthews 1979).

To describe the utterances of speakers/groups in terms of probabilistic laws which are said to be variable rules in a model of grammar is one thing; but to project such rules onto the competence of individual speakers of a language, and then to suppose that speakers or their mental capabilities are in any way constrained by them is, in my opinion, methodologically inadmissible.[9]

9. I think the motivation for the use of probabilistic theories is largely *scientistic* rather than scientific (cf. 9.3.3 and 9.4.1). The two most recent papers on variable rules (Kay and McDaniel 1979; Sankoff and Labov 1979) make no mention of this objection; they are concerned with the technical apparatus of variable rule analysis. Although they too dismiss as relatively minor issues such problems as the interpretation of the competence notion within variable rules and whether the variable rule can be integrated within generative grammar (cf. especially Kay and McDaniel 1979), they do not question the appropriateness of such quantitative methods in the analysis of sociolinguistic data.

9.2 Linguistic and social data: independent or dependent variables?

In the next sections I will consider the extent to which sociolinguistic data can be said to provide the basis for a more coherent theory of change and differentiation than Bailey's wave model, which is based solely on internal linguistic principles. Weinreich et al. (1968) have outlined a research program leading to an empirical theory of language change, which is based on a model of an orderly heterogeneous linguistic system in which the choice between linguistic options carries out social and stylistic functions. Such a system changes with accompanying changes in the social structure. They say (1968: 99):

> a model of language which accommodates the facts of variable usage and its social and stylistic determinants not only leads to more adequate descriptions of linguistic competence, but also naturally yields a theory of language change that bypasses the fruitless paradoxes with which historical linguistics has been struggling for over half a century.

One of the fruitless paradoxes to which they refer is the fact that nothing in Saussurean theory could accommodate a heterogeneous language as the object of a synchronic description. The results of change were recorded through the comparison of successive synchronic analyses, but change itself appeared to elude observation as a process because structuralist descriptions were non-continuous. The only 'mechanism' which entered into the explanation was time. Although Saussure recognized that one of the ways in which language evolved was through speaking, i.e. *parole*, he did not admit that speakers had any part to play in change.

Both Labov's and Bailey's theories are built on the principle that synchronic variation in individuals/groups is or may be itself the vehicle of linguistic change; without variation there can be no change. Weinreich et al. (1968) have identified five relevant problems which a theory of language change must deal with: constraints, transition, actuation, embedding and evaluation. I will discuss some of the empirical findings which relate to these dimensions and evaluate the contribution of both paradigms to the description and explanation of language change. Labov has claimed that there is no distinction to be made between the analysis of the mechanism of a change and its explanation, i.e. he maintains that if we describe the five dimensions given above, then we have 'explained' change. Thus he claims explanatory status for a sociolinguistic theory which is able to describe change. Similarly, Bailey (1972) has suggested that the wave model is explanatory. Therefore, I will be concerned here with examining how these

Table 9.2. *Implicational scale of isoglosses between Low and High German: consonant shift /p t k/ → /(p) f s x/ (data given in Bynon 1977: 177)*

lexical items:		'I'	'make'	'village'	'that'	'apple'	'pound'
Lects Low German	1.	ik	maken	dorp	dat	appel	pund
	2.	ich	maken	dorp	dat	appel	pund
Middle German	3.	ich	machen	dorp	dat	appel	pund
	4.	ich	machen	dorf	dat	appel	pund
	5.	ich	machen	dorf	das	appel	pund
	6.	ich	machen	dorf	das	apfel	pund
High German	7.	ich	machen	dorf	das	apfel	pfund

theories explain what they are claimed to explain and what epistemological status such explanations have.

9.2.1 Transition. Bailey's wave model provides a reasonable account of the transition problem, i.e. how the transition from one state of the language to another occurs in internal linguistic terms, which accords well with certain findings of traditional dialect geography (and in certain respects with my findings in Chapters 6 and 7). Yet, as I mentioned earlier, Bailey's position is that such evidence does not count in the construction of implicational scales, i.e. external evidence is of no interest in the ordering of the environments. It seems to me that it must count, however, if Bailey's claims for the wave model are to have any empirical status. In other words, the ordering of variation in a spatio-temporal network can be tested against the temporal ordering of documented changes. To take an example, I give some data from Wenker's (1878) study of the linguistic boundaries between Low and High German as represented by six words.

The implicational array represents the step-like distribution or patterning of the isoglosses between north and south (Low and High German respectively) in geographical space, and shows how the shift is supposed to have progressed in time by affecting or spreading to different lexical items. The model suggests that the new pronunciations, i.e. the shifted versions, gain in the community while both shifted and unshifted forms coexist. The numbers 1–7 can be conceived of as representing different lects. Stage 1 represents a lect which has undergone no change, and stage 7 shows the completed change; lects 2–6 show the successive phases in the spread of the innovation. This example is however not uncontroversial; there are scholars who argue that the shift proceeded from north to south, and others who think it went from south to north. Thus, stage 7 could be the first stage with the change weakening as it goes north, or 2 could be the first with the shift strengthening as it goes south.

For all practical purposes, if we examine the beginning and end stages, the net effect of the change is the same as if the change had applied uniformly and simultaneously to all members of the speech community, even though the ultimate locus of the transition is one environment in one lect. Like Neogrammarian theory, Bailey's model predicts that the direction of the change is the same for all speakers, and all relevant words are affected in the same way, although not at the same time. The main difference between Bailey's model and Neogrammarian sound change is in the imposition of constraints on the transition period.[10]

Bailey's theory predicts that each lect must differ with respect to the one next to it in terms of only one feature at a time; and that each lect, once affected by the rule change, is internally consistent, i.e. all the items or relevant environments do not change at once discretely. The whole impression is therefore one of gradual and continuous change, but the change proceeds by a series of discrete steps or separate changes, each of which can be thought of as comprising three stages: 1. a grammar prior to innovation; 2. a grammar in innovation, e.g. one old rule and one new one; and 3. a grammar with the innovation, e.g. the old rule lost. Bailey's view fits very well with change which can be characterized as lexically gradual but phonetically abrupt, i.e. lexical diffusion (cf. Wang 1969).

The lack of sharp boundaries resulting from such isogloss patterning had also led some traditional dialect geographers (in particular, Gillieron (1902–10) and the Romance dialectologists) to the conclusion that Bailey and Bickerton have adopted; namely, there are no dialects, or at least, there are no objective dialect boundaries, only subjective ones. Gilliéron might in fact be said to be among the first advocates of polylectal or panlectal grammars; he maintained that none of the Romance dialects was sufficient

10. Bailey's wave model is in many respects a more formalized revival of Schmidt's (1872) wave theory, which was put forward to account for some discrepancies in the classification of the Indo-European languages within a *Stammbaum* framework. Schmidt's wave model accommodated both linguistic convergence and divergence in geographical space, regardless of the genetic relationship of the languages involved. The point of origin of the diffusion of linguistic features was assumed to be the cultural center or focal point (i.e. *Kernlandschaft*) from which change radiated out into the neighboring territory. Such a core area was then surrounded by transitional areas of isogloss bundles. The Rhenish fan is a classic example of this pattern of distribution in which different isoglosses illustrate the extent of the sphere of influence of Cologne from the middle ages onwards (cf. also Trudgill 1973).

on its own to represent the developments which had taken place from Latin to French, but that only the totality of the modern dialects could provide a framework within which individual deviations could be accommodated and explained.

The dynamic paradigm does not appear to be very dynamic if no lect may have variation in more than one environment. Bailey has referred to the theory as dynamic because it dispenses with the structuralist distinction between synchronic and diachronic in favor of a three-dimensional model of linguistic variation which is intended to represent a panlectal competence of speakers. Variation is itself change. Whatever explanations the wave model is capable of presenting must be supported on the basis of the ordering of the rows and columns in an implicational scale which represents speakers and linguistic environments (and features), and checked against a temporal sequence in either real or apparent time.

Bickerton's (1975) data on the process of consonant cluster simplification represent an example where Bailey's wave model predicts the wrong sequence of events in decreolization.[11] Bailey claims that the simplification of consonant clusters consists of a rule containing a number of environments favoring or inhibiting deletion, which are introduced variably and then ordered temporally, so that first one becomes categorical and then another, etc. The difference between adjacent lects in the resulting implicational array represents a difference in time.

Yet, there is no historical evidence which supports Bailey's temporal ordering of the rules. The actual temporal sequence and the process are the reverse of what Bailey predicts. What seems to happen under decreolization is the inhibition of consonant cluster reduction, not the spread of it. The rule seems to be progressively limited so it is allowed to apply in fewer environments. The process appears to be better described as the spread of the inhibition of the rule.

I suggested in Chapter 7 that Bailey's wave model presented a good graphic illustration of the diffusion of the WH relativization strategy in English in terms of the ordering of internal linguistic constraints, i.e. syntactic positions in a case hierarchy which correlate well with intuitive impressions of syntactic complexity (cf. Table 7.15). Yet the wave model which the implicational scale represents does not 'account' for the change, since there is no real time basis for the ordering of the lects (or texts) in this way, i.e. all the modern texts do not fall into one group which can be

11. Bailey (1973: 46) says that his model holds only for natural changes, and that the reverse process occurs under decreolization.

distinguished from the Middle Scots texts. We cannot really say, then, that change took place in the relative system in Middle Scots when the process is apparently still on-going in modern Scots.

Even if the change in primary relativization strategy from TH to WH is a 'dead' issue with respect to the standard language (both spoken and written, and hence Quirk's findings are rather different from those I have reported here), this study adds to our understanding of the implementation phase (or what Weinreich et al. (1968) call the transition and embedding stages) of linguistic change. The evidence from apparent time is inconclusive in itself; but, compared with the evidence from real time, we can see that the process never completed itself in the spoken language, particularly in modern Scots. Thus a similar process of diffusion in response to stylistic constraints manifests itself in successive stages of the language.

Bailey does not provide an account of stable variation, since within his framework, all variation implies change; and there is no distinction between real and apparent time. Labov's work, however, demonstrates that the way in which linguistic differentiation is patterned with respect to age-grading contributes perhaps the most to our understanding of the transition dimension of change. He distinguishes between age-grading which repeats itself each generation and age-grading which represents a stage in long term change.

The simplest evidence which can be offered in favor of the existence of a linguistic change is differing behavior between two successive stages of a language with regard to a particular feature. Such data are, of course, the familiar stock-in-trade of historical linguists. The only meaningful sense in which sound change could be observed is in retrospect, i.e. through a comparison of the results of a change with some stage prior to the change recorded in earlier documents.

Weinreich et al. (1968) proposed that no useful distinction could be made between a change and its propagation, so that change might be observed in comtemporary variation seen as a stage in long term linguistic change.[12] Working from this assumption, change in progress can be observed by comparing 'change in apparent time', i.e. age-grading, or the fluctuating language behavior in different generations of speakers in a population at a given point in time, with 'change in real time', i.e. usage reported in earlier records.

The first demonstration of the importance of age-grading as a mecha-

12. A number of linguists (particularly structuralists and generativists) argued that only the *propagation* of a change could be observed, not the change itself (cf. for example, King 1969 and Hockett 1950).

Table 9.3. *Data from three generations of Charmey speakers (Gauchat 1905: 205)*

Generation	I (90–60 yrs.)	II (60–30 yrs.)	III (under 30)
	l'	l' – y	y

nism in the transmission of change is found in Gauchat's (1905) study of Charmey. Gauchat's work does not seem to have aroused much interest (apart from Hermann's investigation of Gauchat's results in 1929) until its mention by Labov (1963) and Weinreich et al. (1968), probably because Gauchat's findings were so controversial at the time of the study. In any case, I think Gauchat's study must now be seen as a superb piece of sociolinguistic research.

Gauchat found that there was fluctuation among the middle generation of speakers with respect to the use of both old and new norms in the language (see Table 9.3), the case in point being a change from [ʎ] to [j], Gauchat's [l'] and [y]. In 1929 Hermann concluded that Gauchat had obtained a record of sound change in progress in this observation of age-grading differences by comparing the differences between Gauchat's records and his own later ones.

Gauchat's results were striking for a number of reasons. Firstly, they challenged the homogeneity of the idiolect; and secondly, they indicated that one way in which change could take place within the system was by oscillation between old and new norms. The latter finding challenged the Neogrammarian view of a linguistic system as a set of uniform and homogeneous rules which changed discretely from generation to generation.

Gauchat's conclusions were all the more damaging to Neogrammarian ideas about sound change since he had chosen Charmey for the study precisely because the conditions there seemed most likely to support the existence of a homogeneous speech community. Thus Gauchat observes (1905: 222):[13]

Cependant il importe de constater qu'à Charmey, où toutes les conditions sont plutôt favorables à l'unité, la diversité est beaucoup forte que je ne le serais imaginé

13. Hermann (1929: 198) challenged Gauchat's belief that Charmey was a likely spot to look for homogeneity. His opinion was that 'die Mundart von Charmey bildet also einen Ausnahmefall; denn sonst ist eine Mundart nach allen Seiten von derselben Sprachen umgeben', and Gauchat had had 'eine falsche Vorstellung über die Abgeschlossenheit Charmeys'.

après une courte visite ... L'unité du patois de Charmey après un examen plus attentif, est nulle.

Despite the Neogrammarian belief that language was a property of the individual (cf. e.g. Paul 1920), individuals did not have a part to play in transition from one stage of the language to another. The locus of change lay in the discontinuity of different generations of speakers in the community; one way in which change originated was through the imperfect acquisition or imitation of children (i.e. *Einübungstheorie*). Both Gauchat and Hermann found evidence which contradicted the notion that idiolects remained stable after childhood; but Gauchat, in particular, seemed puzzled by the role of the individual in transmitting sound change. He says (1905: 230–2).

Nos matériaux nous obligent à chercher les motifs immédiats d'une loi phonétique *à l'intérieur d'une génération.* La part active de l'enfant consiste à Charmey à généraliser un fait qui paraît capricieux dans la prononciation de sa mère ... Les lois naîtraient dans la bouche de l'individu et se généraliseraient dans les conditions favorables ... Mais alors, comment s'explique le changement de l'articulation des débutants, et comment faut-il que ces débutants soient faits pour devenir influents? Faut-il être un enfant de maître d'école pour jouer un rôle dans l'évolution linguistique? ... Nos matériaux n'offrent aucunc trace d'influence personnelle. La formule *dow pã* (*du pain*) peut devenir *du pã* dans la bouche de n'importe quelle personne. La faute *du pã* ne devient loi qu'après avoir été faite indépendamment par un très grand nombre de personnes. Seules les fautes génériques ont des chances de s'imposer ... Enfin l'état des choses que nous avons observé à Charmey ne donne pas raison à ceux qui croient encore à l'infallibilité des lois phonétiques. Les personnes ne jouent pas un rôle très important dans la transformation de la langue, mais bien les mots.

The problem which bothered Gauchat was how to define the origin of change if the individual himself could not change the language. By equating selection with origin, the transition factor was effectively shifted onto society, i.e. individuals vary, but the group changes the language by selecting among the variants.[14] This is also the position taken by Weinreich et al. (1968: 187):

14. Sapir's (1921: 165–6) often-quoted statement about language drift incorporates the notion of linguistic evolution consisting of two processes, variation and selection:

    What significant changes take place in it [i.e. language drift] must exist to begin with as individual variations ... the drift of a language is constituted by the unconscious selections on the part of its speakers of those individual variations that are cumulative in some special direction.

    The conflation of selection and origin obscures the exact point of spatio-temporal actuation of a change in Labov's theory, but not Bailey's. Of course, it is highly unlikely that such a point would be recorded (except maybe by accident, cf. Longmire 1976); and we would recognize such an innovation in an individual as the origin of a sound change only in retrospect anyway.

Linguistic change is not to be identified with random drift proceeding from inherent variation in speech. Linguistic change begins when the generalization of a particular alternation in a given subgroup of the speech community assumes direction and takes on the character of orderly differentiation.

Thus, the introduction of a new variant into the speech use of an individual does not constitute change. A whole group has to show a change before it is considered a real change. This suggests that changes or innovations have to keep recurring within individuals until they are selected and then transmitted.[15] Paul (1920: 39) believed that change occurred in the idiolect by selective adaptation to other idiolects during social interaction. The theory of biological evolution provided an analogy for linguistic evolution in the principle of natural selection as a proposed explanation for change and diversity.[16]

The biological metaphor is still productive in current views on change which emphasize the role of the individual; for example, Stross comments (1975: 24):[17]

Generation, transmission, and extinction of particular variants is essentially an individual phenomenon, but variation can also be viewed from the perspective of the speech community in terms of competition and selection. Variants compete for dominance in the community repertoire as the pressures of natural selection acting upon the human bearers of variants tend to remove some variants from the repertoire while allowing others to continue the struggle for survival and dominance.

As an explanatory principle, however, the concept of natural selection is meaningless, unless some independent criterion for survival can be established; there does not appear to be a convincing argument in favor of the adaptive function of linguistic diversity and change.[18]

15. Kruszewski (1881) distinguished between *Lautwandel* and *Lautwechsel*; the former are synchronic sound shifts and the latter alternations which may be remnants of *Lautwandel*.
16. The parallels between the theory of biological evolution and linguistic change were recognized by Max Müller (before Darwin) and by Schleicher (1863), i.e. origin from a common ancestor; but it was Darwin who in a sense completed the analogy by arguing for the 'survival of the fittest', a principle which he had read in the work of Müller.
17. Cf. also Longmire (1976), who suggests that /s/ deletion in Spanish is a reappearance of an innovation which began in early Latin. She discusses the problem of how to bridge the gap between language as a property of the individual and that of the group apart from the individual. She (like Sapir) seems to be saying that languages have inherited tendencies transmitted either known (?) or unknown to their speakers which can then reappear (cf. Mendel's idea that the reappearance of traits within organisms after several generations constituted the transfer or inheritance of a trait).
18. Lass (1980) has given a detailed discussion of some of the functionalist arguments used in theories of language change in order to show their explanatory inadequacy. He cites the particular difficulty in defining the locus of a function, i.e. individual or collective; in order for a change to be propagated, the function must be propagated along with it. A better case (or one equally as good) can be made for the maladaptive function of linguistic change and diversity if one examines the social and political

One of the most important similarities between the Darwinian theory of evolution and the theory of sound change accepted by many of the Neogrammarians was the random nature of the process. In other words, speakers were thought to make no conscious effort in producing innovations; but in speaking, each individual tried to reproduce sounds without always hitting the target he aimed for. In each case, however, he produced a chance deviation from the original, since exact replication was impossible. Eventually, the mean of these scattered performances shifted towards a new norm. Such a shift could take place without attracting the attention of speakers because it was assumed to take place so gradually, i.e. by infinitesimal steps. This is also Hockett's (1958: 443) view of allophonic drift by a series of shifts in local frequency maxima. The only way in which A could become or change into B was through a continuous process with a number of intermediate steps.

The idea of intermediate forms is essential in a theory of language change which assumes articulatory gradualness as the mechanism by which phonetic change is accomplished. The problem, however, is that not all sound changes could be credibly described as proceeding through intermediate positions, e.g. those which involve discontinuous articulators. Gauchat's study of the replacement of [l'] by [y] in Charmey challenged the classical model of regular and gradual change with the discovery that the middle generation did not display an intermediate phonetic value between [l'] and [y]; instead, he found fluctuation between the two, thus establishing alternation between variants as a mechanism of linguistic change.[19]

As more information on sound change becomes available (cf. especially Labov et al. 1972), it is becoming more widely accepted that not all sound change has to take place gradually; and in particular, that it is a mistake to fail to discriminate gradualness from change by infinitesimal steps (cf. e.g.

consequences of linguistic heterogeneity (cf. e.g. Fishman 1968). The Neogrammarians claimed that sound change was dysfunctional (but cf. Weinreich et al. 1968: 101); and indeed linguistic *homogeneity* is significantly correlated with economic and social advantages. In spite of this, however, there is also evidence to support the observation that dialect diversification is continuing, even in the face of expanding communications. A strict interpretation of evolutionary theory requires that diversification and complexity be seen as an advance since, functionally speaking, this allows an increase in the range and variety of adaptations to the environment (cf., however, Jespersen 1894).

19. One way out of the dilemma in Charmey would have been to explain the behavior of the second generation as dialect mixture or borrowing (or even internal borrowing, i.e. the middle generation could 'borrow' a form from the older or younger generation). Gauchat, however, claimed that there were no external influences in Charmey; the village had been selected precisely for its supposed homogeneity (cf. n. 13, this chapter). Transformational grammar could not provide an account for such findings either, even though it was accepted by some transformationalists that sound change could be either gradual or discrete. Change could not, however, proceed by oscillation; either the grammar had a rule or it did not, with nothing in-between (cf. King 1969).

Lass 1978: 225–9 for a discussion of the latter). Labov's work, for example, has established that allophonic variation is important in change and has shed some light on the discreteness vs. continuity issue. The plotting of vowels in F_1/F_2 space (cf. Labov et al. 1972: Vol. II) for a number of on-going changes in various English dialects illustrates the movement of a range of variant realizations in certain directions in phonetic space.

Labov has also established that fluctuation of the type Gauchat found in Charmey is a common mechanism of change, i.e. the frequency of occurrence of one or more competing variants increases or decreases in certain environments, and then spreads.[20] Chen (1976: 228) has argued too for the existence of a stage in the process of change from A to B in which A alternates with B. With respect to evidence for this kind of change, there seems to be a good case to be made for the quantitative paradigm. Individual grammars do seem to be characterized by inherent variability; and change in an environment need not take place by categorical innovations, but may take place by changes in the relative proportions of variant realizations.

The restriction that no lect may have variation in more than one environment at a time in Bailey's model has the consequence that variable environments in an implicational scale must occur between an environment in which the rule operates categorically and one in which the rule does not operate at all. Therefore, Bailey's wave model does not handle very well either change by oscillation (which may or may not be phonetically gradual), or a type of change which might be characterized as phonetically gradual, but lexically abrupt, i.e. classical gradual change (cf. Wang 1969).

The existence of gradual lexical diffusion, however, presents some problems for the variable rule model, which predicts shifts in probabilities associated with different environments in the rule. Labov's rules assume that the rate of application will be the same throughout the lexicon; but Wang's (1969) data indicate that the rate of rule application will vary for individual lexical items. In fact, a great deal of the data Labov et al. (1972) present show differences in lexical items with respect to certain phonetic processes, e.g. raising of /æ/. For this reason Wang has questioned whether there is any advantage in using the variable coefficients as a model of change.[21]

20. Milroy (1978: 112) claims that there is no reason to suppose that there is any stage of a language which does not exhibit a wide range of such alternations.
21. Cf. Milroy (1978) for a description of on-going lexical diffusion in Belfast working class vernacular, which appears to be a combination of both lexical diffusion and phonetically gradual change.

Furthermore, Labov's conception of change as innovation occurring in the grammar of a speech community depends on coherent notions of speech community and sociolectal grammar. His conflation of the origin and propagation of a change into one factor shifts the search for explanations of change from the individual to external forces in society. Within the quantitative paradigm there no longer seems to be any argument about whether social factors are involved in linguistic change, but how deeply they are involved. For Labov the focal point of linguistic change is social class. In the next section I discuss his claim that a viable account of language change and differentiation depends on consideration of the social aspect of the embedding problem.

9.2.2 The social dimension of linguistic change. DeCamp, Bailey and Bickerton all maintain that implicational scales and relationships are purely linguistic, and that the addition of a social component to implicational scales can contribute nothing to our knowledge of the patterning of linguistic structure or to an explanation of change. DeCamp and Bickerton, in particular, have said a great deal about this issue; although DeCamp's remarks are, I think, the least challenging to Labov's arguments.

DeCamp (1970, 1971a) has criticized Labov for his assumption that social categories are discrete, and can therefore serve as independent variables. He argues that the only valid approach is to start with linguistic features, which, once scaled, can serve as discrete categories and can be correlated with social data. This difference in approach reflects the methodological boundary between sociolinguistics and the sociology of language (if a distinction between the two is tenable; cf. my comments in Chapter 1). I comment later on the reasons why I do not think DeCamp's criticism can provide a rational basis for choosing between the dynamic and quantitative paradigms.

Labov's work has been essentially correlative, with social structure serving as an independent variable and speech data as the dependent one. The assumption behind this approach is that social structure is reflected in linguistic behavior (cf. Chapter 6, n.1). By interviewing individuals/groups representative of different social categories in different situations certain differences in the speech of the members of the community can be found to covary or correlate with social factors in a systematic way. These linguistic differences are organized along two dimensions: social distance and stylistic function.

In the first large-scale study employing this methodology, Labov (1966) identified a number of aspects of the social context of language use which appeared to be closely connected with linguistic differentiation and on-going change in New York City. He also demonstrated that the social evaluation of competing forms involved in these processes was often the first catalyst towards a change which would eventually complete itself in the speech community.

Social class differences were, of course, known to be connected with the transmission of change before Labov's study. Wyld (1920), for example, noticed the social class correlation in the study of *er/ar* alternation (e.g. *person/parson*), in London English. He suggested that *ar* was a feature of regional speech which entered standard London speech and was later ousted by pressure from the middle class, but this time in favor of the spelling pronunciation. Labov's work has since established this pattern of movement as typical of a certain type of linguistic change.

A number of sociolinguistic studies have illustrated the embedding of linguistic change in social class (cf. e.g. Reichstein 1960; Labov 1966; Trudgill 1974). So far, examples seem to be of two types, which are described by Labov (1966: 328) as 'change from above' and 'change from below'. Each illustrates a process in which social pressures and attitudes come to bear on linguistic structure. Although change does not seem to be unidirectional, i.e. from the upper down to the lower classes, what does seem to be characteristic is that the originating group is neither the lowest or highest in the social hierarchy. Change originates from within the system rather than on the periphery.[22]

Change from below is initiated by a group which is near the bottom of the social class scale; it spreads until it becomes more generalized in the speech of other groups higher up, where social reaction may fasten onto it and suppress or reverse it. Such change is typically below the level of conscious awareness. Change from above, by contrast, comes from the upper social stratum and is generally noticed because it is associated with a high prestige group. This change is then adopted by groups lower in the social scale. During the earliest and latest stages of a change there may be little correlation with social factors, but Labov (1972c: 293) has commented that in every case that has been closely studied, 'one social group or another has been found to lead strongly in the development of a linguistic change'.

Similarly, in societies where social groups are stratified by caste and/or

22. This aspect of embedding is not well handled within Bailey's model; neither is the cross-over pattern of hypercorrection by the lower middle class in more formal styles. The latter has to be dealt with in a side scale.

ethnic group, ethnic identity may be a component of the social context of linguistic change. Bright and Ramanujan (1964) report findings similar to Labov's; namely, that upper and lower class Tamil dialects innovate independently. Furthermore, the Brahmins were chief innovators in conscious change, while the less conscious changes affected both classes. In New York City Labov found that ethnic identity played a more important role than social class in the differentiation of some of the variables. Labov (1963) has also demonstrated the importance of local identity rather than other factors such as occupation, geography, education or sex, in the centralization of /ay/ and /aw/ on Martha's Vineyard.

The importance of sex differentiation and, in particular, the role of women as a factor in linguistic change has been known since Gauchat's study of Charmey (1905).[23] Virtually every sociolinguistic study since Labov (1966), as well as a number of studies prior to it, e.g. Fischer (1958) and Reichstein (1960), have revealed a pattern of sex differentiation with respect to the use of certain linguistic features. One repeated conclusion of such studies is that women are typically the leaders in furthering linguistic change in western society; they use more of the newer linguistic forms than men. Not only do they use more advanced forms in their casual speech, but they also correct more sharply in formal styles. Nordberg (1971, 1975) has concluded that this pattern of sex differentiation, which seems ubiquitous in the United States and western Europe, could almost serve as a criterion for determining which speech forms are stigmatized, and which carry prestige in a given community.[24]

It is not always the case, however, that women lead in all types of linguistic change; men also seem to be responsible for the introduction of new norms, although these are usually vernacular norms which are said to have 'covert prestige' (cf. Trudgill 1972), rather than 'overt prestige'. The most important factor involved in linguistic change seems to be the more general phenomenon of sex differentiation rather than the role of men or women. Trudgill (1972: 179) has stressed the importance of this pattern in linguistic change; he says that 'patterns of sex differentiation deviating from the norm indicate that a linguistic change is taking place'.

The structure of stylistic variation is also known to be an important factor in language differentiation and change. Labov's research in par-

23. Gauchat's (1905: 218) explanation of the role of women was that somehow innovations became selected as changes by occurring more and more frequently; and women talked more than men, thus advancing sound change. Hermann (1929: 213), however, questioned Gauchat's finding that women were ahead of men in certain sound changes in Charmey.

24. Sociolinguistic work in rural societies, however, has obtained different results (cf. e.g. Albó 1970; Irvine 1978).

ticular has shown that social and stylistic variation do not differ in kind. The classic finding seems to be that a socially diagnostic variable will also show stratification along a stylistic dimension (cf. 5.3); deviations from one axis of variation are usually accompanied by deviations from the other. Patterns of stylistic variation of socially diagnostic variables differing from this characteristic type can be seen in the light of repeated sociolinguistic investigations as a recurrent aspect of a linguistic change in progress.

The intimate connection between social and stylistic variation is reflected in the social evaluation of linguistic differentiation. Lower middle class speakers typically exceed the upper middle class in their use of prestige norms in more formal styles, i.e. they hypercorrect. Evidence from subjective reaction tests and self-evaluation reports indicates that this same group is 'hypersensitive' to the use of stigmatized features, so that the lower middle class not only shows the greatest use of the stigmatized feature in their casual speech, but also displays the greatest sensitivity to it in subjective reactions. Labov has suggested that this pattern of hypercorrection of the lower middle class, which manifests itself as a tendency to adopt the formal speech pattern of younger, upper middle class speakers, serves as a critical mechanism of linguistic change by providing a feedback system which is potentially capable of accelerating the introduction of a prestige feature.

I turn now to a number of unanswered questions or contradictory findings which are indicated in the repeated correlations between social and linguistic structure (or what Labov has referred to as 'sociolinguistic patterns'), to examine the extent to which these can be considered explanatory. Linguistic variables can be classified into three different types depending upon the social evaluation they receive and the external factors with which they are correlated (cf. Labov 1972c: 314):

1. Stereotypes – socially stigmatized features.
2. Indicators – features embedded in a social matrix which show social differentiation by age or class, but have no pattern of style shifting and little evaluative force.
3. Markers – features which show both stylistic and social stratification in either of two ways: (a) sharp stratification – distribution over the social classes is not continuous, but discrete, i.e. classes cluster in their use or avoidance of a variable, e.g. most grammatical variables in American English; or (b) fine stratification – feature displays continuously differentiated values with stratification preserved at each stylistic level, e.g. most phonological variables.

I have grouped these types of variables in Table 9.4. Labov's work does

Table 9.4. *Types of linguistic variables in relation to demographic stratification and style shifting*

Type of variable		Demographic stratification	Style shifting
stereotype		–	–
indicator	type 1	+	–
	type 2	–	+
marker		+	+

Table 9.5. *Variable type and linguistic change*

	Change in progress		
Markers	Below	Above	No change in progress
prestige variants	?	(r)	?
stigmatized variants	(oh)	(eh)	(th)

not demonstrate the existence of a Type 2 indicator, but that of Fishman et al. (1971) docs, so I have included it here. Labov's findings suggest that contextual and demographic variation always coincide.

The category of markers can be further subdivided according to their relationship to or involvement with the two types of change supported by empirical data so far. I have done this in Table 9.5, and have given examples (all of them from Labov 1966) which represent each category. (The question marks indicate categories that have not been demonstrated empirically.) The gaps suggest some inconsistencies in the explanations Labov has offered for social dialect differentiation and language change.

Labov's theory is based on the assumption that the spread of linguistic innovations depends on the social prestige attached to them. He has proposed the notion of covert prestige to account for the spread of change from below, i.e. from the lower middle or working class. Overt prestige, on the other hand, emanates from the upper social groups. If, however, each group's norm has its own prestige, then why do we not find that change originates in any group? Why is there no change from the very lowest groups, for example? Labov argues that this group is the least affected by prestige norms; although if the above is true, then they must attach covert prestige to their own norm.

Labov does not really offer an explanation for the difference in mechanisms of change which originate from above or below in the hierarchy. Must change from above motivated by overt prestige of the upper classes always be conscious? And must change from below always be unconscious? The dominant group affects change either by inhibiting change from below, or borrowing from external groups; while the lower social groups initiate change through internal borrowing, either of the variants already existing within the group (e.g. centralization on Martha's Vineyard), or of the prestige norms of groups higher up, mainly by hypercorrection.

One empirical finding of Labov's that has gone largely unchallenged is the peculiar behavior of the middle class. Middle class speech is characterized by less internal differentiation and less complex phonetic conditioning than that of the working class (cf. also Berdan 1975: 38). There does not seem to be any reason why this should be so other than the possibility that this result is the artifact of a methodological paradigm which has concentrated almost exclusively on working class speech, which Labov claims is the most consistent. Therefore, most of the vowel shifts discussed in Labov et al. (1972) originate in working class vernacular. There is also the added fact which I mentioned in the previous chapter that the speech of the lower classes is defined in terms of its deviation from the standard speech of the middle class and change is assumed to take place in that direction.

Once we acknowledge the existence of different norms of speaking and prestige attached to them as co-existent within the same speech community, then the notion of the speech community describable in terms of its usage of a linguistic variable controlled by a single variable rule breaks down (cf. 8.5 and Romaine 1980b). Within the context of the increasing number of sociolinguistic studies being carried out in new settings, the idea that a speech community can move as a whole in a certain direction in the way Labov suggests appears to be too simplistic.[25]

Irvine (1978), for example, has recently reported an instance of on-going change in Wolof noun classification, which is being accomplished by competing pressures from two social groups. What is particularly interesting about Irvine's study is that the nature of the participation of the social factors runs counter to what is predicted by Labov in two important respects. Firstly, Irvine finds that a spread of the innovating tendencies in the noun classification system, which is associated with the upper class of

25. Cf. also Popper's (1961: 124) criticism of historicism. He comments on the 'holistic confusion' in the belief that society, like a physical body, can move as a whole along a certain path and in a certain direction.

nobles, is operating to move the system towards the norm of high status speaking. High status speaking in Wolof is characterized by a reduction in surface elaboration.

The overall trend is a familiar one, i.e. language change as ostensible simplification, but the social mechanism or agent which is responsible for carrying it out (in this case, change by the highest ranking social group) is not what we would expect. Labov's work shows that the lower class typically leads in simplificatory processes (at least at the phonetic level).[26] Secondly, in Irvine's case, it is the lower class that is more conservative and tends towards elaboration of the noun classification system and maintaining it intact.

Irvine claims (as I have also, cf. Romaine 1979c) that these sorts of competing changes represent cases in which norms of speaking associated with different groups in the same community are crucial in providing an account of differentiation and change in the system. Covert prestige (if there is such a thing) can be just as powerful a factor in the maintenance of vernacular norms as change, as Milroy and Margrain's (1978) account of pressure towards vernacular norm maintenance in Belfast demonstrates. It also seems that the norms of the upper and lower groups may coincide in certain cases (cf. e.g. my analysis of /r/ in Scottish English presented in Chapter 8, and Milroy's (1978) account of lexical diffusion in Belfast), which does not seem interpretable as change from above by conscious imitation of a prestige norm, or as conscious movement towards a more standard form of speech.

It should not be surprising that Labov's (or Bailey's) theory does not account for all possible mechanisms of change. Despite its complexity, New York City must not be seen as the archetypical sociolinguistic model for the relationship between social and linguistic differentiation, but rather as an important prototype illustrating one way in which social and linguistic structures interact in a particular urban speech community.

In the next section I return to the following statement by Weinreich et al. (1968:102n):

> The transition, embedding, and evaluation problems were discussed ... under the heading of *mechanism* of a change. However, it seems difficult to give a precise meaning to the term *mechanism of a change*, and here we do not distinguish between explanation of a change and the analysis of the mechanism itself.

26. There is, of course, the possibility that Irvine's data point primarily to the conclusion that grammatical/syntactic variation is governed by somewhat different constraints than phonetic/phonological (cf. Chapter 2).

In my examination of the next two dimensions of change, i.e. constraints and actuation, I will attempt to show why Labov's sociolinguistic patterns (which are to be understood as statements of covariation between social and linguistic structure, cf. Tables 9.4 and 9.5) and Bailey's wave model are not, strictly speaking, *explanatory* of linguistic differentiation and change. The conflation of explanation and analysis of mechanism merely begs the question. I will look closely at one particular example, where an attempt has been made at a causal explanation of the relationship between linguistic and social factors in order to illustrate my argument that even if this type of explanation were valid in linguistics (and I claim later that it is not) it is not anyway the kind of explanation that we want within a sociolinguistic theory.

9.2.3 Constraints and actuation: what can be explained? Bickerton (1973c: 30) and Bailey (1969b: 129) both agree that although the wave model is capable of representing change by varying the order of constraints, it cannot explain change or predict the course that a given change will take. Bailey (1969b: 129) has said that 'At least two points cry for an explanation, besides the fundamental question of why a change starts spreading. We do not know what factors make one word or one environment more favorable for the operation of one rule than another.' Thus, there is no 'explanation' offered for the various types of implicational patterns or of the actuation problem, i.e. why this, now?

Weinreich et al. (1968: 127) appear to regard the question of actuation as potentially answerable, at least in the following statement:

> Of maximum importance is ... the proposal of new causes of change based on a theory of language states so firmly established that one change in a language state necessarily implies another change ex hypothesi, so that event A can be designated a cause of change B ... It is only rarely that historical linguistics has had glimpses of such causal theories.

I raise now the question of whether there can be causal explanations of this type in accounting for change and linguistic differentiation in sociolinguistic theory. I take as the definition of a causal explanation one which is accepted within philosophy of science (cf. e.g. Braithwaite 1960: 320), namely: q because p. In other words, we understand q because we know that event p was nomically sufficient to determine the event to be explained, q.[27] In the absence of specifiable causal mechanisms, statistical expla-

27. Lass (1980) has examined the epistemological status of certain kinds of explanations in historical linguistics and reached similar negative conclusions.

nations are often accepted as special cases of incomplete deductive–nomological explanations. The assumption is made that we lack the means at present of formulating the precise laws which govern the events to be explained, through ignorance, lack of technical apparatus, etc. (cf. Scheffler 1963: 75). This seems to be Labov's position in proposing that probabilistic statements describing the covariation between social and linguistic structure in the form of variable rules can provide sociolinguistics with an empirical base.

A similar assumption seems to be at work in Milroy and Margrain's (1978) attempt to make a quantitative statement of the extent to which an individual's network structure predicts his linguistic behavior. I am taking their analysis here as an example of an attempt to construe a statement of covariation as a causal explanation; this will serve as a convenient point of departure for the methodological discussion which follows.

Milroy and Margrain (1978) invoke the concept of social network as a causal mechanism in explaining change and variation among working class speakers in Belfast for reasons which I have mentioned (cf. 8.5); namely, the inability of index scores of the group as a whole to account for or predict individual variation within the group. I omit the details of their defense of the notion of social network and concentrate on the structure of their argument and their conclusions.[28]

The authors observe (1978: 6) that 'urban sociolinguistic studies tend to correlate linguistic and extralinguistic variables rather than to use one set of variables to explain the other in any specific way'. They then cite the belief of social scientists that the social network concept 'has a powerful capacity to *explain* social behaviour, rather than simply to *describe* correlations between network type and behaviour'. Their finding is that there is a reliable, i.e. statistically significant, relationship between a speaker's use of language and the structure of his social network.

The conclusion which Milroy and Margrain (1978: 32–4) draw from this correlation is that:

If we accept the general thesis that a dense, multiplex network structure supports vernacular norms intact, we may consider changes in network structure to be

28. Milroy and Margrain (1978) suggest that a particular type of social network characterized by density and multiplexity of relationships is an indicator of the pressures a person is under to adopt the norms of local vernacular. I am not attacking the use of the social network per se (cf. Albó 1970 and Gal 1978 for use of this concept, though not in a causal way). I personally find their analysis illuminating and compelling (though *not* in a causal sense). It is the first satisfying account that I have found of the differential behavior of men and women with respect to the use of certain variables (cf. Milroy and Margrain 1978: 16, 30) by showing how sex and network interact.

responsible for some linguistic change ... Thus it would appear that a dense, multiplex network structure is often associated with strongly vernacular speakers well outside working class Belfast. We would suggest a *causal relationship* here; this particular network structure can function powerfully to maintain vernacular norms ... heavy users of the vernacular with high network scores are in fact *less free to choose how they will speak*. [emphasis mine SR]

The objection which I (and others) have against causal explanations of this type is summed up in the deterministic view of individual behavior contained in the last line of their startling conclusion. Thus, Milroy and Margrain's answer to the question which Labov (1972b: 114) has posed as the 'sociolinguistic conundrum', i.e. why does anyone say anything?, appears to be, because they *have* to. I think I am correct in assuming that this is the type of explanation or argument which so many sociolinguists (Labov included, implicitly at least) find so disturbing in Bernstein's work, and which initially provided the impetus for a lot of sociolinguistic studies in urban areas.[29]

I think it is misleading to believe that all linguistic variability can be accounted for deterministically through attempts to correlate an ever increasing amount of linguistic data with more and more social factors; it is the latter possibility which so many of Labov's followers appear to find so attractive in the use of the Cedergren–Sankoff program. Indeed, Labov himself seems to be suggesting this in the following statement (1978: 4):

This might indeed be described as the proper goal of a sociolinguistic theory: to apportion the variance in any sub-section of a linguistic system to the functions of representation, identification, and accommodation, and to predict for any new language the probable distribution of the information conveyed in prosody, the vowel system, the quantifier system, and so on.

Even if we do accept variable rules as making predictions of great accuracy about the occurrences of speakers' utterances, we still do not understand *why* anyone said anything. Furthermore, I submit causal predictions of the type I cited above as precisely the kind of explanations we do *not* want. There is another problem with Milroy and Margrain's analysis, apart from the deterministic or behavioristic view it implies. I refer to their confusion between explanation and prediction. The relation between the two is a unilateral implication, i.e. explain implies predict, but a prediction need not be an explanation. Furthermore, Milroy and Margrain's notion of causality is lacking in the empirical relevance typically associated with

29. There is also the added difficulty with Bernstein's work (which I will not go into here), that it is based on dubious data collection procedures; and Bernstein himself is so contradictory.

deductive–nomological explanations; it is therefore actually 'pseudo-causal' (cf. 9.3.3).

Although I do not accept Bickerton's (1973b) arguments that the constraints which limit utterances are purely external and hence no business of the linguist; or his claim that information about the social constraints which operate in a given situation cannot have any theoretical interest, because the assignment of utterances to situations is just as arbitrary as the assignment of these to phonological shapes, I do agree with his defense (1973b: 8) of 'human autonomy':

> by human autonomy I mean, simply, two things: first, that in any society, no matter how controlled or hierarchized, there is a spectrum of variant codes, social and linguistic, and therefore a lot of ways for the individual to go, and second, that out of the total repertoire which this spectrum provides for him, what the individual selects on any given occasion is, ultimately, his own inalienable choice.

Bickerton (1973b: 17) makes clear the danger in carrying the implications of relationships of covariation too far; but, in all fairness, not all sociolinguists have tried to argue from Labovian quantitative correlations (and I stress that this represents only one way to do sociolinguistics) to cause and effect laws, as Bickerton seems to suggest:[30]

> If linguistic variation existed solely as a carrier of extralinguistic information, we would have to explain why it is that a creole community, which has no more and no grosser social distinctions to make than any other community, should require such a fantastic apparatus to make them with ... Once that continuum existed, it was naturally put to social uses; naturally sections of it became associated with different classes of people, different situations, different styles, and served to distinguish those classes, situations and styles from one another. But to argue that variants within the continuum came into existence simply in order to express those distinctions is a plain reversal of the laws of cause and effect.

I do not find Bickerton's discussion sufficient argument against the inclusion of a social component of language use within a linguistic theory. Oddly enough, I suspect it is from the formation of post-creole continua

30. Wolfram (1971: 96) has made a strong claim about the social causation of linguistic differences:

> It should be noted that I have deliberately used the term *result from* in describing the relationship of linguistic and social differences [i.e. that language differences result from social differences], since I wish to imply that this relationship is one of cause and effect. Although the term correlation is often used to describe this relationship and may be accurate in terms of a particular descriptive model, it is not used here because of its neutrality with respect to cause and effect.

Cf. also Kroch and Small (1978), who are followers of Labov's methodology; they have presented an analysis which is in some respects a counterpart of Milroy and Margrain's, namely, the effect of conscious prestige norms, which they have called 'grammatical ideology'. They claim (1978: 52) to have confirmed the hypothesis 'that grammatical ideology is the cause of the intergroup differences [in the use of certain grammatical variables]'.

(which are more often than not being investigated by those who, like Bickerton, have objected most strongly to the use of social factors in the description of linguistic processes) that we stand to learn the most about the interaction between social processes and linguistic structure. A theory which emphasizes the importance of individual choice in these processes need not be asocial, as Le Page (1975) convincingly demonstrates.[31]

Bickerton is, however, correct in rejecting the quantitative paradigm as an adequate basis for a sociolinguistic theory, although not on the strength of empirical evidence. Both paradigms, the quantitative and dynamic, rest on shaky epistemological foundations with regard to their empiricist claims, as I will argue next.

9.3 Is a sociolinguistic theory possible?

Any serious consideration of this question depends upon a careful evaluation of the status which is claimed for a sociolinguistic theory. My view is that the arguments for an autonomous linguistic theory are misguided; the more comprehensive the set of facts a linguistic theory seeks to explain, the better. What I would not accept, however, is Bickerton's and Labov's belief that there can be an empirical basis for such arguments.

Bickerton (1973b: 8), for example, maintains that the choice between a socially constituted and an asocial linguistics is an empirical issue:

> Those whose choice it is to go beyond freedom and dignity whether with the Skinnermen, the Chomskyans or the Contextualists, are, of course, equally free to do so, not with, but against, the balance of the evidence; and that those who still believe in a more libertarian model of human behavior are doing so, not merely on moral grounds, but because there is solid empirical support for this position.

The so-called solid empirical support which Bickerton offers, however, consists of a selection from the many examples he claims illustrate apparent inconsistencies between language and context. These examples, he says, demonstrate that the connection between context and rule application is merely relativistic or probabilistic, not absolute. Bickerton's latter statement is, of course, true; and there are counterexamples to most of the variable rules which have been proposed so far.

31. Cf. also Wolfson (1978) for a social approach which takes the individual into account. In her study of the use of the conversational historical present in American English, Wolfson concludes that there is no direct correlation between this feature and the background of the speaker. Its use depends on the speaker's assessment of addressee appropriateness.

Labov (1972b: 98) also believes that the choice between theories is subject to empirical verification:

> The luxury of methodology first becomes a necessity when continued investigations produce several competing theories, and we have to find out which one is right. This paper is in fact designed to hold up as the highest goal of linguistics the possibility of being right . . . My own view is that such equivalent theories are trivial variants, and to confine ourselves to arguing their merits is to engage in an aesthetic pursuit rather than a scientific one.

My view is that it is really an aesthetic rather than a scientific pursuit that we are engaged in. Labov's alleged empirical foundations for a sociolinguistic theory are based on a mistaken idea of what constitutes the method of natural science and the nature of the issues which can properly be empirical within a linguistic theory.

9.3.1 On the empirical foundations of a sociolinguistic theory. Labov has proposed in a number of places that the data of a sociolinguistic theory should contain facts which are capable of showing intersubjective agreement. He has said (1975b: 77), for example, that 'data from introspection, observation and experiment can be jointly used to build a theory which rests on the evidence of clear cases'. A similar view is also expressed by Berdan and Legum (1976: 97) who argue for a linguistic theory based on experimental evidence:

> if linguistics is to be regarded as an empirical science, its theories of human language must be subject to empirical verification. Such theory-testing requires the accumulation of reliable, researcher-independent facts. The goal of Experimental Linguistics is to further the *simultaneous* progress of data accumulation and theory verification . . . Linguistic theories are of limited interest for explaining human language if they cannot be subjected to empirical verification.

There are two points in these quotations which deserve further comment: 1. the idea that empirical research rests on 'clear cases' and verification of hypotheses; and 2. the belief that empirical theories are the only interesting linguistic theories.

Labov views sociolinguistics as an inductive theory, i.e. one which collects data first, and then formulates a theory on the basis of that data. I pointed out in the first chapter that there is no basis for accepting the belief that there can be theory-free observation; selection and interpretation take place at the level of observation, thus the observer plays an active part in the process of observation. A number of philosophers of science (e.g.

Popper 1972: 342–3; Feyerabend 1978: 272) have treated this problem extensively. Popper (1961: 105) claims that this picture of scientific method, i.e. collecting observations and drawing conclusions from them, is often mistaken as the method of natural science, but is an illusion. Such a method is non-existent.

Labov also appears to believe that the choice of a particular set of observations or perceptions can be demonstrated to correspond to reality. He has argued (1972b: 259), for example:

By enlarging our view of language, we encounter the possibility of being right ... there are many linguists who do not believe that there is a right or wrong side to theoretical alternatives ... I do not mean, of course, that a particular solution offered is right in any absolute sense. But within the framework provided in this chapter, we can say that the kind of solutions offered to problems such as consonant cluster simplification, copula deletion, and negative concord represent abstract relations of linguistic elements that are deeply embedded in the data. It is reasonable to believe that they are more than the constructions of the analyst – that they are the properties of language itself.

There is nothing 'wrong' with realism per se (though I will argue later that this position must be abandoned as a foundation for a sociolinguistic theory); the difficulty in defending this point of view lies in deciding when/if candidates for real status are demonstrable or non-demonstrable (cf. e.g. Harré 1976: 90–5).[32] Under some conditions, e.g. developments of more appropriate or more powerful instruments, some candidates for reality achieve the status of real things – the virus, for example. I do not think that such conditions exist in linguistics; although, as I pointed out in Chapter 7 (cf. especially n.2), Labov seems to think that probability theory and the Cedergren–Sankoff program provide confirmation of the existence of things like rule schemata, etc. as properties of the data. Thus (Labov 1975a: 196):

Quantitative synthesis, which follows measurement, can give us the objective justification we need; we can show that our rule synthesis is a property of the data itself, and not the result of habit, ideology, or speculative assumptions about the human brain.

Labov seems to retreat a bit from this position in more recent writings, as indicated by the first part of the following statement. Yet the conclusion

32. By realism I mean the view that statements of the theory are true or false and that some of the entities referred to in the theory have an existence in the real world.

seems contradictory, and I think it is fair to say that Labov has not really altered his views on the power of variable rules. Thus (Labov 1978: 12–13):

> Linguistic variables or variable rules are not in themselves a 'theory of language'. They are all heuristic devices. But it is not accidental that linguistic theory has profited from the analysis of variable ways of saying the same thing. Powerful methods of proof proceed from quantitative studies, and this fact is itself a significant datum for our understanding of language structure and language function ... Thus a variable rule analysis is not put forward as a description of the grammar, but a device for finding out about the grammar. Some results support the initial model, others discredit it. We are left with a statement of the degree of objective evidence for a certain abstract grammatical relation in the rule system used by a given speaker or a speech community ... It is the explanation of the variable constraints that lead us to conclusions about the form of the grammar. When we reach these conclusions we will not hesitate to place probabilistic weights upon our grammatical rules, no matter where they occur.

At any rate, it is evident from Labov's repeated emphasis on quantitative methods, instrumental analysis, etc., to the exclusion of all else, that he is very much an operationalist (cf. e.g. Harré's (1976: 78) comments on Eddington). Labov endorses (both implicitly and explicitly) the view that quantitative data are the best; he reifies calculations and numerical measurements to the point where they become ultimate phenomena. In other words, he passes from n as a measure of some property (p) to the belief that n itself is the phenomenon; and p is eliminated from the system of concepts. Both Labov and Bailey trivialize models by claiming real status for them, as I claimed earlier (cf. Chapter 7; and also Lass 1976c: 191); but I have more to say about the function of models in a sociolinguistic theory later.

I take up now the problem of demonstrating the reality of hypothetical entities in linguistic theory and the so-called verification of linguistic hypotheses. Labov claims (1975a: 42):

> The significance of such figures [i.e. the probability coefficients assigned to the environments in a variable rule] can be tested best by replication. If they appear in all probability models, are repeated for many samples taken, and repeated for subsamples within samples, we can have confidence that they represent the real situation. This is the case.

Most modern philosophies of science have challenged the basic tenets of empiricism by emphasizing that no amount of replication of event-pair occurrences is evidence for the truth of a generalization (cf. e.g. Popper 1972, 1977 on the problem of induction). Labov's position is representative of a rather outdated view of empiricism and the role of falsification in empirical research. His positivistic philosophy is apparent in his misunderstanding of the notion of probability and the role of probability statements in linguistics, or in empirical science in general.

9.3.2 On falsification and the role of probability theories in linguistics. In one of his most important papers on sociolinguistic methodology, Labov (1972b) cites Popper's belief in the role of falsification in science, but seems to have misunderstood it. He comments (1972b: 99) that scientific methodology consists in 'trying to prove to yourself that you are wrong. To be right means that you have finally abjectly, hopelessly failed to prove yourself wrong'. This statement reveals a rather naive view of falsificationism, and one which is certainly not Popper's; for Popper excludes the possibility of being right (or says that even if we were, we would have no way of knowing it). There is no sense in which we can ever consider that we have once and for all failed to falsify a theory, and hence must be right by default. The process of conjecture and refutation, which is the hallmark of Popper's philosophy, is an on-going one; it is never completed. Thus, Popper (1972: 15):

> By this method of elimination, we may hit upon a true theory [i.e. by falsifying or refuting one or more competing theories]. But in no case can the method *establish* its truth, even if it is true; for the number of *possibly* true theories remains infinite, at any time and after any number of crucial tests. (This is another way of stating Hume's negative result.) The actually proposed theories will, of course, be finite in number; and it may well happen that we refute all of them, and cannot think of a new one.

Labov has clearly not given any thought to the problem of falsifying variable rules or other linguistic hypotheses; he is concerned with verifying them and being absolutely right. There is a twofold difficulty here with Labov's attempt to provide linguistics with an empirical base. One is the use of probability statements in variable rules; the second is the confusion of probability with theory corroboration. I examine now the conditions under which probabilities are assigned in empirical science.

The concept of probability has to do with events in the real world. Harré (1972: 157) indicates two characteristics of events which scientists describe by probability theories: 1. things in state A can become either B or C, but not both; and 2. the causes of the differential manifestation of B and C are not known. Harré (1972: 162) also accepts the view that statistical knowledge embodied in probabilities is primitive, i.e. it is essentially preliminary to a complete understanding of the mechanism or law of nature which is responsible for the statistics of those events.

Variable rules can be understood, then, as describing a set of events which consists of tokens of utterances; probabilities of the type used in variable rule analysis must, I think, be understood as numerical probability statements (cf. e.g. Popper 1977: 149). In other words, they are statements about the relative frequency with which an event of a certain kind occurs within a sequence of occurrences, i.e. they predict over an aggregate, but never in an individual instance. The grounds for making such probability statements are, however, objective and have nothing to do with degree of belief in assertions. For Popper, degree of corroboration is not a probability.

Polanyi (1973: 24–5) makes a distinction between probability statements on the one hand, and the probability of a statement, or degree of belief in a statement, on the other. Probable statements about events are not the same as statements about probable events. Failure to falsify a theory or a hypothesis leads to a suspension of judgement, not to 'the probability of being right'.

It follows from the nature of probability statements as defined above, i.e. that they predict over an aggregate, that they can never be falsified by any individual event. Thus, neither Bailey nor Bickerton can claim to have evidence which will falsify the predictions of variable rules, since there is no basis for distinguishing the behavior of an individual who is applying the rule and one who is not. Popper has commented extensively on the role of probability statements in empirical science and the problem of their decidability. He says (1977: 189–90):

> Probability statements will not be falsifiable. Probability hypotheses do not rule out anything observable; probability estimates cannot contradict or be contradicted by, a basic statement; nor can they be contradicted by a conjunction of any finite number of basic statements, and accordingly not by any finite number of observations either... Only an infinite sequence of events – defined intensionally by a rule – could contradict a probability estimate... Probability estimates are unfalsifiable because their dimension is infinite. We should therefore really describe them as empirically uninformative, as void of empirical content.

The consequence of the unfalsifiability of probability statements is, among other things, that it must always be possible to account for any regularity by probability estimates. This does not of course mean that theories, linguistic or otherwise, should not be based on probability statements (though there is another reason why they should not form the basis of a linguistic theory, as I explain below). Popper notes the successes which physics has achieved with predictions arising from hypothetical estimates of probability. Likewise, a number of interesting, and what might be called successful, predictions seem to be possible in linguistics through the use of variable rules.

But Popper has also said (1977: 198) that if theories involving probability are applied without special precautions, they are not to be regarded as scientific. Their metaphysical use must be ruled out if they are to have any use in the practice of empirical science. Popper claims that under certain conditions probability statements can be incorporated into empirical theories; namely, if we assume that they can be falsified by reproducible deviations from a macro-effect which has been deduced from a probability estimate. The assumption here is that extremely improbable events are not reproducible at will. Hence the predictable and reproducible occurrence of systematic deviations from a probability estimate constitutes a falsification of a probability statement (cf. Popper 1977: 203).

I think it is fair to say that the use of probability theory in sociolinguistics as exemplified in the Cedergren–Sankoff variable rule program is not scientific in this sense; it is instead metaphysical. As I explained in Chapter 7 (cf. especially nn. 9 and 11), the criterion of acceptance/rejection does not allow a decision of the degree of fit between the data and any one set of frequency statements or range of observations, but only between competing models on the basis of the values of chi-square (cf. e.g. Labov 1975a: 242). The choice then is that of accepting one model and rejecting the other; but this is not an acceptable basis for deciding between two alternate statistical hypotheses (cf. e.g. Braithwaite 1960: ch. 7).

To reject a hypothesis is a different matter from accepting it; if a rejection criterion eliminated one of two hypotheses, this would not imply that the other one should be accepted, unless we assume that one of the hypotheses is true. This need not be the case. Braithwaite (1960: 200), for instance, gives the example that it need not be the case either that 50 percent or less of births are male births, or that more than 50 percent of births are male births; for there may well be *no* statistical hypothesis at all about the proportion of male births, which is true. All estimations of statistical significance depend on the assumption that there *is* a statistical law which can be realized as a probability value and which is true.

I am not trying to be perverse in my argument about criteria for statistical significance; but merely point out that the proponents of the Cedergren–Sankoff program have not given careful thought to this question. In fact, I would assume that it is not a formidable problem to devise a statistically acceptable measure of significance, which would then qualify the program to be used for empirical purposes; but I leave that to those with more mathematical sophistication. The real issue that I see here is not whether the use of probability theories can be made to conform to the standards of empirical science, but rather, whether they are appropriate to the description of linguistic facts and reveal anything interesting.

9.3.3 Defining a sociolinguistic methodology. There is no real question that some aspects of a speaker's utterances, considered as linguistic facts which have an objective existence in the real world, can be brought within the scope of a statistical or probabilistic law, thus enabling a certain degree of success in predicting the likelihood of further occurrences. The question is whether linguistic behavior can be thought of as law-governed, and whether the extension of probability theories from physics to linguistics makes sense. Physicists, for example, speak of the behavior of atoms or of sub-atomic particles as predictable on the basis of probabilistic laws; but as far as I know, there is no talk among physicists about the 'competence' of atoms or what knowledge the atoms might have, which enables them to behave in such a fashion, nor of the 'meaningfulness' of the various movements of atoms. The problem, even in a metaphorical extension of probabilistic explanations from physical macro-domains to linguistic micro-domains, is this: linguists presumably *do* want to talk about competence and the meaningfulness of individual linguistic behavior.[33]

Since, as I pointed out earlier in this chapter, a sociolinguistic theory with a probabilistic base would not seem to provide us with the means for saying anything about these questions in any interesting way, one solution would be to cease all speculation about such matters, and try to make sociolinguistics empirical; or settle for a sociolinguistic theory which is a lot less

33. I am, of course, greatly simplifying the state of affairs in physics with regard to the use of probability theories. One of the most important philosophical problems in physics centers on the transition from causal to probabilistic laws (cf. e.g. the essays in Feigl and Brodbeck 1953: ch. 5). Not all physicists, for example, accept Heisenberg's principle of indeterminacy, which forms the center of quantum mechanics. Einstein was one who did not abandon the causal 'clockwork' picture of the universe. Heisenberg's followers claim that quantum mechanics is incompatible with a belief in causality. Von Neumann argued that the principle of indeterminacy was not only fundamental, but also final. In other words, in the macroscopic world, statistical statements are reports of averages of large numbers of individual events; but in the microphysical domain, there does not seem to be any way of interpreting statistical statements as averages over large numbers of subquantum events. Microphysical statements are statistical in an absolute sense, and therefore no meaning can be given to statements about these events. The real issue for Einstein was whether quantum mechanics was complete, i.e. he regarded it as only provisional.

empirical. I would opt for the latter, since it is the less restrictive alternative.

This raises the question of whether explanation and methodology in sociolinguistics has the same structure as in the physical sciences; and if proper understanding of sociolinguistic phenomena requires different types of argumentation, i.e. other than causal and/or probabilistic connections. There has been a great deal of discussion of the so-called unity of method doctrine among philosophers of science and of the social sciences (cf. e.g. Winch 1958; Popper 1961; Hempel 1965; Rudner 1966).

Popper (1961: 130–1) supports the unity of method doctrine, i.e. that all theoretical or generalizing sciences make use of the same method, whether they are natural or social sciences. If all disciplines share certain methods of assembling facts and connecting theory with hypotheses, then it follows that the structural characteristics of a theory in social science (and, I would add, a sociolinguistic theory) are precisely the same as those of any other scientific theory (cf. Rudner 1966: 10).

Popper (1961) furthermore maintains that the method of science always consists in offering deductive causal explanations and testing them by way of predictions, i.e. the hypothetical–deductive method. Explanation, prediction and testing is thus the job of all science which is theoretical; and empirical science backs up its explanations and predictions by observable facts. I have already questioned whether explanations of this type are available in sociolinguistics in my examination of Milroy and Margrain's (1978) attempt to make a statement of covariation a causal explanatory one. The result speaks for itself.

Must a sociolinguistic theory employ a radically different method from the one outlined above; or must it fail to achieve the status of an explanatory science in Popper's sense? I accept Winch's argument (1958: 95) that the conceptions according to which we usually think of social events are incompatible with the types of explanations required by the hypothetical–deductive method of science. He claims (1958: 51–2) that any analysis of meaningful or symbolic behavior must allot a central role to the notion of 'rule'. Therefore, all behavior which is meaningful, i.e. all human behavior, is ipso facto rule-governed.

Phenomena like social networks, social groups and variable rules as such are not given to us as definite observable objects or natural units. They refer to certain structures of relationships between some of the many things we observe within spatio-temporal limits. We select certain aspects of such complex phenomena because we think we may perceive connections between them – connections which may or may not in fact exist (cf. Hayek

1952: 54–6). Quantitative analysis in these cases does not measure empirical constructs, but assigns numerical values to relationships within a model.

Furthermore, rules, as opposed to laws, have no implications of nomic necessity. Rules may be broken, but laws are never violated. What this distinction entails for a sociolinguistic theory is this: if the proper domain for a sociolinguistic theory is the study of the use of language in society, then statements of covariation are not laws in the strict sense, and there can be no possibility of their becoming causally explanatory. They may, however, form the basis of taxonomies, as I will explain below.

9.4 Suggestions for a sociolinguistic research program

What I intend to offer here is more in the nature of some methodological guidelines for a sociolinguistic research program rather than a detailed exposition of the foundations of a sociolinguistic theory such as that found in Hymes (1974a). I will be much more programmatic and confine myself to proposing two methodological principles:

1. Avoid scientism.
2. Develop a non-deductivist epistemology.

The first guideline is really a caveat or a negative suggestion; it tells us what *not to do*. By 'scientism' I intend a form of criticism, i.e. the imitation of the language and methods of natural science by social scientists based on a mistaken view of the nature of scientific method and practice. My second point raises the question (for those who will ask it) of what a non-empirical (or only partially empirical) sociolinguistic theory can and should do. The answer I would suggest is to develop taxonomies. I will expand both points before considering the final question of what place a sociolinguistic theory has vis-à-vis a linguistic theory.

9.4.1 Avoiding scientism. I accept Feyerabend's (1978: 179) belief that science is much more sloppy and irrational than its methodological image. Yet some linguists (especially those who follow the quantitative paradigm) seem to have an excessive respect for the prestige and authority conveyed by science; this has resulted in a dangerous misconception of the validity of science as well as in illicit application of images, techniques of analysis, etc. to add inappropriate weight to linguistic arguments, where such a transfer is not warranted. Scientism affects practitioners of other disciplines too, even scientists, to the point where some have argued for the superiority of scientific ethos over all other ethical systems (cf. e.g. the discussion in Hayek 1952, from whom I have taken the term 'scientism'). Popper argues (1972: 295) that 'It is not science but dubious philosophy (or outdated science) which leads to idealism, phenomenalism, and positivism, or to materialism and behaviorism, or to any other form of anti-pluralism.' Feyerabend (1978: 307) has also maintained that a science that insists on possessing the only correct method and the only acceptable results is ideology, and not science. I think that a number of the supporters of the dynamic and quantitative paradigms are guilty of promoting ideology based on a misunderstanding of the function of scientific research, i.e. the view that scientific theories must penetrate the essence of things in order to explain them. This essentialism is particularly apparent in Labov's insistence on being right and on the reality of certain theoretical constructs.

The models which Bailey and Labov propose to 'explain' change and variation are ultimately metaphorical. All theory construction is essentially model building; and models often contain imagined entities and processes which may invite existential questions. Harre (1972: 38f.) has given careful consideration to the role of models in theory construction, which I find insightful here. He distinguishes between models, analogies and metaphors which, although closely related, are not identical tools. In particular, he strikes a distinction between the use of models as the source of picturesque terminology and models as the source of genuine science-extending existential hypotheses.

Harré defines a model as a thing or process analogous to that of which it is a model, which can be described in the language of simile. He gives as an example a model of the economy, which makes use of cycles of inflation, depression and boom. He observes (1972: 47), however, that 'The model offers us nothing by way of explanation, and no existential hypotheses, but it does provide, in the system of metaphors, a picturesque terminology.' According to Harré, a metaphor is a set of concepts derived as in the standard process of model building, but which have no causal connections with phenomena. This seems to me to be an accurate description of the function of models in linguistics. The function of such models cannot be to generate existential hypotheses; therefore, Harré says, a model of this type does not form part of an explanation in the usual sense. Its function is to illuminate the facts, throw them into a new light, or make them more readily memorable.

I think it is a mistake to put questions about the reality or existence of theoretical entities into the center of linguistic theories. Belief in a theory need not entail essentialism or realism, but only a commitment to a belief that a phenomenon can be described by the application of a theory. It is naive to argue that the question of the nature of language is exhausted by the question of the nature of a grammar based on variable rules or implicational scales. If the success of a sociolinguistic theory is to be determined by its ability to say correct things about the nature of language, then it will almost certainly preside over its own demise.

9.4.2 Developing a non-deductivist epistemology. To take a more positive outlook, I will suggest that there are a number of interesting things that a sociolinguistic theory can do without being empirical or insisting on a particular view of the nature of language. Such a theory can still be partially empirical. Although there can be no question that decisions between competing theories which describe variation and change are not empirical ones, we do have evidence (thanks largely to Labov) that descriptions of linguistic variability can be involved in empirical issues, and can help to provide answers to some of the basic theoretical issues in linguistics. Lass (1976a: 221), for example, has observed that it can be an empirical matter which of the complementary aspects of language, i.e. the variable or categorical, is more crucially involved in linguistic change.

It can be reasonably argued that the incorporation of variability into a theory of grammar provides a framework for describing a number of interesting things about language, such as social dialect differentiation and language change. The pursuit of these descriptive goals is both realistic and worthwhile.[34] For example, statements of covariation, even if they are non-causal, and hence non-explanatory in a strict sense, can form the basis of a taxonomy. Labov's work has made important contributions here.

I have given an illustration of this in Tables 9.4 and 9.5, which display sets of empirical facts about types of variables and their relationship with social factors and involvement in linguistic change. Such taxonomies do not explain change, but they suggest useful questions and directions for further research; and they generate new facts and problems which stand in need of explanation. For instance, why have certain combinations of linguistic and social factors not been observed? Are we likely to find a

34. Lass (1976d: 219) has observed that the word 'empirical' carries such prestige that it has blinded linguists to the respectability of non-empirical theories. He argues that there is nothing wrong with a partially non-empirical linguistics, and that metaphysical theories have a worthwhile place in linguistics. He does not, however, deny the possibility that linguistics can be a fundamentally empirical science; but it would have to do so at the expense of restricting its domain to those aspects of linguistics which are capable of supporting empirical claims.

variable originating as a social stereotype with stylistic stratification which emerges at a later stage as a social variable without stylistic shift? How do indicators 'become' markers? And finally, from a historical point of view, what is the life cycle of a variable, i.e. does, for example, social variation imply the development of stylistic variation?

Some of these questions are empirical ones, and I think my study of variation in the relative marker in Middle Scots has indicated that sociolinguistic methodology has important contributions to make to historical linguistics. My results suggest, for example, that variability which is stylistically stratified can persist over long periods of time without necessitating change; and they illustrate how such variation may then become socially diagnostic as well. Non-standard varieties of English, like Scots, may lag behind standard English in integrating the WH relativization strategy in both the spoken and written language.

Hymes (1974a: 44) also agrees that a more reasonable (and, according to his view, also more urgent) goal for sociolinguistics is the development of a specific and explicit mode of description and taxonomies through the collection of more and new data sets. He comments that it was:

> thc development of a specific mode of description that ensured the success of linguistics in the United States and the lack of it that led to the peripheral status of folklore although both linguistics and folklore had started from a similar convergence of interests of scholars working in separate fields.

9.5 The place of sociolinguistic theory vis-à-vis linguistic theory

I have already argued that a sociolinguistic theory need not be empirical to be viable or respectable. The question I raise now is whether a sociolinguistic theory need be coterminous with linguistic theory to qualify as a legitimate discipline. Labov does not acknowledge either possibility, i.e. that sociolinguistics need not be empirical or be linguistics to be successful. I am not sure whether there is any point in having a sociolinguistic theory which *is* linguistics. To argue for this position seems to me to misunderstand the nature of linguistics as a discipline as well as to endorse, implicitly at any rate, the belief that success can be related to a unique theory or set of standards (cf. e.g. Feyerabend 1978: 216).

I take DeCamp's arguments against the possibility of a sociolinguistic theory as illustrative of what I do not see as a realistic position for such a theory to occupy. He says (1970: 158) that 'Sociolinguistics is still in the pre-theoretical, butterfly-collecting stage, with no theory of its own and uncertain whether it has any place in general linguistic theory.' But his view stems from a firm commitment to transformational generative grammar. Generative theory, he suggests, should incorporate sociolinguistic questions, data, etc., within itself, adding, as it were, a sociolinguistic amendment to a transformational constitution. The above comment is based on a very limited conception of the scope and place of a linguistic theory. He proposes a no more satisfactory solution to the problem of the place of a sociolinguistic theory in relation to linguistic theory, than the 'additive' approach (cf. Chapter 1), which he himself condemns. Thus he rejects both the possibility of the incorporation of social aspects of language into sociological theory (but not linguistic theory), as well as the independent existence of sociolinguistics as a theoretical discipline separate from both linguistics and sociology.

He does not consider the strongest possible claim, however, which is that linguistics is sociolinguistics. Yet, I think there is an interesting reason why he does not, which results from a misconception of the relationship between competing theories within the context of the history of linguistics. The equation of linguistics with sociolinguistics necessitates, in DeCamp's view, a change of paradigm, rather than a modification of an existing one. (And here I think we have another instance of scientism.)[35]

DeCamp professes to have a disparaging view of linguists who tend to see the areas of concern outlined by Chomsky as constituting 'linguistics proper' or 'theoretical linguistics', and all other aspects of language study as ancillary fields, or 'hyphenated' linguistics. He no doubt conceives himself to be broad-minded in proposing the accommodation of sociolinguistics within generative grammar without incorporating fundamental changes in the generative machinery.

Nevertheless, this generosity seems to be motivated by the fear that if transformational theory does not take in sociolinguistics, then the latter will take over generative grammar; and that in doing so, it will somehow thwart the well-established theoretical concerns and procedures which form the basis of linguistics; or worse yet, it will abolish them. This fear is

35. I say scientistic here because the mistaken idea seems to be implied that if a field does not have paradigms, it is not a science (cf. e.g. Percival 1976). I agree with Feyerabend (1978) that the separation of science and non-science is artificial. Feyerabend (1970: 198) suggests that Kuhn's work has had a disadvantageous effect on some social scientists. He comments:

> More than one social scientist has pointed out to me that now at last he had learned how to turn his field into a 'science' – which of course meant that he had learned how to *improve* it. The recipe according to these people, is to restrict criticism, to reduce the number of comprehensive theories to one, and to create a normal science that has this one theory as its paradigm.

unfounded, but it seems to underlie the following remark (DeCamp 1970: 159):

> The thesis of this paper, however, is that for at least the third time in history, a prevailing linguistic theory has been suspected of failing to provide a place for sociolinguistics, that this lack was indeed a significant factor in the demise of the two earlier theories, and that it is therefore of great importance to general linguistics that we now examine current linguistic theory to determine whether it can accommodate sociolinguistic questions.

There are at least two fallacies in this argument: one is the assumption that a reasonable sociolinguistic theory can be incorporated into generative grammar; the other is the hope that the inclusion of some sort of sociolinguistics will ensure the longevity of generative grammar by keeping the wolves who would do away with it from the door. Both these expectations are, in my opinion, unreasonable.

The import of DeCamp's statement seems to be not whether generative grammar can accommodate sociolinguistic questions, but whether it can afford *not* to. DeCamp is not alone in his desire for self-preservation.[36]

Such sentiments are the product of what might be called a 'king of the mountain' view of linguistics (cf. Hymes 1974c), in which different interests and orientations are seen to be competing with each other 'to be' linguistics, with one succeeding in displacing each other at intervals. This corresponds to Kuhn's view of the structure of a scientific community.[37] I think that Hymes is correct in thinking that the prestige of Kuhn's notion of paradigm (1962) may well have a disabling effect on linguistics as a discipline. The attractiveness of describing linguistics as a succession of paradigms confers a badge of status to a conception (and a scientistic one, I would say) of linguistics as an empirical science; but it does so at the expense of making the history of linguistics discontinuous.

Kuhn's definition of a paradigm assumes that a new paradigm is not just different from an old one, but that it is also superior in the sense that it explains things that the old one could not, i.e. new and different things, while it continues to be able to explain what the old one could. I agree with

36. A recent report in the *Newsletter of the American Dialect Society* (1977) indicates that a similar problem was discussed by dialectologists, i.e. 'how to keep dialectology viable in the face of a sociolinguistics which seems to appropriate all subjects'.
37. Kuhn's view of paradigms and so-called normal science has been the subject of a great deal of controversy in the philosophy of science (cf. e.g. the papers in Lakatos and Musgrave 1970). Masterman (1970) has observed that Kuhn uses the term 'paradigm' in no fewer than twenty-one different senses.

Hymes that paradigms in this sense cannot be identified in the history of linguistics.[38]

Hymes suggests that the history of linguistics is more profitably viewed as a succession of traditions or cynosures (cf. Kanngiesser 1972a: 1), in which each dominant approach or tradition was the cynosure of the discipline, and had a paradigmatic community associated with it; but no cynosure has ever been equivalent to the whole of the discipline because none has succeeded in establishing complete authority. Furthermore, as Verburg (1974: 193) has pointed out, there were a number of sciences or other disciplines which influenced, or even dominated linguistics from time to time, but their impact was generally neutralized and incorporated into a specific subdiscipline within linguistics.

Hymes' ideas on the difference between a view of linguistics as a succession of paradigms and one of linguistics as a succession of cynosures are, I think, particularly insightful in deciding what a reasonable goal for a sociolinguistic theory is. Hymes (1974c: 15) argues that if the qualitative study of grammatical structure should be succeeded as a cynosure by a quantitative paradigm (such as Labov proposes, which is concerned with variation and use), structural linguistics will still continue to develop. What changes from one to the other is not so much the explanation of the same phenomena, but rather the phenomena one wants most to explain. Because one cynosure does not really supersede another, but only shunts it from the center of attention (and it often chooses to address a different set of facts about language), cynosures have never really been able to command complete authority over the field as Kuhn claims that true paradigms in the history of science do.

The gap between what Hymes calls true paradigmatic status and the lesser authority of the cynosure has a number of interesting consequences in linguistics. Hymes suggests, for one thing, that this gap may help explain the 'polemical overkill' that has characterized an ascendent cynosure's treatment of both its predecessors and its competitors. He has also quite rightly pointed out that the implicit scenario for succeeding as a cynosure seems often to consist as much of discrediting, forgetting or ignoring other

38. Metcalf (1974: 253) has suggested that the field of linguistics as a whole has not emerged as a science for lack of a paradigm which is sufficiently comprehensive to encompass all of language, although there are parts of the field which have developed ascendent paradigms. I accept, however, Lakatos' (1970: 155) criticism of this view of normal science as monistic:

> The history of science has been and should be a history of competing research programmes (or, if you wish, 'paradigms'), but it has not been and must not become a succession of periods of normal science: the sooner competition starts, the better for progress. 'Theoretical pluralism' is better than 'theoretical monism': on this point Popper and Feyerabend are right and Kuhn is wrong.

work as of making new discoveries; insistence on rectitude seems to become all the more intense when the cynosure's claim to respectable status is not universally granted.

My final point is that a great deal can be done with a sociolinguistic theory of language without the necessity of commiting ourselves to one research program, or to one aspect of language. In any event, the search for an answer to the question of what language is like as a whole is elusive.[39] The dilemma is illustrated very well in the story of the blind men who tried to explain what an elephant was like after touching different parts of it. The difference among the seven resulting descriptions was not so much a problem of sampling error as of incautious extrapolation from the data.

All description is selective and deals only with an aspect of any phenomenon, which suggests that pluralism or complementarity in our approach to the description of language is a healthier attitude than insistence on one research strategy (cf. also Lass 1976d). Furthermore, descriptions are idealizations; Rudner (1966: 57) has commented that there is 'no entity, process, or state of affairs to which the idealization stands in designatory or descriptive relationship'.

Paul (1920), prior to Saussure's dichotomy between synchronic and diachronic linguistics, believed that a theory of language change and a theory of language were one and the same thing. And it was Labov who demonstrated that a close examination of the way in which language varies is crucial in understanding how linguistic change takes place. A sociolinguistic theory which is based on descriptions of variability shifts the emphasis away from what Chomsky (1973: 232) has called the fundamental empirical problem of linguistics, namely, to explain how a person can acquire knowledge of a language, to a rediscovery of the importance of explaining, as well, how language changes.

39. Popper claims (1961: 77):

> If we wish to study a thing, we are bound to select certain aspects of it. It is not possible for us to observe or to describe a whole piece of the world, or a whole piece of nature; in fact, not even the smallest whole piece may be so described, since all description is necessarily selective.

Harris' (1965: 365) idea of the complementarity of string analysis, transformational analysis and constituent grammar (which Labov (1972b) takes as an example of an aesthetic rather than a scientific attitude towards theories) seems more realistic. He says:

> To interrelate these analyses, it is necessary to understand that they are not competing theories, but rather complement each other in the description of sentences. It is not that grammar is one or another of these analyses, but that sentences exhibit simultaneously all of those properties.

Bibliography

Aarts, F. (1971). On the distribution of noun phrase types in English clause structure. *Lingua* 26: 281–93.

Abercrombie, D. (1965). What is a 'Letter'? In Abercrombie, D. *Studies in Phonetics and Linguistics*. London: Oxford University Press. pp. 76–86.

(1967). *Elements of General Phonetics*. Chicago: Aldine Publishing Co.

Addison, J. (1711). Humble petition of *who* and *which*. *The Spectator*, No. 78. 30 May.

Adorno, T. (1978). Sociology and empirical research. In Connerton, P. (ed.) *Critical Sociology*. Harmondsworth: Penguin. pp. 237–58.

Aitken, A.J. (1971). Variation and variety in Middle Scots. In Aitken, A.J. et al. (eds.) *Edinburgh Studies in English and Scots*. London: Longman. pp. 177–210.

(1973). The language of Older Scots poetry. Unpublished MS.

Aitken, A.J., McIntosh, A. and Pálsson, H. (eds.) (1971). *Edinburgh Studies in English and Scots*. London: Longman.

Alatis, J. (ed.) (1970). *Linguistics and the Teaching of Standard English to Speakers of other Languages or Dialects*. Washington, DC: Georgetown University Press.

Albert, E. (1972). Culture patterning of speech behavior in Burundi. In Gumperz, J.J. and Hymes, D. (eds.) *Directions in Sociolinguistics*. New York: Holt, Rinehart and Winston. pp. 72–106.

Albó, X. (1970). Social constraints on Cochabamba Quechua. PhD dissertation. Cornell University.

Allen, C. (1977). Topics in diachronic English syntax. PhD dissertation. University of Massachusetts.

Allen, H. (ed.) (1958). *Readings in Applied English Linguistics*. New York: Appleton-Century-Crofts.

Alston, R. (ed.) (1967). Bishop Lowth. 1762. *A Short Introduction to English Grammar*. Facsimile reprint edition. Menston: The Scolar Press.

Andersen, H. (1973). Abductive and deductive change. *Language* 49: 765–93.

Anderson, J.M. (1971). *The Grammar of Case: Towards a Localist Theory*. Cambridge: Cambridge University Press.

Anderson, J.M. and Jones, C. (eds.) (1974). *Historical Linguistics: Proceedings of the First International Conference on Historical Linguistics*. 2 vols. Amsterdam: North Holland.

Anderson, S. and Kiparsky, P. (eds.) (1973). *A Festschrift for Morris Halle*. New York: Holt, Rinehart and Winston.

Anttila, R. (1974). Formalization as degeneration in historical linguistics. In Anderson. J.M. and Jones, C. (eds.) *Historical Linguistics*. Amsterdam: North Holland. Vol. I: 1–32.

(1975). Was there a generative historical linguistics? In Dahlstedt, K.-H. (ed.) *The Nordic Languages and Modern Linguistics*. Stockholm: Almqvist & Wiksell. pp. 70–92.

Aracil, L. (1974). Sociolinguistics; revolution and paradigm. Unpublished MS.

Austerlitz, R. (ed.) (1975). *The Scope of American Linguistics*. Lisse: The Peter de Ridder Press.

Bach, E. (1968). Nouns and noun phrases. In Bach, E. and Harms, R. (eds.) *Universals in Linguistic Theory*. New York: Holt, Rinehart and Winston. pp. 91–125.

(1974). *Syntactic Theory*. New York: Holt, Rinehart and Winston.

Bach, E. and Harms, R. (eds.) (1968) *Universals in Linguistic Theory*. New York: Holt, Rinehart and Winston.

Bailey, C.-J. (1969a). Some implicational phenomena in dialectology. *Working Papers in Linguistics* 1.8: 105–22. University of Hawaii.

(1969b). Implicational scales in diachronic linguistics and dialectology. *Working Papers in Linguistics* 1.8: 123–38. University of Hawaii.

(1970). Using data variation to confirm, rather than undermine, the validity of abstract syntactic structures. *Working Papers in Linguistics* 2.8: 77–86. University of Hawaii.

(1971). Trying to talk in the new paradigm. *Papers in Linguistics* 4: 312–38.

(1972). How the wave model explains what it explains. Unpublished MS.

(1973). *Variation and Linguistic Theory*. Washington, DC: Center for Applied Linguistics.

Bailey, C.-J. and Shuy, R. (eds.) (1973). *New Ways of Analyzing Variation in English*. Washington, DC: Georgetown University Press.

Bartsch, R. (1973). Gibt es einen sinnvollen Begriff von linguistischer Komplexität? *Zeitschrift für linguistische Germanistik* 1.1: 6–31.

Basso, K. (1974). The ethnography of writing. In Bauman, R. and Sherzer, J. (eds.) *Explorations in the Ethnography of Speaking*. Cambridge: Cambridge University Press. pp. 425–33.

Bately, J. (1965). *Who* and *which* and the grammarians of the 17th century. *English Studies* 46: 245–50.

Battison, R., Markowicz, H. and Woodward, J. (1975). Variable phonology in American sign language. In Fasold, R. and Shuy, R. (eds.) *Analyzing Variation in Language*. Washington, DC: Georgetown University Press. pp. 291–303.

Bauman, R. and Sherzer, J. (eds.) (1974). *Explorations in the Ethnography of Speaking*. Cambridge: Cambridge University Press.

Bender, H. (1912). ἀπὸ κοινοῦ in *Gudrun*. *Journal of English and Germanic Philology* XI: 565–73.

Benveniste, E. (1971). The relative clause, a problem of general syntax. In

Benveniste, E. (trans. M. Meek). *Problems in General Linguistics*. Miami: University of Miami Press.

Berdan, R. (1975). On the nature of linguistic variation. PhD dissertation. University of Texas.

Berdan, R. and Legum, S. (1976). The goals of experimental linguistics. *Language in Society* 5: 97–8.

Bernstein, B. (1973). *Class, Codes and Control*, vol. II. London: Routledge and Kegan Paul.

Bever, T. and Langendoen, T. (1971). A dynamic model of evolution of language. *Linguistic Inquiry* 2: 433–65.

(1972). The interaction of speech perception and grammatical structure in the evolution of language. In Stockwell, R.P. and Macaulay, R.K.S. (eds.) *Linguistic Change and Generative Theory*. Bloomington: Indiana University Press. pp. 32–95.

Bickerton, D. (1971). Inherent variability and variable rules. *Foundations of Language* 7: 457–92.

(1972). The structure of polylectal grammars. In Shuy, R. (ed.) *Sociolinguistics*. 23rd Annual Roundtable. Washington, DC: Georgetown University Press. pp. 17–43.

(1973a). On the nature of a creole continuum. *Language* 49: 641–69.

(1973b). The chimera of context. *Working Papers in Linguistics*. University of Hawaii.

(1973c). Quantitative vs. dynamic paradigms: the case of Montreal *que*. In Bailey, C.-J. and Shuy, R. (eds.) *New Ways of Analyzing Variation in English*. Washington, DC: Georgetown University Press. pp. 23–44.

(1975). *Dynamics of a Creole System*. Cambridge: Cambridge University Press.

(1977). *Change and Variation in Hawaiian English*, Vol. II: *Creole Syntax*. Social Sciences and Linguistics Institute, University of Hawaii.

Bickerton, D. and Odo, C. (1976). *Change and Variation in Hawaiian English*, Vol. I: *General Phonology and Pidgin Syntax*. Social Sciences and Linguistics Institute, University of Hawaii.

Binnick, R. et al. (eds.) (1969). *Papers from the Fifth Regional Meeting of the Chicago Linguistic Society*. Department of Linguistics, University of Chicago.

Bloch, B. (1948). A set of postulates for phonemic analysis. *Language* 24: 3–46.

Bloom, L. (1970). *Language Development: Form and Function*. Cambridge, Mass.: MIT Press.

Bloomfield, L. (1926). A set of postulates for the science of language. *Language* 2: 153–64.

Bodine, A. (1975). Androcentrism in prescriptive grammar: singular 'they', sex-indefinite 'he', and 'he or she'. *Language in Society* 4: 129–47.

Braithwaite, R.B. (1960). *Scientific Explanation*. New York: Harper.

Braunmüller, K. (1978). Remarks on the formation of conjunctions in Germanic languages. *Nordic Journal of Linguistics* 1: 99–120.

Bresnan, J. (1972). Theory of complementation in English syntax. PhD dissertation. Massachusetts Institute of Technology.

(1977). Variables in the theory of transformations. In Culicover et al. (eds.)

Formal Syntax. New York: Academic Press. pp. 157–97.
Bright, W. (1966). (ed.) *Sociolinguistics*. The Hague: Mouton.
Bright, W. and Ramanujan, A. (1964). Sociolinguistic variation and language change. In Lunt, H. (ed.) *Proceedings of the 9th International Congress of Linguists*. The Hague: Mouton.
Brown, P. and Levinson, S. (1979). Social structure, groups and interaction. In Scherer, K. and Giles, H. (eds.) *Social Markers in Speech*. Cambridge: Cambridge University Press. pp. 291–341.
Bühler, K. (1934). *Sprachtheorie*. Jena.
Burtt, E.A. (1924). *The Metaphysical Foundations of Modern Science*. New York: Doubleday Anchor Books.
Bynon, T. (1977). *Historical Linguistics*. Cambridge: Cambridge University Press.
Caldwell, S. (1974). *The Relative Pronoun in Early Scots*. Mémoires de la Société Néophilologique de Helsinki. Vol. XLII. Helsinki.
Carden, G. (1972). Dialect variation and abstract syntax. In Shuy, R. (ed.) *Some New Directions in Linguistics*. Washington, DC: Georgetown University Press. pp. 1–35.
(1976). Syntactic and semantic data: replication results. *Language in Society* 5: 99–104.
Cedergren, H. (1973). The interplay of social and linguistic factors in Panama. PhD dissertation. Cornell University.
Cedergren, H. and Sankoff, D. (1974). Variable rules: performance as a statistical reflection of competence. *Language* 50: 333–55.
Chalmers, A.F. (1978). *What Is This Thing Called Science?* Open University Press.
Charnley, M.B. (1958). The syntax of deferred prepositions. In Allen, H. (ed.) *Readings in Applied English Linguistics*. New York: Appleton-Century-Crofts. pp. 275–86.
Chen, M. (1976). Relative chronology: 3 methods of reconstruction. *Journal of Linguistics* 12: 209–58.
Chiang, K.Y. (1977). Restrictive relative clauses in Bahasa Malaysia. *Studies in Linguistic Science*. No. 17. Department of Linguistics, University of Illinois.
Chomsky, N. (1965). *Aspects of the Theory of Syntax*. Cambridge, Mass.: MIT Press.
(1966). *Cartesian Linguistics*. New York: Harper and Row.
(1973). Conditions on transformations. In Anderson, S. and Kiparsky, P. (eds.) *A Festschrift for Morris Halle*. New York: Holt, Rinehart and Winston. pp. 232–86.
(1976). *Reflections on Language*. Glasgow: Fontana/Collins.
(1977). On WH movement. In Culicover et al. (eds.) *Formal Syntax*. New York: Academic Press. pp. 71–133.
Chomsky, N. and Halle, M. (1968). *The Sound Pattern of English*. New York: Harper.
Cofer, T. (1972). Linguistic variability in a Philadelphia speech community. PhD dissertation. University of Pennsylvania.
Cohen, D. (ed.) (1974). *Explaining Linguistic Phenomena*. Washington, DC: Hemisphere Publishing Corporation.

Cohen, D. and Wirth, J. (eds.) (1975). *Testing Linguistic Hypotheses*. Washington, DC: Hemisphere Publishing Corporation.

Connerton, P. (ed.) (1978). *Critical Sociology*. Harmondsworth: Penguin.

Corum, C., Smith-Stark, T. and Weiser, A. (eds.) (1973). *You take the high node and I'll take the low node*. Papers from the Comparative Syntax Festival. Chicago: Chicago Linguistics Circle.

Crystal, D. and Davy, D. (1976). *Investigating English Style*. London: Longman.

Culicover, P., Wasow, T. and Akmajian, A. (eds.) (1977). *Formal Syntax*. New York: Academic Press.

Curme, G. (1911). The history of the development of the relative pronoun in the Germanic languages. *Journal of English and Germanic Philology* 10: 225–377.

(1912). A history of the English relative constructions. *Journal of English and Germanic Philology* 11: 10–29, 180–204, 355–80.

Dahlstedt, K.-H. (1973). Synpunkter på sociolingvistiken. In *Svenska studier från runtid till nutid tillägnade Carl Ivar Stahle*. Skrifter utgivna av Nämnden för mensk språkvård 48. Lund. pp. 235–50.

(ed.) (1975). *The Nordic Languages and Modern Linguistics*. Stockholm: Almqvist & Wiksell.

Day, R. (1972). Patterns of variation and tense in the Hawaiian post-creole continuum. PhD dissertation. University of Hawaii.

Dean, J. (1967). Determiners and relative clauses. Unpublished MS.

DeCamp, D. (1970). Is a sociolinguistic theory possible? In Alatis, J. (ed.) *Linguistics and the Teaching of Standard English to Speakers of other Languages or Dialects*. Washington, DC: Georgetown University Press. pp. 151–73.

(1971a). Towards a generative analysis of a post-creole continuum. In Hymes, D. (ed.) *Pidginization and Creolization of Languages*. Cambridge: Cambridge University Press. pp. 349–70.

(1971b). Implicational scales and sociolinguistic linearity. *Linguistics* 73: 30–43.

(1973). What do implicational scales imply? In Bailey, C.-J. and Shuy, R. (eds.) *New Ways of Analyzing Variation in English*. Washington, DC: Georgetown University Press. pp. 141–9.

DeCamp, D. and Hancock, I. (eds.) (1974). *Pidgins and Creoles: Current Trends and Prospects*. Washington, DC: Georgetown University Press.

Dekeyser, X. (1975). *Number and Case Relations in 19th Century British English*. Antwerpen: De nederlansche Boekhandel.

Dorian, N. (1973). Grammatical change in a dying dialect. *Language* 49: 414–38.

(1977). A hierarchy of morphophonemic decay in Scottish Gaelic language death: the differential failure of lenition. *Word* 28: 96–109.

(1981). *Language Death: The Life Cycle of a Scottish Gaelic Dialect*. Philadelphia: University of Pennsylvania Press.

Drachman, G. (ed.) (1975). *Akten der I Salzburger Frühlingstagung für Linguistik*. Tübingen: Narr.

Dreyfuss, G. (1977). Relative clause structure in four creole languages. PhD dissertation. University of Michigan.

Durkheim, E. (1964). *The Rules of Sociological Method*. New York: The Free Press.

Dykema, K. (1958). Historical development of the concept of grammatical properties. In Allen, H. (ed.) *Readings in Applied English Linguistics*. New York: Appleton-Century-Crofts. pp. 2–9.

Earle, J. (1871). *The Philology of Language*. London: Macmillan.

Einenkel, E. (1891–2). Die Quelle der englischen Relativellipse. *Anglia* 13: 348–52; 14: 122–32.

(1906). Die dänischen Elemente in der Syntax der englischen Sprache. *Anglia* 29: 120–8.

Elliot, D., Legum, S. and Thompson, S. (1969). Syntactic variation as linguistic data. In Binnick, R. et al. (eds.) *Papers from the Fifth Regional Meeting of the Chicago Linguistic Society*. Department of Linguistics, University of Chicago. pp. 52–9.

Emonds, J. (1970). Root and structure-preserving transformations. PhD dissertation. Massachusetts Institute of Technology.

Ervin-Tripp, S. (1972). On sociolinguistic rules: alternation and co-occurrence. In Gumperz, J.J. and Hymes, D. (eds.) *Directions in Sociolinguistics*. New York: Holt, Rinehart and Winston. pp. 213–50.

Fasold, R. (1970). Two models of socially significant variation. *Language* 46: 551–63.

(1978). Language variation and linguistic competence. In Sankoff, D. (ed.) *Linguistic Variation*. New York: Academic Press. pp. 85–95.

Fasold, R. and Shuy, R. (eds.) (1975). *Analyzing Variation in Language*. Washington, DC: Georgetown University Press.

(eds.) (1977). *Studies in Language Variation*. Washington, DC: Georgetown University Press.

Feigl, H. and Brodbeck, M. (eds.) (1953). *Readings in the Philosophy of Science*. New York: Appleton-Century-Crofts.

Feyerabend, P. (1970). Consolations for the specialist. In Lakatos, I. and Musgrave, A. (eds.) *Criticism and the Growth of Knowledge*. Cambridge: Cambridge University Press. pp. 197–231.

(1978). *Against Method*. London: Verso.

Fillmore, C. and Langendoen, T. (eds.) (1971). *Studies in Linguistic Semantics*. New York: Holt, Rinehart and Winston.

Fischer, J.L. (1958). Social influences on the choice of a linguistic variant. *Word* 14: 47–56.

Fishman, J. (1968). Some contrasts between linguistically heterogeneous and linguistically homogeneous polities. In Fishman, J., Ferguson, C. and Das Gupta, J. (eds.) *Language Problems of Developing Nations*. New York: Wiley. pp. 53–68.

(ed.) (1971). *Advances in the Sociology of Language*. 2 vols. The Hague: Mouton.

Fishman, J., Cooper, R., Ma, R. et al. (1971). *Bilingualism in the Barrio*. Bloomington: Indiana University Press.

Fishman, J., Ferguson, C. and Das Gupta, J. (eds.) (1968). *Language Problems of Developing Nations*. New York: Wiley.

Fisiak, J. (ed.) (1978). *Recent Developments in Historical Phonology*. The Hague: Mouton.

Flebbe, Dr. (1878). Der elliptische Relativsatz im Englischen. *Archiv für das Studium der neueren Sprachen und Litteraturen* 60: 85–101.
Fowler, H. (1926). *A Dictionary of Modern English Usage*. Oxford: Clarendon Press.
Fowler, R. (1966). Linguistics; Stylistics; Criticism? *Lingua* XVI: 153–65.
Friedrich, P. (1972). Social context and semantic feature: the Russian pronominal usage. In Gumperz, J.J. and Hymes, D. (eds.) *Directions in Sociolinguistics*. New York: Holt, Rinehart and Winston. pp. 270–301.
Friedrich, P. and Redfield, J. (1978). Speech as a personality symbol. *Language* 54: 263–89.
Gal, S. (1978). Peasant men can't get wives: language change and sex roles in a bilingual community. *Language in Society* 7: 1–16.
Gardner, R.A. and Gardner, B. (1969). Teaching sign-language to a chimpanzee. *Science* 165: 664–72.
Gauchat, L. (1905). L'unité phonétique dans le patois d'une commune. In *Aus Romanischen Sprachen und Litteraturen: Festschrift Heinrich Morf*. Halle: Max Niemayer. pp. 175–232.
Giglioli, P. (ed.) (1973). *Language and Social Context*. Harmondsworth: Penguin.
Gilliéron, J. (1902–10). *Atlas linguistique de la France*. 13 vols. Champion.
Girvan, R. (1939). *Ratis Raving and other early Scots poems on morals*. Scottish Text Society III. Edinburgh.
Greene, J. (1977). The use of WHICH as a non-restrictive relative marker. PhD dissertation. Georgetown University.
Guðmundsson, H. (1972). The pronominal dual in Icelandic. PhD dissertation. Institute of Nordic Linguistics, University of Reykjavík.
Gumperz, J.J. (1968). The speech community. In *International Encyclopedia of the Social Sciences*. MacMillan. pp. 381–6.
Gumperz, J.J. and Hymes, D. (eds.) (1972). *Directions in Sociolinguistics*. New York: Holt, Rinehart and Winston.
Guttman, L. (1944). A basis for scaling quantitative data. *American Sociological Review* 9: 139–50.
Guy, G. (1974). Variation in the group and individual: the case of final stop deletion. *Pennsylvania Working Papers on Linguistic Change and Variation* II. 4.
(1975). The Cedergren–Sankoff variable rule program. In Fasold, R. and Shuy, R. (eds.) *Analyzing Variation in Language*. Washington, DC: Georgetown University Press. pp. 59–70.
(1977). A new look at *-t*, *-d* deletion. In Fasold, R. and Shuy, R. (eds.) *Studies in Language Variation*. Washington, DC: Georgetown University Press. pp. 1–12.
Hackenberg, R. (1972). Appalachian English: a sociolinguistic study. PhD dissertation. Georgetown University.
Hale, K. (1976). The adjoined relative clause in Australia. In Dixon, R. (ed.) *Grammatical Categories in Australian Languages*. Canberra: Institute of Aboriginal Studies. pp. 78–105.
Hale, K., Jeanne, L. and Platero, P. (1977). Three cases of overgeneration. In Culi-

cover et al. (eds.) *Formal Syntax*. New York: Academic Press. pp. 379–417.
Halliday, M.A.K. (1964). The linguistic study of literary texts. In Lunt, H. (ed.) *Proceedings of the 9th International Congress of Linguists*. The Hague: Mouton. pp. 302–8.
(1978). *Language as a Social Semiotic*. London: Edward Arnold.
Hamp, E. (1975). On the disappearing English relative particle. In Drachman, G. (ed.) *Akten der I Salzburger Frühlingstagung für Linguistik*. Tübingen: Narr.
Harré, R. (1972). *The Principles of Scientific Thinking*. London: MacMillan.
(1976). *The Philosophies of Science*. London: Oxford University Press.
Harris, Z. (1965). Transformational theory. *Language* 41: 363–401.
Hastings, A.J. and Koutsoudas, A. (1976). Performance models and the generative-interpretive debate. In Wirth, J. (ed.) *Assessing Linguistic Arguments*. Washington, DC: Hemisphere Publishing Co. pp. 187–216.
Haugen, E. (1975). Pronominal address in Icelandic: from you-two to you-all. *Language in Society* 4: 323–39.
Haugen, E. and Chapman, K. (1964). *Spoken Norwegian*. New York: Holt, Rinehart and Winston.
Hawkins, S. and Keenan, E. (1974). The psychological validity of the accessibility hierarchy. Paper given at the Linguistic Society of America Summer Meeting.
Hayek, F. (1952). *The Counter-Revolution of Science*. Glencoe, Ill.: The Free Press.
Hempel, C.G. (1965). *Aspects of Scientific Explanation and Other Essays in the Philosophy of Science*. New York: The Free Press.
Herdan, G. (1960). *Type–Token Mathematics*. 'S-Gravenhage: Mouton.
Hermann, E. (1929). Lautveränderungen in den Individualsprachen einer Mundart. *Nachrichten der Gesellschaft der Wissenschaften zu Göttingen. Philosophisch-Historische Klasse* II: 195–214.
Hill, A.A. (1958). *Introduction to Linguistic Structures*. New York: Harcourt, Brace and World.
Hill, J. (1973). Subordinate clause density and language function. In Corum, C. et al. (eds.) *You take the high node and I'll take the low node*. Papers from the Comparative Syntax Festival. Chicago: Chicago Linguistics Circle. pp. 33–52.
Hjelmslev, L. (1953). *Prolegomena to a Theory of Language*. (trans. F.J. Whitfield). Baltimore: Waverly.
Hockett, C.F. (1950). Age-grading and linguistic continuity. *Language* 26: 449–57.
(1958). *A Course in Modern Linguistics*. New York: MacMillan.
Hoenigswald, H. (1960). *Language Change and Linguistic Reconstruction*. Chicago: University of Chicago Press.
(1973). On the notion of an intermediate stage in traditional historical linguistics. In *Studies in Formal Historical Linguistics*. Formal Linguistics Series 3. Dordrecht.
Householder, F. (1971). *Linguistic Speculations*. Cambridge: Cambridge University Press.
Huff, D. (1973). *How to Lie with Statistics*. Harmondsworth: Pelican.
Hunt, K.W. (1970a). How little sentences grow into big ones. In Lester, M. (ed.) *Readings in Applied Transformational Grammar*. New York: Holt, Rinehart and Winston. pp. 170–187.

(1970b). Recent measures in syntactic development. In Lester, M. (ed.) pp. 187–200.

Hymes, D. (1968). The ethnography of speaking. In Fishman, J. (ed.) *Readings in the Sociology of Language*. The Hague: Mouton. pp. 99–139.

(ed.) (1971). *Pidginization and Creolization of Languages*. Cambridge: Cambridge University Press.

(1974a). *Foundations of Sociolinguistics*. Philadelphia: University of Pennsylvania Press.

(1974b). Ways of speaking. In Bauman, R. and Sherzer, J. (eds.) *Explorations in the Ethnography of Speaking*. Cambridge: Cambridge University Press. pp. 433–51.

(ed.) (1974c) *Studies in the History of Linguistics: Traditions and Paradigms*. Bloomington: Indiana University Press.

Irvine, J. (1978). Wolof noun classification: the social setting of divergent change. *Language in Society* 7: 37–65.

Jackendoff, R. (1972). *Semantic Interpretation in Generative Grammar*. Cambridge, Mass.: MIT Press.

(1977). *$\bar{X}$ Syntax: A Study of Phrase Structure. Linguistic Inquiry* Monograph No. 2. Cambridge, Mass.: MIT Press.

Jacobs, R.A. and Rosenbaum, P.S. (1968). *English Transformational Grammar*. Waltham, Mass.: Blaisdell Publishing Co.

Jacobsen, S. (1965). Review of Rydén, M. (1966). *Relative Constructions in Early 16th Century English. Linguistics* 45: 118–127.

Jacobsson, B. (1963). On the use of *that* in non-restrictive relative clauses. *Moderna Sprak* 57: 407–416.

Jakobson, R. (1960). Linguistics and poetics. In Sebeok, T. (ed.) *Style in Language*. Cambridge, Mass.: MIT Press. pp. 350–78.

Jespersen, O. (1894). *Progress in Language with Special Reference to English*. London: Swan Sonnenschein and Co.

(1909–49). *A Modern English Grammar on Historical Principles*. London: George Allen and Unwin.

(1926). Notes on relative clauses. *Society for Pure English*. Tract No. 24. London: Oxford University Press.

(1968). *Growth and Structure of the English Language*. New York: The Free Press.

Joos, M. (1967). *The Five Clocks*. New York: Harcourt, Brace and World.

Kanngiesser, S. (1972a). Untersuchungen zur Kompetenztheorie und zum sprachlichen Handeln. *Zeitschrift für Literaturwissenschaft und Linguistik* 7: 13–45.

(1972b). *Aspekte der synchronen und diachronen Linguistik*. Tübingen: Max Niemayer.

Karttunen, L. (1971). Definite descriptions with crossing coreference. *Foundations of Language* 7: 157–82.

Kay, P. (1978). Variable rules, community grammar and linguistic change. In Sankoff, D. (ed.). *Linguistic Variation*. New York: Academic Press. pp. 71–82.

Kay, P. and McDaniel, C. (1979). On the logic of variable rules. *Language in Society* 8: 151–89.

Kay, P. and Sankoff, G. (1974). A language-universals approach to pidgins and creoles. In DeCamp, D. and Hancock, I. (eds.) *Pidgins and Creoles*. Washington, DC: Georgetown University Press. pp. 61–73.

Keenan, E.L. (1972). Relative clause formation in Malagasy. In Peranteau, P. et al. (eds.) *The Chicago Which Hunt*. Papers from the Relative Clause Festival. Department of Linguistics, University of Chicago. pp. 169–190.

(1975). Variation in universal grammar. In Fasold, R. and Shuy, R. (eds.) *Analyzing Variation in Language*. Washington, DC: Georgetown University Press. pp. 136–49.

(ed.) (1977). *Discourse across Time and Space*. SCOPIL No. 5. Department of Linguistics, University of Southern California, Los Angeles.

Keenan, E.L. and Comrie, B. (1972). Noun phrase accessibility and universal grammar. Paper presented at the Linguistic Society of America Meeting.

(1977). Noun phrase accessibility and universal grammar. *Linguistic Inquiry* 8: 63–99.

(1979). Data on the noun phrase accessibility hierarchy. *Language* 55: 332–52.

Kellner, L. (1892). *Historical Outlines of English Syntax*. London.

Kendall, M. and Babington Smith, B. (1938). Randomness and random sampling numbers. *Journal of the Royal Statistical Society* 101, 147.

King, R.D. (1969). *Historical Linguistics and Generative Grammar*. Englewood Cliffs, NJ: Prentice-Hall.

Klima, E. (1969). Relatedness between grammatical systems. In Reibel, D. and Schane, S. (eds.) *Modern Studies in English*. Englewood Cliffs, NJ: Prentice-Hall.

Kock, A. (1897). *The English Relative Pronouns*. Lund.

Koestler, A. (1975). *The Act of Creation*. London: Pan Books.

(1978). *Janus: A Summing Up*. London: Hutchinson.

Koutsoudas, A. (1968). On WH-words in English. *Journal of Linguistics* 4: 267–73.

Kroch, A. and Small, C. (1978). Grammatical ideology and its effect on speech. In Sankoff, D. (ed.) *Linguistic Variation*. New York: Academic Press. pp. 45–55.

Kroll, B. (1977). Combining ideas in written and spoken English: a look at subordination and coordination. In Keenan, E. (ed.) *Discourse across Time and Space*. SCOPIL No. 5. Department of Linguistics, University of Southern California, Los Angeles.

Kruszewski, M. (1881). *Über die Lautabwandlungen*. Kazen.

Kuhn, T.S. (1962). *The Structure of Scientific Revolutions*. Chicago: University of Chicago Press.

Kuroda, S.-Y. (1969). English relativization and certain related problems. In Reibel, D. and Schane, S. (eds.) *Modern Studies in English*. Englewood Cliffs, NJ: Prentice-Hall. pp. 264–87.

Labov, W. (1963). The social motivation of a sound change. *Word* 19: 273–309.

(1966). *The Social Stratification of English in New York City*. Washington, DC. Center for Applied Linguistics.

(1969). Contraction, deletion and inherent variability of the English copula. *Language* 45: 715–62.

(1970). On the adequacy of natural language: I the development of tense. LAUT paper no. 23. Linguistic Agency, University of Trier.

(1972a). The study of language in its social context. In Labov, W. *Sociolinguistic Patterns*. Philadelphia: University of Pennsylvania Press. pp. 183–259.

(1972b). Some principles of linguistic methodology. *Language in Society* 1: 97–120.

(1972c). The social setting of linguistic change. In Labov, W. *Sociolinguistic Patterns*. Philadelphia: University of Pennsylvania Press. pp. 260–327.

(1972d). For an end to the uncontrolled use of linguistic intuitions. Paper given to the Linguistic Society of America Winter Meeting. Atlanta.

(1973). The logic of non-standard English. In Giglioli, P. (ed.) *Language and Social Context*. Harmondsworth; Penguin. pp. 179–217.

(1975a). The quantitative study of linguistic structure. In Dahlstedt, K.-H. (ed.) *The Nordic Languages and Modern Linguistics*. Stockholm: Almqvist & Wiksell. pp. 188–245.

(1975b). Empirical foundations of linguistic theory. In Austerlitz, R. (ed.) *The Scope of American Linguistics*. Lisse: The Peter de Ridder Press. pp. 77–135.

(1977). The unity of sociolinguistics. LAUT Series B. paper no. 22. Linguistic Agency , University of Trier.

(1978). Where does the sociolinguistic variable stop? A response to B. Lavandera. *Working Papers in Sociolinguistics*. No. 44. Southwest Educational Development Laboratory, Austin, Texas.

Labov, W. and Weiner, J. (1977). Constraints on the agentless passive. Paper given to the Linguistic Society of America Summer Meeting. Honolulu.

Labov, W., Cohen, P., Robins, C. and Lewis, J. (1968). *A Study of the Non-standard English of Negro and Puerto Rican Speakers in New York City*. 2 vols. Final Report. Cooperative Research Project 3288. Philadelphia: U.S. Regional Survey.

Labov, W., Yaeger, M. and Steiner, R. (1972). *A Quantitative Study of Sound Change in Progress*. 2 vols. Final Report on NSF Contract 3287. Philadelphia: U.S. Regional Survey.

Ladefoged, P. (1975). *A Course in Phonetics*. New York: Harcourt, Brace, Jovanavich.

LaGaly, M., Fox, R. and Bruck, A. (eds.) (1974). *Papers from the Tenth Regional Meeting of the Chicago Linguistic Society*. Department of Linguistics, University of Chicago.

Lakatos, I. (1970). Falsification and the methodology of scientific research programmes. In Lakatos, I. and Musgrave, A. (eds.) *Criticism and the Growth of Knowledge*. Cambridge: Cambridge University Press. pp. 91–197.

Lakatos, I. and Musgrave, A. (eds.) (1970). *Criticism and the Growth of Knowledge*. Cambridge: Cambridge University Press.

Lakoff, G. (1970). *Irregularity in Syntax*. New York: Holt, Rinehart and Winston.

Lass, R. (ed.) (1969). *Approaches to English Historical Linguistics*. New York: Holt, Rinehart and Winston.

(1976a). Variation studies and historical linguistics. *Language in Society* 5: 219–29.

(1976b). On generative taxonomy, and whether formalizations 'explain'. *Studia*

Linguistica 30: 139–55.
(1976c). Review of Dahlstedt, K.-H. (ed.) (1975). *The Nordic Languages and Modern Linguistics. Studia Linguistica* 30: 183–97.
(1976d). *English Phonology and Phonological Theory*. Cambridge: Cambridge University Press.
(1978). Mapping constraints in phonological reconstruction: on climbing down trees without falling out of them. In Fisiak, J. (ed.) *Recent Developments in Historical Phonology*. The Hague: Mouton. pp. 245–86.
(1980). *On Explaining Language Change*. Cambridge: Cambridge University Press.

Lavandera, B. (1975). Linguistic structure and sociolinguistic conditioning in the use of verbal endings in si-clauses (Buenos Aires Spanish). PhD dissertation. University of Pennsylvania.
(1978). Where does the sociolinguistic variable stop? *Language in Society* 7: 171–83.

Laver, J. (1976). The semiotic nature of phonetic data. *York Papers in Linguistics* 6: 55–62.

Leech, G. (1969). *A Linguistic Guide to English Poetry*. London: Longman.
(1974). *Semantics*. Harmondsworth: Penguin.

Lees, R.B. (1960). *The Grammar of English Nominalizations*. Bloomington, Ind.: Indiana University Press.

Legum, S. (1975). Strategies in the acquisition of relative clauses. Southwest Regional Laboratory for Educational Research and Development.

Lehmann, W.P. and Malkiel, Y. (eds.) (1968). *Directions for Historical Linguistics*. Austin: University of Texas Press.

Le Page, R.B. (1975). Projection; focussing; diffusion; steps towards a sociolinguistic theory of language. Paper given to the Linguistics Association of Great Britain Meeting. Nottingham.
(1979). Theoretical aspects of sociolinguistic studies in pidgin and creole languages. Paper given at the Conference on Directions of Theoretical Orientations in Creole Studies. St. Thomas, Virgin Islands.

Lester, M. (ed.) (1970). *Readings in Applied Transformational Grammar*. New York: Holt, Rinehart and Winston.

Lewis, C.S. (1954). *English Literature in the 16th Century excluding Drama*. Oxford: Clarendon Press.

Lightfoot, D. (1979). *Principles of Diachronic Syntax*. Cambridge: Cambridge University Press.

Linell, P. (1976). Is linguistics an empirical science? *Studia Linguistica* 30: 77–94.

Lohmann, O. (1880). Über die Auslassung des englischen Relativpronomens. *Anglia* 3: 115–50.

Lomax, A. (1977). A stylistic analysis of speaking. *Language in Society* 6: 15–49.

Lomax, A. et al. (1968). *Folksong Style and Culture*. American Association for the Advancement of Science. Publication no. 88. Washington, DC.

Longmire, B.J. (1976). The relationship of variables in Venezuelan Spanish to historical sound changes in Latin and the Romance languages. PhD dissertation. Georgetown University.

Lunt, H. (ed.) (1974). *Proceedings of the 9th International Congress of Linguists*. The Hague: Mouton.

Lyons, J. (1977). *Semantics*, vol. I. Cambridge: Cambridge University Press.

Macaulay, R.K.S. (1970). Review of Wolfram, W. (1969). *A Sociolinguistic Description of Detroit Negro Speech*. *Language* 46: 764–73.

(1973). *Language, Education and Employment in Glasgow*. Report to the Social Science Research Council.

(1976). Review of Trudgill, P. (1974). *The Social Differentiation of English in Norwich*. *Language* 52: 266–70.

(1977). *Language, Social Class and Education: A Glasgow Study*. Edinburgh: Edinburgh University Press.

McClure, J.D. (1975). Modern Scots prose writing. In McClure, J.D. (ed.) *The Scots Language in Education*. Association for Scottish Literary Studies Occasional Papers No. 3. pp. 54–68.

McIntosh, A. (1948). The relative pronouns *þe* and *þat* in Early Middle English. *English and Germanic Studies* 1: 73–87

(1963). Language and style. *Durham University Journal* XXIV: 116–23.

(1969a). The analysis of written Middle English. In Lass, R. (ed.) *Approaches to English Historical Linguistics*. New York: Holt, Rinehart and Winston. pp. 35–58.

(1969b). A new approach to Middle English dialectology. In Lass, R. (ed.) *Approaches to English Historical Linguistics*. New York: Holt, Rinehart and Winston. pp. 392–404.

(1978). The dialectology of Medieval Scots: some possible approaches to its study. *Scottish Literary Journal*. Supplement No. 6: 38–44.

McQueen, L. (1957). The last stages of the older literary language of Scotland. PhD dissertation. University of Edinburgh.

Martinet, A. (1963). Preface to Weinreich, U. *Languages in Contact*. The Hague: Mouton.

Masterman, M. (1970). The nature of a paradigm. In Lakatos, I. and Musgrave, A. (eds.) *Criticism and the Growth of Knowledge*. Cambridge: Cambridge University Press. pp. 59–91.

Matthews, P. (1979). *Generative Grammar and Linguistic Competence*. London: Allen and Unwin.

Meier, H. (1967). The lag of relative *who* in the nominative. *Neuphilologus* 51: 277–86.

Mendelsohn, D. (1977). The factor structure of foreign learners' English. PhD thesis, University of Edinburgh.

Meritt, H.D. (1938). *The Construction* ἀπὸ κοινοῦ *in the Germanic Languages*. University Series. Language and Literature VI. 2. Stanford: Stanford University Publications.

Metcalf, G. (1974). The Indo-European hypothesis in the sixteenth and seventeenth centuries. In Hymes, D. (ed.) *Studies in the History of Linguistics*. Bloomington: Indiana University Press. pp. 233–58.

Milroy, J. (1978). Lexical alternation and diffusion in vernacular speech. *Belfast Working Papers in Language and Linguistics* 3: 100–15.

Milroy, J. and Milroy, L. (1977). Speech and context in an urban setting. *Belfast*

Working Papers in Language and Linguistics. 1: 1–85.
Milroy, L. and Margrain, S. (1978). Vernacular language loyalty and social network. *Belfast Working Papers in Language and Linguistics* 3: 1–59.
Mitchell, B. (1965). *A Guide to Old English*. Oxford: Basil Blackwell.
Mitchell, J. (ed.) (1974). *Computers in the Humanities*. Edinburgh: Edinburgh University Press.
Moser, C.A. and Kalton, G. (1971). *Survey Methods in Social Investigation*. London: Heinemann.
Mustanoja, T. (1960). *A Middle English Syntax*, Part I: Parts of Speech. Helsinki: Mémoires de la Société Néophilologique 23.
Napoli, D.J. (1977). Variations on relative clauses in Italian. In Fasold, R. and Shuy, R. (eds.) *Studies in Language Variation*. Washington, DC: Georgetown University Press. pp. 37–51.
Naro, A. (1981). The social and structural dimensions of a syntactic change. *Language* 57: 63–99.
Naro, A. and Lemle, M. (1977). Syntactic diffusion. *Ciencia e Cultura* 29.3: 259–68.
Newsletter of the American Dialect Society. 9.3, October 1977. Panel discussion: Is dialectology a part of sociolinguistics? Rocky Mountain Regional Meeting.
Nisbet, R. (1977). *Sociology as an Art Form*. New York: Oxford University Press.
Noizet, G., Deyts, F. and Deyts, J.-P. (1972). Producing complex sentences by applying relative transformations: a comparative study. *Linguistics* 89: 49–67.
Nordberg, B. (1971). En undersökning av språket i Eskilstuna. *Språkvård* 3: 7–15.
(1975). Contemporary social variation as a stage in long term phonological change. In Dahlstedt, K.-H. (ed.) *The Nordic Languages and Modern Linguistics*. Stockholm: Almqvist & Wiksell. pp. 587–608.
Offir, C. (1973). Recognition memory for relative clauses. *Journal of Verbal Learning and Behavior* 12: 636–43.
O'Neil, W. (1976). Clause adjunction in Old English. *General Linguistics* 17: 199–211.
Paul, H. (1920). *Prinzipien der Sprachgeschichte*. Halle: Niemayer.
Paulston, C. (1976). Pronouns of address in Swedish: social class semantics and a changing system. *Language in Society* 5: 359–87.
Peet, W. (1974). Omission of subject relative pronouns in Hawaiian English restrictive relative clauses. In Shuy, R. and Bailey, C.-J. (eds.) *Towards Tomorrow's Linguistics*. Washington, DC: Georgetown University Press. pp. 253–67.
Peranteau, P., Levi, J. and Phares, G. (eds). (1972). *The Chicago Which Hunt*. Papers from the Relative Clause Festival. Department of Linguistics, University of Chicago.
Percival, K. (1976). The applicability of Kuhn's paradigms to the history of linguistics. *Language* 52: 285–92.
Perry, J. (1970). The influence of the literary Scot on the diction of popular English prose (1738–1774). PhD dissertation. University of Pennsylvania.
Pike, K.L. (1968). *Phonemics*. Ann Arbor: University of Michigan Press.
Polanyi, M. (1973). *Personal Knowledge*. London: Routledge and Kegan Paul.
Popper, K. (1961). *The Poverty of Historicism*. London: Routledge and Kegan Paul.
(1972). *Objective Knowledge*. Oxford: Clarendon Press.

(1977). *The Logic of Scientific Discovery*. London: Hutchinson.

Posner, R. (1963). The use and abuse of stylistic statistics. *Archivum Linguisticum* xv: 111–39.

Postal, P. (1971). *Cross-over Phenomena*. New York: Holt, Rinehart and Winston.

Poutsma, H. (1904). *A Grammar of Late Modern English*. 2 vols. Groningen: Noordhof.

Quirk, R. (1957). Relative clauses in educated spoken English. *English Studies* 38: 97–109.

(1958). Substitutions and syntactical research. *Archivum Linguisticum* 10: 37–42.

Quirk, R., Greenbaum, S., Leech, G. and Svartvik, J. (1972). *A Grammar of Contemporary English*. London: Longman.

Reibel, D. and Schane, S. (eds.) (1969). *Modern Studies in English. Readings in Transformational Grammar*. Englewood Cliffs, NJ: Prentice-Hall.

Reichstein, R. (1960). Study of social and geographical variation of linguistic behavior. *Word* 16: 55–99.

Reuter, O. (1937). Some notes on the origin of the relative construction *the which*. *Neuphilologische Mitteilungen* 38: 146–88.

(1938). *On Continuative Relative Clauses in English*. Societas Scientarum Fennica. Commentationes Humanarum Litterarum IX. 3. Helsinki.

(1939). Instances of *the which* in the glossed prose Psalter and their relation to the French original. *Neuphilologische Mitteilungen* 40: 75–82.

Rickford, J. (1975). Carrying the new wave into syntax: the case of Black English BIN. In Fasold, R. and Shuy, R. (eds.) *Analyzing Variation in Language*. Washington, DC: Georgetown University Press. pp. 162–84.

Riecke, O. (1884). *Die Construction der Nebensätze im Oxforder Texte des altfranzösischen Rolandliedes*. Münster.

Ringen, J. (1975). Linguistic facts: a study of the empirical scientific status of transformational generative grammars. In Cohen, D. and Wirth, J. (eds.) *Testing Linguistic Hypotheses*. Washington, DC: Hemisphere Publishing Corporation. pp. 1–41.

Romaine, S. (1975). Linguistic variability in the speech of some Edinburgh schoolchildren. M. Litt. thesis. University of Edinburgh.

(1978a). Postvocalic /r/ in Scottish English: sound change in progress? In Trudgill, P. (ed.) *Sociolinguistic Patterns in British English*. London: Edward Arnold. pp. 144–58.

(1978b). *A Sociolinguistic Investigation of Edinburgh Speech*. Report to the Social Science Research Council.

(1978c). Problems in the investigation of linguistic attitudes in Scotland. *Work in Progress* 11: 11–30. Department of Linguistics, University of Edinburgh.

(1979a). The language of Edinburgh schoolchildren: the acquisition of sociolinguistic competence. *Scottish Literary Journal* 9: 55–61.

(1979b). On the non-decisiveness of quantitative solutions: Why Labov was wrong about contraction and deletion of the copula. *Work in Progress* 12: 10–17. Department of Linguistics, University of Edinburgh.

(1979c). The social reality of phonetic descriptions. *Northern Ireland Speech and Language Forum Journal* 5: 21–36.

(1980a). The relative clause marker in Scots English: diffusion, complexity and style as dimensions of syntactic change. *Language in Society* 9: 221–49.

(1980b). What is a speech community? *Belfast Working Papers in Language and Linguistics* 4: 41–60.

(1980c). A critical overview of the methodology of urban British sociolinguistics. *English World Wide* 1/2: 163–98.

(1980d). Stylistic variation and evaluative reactions to speech. *Language and Speech* 23: 213–32.

(1981a). The status of variable rules in sociolinguistic theory. *Journal of Linguistics* 17: 93–119.

(1981b). Syntactic complexity, relativization and stylistic levels in Middle Scots. *Folia Linguistica Historica* 2: 56–77.

(forthcoming a). The English language in Scotland. In Bailey, R.W. and Görlach, M. (eds.) *English as a World Language*, Vol. I. Ann Arbor: University of Michigan Press.

(ed.) (forthcoming b). *Sociolinguistic Variation in Speech Communities*. London: Edward Arnold.

(forthcoming c). On the problem of syntactic variation. To appear in *Working Papers in Sociolinguistics*. Austin. Texas.

(forthcoming d). Review of Lass, R. (1980). *On Explaining Language Change*. *Language in Society*.

(forthcoming e). Syntactic change as category change and diffusion: some evidence from the history of English. Paper given at the Second International Conference on English Historical Linguistics. Odense, Denmark.

(forthcoming f). Towards a typology of relative clause formation strategies in Germanic. To appear in Fisiak, J. (ed.) *Historical Syntax*. The Hague: Mouton.

Ross, J.R. (1967). Constraints on variables in syntax. PhD dissertation. Massachusetts Institute of Technology.

(1969). Auxiliaries as main verbs. In Todd, W. (ed.) *Studies in Philosophical Linguistics*. Series I. Evanston, Ill.: Great Expectations.

Rousseau, P. and Sankoff, D. (1978). Advances in variable rule methodology. In Sankoff, D. (ed.) *Linguistic Variation*. New York: Academic Press. pp. 57–68.

Rudner, R. (1966). *Philosophy of Social Science*. Englewood Cliffs, NJ: Prentice-Hall.

Rydén, M. (1966). *Relative Constructions in Early 16th Century English*. Studia Anglistica Upsaliensia 3. Uppsala.

Rynell, A. (1952). Parataxis and hypotaxis as a criterion of syntax and style especially in Old English poetry. *Lunds Universitetets Arsskrift NF*. Series 1. 48.3.

Sanders, G. (1974). Introduction. In Cohen, D. (ed.) *Explaining Linguistic Phenomena*. Washington, DC: Hemisphere Publishing Corporation. pp. 1–20.

Sankoff, D. (ed.) (1978). *Linguistic Variation: Models and Methods*. New York: Academic Press.

Sankoff, D. and Labov, W. (1979). On the uses of variable rules. *Language in Society* 8: 189–223.

Sankoff, D. and Rousseau, P. (1974). A method for assessing variable rule and implicational scaling analyses of linguistic variation. In Mitchell, J. (ed.) *Computers in the Humanities*. Edinburgh: Edinburgh University Press. pp. 3–16.

Sankoff, G. (1973). Above and beyond phonology in variable rules. In Bailey, C.-J. and Shuy, R. (eds.) *New Ways of Analyzing Variation in English*. Washington, DC: Georgetown University Press. pp. 44–62.

(1974). A quantitative paradigm for the study of communicative competence. In Bauman, R. and Sherzer, J. (eds.) *Explorations in the Ethnography of Speaking*. Cambridge: Cambridge University Press. pp. 18–50.

Sankoff, G. and Brown, P. (1976). The origins of syntax in discourse: a case study of Tok Pisin relatives. *Language* 52: 631–66.

Sapir, E. (1921). *Language*. New York: Harcourt, Brace and World.

Saussure, F. de (1966). *Course in General Linguistics* (trans. Baskin, W.). New York: McGraw Hill.

Schachter, P. (1973). Focus and relativization. *Language* 49: 19–46.

Scheffler, I. (1963). *The Anatomy of Inquiry: Philosophical Studies in the Theory of Science*. New York: Knopf.

Scherer, K. and Giles, H. (eds.) (1979). *Social Markers in Speech*. Cambridge: Cambridge University Press.

Schleicher, A. (1863). *Die Darwinsche Theorie und die Sprachwissenschaft*. Berlin.

Schmidt, J. (1872). *Die Verwandtschaftsverhältnisse der indogermanischen Sprachen*. Weimar: Böhlau.

Schulz, G. (1972). Über die dürftige Syntax im restringierten Kode. *Zeitschrift für Literaturwissenschaft und Linguistik* 7: 97–116.

Sebeok, T. (ed.) (1960). *Style in Language*. Cambridge, Mass.: MIT Press.

Sheldon, A. (1973). The role of parallel function in the acquisition of relative clauses in English. *University of Minnesota Working Papers in Linguistics and Philosophy*.

Sherzer, J. (1970). Talking backwards in Cuña: the sociological reality of phonological descriptions. *Southwestern Journal of Anthropology* 26: 343–53.

Shiels, M. (1972). Dialects in contrast: a sociolinguistic analysis of Puerto Rican English and Black English in Harlem. PhD dissertation. Georgetown University.

Shuy, R. (ed.) (1972a). *Some New Directions in Linguistics*. Washington, DC: Georgetown University Press.

(ed.) (1972b). *Sociolinguistics: Current Trends and Prospects*. Georgetown University Round Table on Languages and Linguistics, 1972. Washington, DC: Georgetown University Press.

Shuy, R. and Bailey, C.-J. (eds.) (1974). *Towards Tomorrow's Linguistics*. Washington, DC: Georgetown University Press.

Skeat, W.W. (ed.) (1894). John Barbour. *The Bruce*. 2 vols. Scottish Text Society. Edinburgh.

Smith, C.S. (1964). Determiners and relative clauses in a generative grammar of English. *Language* 40: 37–52.

Smith, G. (1902). *Specimens of Middle Scots*. Edinburgh: William Blackwood and Sons.

Smith, M.D. (1974). The adequacy and reality of underlying representations: relative clause formation. In LaGaly, M. et al. (eds.) *Papers from the Tenth Regional Meeting of the Chicago Linguistic Society*. Department of Linguistics, University of Chicago. pp. 643–56.

Söderlind, J. (1964). The attitude to language expressed by or ascertainable from English writers of the 16th and 17th centuries. *Studia Neophilologica* XXXVI: 111–26.

Stahlke, H.F. (1976). Which that. *Language* 52: 584–611.

Steinki, J. (1932). *Die Entwicklung der englischen Relativpronomina in spätmittelenglischer und früneuenglischer Zeit*. Breslau.

Stockwell, R.P. (1977). *Foundations of Syntactic Theory*. Englewood Cliffs, NJ: Prentice-Hall.

Stockwell, R.P. and Macaulay, R.K.S. (eds.) (1972). *Linguistic Change and Generative Theory*. Bloomington: Indiana University Press.

Stockwell, R.P., Schachter, P. and Partee, B. (eds.) (1973). *The Major Syntactic Structures of English*. New York: Holt, Rinehart and Winston.

Stolz, W. and Bills, G. (1968). An investigation of the standard-non-standard dimension of Central Texan English. Unpublished MS.

Stross, B. (1975). *Variation and Natural Selection as Factors in Linguistic and Cultural Change*. Lisse: Peter de Ridder Press.

Sweet, H. (1900). *A New English Grammar: Logical and Historical*. Oxford: Clarendon Press.

Taglicht, J. (1973). The choice of relative pronouns in written English. *Scripta Hierosolymitana* 25: 327–36.

Thompson, S.A. (1971). The deep structure of relative clauses. In Fillmore, C. and Langendoen, D.T. (eds.) *Studies in Linguistic Semantics*. New York: Holt, Rinehart and Winston. pp. 79–97.

Thorne, J.P. (1965). Stylistics and generative grammar. *Journal of Linguistics* 1: 49–59.

(1972). On non-restrictive relative clauses. *Linguistic Inquiry* 3: 552–6.

Todd, W. (ed.) (1969). *Studies in Philosophical Linguistics*. Series I. Evanston, Ill.: Great Expectations.

Traugott, E.C. (1972). *The History of English Syntax*. New York: Holt, Rinehart and Winston.

(1979). From propositional to textual and expressive meanings; some semantic–pragmatic aspects of grammaticalization. Paper given at the First International Conference on English Historical Linguistics.

Trudgill, P. (1972). Sex, covert prestige and linguistic change in the urban British English of Norwich. *Language in Society* 1: 179–96.

(1973). Linguistic change and diffusion: description and explanation in sociolinguistic dialect geography. *Language in Society* 2: 215–46.

(1974). *The Social Differentiation of English in Norwich*. Cambridge: Cambridge University Press.

(ed.) (1978a). *Sociolinguistic Patterns in British English*. London: Edward Arnold.

(1978b). Creolization in reverse. *Transactions of the Philological Society 1976–7*, 32–50.

Turner, G.W. (1973). *Stylistics*. Harmondsworth: Penguin.

Uldall, H.J. (1944). Speech and writing. *Acta Linguistica* 4: 11–16.

Vachek, J. (1964a). Zum Problem der geschriebenen Sprache. In Vachek, J. (ed.) *A Prague School Reader in Linguistics*. Bloomington: University of Indiana Press. pp. 441–53.

(1964b). Written language and printed language. In Vachek, J. (ed.) *A Prague School Reader in Linguistics*. Bloomington: University of Indiana Press. pp. 453–63.

Van den Broeck, J. (1977). Class differences in syntactic complexity in the Flemish town of Maaseik. *Language in Society* 6: 149–83.

Van der Geest, T., Gerstel, R., Appel, R. and Tervoort, B. (1973). *The Child's Communicative Competence*. The Hague: Mouton.

Verburg, P. (1974). Vicissitudes of paradigms. In Hymes, D. (ed.) *Studies in the History of Linguistics*. Bloomington: University of Indiana Press. pp. 191–233.

Visser, F. (1963). *An Historical Syntax of the English Language*. 3 vols. Leiden: Brill.

Wang, W. (1969). Competing changes as a cause of residue. *Language* 45: 9–25.

Wang, W. and Crawford, J. (1960). Frequency studies of English consonants. *Language and Speech* 3: 131–9.

Weinreich, U. (1963). *Languages in Contact*. The Hague: Mouton.

(1966). *Explorations in Semantic Theory*. The Hague: Mouton.

Weinreich, U., Labov, W. and Herzog, M. (1968). Empirical foundations for a theory of language change. In Lehmann, W.P. and Malkiel, Y. (eds.) *Directions for Historical Linguistics*. Austin: University of Texas Press. pp. 95–189.

Wenker, G. (1878). *Sprachatlas der Rheinprovinz nördlich der Mosel. sowie des Kreises Siegen*. Unpublished MS.

Winch, P. (1958). *The Idea of a Social Science and its Relation to Philosophy*. London: Routledge and Kegan Paul.

Winter, W. (1961). Relative Haufigkeit syntaktischer Erscheinungen als Mittel zur Abgrenzung von Stilarten. *Phonetica* 7: 193–216.

(1964). Styles as dialects. In Lunt, H. (ed.) *Proceedings of the 9th International Congress of Linguists*. The Hague: Mouton. pp. 324–30.

Wirth, J. (ed.) (1976). *Assessing Linguistic Arguments*. Washington, DC: Hemisphere Publishing Corporation.

Wolfram, W. (1969). *A Sociolinguistic Description of Detroit Negro Speech*. Washington, DC: Center for Applied Linguistics.

(1971). Social dialects from a linguistic perspective. In Shuy, R. (ed.) *Sociolinguistics*. Washington, DC: Center for Applied Linguistics. pp. 86–135.

(1973). *Sociolinguistic Aspects of Assimilation: Puerto Rican English in New York City*. Washington, DC: Center for Applied Linguistics.

(1975). Variable constraints and rule relations. In Fasold, R. and Shuy, R. (eds.) *Analyzing Variation in Language*. Washington, DC: Center for Applied Linguistics. pp. 70–89.

Wolfram, W. and Christian, D. (1976). *Appalachian Speech*. Washington, DC: Center for Applied Linguistics.

Wolfram, W. and Fasold, R. (1974). *The Study of Social Dialects in American English*. Englewood Cliffs, NJ: Prentice-Hall.

Wolfson, N. (1976). Speech events and natural speech: some implications for sociolinguistic methodology. *Language in Society* 5: 189–211.

(1978). A feature of performed narrative: the conversational historical present. *Language in Society* 7: 215–39.

Wood, H. (1933). *The Poems and Fables of Robert Henryson*. Edinburgh: Oliver and Boyd.

Woodward, J. (1975). Variation in American sign language syntax. In Fasold, R. and Shuy, R. (eds.) *Analyzing Variation in Language*. Washington, DC: Georgetown University Press. pp. 303–12.

Wunderlich, D. (1974). *Grundlagen der Linguistik*. Reinbeck bei Hamburg: Rowohlt Taschenbuch Verlag.

Wyld, H.C. (1920). *A History of Modern Colloquial English*. Oxford: Basil Blackwell.

Primary texts

Acts of the Lords of Council in Public Affairs. Hannay, R.K. (ed.) (1932). *Selections from the Acta Dominorum Concilii introductory to the register of Scotland. 1501–1554*. Edinburgh.

Ane Satyre of the Thrie Estaitis. Lindsay, Sir David (1542). *Ane Satyre of the Thrie Estaitis*. Early English Text Society edition. Edinburgh: Robert Charteris. 1602.

The Bannatyne Manuscript. Ritchie, W.T. (ed.) (1934). *The Bannatyne Manuscript*. 1568 by George Bannatyne. 4 vols. Scottish Text Society. Edinburgh.

Boece. Bellenden, J. (1531). *The Chronicles of Scotland compiled by Hector Boece and translated into Scots by John Bellenden*. Scottish Text Society. 2 vols. Edinburgh. 1938–41.

Burgh Records for the Burgh of Edinburgh. Marwick, Sir J.D. (ed.) (1869–92). *Extracts from the Records of the Burgh of Edinburgh A.D. 1430–1528 (1589)*. 5 vols. Edinburgh: Scottish Burgh Society Records.

The Scottish Correspondence of Mary of Lorraine. Cameron, A.I. (ed.) (1927). *The Scottish Correspondence of Mary of Lorraine including some 300 Letters from 20 Feb. 1542–3 to 15 May 1560*. Edinburgh: Scottish Historical Society Publications. Third Series. Vol. 10.

Sheriff Court Book of Fife. Dickinson, W.C. (ed.) (1928). *The Sheriff Court Book of Fife*. Edinburgh: Scottish Historical Society Publications. Third Series. Vol. 12.

Other texts cited:

The Anglo-Saxon Chronicle. Plummer, C. and Earle, J. (eds.) (1892–9). *Two of the Saxon Chronicles Parallel*. 2 vols. London: Oxford University Press.

Chaucer, G. *The Canterbury Tales*. Skeat, W.W. (ed.) (1889–1900). *Chaucer: Complete Works*. 7 vols. London: Oxford University Press.

Index

acquisition, 30, 54n, 103–4, 211, 221, 237, 258, 289
acrolect, 211, 213, 221
age-grading, 255–7. *See also* change
agentless passive, *see* passive
anaphora, 82, 86
anglicization, 23–4, 136, 157
animacy: as factor in relativization, 2, 58, 60–1, 63, 69, 81, 88–9, 95, 142–3, 191–4
ἀπὸ κοινοῦ, 72–6. *See also* contact clause, deletion, ellipsis
aspiration: and deletion of /s/, 28, 200, 224, 228, 259n
autonomy: vs. determinism, 271–3, 283; principle, 4n; thesis (in extended standard theory), 216

basilect, 211, 221
BEV (Black English Vernacular), 28, 30, 36–7, 76, 177, 184–5, 218–21, 237

case: agreement, 134–5, 137, 208; coding/marking, 57–8, 63, 68, 93, 95, 132; hierarchy, *see* NP accessibility
causality, 55n. *See also* explanation
centralization: of diphthongs on Martha's Vineyard, 235–6, 264, 267
Cedergren–Sankoff variable rule program: and *a*-prefixing, 226–7; and change, 210–11; and post-vocalic /r/, 230–2; and probability theory, 271, 275, 279; and relatives, 26–7, 188–209, 218; and variable rules, 31, 139, 173–4, 183–8. *See also* variable rule
channel, 14, 19–20, 26; cues, 119–20, 125. *See also* medium
change, linguistic: and age-grading, 255–7; as diffusion, 152n, 212–14, 255–6; direction of, 171–3, 180, 208, 211–12, 236, 254–6, 263, 267; from above, 213, 263, 266–8; from below, 173, 263, 266–7; function of, 259–60; gradual vs. discrete, 254–61; and identity, 264; intermediate stages in, 260, 229–31; and linguistic theory, 240, 252–73; natural, 212, 255n; Neogrammarian theory of, 254–60; origin vs. propagation, 244, 256, 258, 262; in relativizers, 199–204; by reordering/reweighting of constraints, 27, 174, 199–204, 210–11, 219, 232; and role of individual, 257–8; and role of social factors, 19, 210, 234, 262–9; by rule decomposition, 200; and sex differentiation, 264; and social class, 263, 266; vs. stable variability, 25, 200–4, 236, 256; and style, 264–5; and types of variables, 265–6, 284; and variation, 25, 200, 204, 209, 218, 231, 252, 255
chi-square, 186, 191n, 193, 207, 279
coexistent systems, 65, 115, 209, 217, 236
colloquialisms: and colloquial speech, 77, 101, 120, 137, 213; in Old English, 74; in Middle English, 62, 70, 74, 167; in Middle Scots, 22–4, 125, 154, 167, 169; in seventeenth century, 17, 87. *See also* non-standard speech, vernacular, written language
competence, 14, 280; communicative, 157n, 251; and *langue* vs. *parole*, 106; vs. performance, 10, 26, 35–7, 240–1, 243, 247–51; polylectal/panlectal, 231n, 249; and variable rules, 185–8. *See also* performance
complementation, 42, 77, 82
complementizer: as COMP node, 50, 214–17; *que* deletion, 162n, 241–2; *that* deletion, 23, 116, 208, 215; vs. relativizer status of *that*, 38, 46–8, 58–9, 60n, 76–7, 79, 135. *See also* deletion, relativization, TH
constraint hierarchy (in variable rule): and competence, 249–50; explanation of, 276; interaction between social and linguistic, 199–204, 216–17, 226–34; mirror image, 192, 227; ordering in, 189, 192, 197; reordering as a factor in change, 174, 200,

octosyllabic vs. decasyllabic, 175–6; rhymed vs. alliterative, 22, 175; as a stylistic category, 2, 16, 72, 114, 163–6, 175–6, 180, 194. *See also* prose

wave model (Baileyan), 31, 170–4, 254n, 261, 269; vs. variable rule, 209–11, 252–73. *See also* implicational scales, variable rule
WH: attachment, 44–6, 49, 116; forms, 2, 22, 27n, 38–51, 59–72 *passim*, 81–99 *passim*, 140–74 *passim*, 184–209 *passim*; fronting, 45–6, 50, 189n; movement, 208, 215. *See also* relativization
word order, 67, 75–6, 77–9, 137, 173
written language: and complexity, 53–5, 64–5, 212–13, 256, 285; and deletion, 78–9; and socio-historical reconstruction, 122; vs. spoken, 3, 14–22, 202–3; variation in, 13, 70–1; and *which* vs. *that*, 137. *See also* medium

zero clauses/relatives, see *ἀπὸ κοινοῦ*, contact clause, deletion, ellipsis